JOHN WAYNE

JOHN WAYNE

BY ALLEN EYLES
Introduction by LOUISE BROOKS

Memorial Edition

South Brunswick and New York: A. S. Barnes and Co.
London: The Tantivy Press

This book is for my mother
and to the memory of my father

© 1976, 1979 by Allen Eyles

Library of Congress Catalogue Card Number: 79-5416

A. S. Barnes and Co., Inc.
Cranbury, New Jersey 08512

The Tantivy Press
Magdalen House
136-148 Tooley Street
London SE1 2TT, England

ISBN 0-498-02487-3
Printed in the United States of America

Presidential Tributes to John Wayne

John Wayne was bigger than life. In an age of few heroes, he was the genuine article. But he was more than just a hero—he was a symbol of many of the most basic qualities that made America great. The ruggedness, the tough independence, the sense of personal conviction and courage—on and off the screen—reflected the best of our national character.

It was because of what John Wayne said about what we are and what we can be that his great and deep love of America was returned in full measure...

President Jimmy Carter

John Wayne was a unique, magnificent person who met every challenge in his own life and responded to the Nation's problems with courage, wisdom and conviction.

President Gerald R. Ford

Contents

1. Duke by Divine Right

An Introduction by Louise Brooks

PROMPTED by some inner sense which proved correct, I felt that I was reaching the end of my career in 1938 when I signed to make a Western picture with a two week schedule, *Overland Stage Raiders* at the Republic studio. And the sorely needed three hundred dollar salary did little to cheer me up at the prospect of working in a typical Hollywood Western whose unreality disgusted me.

In 1870 my great grandfather, John Brooks, with his family, made the hazardous journey by covered wagon from Tennessee to a homestead in Kansas. The cavalry galloped from Fort Scott to defend the Kansans against the Indian raids, but they had to defend themselves against the Texas cattle drivers. After forty days on the trail, driving twenty-five hundred head of cattle under the brutal July sun, the cowboys attacked the cow towns like mad dogs. Until the cattle were fattened for shipment in August or September and they returned to Texas, the cowboys ran wild in a mindless fury of boozing, whoring and gun fighting. They could be restrained only by the buffalo hunters who, after exterminating those beasts, kept themselves in business as professional killers.

Growing up on this history, it is not surprising that I did not share Hollywood's romantic view of the cowboy hero.

Returning to 1938, at sunrise one August morning I was driven in a company car to location on the ranch where Republic shot all its Westerns. Where was I supposed to go, I wondered, after I got out of the car and stood alone in a cloud of dust kicked up by a passing string of horses — that damned dust so cherished by Western cameramen. Up the road a bunch of cowboys were talking and laughing with two men who stood slightly apart from them. When the company car honked for them to get off the road, the two men looked around, saw me, and came to greet me. One was a cherub, five feet tall, carrying a bound script; the other was a cowboy, six feet four inches tall, wearing a lovely smile. The cherub, who was the director, George Sherman, introduced me to the cowboy who was John Wayne, the star of The 3 Mesquiteers series. Looking up at him I thought, this is no actor but the hero of all mythology miraculously brought to life.

During my thirteen years in films I had made a study of the manner in which the reigning stars of Hollywood exercised their power. My first study had been of Queen Gloria Swanson who knocked people about like bowling pins. My last study had been of King Clark Gable who wore his crown at a humorously apologetic angle. Now, for the first time I beheld a Duke born to reign. John was, in fact, that which Henry James defined as the greatest of all works of art — a purely beautiful being.

John Wayne and Louise Brooks: happy co-stars of Overland Stage Raiders *(1938).*

2. "God Loves John Wayne"

John Wayne saw the American dream come true.

He wasn't born in a log cabin and he didn't grow up to be President. But he did come from a quiet, small-town background and he grew up to be the most popular film star of all time. He spent more than twenty years at the very top of his profession within the golden circle of the top ten box-office draws. Right through his sixties and into his early seventies, he maintained his appeal when other stars reaching his age had been shuffled off to character work and television series, or soldiered on in largely ignored movies. Wayne's participation in the making of *The Cowboys* upped its budget to six million dollars, the largest amount allocated for a film made within the United States during 1971. A 1968 poll in America revealed that he was the most popular artist on TV, largely through showings of his old films, and in a list of the top ten most heavily watched programs in American TV history, the Academy Awards telecast of 1970 had top place. It would be very plausible to deduce that interest in whether Wayne would gain the Oscar for *True Grit* (which he did) made all the difference. Also, in seventh place, after football games, Christmas shows and one movie *(Ben-Hur),* came a 1970 program called simply "John Wayne"—a TV special (Wayne's first) in which he looked back on America's past. In Britain, Christmas wouldn't be Christmas without a John Wayne Western on BBC TV, frequently shown in the key spot on Christmas evening. A 1972 poll by the American "Photoplay" magazine revealed him to be its readers' male favourite, and it said something for Wayne's business acumen as a producer-star that he had already engaged the poll's female choice, Ann-Margret, to be the leading lady in his next picture, *The Train Robbers.*

Wayne became more than just a much-loved actor. He became a symbol like—as a writer once put it— "an extra star on the American flag." There was even a car sticker, seen displayed in director John Ford's home that read "God loves John Wayne." His universal appeal was based on the parts he played and the beliefs he expressed in them; and for a great many Americans his popularity was enhanced by the role he had undertaken as a spokesman for the "silent majority," propounding views on politics, the war in Vietnam, minority rights and patriotism of an arch-conservative nature.

Even those who despised his opinions often admitted to a grudging admiration for the forthright manner in which Wayne expressed them. He was, for example, the only prominent figure in the film industry to remain publicly proud of the role he had in the blacklisting era in helping to eliminate supposed Communists, and he kept up his admiration for the late Joe McCarthy.

His reputation as an actor became almost inextricably bound up with his role as a public figure. He exerted a strong appeal on the Armed Services and when in July, 1971 it was announced that the Marine Corps League had named him to be the recipient of their award for the man "who best exemplified the word 'American'," it was as much a tribute of American involvement in Vietnam as to his work as a hero of war films (and in *The Green Berets* he was both hero *and* advocate of a cause). A cartoon strip once introduced the engaging notion of a "John Wayne TV Movie Alert System," notifying officers of opportunities to watch their hero in action. This image was exploited for satirical purposes by Jak, the cartoonist of the London *Evening Standard,* when in November, 1970 he depicted a battered squad of troops returning to the briefing room after a goofed-up mission in Vietnam to learn that John Wayne would personally be leading their next attack with a map on the wall showing a large arrow pointed straight at Peking.

Given his own great success within the American system as it has stood for decades, it was not surprising that he believed it needed little adaptation to meet the future and that he could tell a Republican convention several years back, "I am proud of every day in my life I wake up in the United States of America." Wayne carried the guidon for those Americans who feared change and saw behind the pressures

Hero and advocate of a cause: John Wayne as star/producer of The Green Berets *(1968) with sons Patrick (left) and Michael.*

on the present form of American society the forces of Communism and anarchy.

Wayne's image on screen is attractive for its simple, clear-cut attitudes. In his favourite settings of war and the old West, issues are always clear cut, right and wrong clearly demarcated. Wayne expressed such notions as male chauvinism (allied to old-fashioned gallantry to women), fighting for what you believe in, standing up to being pushed around, and making your own way in life. Wayne stood for a time when self-reliance was the great ideal, when honour, integrity, instinctive generosity, and outright love of country were prized virtues with unequivocal meaning and clear-cut implications to them rather than woolly notions to be argued about. Wayne remained a hero in an age of antiheroes, critical of the new screen permissiveness and of stars like Paul Newman and Kirk Douglas for playing ''weak'' and flawed figures.

Wayne had long ensured that he played parts of which he approved, modifying them to that end. It is more true of him than any other actor that his films be as much John Wayne pictures as those of the director or writer. Whenever Wayne was asked about his basic philosophy, he spoke of the advice he received from his father: 1) Always keep your word. 2) A gentleman never insults anybody intentionally. 3) Don't go around looking for trouble—but if you get into a fight, make sure you win it. These are tenets that Wayne applied in real life where, in the film business, he always stuck to his word and was patient under provocation from ''fans.'' And it is certainly part of Wayne's image on screen. How closely the public and private image merge can be seen in Wayne's interview with *Playboy* magazine (May 1971) when he was talking about the things that were wonderful in life, listing ''a good horse under you'' and ''the sound of a kid calling you Dad for the first time'' and speaking of ''tomorrow'' as the most important thing because ''it's perfect when it arrives and it puts itself in our hands. It hopes we've learned something from yesterday.'' Lines like these sound like dialogue recalled from a John Wayne picture.

Wayne could no longer be interviewed without having to spend more time elaborating on his private views than on his screen work. It became fashionable in sophisticated circles to ridicule him (see the hostile profile in *Time* magazine of August 8, 1969) but Wayne seemed happy to submit, clearly sure that there was a large audience who would be responsive to what he had to say, no matter how it was packaged. It should be added that Wayne backed up his arguments on such subjects as student unrest with hard-hitting detail, suitable quotes from other authorities ready to hand (as shown by the *Playboy* interview).

Part of this hostility would seem to be based on a lack of respect for Wayne as an actor: if he couldn't act, he couldn't have been a great thinker either. This arose in part because Wayne mainly made Westerns and popular ones at that: both the *genre* and popular success were apt to be looked down on by many

reviewers. It was not the urban areas of America, where critics' opinions have most sway, that gave Wayne his box-office power: it was the rest of the country. (Even in London, his films were not sure-fire West End material. *The Cowboys* performed as weakly there as in New York, and many other Wayne films had gone straight into release without a prestige opening.)

Wayne himself was extremely modest about his acting abilities and his record of work. ''I don't act, I react,'' he was fond of saying (but this, of course, was a style of acting); ''I always look for a story with basic emotions. A dog, a kid, a woman's love, a man's love''; ''I've been in more bad pictures than just about anyone in the business.'' This was hardly the sound of a great actor speaking profoundly about his craft. Even John Ford contributed to the general picture of Wayne the screen personality rather than Wayne the serious actor. On the set of *The Cowboys* Ford was overheard saying ''That guy was one of the greatest stars I ever worked with; it's too bad he never could act.'' But, evasive always, Ford has also been recorded saying that Wayne was ''a splendid actor who has had very little chance to act.'' Howard Hawks, though, in an interview in *Cinema* (Vol. 1, no. 6) summed it up best. ''Wayne is underrated. He's a much better actor than he's given credit for being. He's an awfully good actor. He holds a thing together, he gives it a solidity and honesty, and he can make a lot of things believable. If he's kind of grousing around in a scene, you know that there's something wrong with the scene. He maybe can't tell you, but you can find out what's bothering him. He has a very true sense of cinema.''

Even those who respond to Wayne's efforts on screen sometimes have problems of reconciling the effect he had on them with their feelings about the real-life John Wayne. This led French director and intellectual Jean-Luc Godard to ask himself how he could ''hate John Wayne upholding Goldwater and love him tenderly when abruptly he takes Natalie Wood into his arms in the next-to-last reel of *The Searchers*.''

It could be said that only the public really liked him.

Yet Wayne deserved intelligent respect. It was not that he just happened to be in some good films by John Ford, Howard Hawks and others. He was indispensable to them. He may have always been playing himself, but this has come to mean something unusually forceful and resonant on the screen. It made him watchable in even his bad films. And it was perfectly possible to accept his conduct and attitudes in the particular context of a film without applying them to modern life. The more Wayne's films were divorced from immediate reality, the more effective they became. In stylized settings like the old West, the films could confront age-old issues of personal conduct and integrity in meaningful terms, giving us clear-cut issues to respond to and satisfy that need, inhibited by the complexity and restraints of modern

The most popular film star of all time meets his fans and poses (during shooting of Hatari!, 1962) *for a sculptor.*

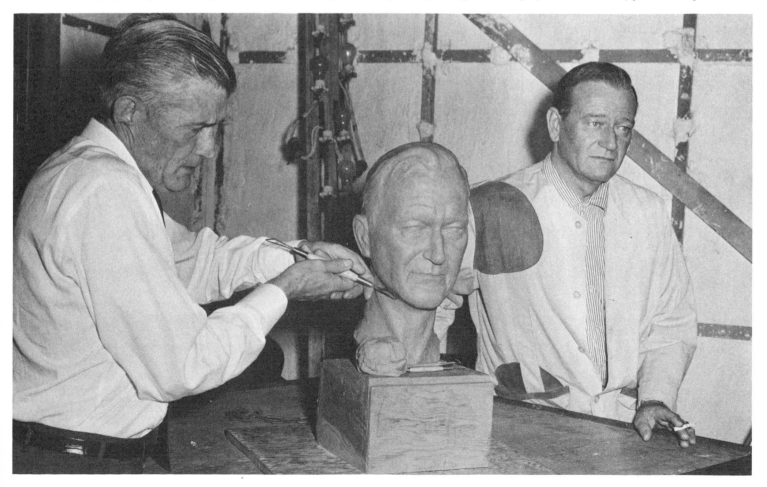

life, to be involved in matters of decision and to see them resolved cleanly and finally. Life itself is not so neat and it is facile to expect it to be so.

This book, then, is partly the result of a continuing enthusiasm for Wayne, strained at times, but always intrigued, often touched, by the charisma of the man. It has also been an adventure in film research, charting a career of formidable length. The more one goes into detail, the more difficult it is to draw general conclusions, but I hope that I have developed a full picture of the Wayne image in following through aspects of it as they occur at their most significant in particular films.

Ideally, I would have sat down and watched every single Wayne film in proper order, but of necessity this book has had to be done in a less satisfactory fashion. I have been able to renew my acquaintance with almost all the key Wayne films during the period of compiling this book. Otherwise, I have relied on reinforcing old memories of films like *Hondo* by consulting a wide range of comment and documentation and merging it with my own lasting impressions; and for the films that I have not been able to see (mainly from the Thirties, I have carefully explored contemporary reviews to give as accurate an impression of the content and significance of them as possible.

I have tried to concentrate on Wayne's contribution to each picture rather than the picture as a whole and to revive the impression he made on each occasion. I have only gone into more general issues where Wayne has directed the film or made it to put forward a provocative viewpoint (as in *Big Jim McLain*).

Since each picture is essentially "John Wayne in a situation" rather than the character he plays, especially when one thinks back on them, I have referred to Wayne rather than the name of the character in commenting on each film, in the same way that most reviewers do. I have, however, referred to other characters by their names rather than the actors playing them, since it is difficult to draw the line between when the actual performer is well enough known to be remembered and when it is the name of the part that lingers.

3. Working with Wayne

IN SEEKING to explain Wayne's success in both economic and artistic terms, a legitimate field for investigation is his relationship with other film workers. Here an almost uniform portrait of a courteous but firm, hard-working professional emerges from the comments of his collaborators with none of the high-handed temperament that other stars are renowned for. Take the comments of Mark Rydell, the young director of *The Cowboys*, to Gerald Pratley during production: "He was the ideal choice for the role. Yet he represents ideas, opinions, political attitudes, quite different from my own. But he is an individual man, like the character in the film, and that's the man I wanted for the part. And I tell you it's been a stunning shock for me. I came prepared to fight with him, to 'handle' him, and I find him one of the most incredible professionals I have ever met. He is always ready, always listens to reason, our political differences have never interfered with our work, and this is the fourth week of shooting and we are well ahead of schedule; it's very unusual to be charmed by such a figure. But then, I thought, why should I think this? There must be a good reason why for forty-one years this man has captured the world. There are very few stars of his magnitude. All you need is a week with him to realise that his qualities are quite remarkable."

This respect is echoed by one of Wayne's fellow actors in the film, Roscoe Lee Browne: "I came prepared to dislike him, and instead found an intelligent, courteous and well-read man." When *The Cowboys* was being released in Europe, Mark Rydell came over to help promote it, and his opinions of Wayne were as flattering as before. An Irish newspaper reports Rydell as saying: "He never changed one word of the picture in order to project his own political philosophy as a right-wing conservative. He's a literate, genuine, compassionate human being who spent hours discussing Shelley and Keats with Roscoe Lee Browne, a black actor well-known for his liberal, left-wing philosophy. I expected all kinds of clashes on the set, but Duke had everybody eating out of his hand. As we got into the actual work, I found him articulate and sensitive and totally unselfish. The kids crawled all over him like a monkey bar in the Central Park Zoo. The great dictator turned out to be a lamb. He also has a sharp, Shavian wit with an uncanny ability to make pungent observations. A week after we started shooting, his famous 'Playboy' interview came out and I told him: 'We must never discuss anything because we're not even in the same world.' But I found myself listening to him and learning. Roscoe Lee Browne disagreed with him on everything, but they can't get off the phone with each other. The key to his success, I think, is that he is so secure as a man you don't have to worry about stepping on his toes. His toes are invulnerable. At first, I was terrified. To begin with, he's so goddam BIG. He did all of his own riding and fighting in the film, refused to use a stand-in. He's sixty-five years old, has only one lung, and he'll outlive us all. You'll have to beat him to death with a stick."

Rydell elaborated further in an interview with David Castell (published in "Films Illustrated," May 1972): "We had it quite clear from the start that I was producer and director. He was delighted to surrender all managerial rights and be just an actor in this film. He was as happy as a twenty year old and he called me 'Sir' right the way through the shooting. Me! He's been a star for more years than I've even been alive. It was fascinating to go out in public with him because he is one of the ten best-known men in the world. In the middle of meals people would come up and ask for his autograph or want him to go over and meet their friends and relations. He was unfailingly courteous and he resisted no imposition on his time or privacy. In all the time I was with him, I never once knew him to turn anyone away."

The Cowboys *(1972): Wayne takes direction from Mark Rydell and acts with Roscoe Lee Browne.*

Steve Ditlea, visiting the film in production for "Show" magazine, reported in its March 1972 issue: "Prepared for so long to dislike this embodiment of so much that is alien to me, I found myself disarmed by his attentive conversation and affable disposition." He observed Rydell giving Wayne minimal instructions on playing scenes and usually settling for just one take when shots featured him. In small ways, Ditlea found Rydell making a special effort to cater to the star, rather than force arguments. He had the faces of other players darkened for one shot to match the reddish make-up that Wayne's personal make-up man had applied to his features, not allowing for the film stock in use which needed more natural colouring. Extra lighting was then brought in to brighten all the faces. Rydell was also observed settling for less than he wanted from Wayne rather than force him through too many re-takes in a slightly too inexpressive reaction to a scene. Wayne remained ignorant of these small moves which demonstrates an awe that perhaps inhibits directors from obtaining the best that Wayne was capable of.

Yet Wayne was more flexible than was commonly allowed. Writer Wendell Mayes, in an interview published in "Focus on Film" (No. 7), recalled: "In a scene in which I know John Wayne is going to play a role, I will say to myself: 'Well, John Wayne can't *say* that line of dialogue,' so I won't write it. Now in *In Harm's Way*, John Wayne was hired after the screenplay was written. It was not written for John Wayne and if I'd been writing it for him there are certain speeches that I would not have written because I felt he could not read them. As it turned out, John Wayne *was* able to read the lines and read them very well indeed — so that I think it was a better film because I didn't know he was going to play the role." At work on the picture, Wayne earned this tribute from Mayes: "John Wayne's a great pro. John Wayne never blows a line. He'll come in letter perfect. The other actors will blow lines but he will stand there patiently, wait for them to get their lines, say his in his own way."

One can see, however, a certain measure of adjustment to Wayne's presence in a film in Mayes' further recollections: "I wanted Wayne to die and the son to live, and Otto [director Otto Preminger] wanted the son to die and Wayne to live. His argument was — you can't kill John Wayne. So he won, and perhaps he's right. You can cut a leg off, or an arm, or an ear, or something, you can maim him for life, but you can't kill him." Wayne's death in *The Cowboys* was, of course, a big surprise feature of the film, and, though Wayne *has* died on screen (*The Fighting Seabees, Sands of Iwo Jima*), Mayes and Preminger were broadly speaking correct in their assessment of how much the public will stand for in adjusting the Wayne image.

Wayne could, on occasion, bring his views to bear in a decisive fashion. He was always on guard for any actions that would make him seem "mean and petty." Iain Johnstone, in the "Radio Times" (December 11, 1969), recalled Wayne refusing to do a scene in *Chisum* where he was supposed to eavesdrop on a conversation between a father and his son. "I know how to get my way," he is quoted as saying, "I don't argue, I become adamant." As the executive producer of most of his pictures (including *Chisum*), he obviously had the right in such instances to say how things should be done, but his power had extended to pictures on which he was simply an employee, albeit the main reason for such productions being made.

In his book "How to Make a Jewish Movie," Melville Shavelson recalls a brush with Wayne when he co-wrote and produced *Trouble Along the Way* with Wayne starring. Wayne disagreed with certain aspects of the story development and was handed a version of the script tailored to meet his wishes. But Shavelson went ahead with his own ideas in sequences which featured other characters. Wayne came onto the set unexpectedly and found out what was going on behind his back. The picture was then filmed the Wayne Way. "Ordinarily," writes Shavelson, "he is one of the kindest and most level-headed of men. But when crossed, and particularly when double-crossed, he can make an underground nuclear explosion seem like a baby's sigh." However, Wayne subsequently made a point of sending his unsolicited compliments on one of Shavelson's later pictures. While fraternal back-slapping is a Hollywood pastime, Shavelson was im-

Otto Preminger directs Wayne in In Harm's Way *(1965).*

pressed that Wayne *wrote* his praise and thereby displayed his real sincerity. Later still, Wayne was more than willing to listen to Shavelson's proposals that he should appear in the latter's production of *Cast a Giant Shadow*, and gave his handshake on playing a suitable part in it subject to liking the first thirty pages of the screenplay.

Given his years of experience and his own work as a director, Wayne was apt to put in his two cents' worth. Iain Johnstone recalls Wayne tactfully suggesting to a fellow actor in *Chisum*, playing an unsympathetic sergeant, that he should be surprised to be offered a cigar by Wayne. The actor duly looked surprised on the next run-through. When an Indian character had inserted an "Okay" into his lines, Wayne was on hand to point out that it was anachronistic for the period of the film. When Johnstone was setting up BBC TV cameras to film an interview with Wayne, the actor told him that the mountains behind would come out flat. When the cameraman expressed complete confidence in his colour stock, Wayne replied: "I've been making pictures for forty years and they'll come out flat." The interview was conducted elsewhere—in the middle of a stream with Wayne thoughtfully sending a bottle of bourbon to the soundman who had to stand in the water while Wayne perched on some rocks. Johnstone concluded: "Boorish, reactionary, overbearing he may be, but he forces you to like him."

Not all directors are so deferential. When William Wellman was employed by Wayne to direct him in the actor's own production of *The High and the Mighty*, he didn't take kindly to Wayne interfering with his work and recently recalled to me with some relish that he bawled out Wayne in front of the entire cast and crew. Wellman is not nicknamed "Wild Bill" for nothing! Wayne was apparently happy to leave things to the director and Wellman continued to do pictures for him.

Back in the Forties, of course, Wayne had much less say. According to the director Allan Dwan, he became powerful with the success of *Sands of Iwo Jima*. At that point, Wayne was keen to play the part but had to be persuaded to tell the studio boss that he insisted on doing it. Asked by Peter Bogdanovich in the book "Allan Dwan, The Last Pioneer" about working with Wayne, Dwan replied: "Oh, he was fine. He came to me the second day and said, 'You're my kind of director,' shook hands and that was the end—I don't think there was a bit of friction." The only trouble that Wayne caused was that he would tempt other members of the cast to stay up drinking with him late at night. While Wayne could carry his liquor — and was a Hollywood legend in that respect — the other players would be in a sorry state the next morning until a tough drill sergeant got to work on them and they then avoided Wayne at all costs. Dwan was asked if Wayne had taken a hand in the directing. "No" replied the director, "He's particularly good at faking punches. And I let him and Forrest Tucker slug it out. They'd talk over their fight scenes and work them out. And I know one time these two kids weren't doing exactly what I wanted and they were a little sulky about it. And all of a sudden, over my shoulder, Wayne said, 'God damn it!

Will you bastards do what he tells you!' And they did it then. I said, 'Thanks.' "

Even at this stage, we find Wayne concerned to adjust the role to suit his image and abilities, bringing writer James Edward Grant in to change some of his dialogue. "The script was perfect for Wayne, except that he wants to say things in a certain way, and a writer sometimes writes a phrase a little differently. Wayne's very simple and very plain, and he seemed to think that Grant was the only man who could put the words the way he ought to say them." Wayne continued to rely on James Edward Grant up until his death in 1966. For a hostile portrait of the way Grant asserted himself on Wayne's behalf, see Frank Capra's autobiography "The Name Above the Title" regarding *The Magnificent Showman (Circus World)*.

There were only two directors that Wayne trusted implicitly: John Ford and Howard Hawks. They were both older than him and giants of the industry when Wayne came to work for them, and his faith was clearly justified from the great opportunities they have given him in *Stagecoach, Red River, She Wore a Yellow Ribbon, Rio Bravo* and others. Hawks recalls the way he hired Wayne for *Rio Lobo*. "I called him up and said , 'Duke, I've got a story.' He said, 'I can't make it for a year, I'm

Gérard Blain (left) and Howard Hawks (hat) watch Wayne rehearsing some action for Hatari! *(1962).*

all tied up.' And I said 'Well, that's all right, it'll take a year to get it finished.' He said, 'Good, I'll be ready.' And he came down on location and he said 'What's this about?' And I told him the story. He never even read it, he didn't know anything about it.'' (Reported in ''Sight and Sound,'' Spring 1971).

It was always a two-way collaboration between Wayne and Hawks. Hawks said in ''Cinema'' magazine's interview, ''Wayne is like a big cat on his feet, he thinks quickly and he thinks right. Also he contributes to what other people do. If he sees somebody who is not moving he tells 'em to move, and it becomes part of the story.'' Hawks also tells an amusing story of how he tried to sell Wayne the idea of a spot of comic relief in *Red River* in which Wayne was to get his finger mangled between a saddle horn and a rope and be made drunk so that it could be amputated. Wayne failed to see the humorous potential of this scene so Hawks told him he would use it later with a better actor (who turned out be Kirk Douglas in *The Big Sky*). Wayne did, however, allow some finger-cutting into *True Grit* for another veteran director, Henry Hathaway, although it was not Wayne but one of the villains on the receiving end. ''I thought it was going too far,'' Wayne told Gerald Pratley in a radio interview. ''Henry fell in love with this idea. I think he didn't feel that the lines that I had growling at this fellow to try and get him to confess would mean anything unless there was a shocker ahead of it. So he certainly put a shocker ahead of it!''

Perhaps the only director to have completely dominated Wayne was the eccentric Josef von Sternberg on *Jet Pilot*. The latter, in his autobiography ''Fun in a Chinese Laundry,'' relates that Wayne was scared stiff of him. John Huston is another obstinate, singleminded director who didn't fare quite so well working with the actor on *The Barbarian and the Geisha*. Wayne was unusually vocal about his dissatisfaction with Huston and in the book ''King Rebel'' by William F. Nolan there are several grievances quoted that the actor had at the time of shooting. One concerned Huston's apparent refusal to use him as John Ford had done by ignoring his claim that his best profile was on the right, Huston deliberately lining up shots to take in the other profile as much as possible. The film's script was being knocked into shape just ahead of shooting and Wayne was quoted as saying that, when he sought to find out what would be filmed next, Huston would sigh and point out of the window of his room, drawing attention to the magnificence of the view. ''For a while ,'' Wayne said, ''I couldn't make up my mind whether to flat quit and go home and let them sue me or stay on and give this thing a whirl. Guess I'm in so deep now I can't back out —but old Duke's not happy, I tell you that.'' Part of Wayne's dissatisfaction came from seeing the rushes: ''Huston

Maureen O'Hara, director Andrew V. McLaglen and Wayne relax during production of McLintock! *(1963).*

has me walking through a series of Japanese pastels. Hell, my fans expect me to be tall in the saddle.'' Had Wayne left the picture, it wouldn't have been the first time a star of his magnitude has asserted himself that way — and been forgiven for it. But Wayne stuck to his agreement, although, from his point of view, he was right to be concerned about the picture: whether good or bad, it was one of the few box-office flops he starred in.

With younger, hand-picked directors like Andrew V. McLaglen and Burt Kennedy, Wayne knew that his views would be respected. Kennedy had worked as a writer for Wayne before being given the chance to direct *The War Wagon* and told ''Cinema'' (Vol. 4, No. 1) what Wayne was like. ''He's tough to work with and he'll admit it. But I understand his position; he remembers me as a writer. He'll try to help to the point that he may hurt. But there's no doubt he knows what he's doing. He's been doing it long enough. I'd like to do another picture with Duke. I've got my spurs now with him.'' (Kennedy has had that further opportunity with *The Train Robbers.*)

Wayne then, had the respect of almost all the people he has worked with. Even the current crop of stars bow to his reputation as a dedicated worker. Steve McQueen is reported as saying: ''Sometimes kids ask me what a pro is. I just point to the Duke.''

4. Beginning at Fox (1926-31)

IT WAS in 1926 that Wayne first made contact with the world of movie-making. Not yet twenty, he had accepted a football scholarship at the University of Southern California. He was lean and good-looking, born in the maize-growing state of Iowa on May 26, 1907 (though the date is sometimes given as 1908). His father was Clyde Morrison, a hard-up pharmacist who named him Marion Michael. Because of a lung complaint, Mr. Morrison was compelled to move to a warm, dry climate and so he, his wife Mary (née Brown), and young Marion settled on a ranch near Lancaster, California, on the edge of the Mojave desert. Here they struggled to put a smallholding into shape but after a couple of years they lost the battle against an unfriendly environment and Mr. Morrision went to work in a drug store at Glendale, a suburb of Los Angeles, and then set up in business for himself. For Marion (joined by a younger brother, Robert E.) life in the desert had meant

hours of swimming in a huge irrigation ditch and riding a horse to school; now in Glendale he earned pocket money working for his father, delivering medicines and also newspapers; he had a large Airedale dog which he called "Duke" and the nickname also attached itself to the animal's young owner. Marion would spend his pocket money at the local movie house, revelling in the exploits of Douglas Fairbanks and imitating them in play. At school, he showed an outstanding ability at football, and he also made his mark academically, writing a prize essay and joining the debating team. His big ambition was to be selected to attend the Annapolis Naval Academy in Maryland but he narrowly missed being accepted. So it was that he went to the University of Southern California and, seeking employment during a summer vacation, approached his football coach for suggestions. So, when the coach was asked by the great cowboy star, Tom Mix, if he could provide some good

Frame enlargement of Wayne as the excited race spectator in Hangman's House *(1928).*

seats for a game, Mix agreed to the condition that he should find some work for Marion Morrison and another footballer in exchange for tickets. A few days later the two youngsters turned up at the Fox studio and met Mix in his dressing room. He told them that he would be making a Western, *The Great K & A Train Robbery,* later in the summer and they could help him keep in shape by taking exercise runs with him each morning. In the meantime, he found them a place on what was known as the "swing gang," earning a whole thirty-five dollars a week for moving props and set decorations around the studio.

It was while Wayne (to give him his more familiar name) had this lowly position at the studio that he first encountered John Ford, by then a major director on the lot. It was 1927 and Ford was making a film called *Mother Machree* which Wayne joined as a further prop man during production. His chores included looking after a herd of geese who kept straying across a huge outdoor set. Ford had heard that the young man was a footballer, kidded him over the kind of work he was doing, and invited him to demonstrate a football position. Ford then tackled Wayne and tipped him into a mud puddle. Wayne invited Ford to try again and, being prepared this time, put the great director on the ground with a thud. Ford was at first mad but then amused at the youngster's audacity.

It is sometimes said that Wayne appeared as an extra in *Mother Machree**. As no prints of this film are thought to have survived, it is impossible to know for sure. At any rate Wayne went on to work as a prop man

*It has also been reported that Wayne, with other football team-mates, was seen as himself in a 1927 college football drama, *The Drop Kick.*

on Ford's *Four Sons,* released in February 1928. Here again, he made an impression on the director by wandering into the background of a shot, sweeping up some leaves, unaware that the camera was rolling. Spotting his mistake, Wayne ran off to a roar of amusement from the cast and crew.

Three months later, when Ford's next picture, *Hangman's House,* came out, Wayne had progressed to some small bits in front of the camera. This film has survived and Wayne is clearly visible in four shots, two of them centered on him. The film is set in Ireland and includes a horse race. Wayne is first seen from behind, leaning against a fence, glancing at John D'Arcy (played by Earle Foxe) as he passes through a gate in the fence before the race starts. Then, during the race itself, Ford uses three shots of Wayne as a spectator becoming increasingly excited by what he is seeing. In the first, he is banging on the fence, hat rammed on his head, urging the horses on. The second shows him more centrally placed in the shot, leaping up and down and starting to knock the fence apart (it is briefly intercut with a shot of the horses). The third has him breaking through the fence leading other spectators in a surge forward to gather round the winning horse. Shortly afterwards, there's a dusty mêlée when D'Arcy shoots the animal and Wayne was probably in the thick of it; he could also have been one of the blindfolded figures with a noose around his neck who earlier on haunts the judge (Hobart Bosworth) who has sentenced them to die.

Wayne may have done other bits in Fox films around this period but this is the only one to have come to light at the present time. What can be positively asserted is that in *Words and Music*, released more than a year later in August 1929, Wayne had graduated to actual billing for the first time, appearing sixth in the cast list

David Percy, John Wayne and Frank Albertson gather around Lois Moran in Words and Music *(1929).*

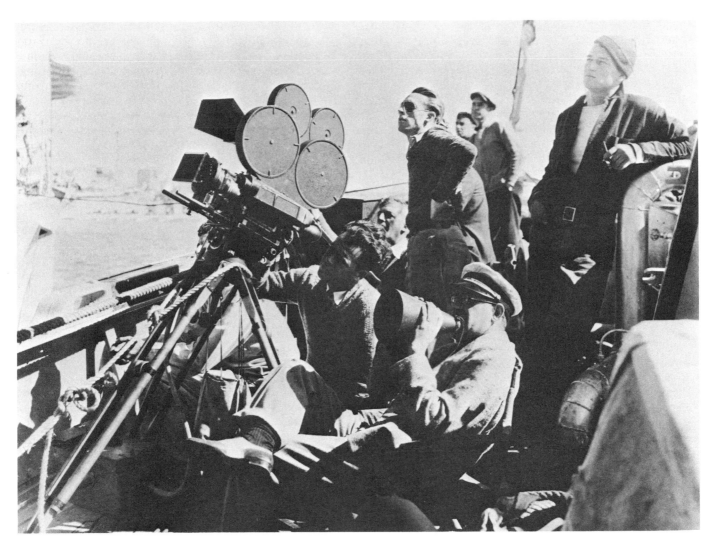

John Wayne (at right) watches director John Ford give instructions through his megaphone during production of Men Without Women *(1930).*

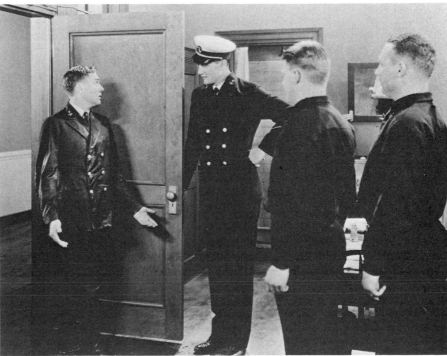

Frank Albertson, John Wayne and players in a moment from Salute *(1929).*

using his real name of Morrison and prefacing it with his nickname, Duke. The film centered on a campus beauty, Mary Brown (Lois Moran) with two students, Phil Denning (David Percy) and Pete Donahue (Wayne), competing for her affections. The two men enter an annual competition for the best musical number written by a collegian and ask Mary to perform their work. She complies with both requests in the annual college revue but it is Phil's entry that wins the contest and Phil who wins the girl. A typical, lavish musical comedy from the early days of sound, it featured an actor called Ward Bond in a very minor role. Bond was to become one of Wayne's closest friends through the years ahead.

By a curious twist of fate, Wayne at last managed to enter the Annapolis Naval Academy in Maryland where he had hoped to enroll as a student. He went as part of the team making *Salute* (1929). This was a drama with a big football game as its climax and Wayne joined Ward Bond and a number of football players that director John Ford had recruited from universities in the Los Angeles area to play out a complete game before the cameras. The second half was dramatically enhanced by driving rain which reduced the players to battling on in the muddiest of conditions. Ford selected footage from the game to blend with shots featuring his principal players. The plot had to do with Army-Navy rivalry as personified by two brothers (George O'Brien, William Janney) who come face to face in the big match, their differences being helped towards a happy resolution by the outcome of the match being a tie. Wayne also had some bits to play off the field as a cadet.

Ford kept Wayne for his next film, a naval drama called *Men Without Women* (1930). The actor had the small role of the sailor who relays the messages from the divers clearing the torpedo tube of a sunken submarine, the S-13, to the officer commanding the rescue operation. He had four or five lines to speak for the talking version but these are rendered as titles in the surviving silent prints. His lines were filmed in a mere couple of camera set-ups but he is clearly visible with earphones and mouthpiece, locks of hair curling over his forehead. However, he made a more impressive contribution to the film as a stuntman. When the regular stuntmen were fearful of the risks involved, Wayne dived boldly into the choppy sea, coming up to the surface several times over to represent the crew of the submarine escaping from the vessel below. His unhesitating assistance did much to cement his friendship with John Ford.

However, it was back to work solely as a prop man that Wayne went on Ford's subsequent picture, *Born Reckless* (1930), though he turned up as a bit actor in two other films made around that time: a George O'Brien outdoor adventure called *Rough Romance*, set in the forests of Oregon, and another college musical comedy, *Cheer Up and Smile*. Neither of these acting chores could have given him much satisfaction, denying him the billing he had gained on *Words and Music* and making his future as an actor seem distinctly bleak. It was a dramatically apt moment for him to be catapulted into an opportunity beyond his wildest dreams.

While carrying props around on *Born Reckless*, he had been noticed by director Raoul Walsh who was busy planning to shoot an epic of Western pioneering days, *The Big Trail*. Gary Cooper had declined to take the leading role and Walsh had decided to look for an unknown as a way of economising . A huge amount had been allocated to reconstruct a wagon train trek on location and there was additional expense to be faced in shooting the film both on conventional 35mm and for 70mm wide-screen presentation in a process called Fox Grandeur.

The tall, commanding figure of the prop boy looked right for the part and, when John Ford vouched for Wayne's dedication to work, Walsh arranged a screen test. Wayne pretended to be the wagon train leader and fielded questions about the journey improvised by other members of the cast. He lost his temper while doing this and Walsh was delighted. He soon had the part and was put into training. He took lessons in knife-throwing and handling tomahawks. He suffered at the hands of a dramatic coach from the East, assigned by the studio to improve his elocution, and hated the fancy delivery that was forced on him. With Walsh's approval, he went back to his normal manner of speech. Meanwhile, the Fox executives started to beat the publicity drum and gave him a fresh start with the name of John Wayne*. His salary was all of a fabulous seventy-five dollars a week.

Reacting so positively against the exaggerated acting encouraged in those early days of sound by the Broadway voice tutors, Wayne turns in a performance that stands up well today. He certainly *looks* the part, making a stirring figure of action and showing himself to be capable of horsemanship. His handling of moments of deep feeling and those of leadership compensate for his occasional weaknesses, the delivery of more routine lines in a monotonous, rushed fashion, and sometimes stiff expressions. Wayne's inexperience still seems overly evident to some viewers; but I side with those who respond to the underlying forcefulness of personality.

In any case, the film did not rest so much on Wayne as on its spectacular highlights and the painstaking recreation of the hazards of pioneering with a buffalo hunt, a massive Indian attack on the wagons grouped in a circle, the fording of a swollen river and the lowering of cattle and wagons down a sheer cliff-face played out against a backdrop of rainstorms, blizzards and desert heat.

Instead of settling for the dramatic effectiveness of these sequences, the film dragged in a subsidiary plot about Wayne's Breck Coleman seeking to avenge the

*Though not given any choice in the matter, Wayne had always and sensibly welcomed the name thrust upon him. It is probably coincidence but one of the characters in a Fox Western starring Buck Jones, *The Arizona Romeo* (1925), had the very same name. In a recent interview, Wayne spoke of being credited under the name of Michael Burn on an early picture. Although he says this was for Republic, he was too well established to have changed his name from John Wayne when that company was formed in the mid-Thirties. In any case, I cannot trace any credit to a Michael Burn (or Byrne or Berne) anywhere during the early years of Wayne's career.

The Big Trail (1930): John
Wayne romances Marguerite
Churchill and talks to
Tyrone Power Sr. on the trail.

murder of a trapper friend besides leading the wagon train. Fortunately, he is able to manage both at the same time, discovering that one of the travellers, Red Flack (Tyrone Power Sr.), is the guilty party and settling the score with him during a snowstorm. There was also some conventional romance to be played out by Wayne and Marguerite Churchill as Ruth Cameron, following the usual course of mutual animosity to Ruth's ultimate respect and lasting affection for Wayne's manliness.

Fittingly, the last image surrenders to the might of nature as Wayne and his girl embrace passionately in a forest and the camera pans up the towering tree trunks that utterly dwarf them.

Because *The Big Trail* was a box-office flop when it came out in late 1930, it has been too readily assumed that Wayne was to blame. It is obviously true that he did not manage of his own accord to stir audiences into flocking to the picture, but the film would have had to do extraordinarily well to recoup its high cost and exhibitors were reluctant to shell out the money to equip their theatres for the 70mm version Fox were stressing. They had already had the expenses of wiring for sound and money was tight during the Depression.

Fox had had enough of taking chances and put their wide-screen process away to gather dust until they were ready for another gamble with CinemaScope in the early Fifties. They also played safe with Wayne, giving him roles with billing under more prominent actresses for a couple of pictures before letting him go.

In *Girls Demand Excitement* (1931), yet another higher education frolic, Virginia Cherrill played the spoiled young student from a wealthy background with Wayne as Peter Brooks, a hard-up figure working his way through college. Wayne is the strong, silent type with no time for girls — in fact, he is trying to end the co-educational system. But the heroine exercises her charm to softening effect. Wayne felt embarrassed at being required by the film's dance director to climb up trees or lean out of windows to kiss girls. Nevertheless, the "New York Times" thought he gave a "manly performance," having earlier gone as far as to extend warm praise for his work in *The Big Trail* ("Mr. Wayne acquits himself with no little distinction. His performance is pleasingly natural.").

However, Wayne had slipped to only acting "fairly well" in the estimation of the "Times" when he was seen in *Three Girls Lost* (1931) but the part of an architect called Gordon Wales was hardly custom-made for him. In the film he is the resident of an apartment block in Chicago who goes out for a walk one night and returns to find one of the other residents, Marcia Tallant (Joan Marsh), locked out. He lets her in, flirts with her, and steals a kiss. She, however, is a heartless gold digger and, when she is murdered after taking up with a bootlegger (Lew Cody), suspicion falls on Wayne of having killed her in a fit of jealousy. He manages to clear his name and finds happiness with one of Marcia's room-mates, Noreen McMann (Loretta Young).

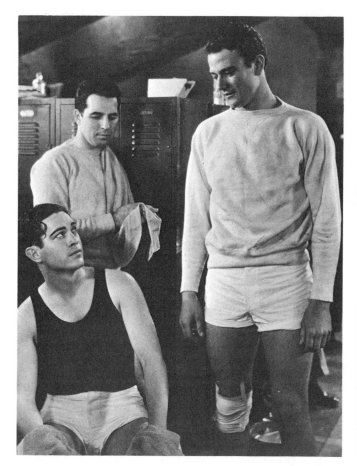

Left, John Wayne and unidentified players in Girls Demand Excitement *(1931).* *Below, Wayne and Joan Marsh in* Three Girls Lost *(1931).*

24

5. A Contract with Columbia (1931-32)

WHEN WAYNE was taken on by Columbia for a six months contract, it was a step down as this was a minor studio at that time compared to Fox (it didn't as yet distribute its own pictures in Britain, handing them to United Artists). Columbia made something of a habit of picking up players and stars from other studios' discards instead of cultivating its own. Like Wayne, Rita Hayworth was to be dropped by Fox and picked up by Columbia; unlike Wayne she became a big star there while he went rapidly downhill.

He began in *Men Are Like That* (1931), released in Britain as *The Virtuous Wife*. Although again supporting a bigger name actress, Laura LaPlante, Wayne at least had a picture with a masculine ring to its American title after two films that emphasised Girls in their titles. It was a strong role as Lieutenant Bob Denton, a West Point cadet and outstanding footballer who is popular with the ladies (the film showed him in action on the field). He breaks off an affair with one girl, Evelyn Palmer (Laura LaPlante) and, when he is posted to Arizona, he finds that she has become the wife of his guardian and commanding officer, Colonel Bonham (Forrest Stanley). He is attracted to her sister Bonita (June Clyde) and his old flame reacts from mixed motives of jealousy and protecting her sister from a similar rebuff by accusing him of trying to embrace her in her husband's absence. Wayne is asked to resign from the Army but when it is revealed that he has already married Bonita, Evelyn confesses and is forgiven by the Colonel. By now Wayne had completely lost the support of the "New York Times" who found him "not convincing" but the fact that he was playing in an updated version of an antiquated play may not have helped.

At this point Wayne fell out of favour with Columbia's boss, Harry Cohn, who heard rumours that

Laura LaPlante, Forrest Stanley and John Wayne in Men Are Like That *(1931).*

Wheeler Oakman, Tim McCoy and John Wayne in Two Fisted Law *(1932).*
Jack Holt instructs the team in Maker of Men *(1931), Wayne at his left shoulder.*

his new star was drinking on the set and playing around with one of the studio's leading actresses, a lady in whom Cohn himself took a keen interest. Cohn declined to believe Wayne's denials of the charges and coarsely told him, "Keep your pants buttoned at my studio." Suddenly Wayne found he wasn't working much, although still receiving his salary under contract, and the films he did get didn't give him any chance to excel. Three were B Westerns in which he was thoroughly eclipsed by their stars.

In *Range Feud,* Buck Jones (another Fox graduate claimed by Columbia) was the new sheriff, Buck Gordon, and Wayne played his foster brother and son of a local rancher. When Wayne, as Clint Turner, is accused of murdering a rival rancher who was an enemy of his father but whose daughter Judy (Susan Fleming) he loves, the sheriff has to arrest him but saves him while the noose is around his neck by exposing the real culprit.

In two Tim McCoy Westerns he was simply a pal of the star with only a handful of lines to speak. These were *Texas Cyclone* and *Two Fisted Law* (both 1932). In the latter, Wayne was called Duke (his real-life nickname) and was down to sixth place in the cast list, just above Walter Brennan as a crooked deputy; he played the ranch hand who has to be paid off by McCoy's Tim Clark after villain Bob Russell (Wheeler Oakman) has

stolen his spread and McCoy decides to go off and look for silver.

In one of his other Columbia pictures, a notch up in size, Wayne took the familiar role of a footballer, this time called Dusty. The film, titled *Maker of Men*, revolved around Richard Cromwell as the sensitive son of a tough University football coach (Jack Holt) who fails to live up to his father's expectations. After being disowned by pater, school and girlfriend when he plays badly in a vital match, he joins a rival college and helps it defeat his father's team. Wayne was one of the students who taunted Cromwell over his apparent cowardice.

The most humiliating part of his stay at Columbia came when he was ordered to play a corpse in *The Deceiver* (1931). The film was a crime mystery in which Ian Keith, who had supported Wayne in *The Big Trail*, played an actor, Reginald Thorpe, found dead in his dressing room with a knife in his back leaving the usual rich bunch of suspects to be sifted through. Keith was not available to appear as the corpse in one scene, and Wayne had to stand in for him. It cannot be coincidental that, while Wayne has worked more than once for every other major studio since he became a top box-office star, he has never returned to Columbia since finishing this early contract on so humiliating a note.

6. Down Poverty Row: The Serial Star (1932-33)

WAYNE escaped from Columbia only to land in "Poverty Row", the name given to the small independent companies who ground out modest features and serials for quick playoff in small theatres. Here he became the star of three serials made by Mascot, one of them released before all his Columbia work had been seen.

On the way to Mascot, he did pause to make an isolated appearance for Paramount in a quite impressive small film called *Lady and Gent* (1932). Here he played Buzz Kinney, former college student and now a young boxer who knocks out the veteran prizefighter Stag Bailey (George Bancroft) when the latter is over confident in the ring. By the end of the film, Wayne has gone to seed, with a cauliflower ear, broken nose, stubbly chin, and a sarcastic, bitter frame of mind. It is the most extreme form of make-up ever applied to Wayne's features and consequently both grotesque and disturbing to see today, as well as a jolt from the kind of bland parts he was playing then.

The first Mascot serial to appear was *Shadow of the Eagle* (1932). The Eagle was one of those master villains beloved of serials who spelt out his threats against a large corporation by writing them in the sky. Nathan Gregory (Edward Hearn), the owner of a travelling fairground, is suspected of being the Eagle, having the flying ability and a grudge against the threatened company for stealing an invention of his. Wayne is Craig

McCoy, one of the fairground attractions, a skilled pilot and skywriter who gets on the track of the Eagle after Gregory mysteriously disappears. He locates the missing Gregory, unmasks the Eagle, and marries Gregory's daughter, Jean (Dorothy Gulliver). Among the highlights of this chapterplay is Wayne's recovery of the stolen plans from one of the villains, Boyle (Yakima Canutt), seizing them from the man's hands as he dashes past on a motorcycle. This was the first of many working associations between Wayne and Canutt.

Wayne was a pilot again in the second Mascot serial *The Hurricane Express* (1932). This time the villain is called The Wrecker and his target is the L & R Railroad. One of the victims of the train wrecks he has caused is the father of Larry Baker (Wayne). As in *Shadow of the Eagle,* a prime suspect is Wayne's employer, the head of an airline competing with the railroad. But there is also Stratton (Edmund Breese), a man falsely charged with embezzlement by the railroad, who has escaped from jail; his daughter, Gloria (Shirley Grey), who is working for the railroad under an assumed name in the hope of clearing her father; a discharged employee (Matthew Betz) anxious to get even; and others with a score to settle. The Wrecker is a master of disguise, capable of assuming the appearance of anyone he chooses, but Wayne battles on to avenge his father, surviving such tight spots as being trapped with Gloria in a blazing plane as it reels through space, and unmasks the criminal mastermind in the final reel.

Aerial exploits had an opening in the third and last of the Wayne serials, *The Three Musketeers* (1933), with Wayne once more cast as a flyer. The production was ''inspired'' by the Dumas story to the extent of making him (playing one Tom Wayne) the modern D'Artagnan who recruits his Musketeers when he rescues three legionnaires from the clutches of some rebels in the Arabian desert. They are Clancy (Jack Mulhall), Renard (Raymond Hatton) and Schmidt (Francis X. Bushman Jr.), and with their help Wayne takes on the enigmatic El Shasta, a man whose face has never been revealed as he stirs up the locals with the aim of wiping out the Foreign Legion.

Later in 1933 Wayne was the star of *His Private Secretary*, made by a small producing and distributing outfit called Showmen's Pictures. This modest venture was a romantic comedy in which Wayne, as Dick Wallace, was the son of a wealthy businessman (Reginald Barlow) who opposes his plans to marry a minister's grand-daughter (Evelyn Knapp) and wants him to settle down and work for the family concern. Wayne's girl overcomes his father's objections by taking a job as his secretary and proving her worth.

Left, George Bancroft and (in background) John Wayne in a battling moment from Lady and Gent *(1932).*
Below left, a scene from episode 8, 'On the Spot', of Shadow of the Eagle *(1932): the Eagle strikes again, leaving Edmund Burns dead on the floor after the lights have gone out. John Wayne has some explaining to do to the directors of the harassed corporation.*
Below, the final episode of The Hurricane Express *(1932): the Wrecker is unmasked – it looks like Conway Tearle.*

28

John Wayne gets his orders from Robert Warwick in The Three Musketeers *(1933). Emile Chautard is at right.*

Above, John Wayne with Francis X. Bushman Jr., Raymond Hatton and Jack Mulhall in The Three Musketeers *(1933).*

Right, Reginald Barlow, John Wayne and Arthur Hoyt in His Private Secretary *(1933).*

John Wayne at Warners –
The Big Stampede *(1932) and
(below)* Ride Him Cowboy *(1932).*

7. Westerns for Warners (1932-33)

WAYNE'S career took a turn for the better when he was signed by Warner Bros. to star in a set of cowboy pictures to be produced by Leon Schlesinger. These gave Warners a series to compete with those being made at other studios by such stars as Fox's George O'Brien and Paramount's Randolph Scott. The six pictures that resulted under the contract were short, well-produced and actional, combining the thrills of the chase and the fistfight with humour, romance and horsemanship in an artless but breezy fashion. Wayne was teamed with a white steed called Duke and billed as either "The Devil Horse" or "The Miracle Horse."

As noted in the filmography, four of the films were direct re-makes of silent Ken Maynard Westerns, so that the appeal of the basic stories had already been tested. In addition, Warners were able to use stock footage from the silent versions — especially the big action sequences or panoramic views which would have been expensive to film again. In one such re-make, *Somewhere in Sonora*, Wayne and the heroine are dressed closely enough to their counterparts in the earlier version to be indistinguishable in long shot. Even in

a Wayne film which was not a re-make, *The Telegraph Trail*, the script was shaped to incorporate a massive Indian attack from Ken Maynard's *The Red Raiders*, and only discrepancies in the quality of photography (with the later version coming off best) and in the film speed give the game away. And the one remaining original from the sextet — *The Man from Monterey* —bears some marked similarities to Ken Maynard's *Senor Americano* (1930) made for Universal and partly written by Lesley Mason who scripted the Wayne film.

Warners made further use of their previous productions where music was concerned. This was usually confined to the opening titles and end fade-out (with an occasional musical interlude somewhere between), and the music of "Under a Texas Moon" from the 1930 talkie of the same name played over the titles and at the end of Wayne's *The Big Stampede*.

It is interesting to note that in these six pictures Wayne always plays a character called "John," and in fact Ken Maynard's part of Tom Drury in his version of *Ride Him Cowboy* becomes John Drury for Wayne. It seems most probable that it was simply a matter of

John Wayne and Paul Hurst in The Big Stampede *(1932).*

Left, Wayne and Mae Madison in The Big Stampede *(1932). Right, Wayne in action from* Haunted Gold *(1932).*

attempting to merge the actor and the part in audiences' minds to help build up a following so that it was John Wayne up there on screen rather than an actor in a role. In his later B Westerns, Wayne continued to play "John" roles most of the time, and other B Western stars like Gene Autry even used their full names for their screen work.

First of the six was *Ride Him, Cowboy* (1932), released in Britain as *The Hawk*. Wayne's John Drury is the wandering cowboy who saves a spirited wild horse from being destroyed after a murderer, whose identity the horse knows, tries to cover up his crime by laying the blame for a rancher's death on the animal. Wayne trains Duke, the horse, to do his bidding and sets about tracking down the killer, a bandit known as the Hawk whose gang have been responsible for terrorising the neighbourhood. The Hawk is in reality the town's leading citizen (Frank Hagney) and he turns the tables on Wayne and has him brought up in court on a faked charge. Here Otis Harlan contributed the humour that was a staple ingredient of the series as a biased judge while Wayne, helped by his horse and a girl (Ruth Hall), is able to establish his innocence and expose the Hawk. Said a British trade paper in a review that could have applied to any of the succeeding films: "The familiar ingredients have been mixed with skill, and the fast pace at which the story unfolds cleverly cloaks the obvious. The horsemanship is excellent, the humour is well above average, and the atmosphere is good in detail. Short and snappy, the film should make a useful second feature."

This was followed by *The Big Stampede* (1932) in which Noah Beery Sr. made a colourful villain, playing a ranch owner who disposes of the local lawmen to allow his men to rustle cattle unchecked. But John Wayne was John Steele, the deputy sheriff dispatched to the area to foil their plans, who recruits a bandit (Luis Alberni, providing the comic relief) to assist him. The film's climax was all that its title promised, thanks to Ken Maynard's work in the silent version. Also in the cast was Berton Churchill, later to play the banker in *Stagecoach* and here portraying the Governor of New Mexico, Lew Wallace (better known as the author of "Ben-Hur").

Next came *Haunted Gold* (1932) which made rather eerie use of the paraphernalia of the mystery chiller: sliding panels, sinister shadows, and hooded figures. Also borrowed from this other genre was the comic relief of Blue Washington as a superstitious black easily alarmed by the unusual goings-on. Wayne (as John Mason) and heroine Sheila Terry played a couple who answer a mysterious letter telling them to visit a ghost town which has an abandoned gold mine. Also in the area are a band of crooks (led by Harry Woods) who are trying to locate a hidden fortune in gold. Wayne, helped by a mysterious figure called The Phantom (who turns out to be the heroine's supposedly-dead father and the rightful owner of the gold), is able to thwart the opposition but doing so involves him in a spectacular fight in a wooden container suspended over a chasm on a cable.

Haunted Gold was followed by *The Telegraph Trail* (1933). Wayne is the U.S. Army scout, John Trent, who volunteers to complete the stringing of the telegraph wire across the plains after the Indians (led by Yakima Canutt and stirred up by Albert J. Smith as a white trader) have killed a good friend of his. "Those red devils!" he snarls with choked rage, his face tightening, the skin shining, and his eyes narrowing to slits as the

Above, Luis Alberni, Noah Beery Sr. and John Wayne in The Big Stampede *(1932).*
Below left, Albert J. Smith and Wayne brawl in The Telegraph
Trail *(1933), watched by Marceline Day and Otis Harlan.*
Below right, Wayne in The Man from Monterey *(1933).*

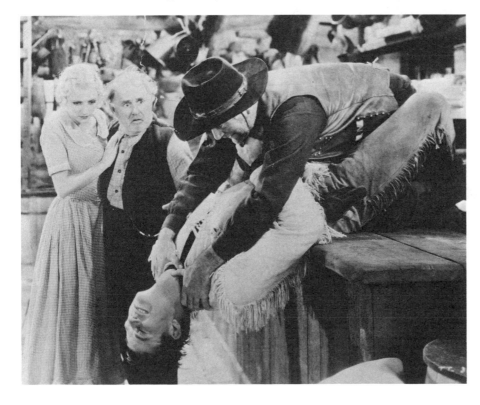

telegraph key ominously stops chattering. Soon he has organised the people of a nearby town to lend a hand at the construction camp and in a pitched battle the Indians are routed. It is, said a contemporary reviewer, "a big picture in miniature." The big picture, in fact, was the old Ken Maynard film that loaned most of the impressive climax, with especially striking shots of an Indian war dance; the miniature picture was the rest. Its romance is woefully contrived at the outset, leading to an exchange of blows and knives between Albert J. Smith as a would-be suitor and John Wayne as an invented *fiancé* whom the heroine says she fears. In fact, Wayne is extraordinarily cordial later on, frequently calling her "dear" as in "Help's on the way, dear." Credibility is not enhanced by having the heroine overhear the plans of the villains by accident on two separate occasions. The comedy relief provided by Frank McHugh and Otis Harlan has dated badly. But Duke the horse does his stuff with aplomb whether carrying a lover's message or harrying an Indian with kicks from the rear. And Wayne is extremely capable in handling the lighter moments (such as joking with his girl) or in issuing orders or recruiting the townspeople, though he seems unsure of himself as an actor when called on to do nothing much but stand around or when displaying intense emotion. In a relaxed moment at the construction camp, he is shown performing on a harmonica, but his singing days have not yet arrived and he leaves the other cowboys with their guitars to render the film's song break.

Somewhere in Sonora (1933) came next. Wayne played John Bishop, the cowboy wrongly accused of

A lively moment from The Man from Monterey *(1933).*

John Wayne, Ruth Hall, Lillian Leighton and Donald Reed in The Man from Monterey

misconduct during a coach race at a rodeo show. Forced to cross the border into Mexico, he learns of a plan to rob a silver mine owned by the father (Ralph Lewis) of the girl he loves (Marceline Day again). He joins up with the plotters, eventually outwits them, and also recovers the missing son of his old boss (Henry B. Walthall, the former star of silent pictures). Playing the son, who has been a captive of the gang, was Paul Fix in the first of a great many associations with Wayne.

The last of this series was *The Man from Monterey* (1933) which was more of a costume adventure than a Western, being set in California in the days of the sword, not the six-gun. Wayne played Army Captain John Holmes who is instructed to persuade an elderly Spanish landowner (Lafe McKee) to register his property under a new act before it goes into public domain. Conflicting advice comes from a neighbour (Donald Reed) but Wayne is able to expose the latter's shady motives as well as save heroine Ruth Hall (co-star of the first of these Warner pictures) from marrying the scoundrel. Luis Alberni was again in charge of the film's moments of humour, and Wayne had one spectacular action scene, thrusting his sword at the villains from a tabletop.

After Wayne's departure, Warners gave up making series Westerns until they made Dick Foran the singing star of a group of pictures in 1936-37. The old Ken Maynards again received the re-make treatment and one story that both Wayne and Maynard had filmed went before the cameras once more.

* * *

While under contract to the studio, Wayne had one fairly important opportunity to act outside the Western field in a main feature. He achieved respectable billing in fifth place in *Baby Face* (1933). Here he was Jimmy McCoy, one of the men who littered the trail of Lily,

alias Baby Face (Barbara Stanwyck), in her ruthless climb to the top from a dubious speakeasy background. Wayne's position in the film as undermanager of a bank made him a useful stepping stone — finding her a job, gaining her promotion, and then being discarded as she goes on to become the mistress of the bank's president, lending a note of *double entendre* to her line when Wayne regrets "Oh, I never see you any more..." and she replies "I never see anybody, I'm working so hard. I have to go to bed early every night."

However, Warners evidently saw no need to waste Wayne's spare time and pressed him into service doing several uncredited bit roles in non-Westerns. His appearances were so slight that none of the contemporary reviews I have consulted bother to mention him and I am grateful to film historians Leonard Maltin and William K. Everson for confirming his presence in *College Coach* and *Central Airport* (both 1933). In the former film, a football story, Wayne can be seen walking up to Dick Powell as a star player and wishing him good luck in a game; in the latter, he doesn't even speak and is barely recognisable as one of the men aboard a downed airplane seen floundering in the ocean at night (a studio tank long shot).

Better known is Wayne's bit as a confident boxer called Smith in *The Life of Jimmy Dolan* (also 1933, released in Britain as *The Kid's Last Fight)* but his part was so peripheral that he could go off to be knocked out in the ring without the camera bothering to follow, focusing instead on Douglas Fairbanks Jr. as the star of the picture.

Though Warners' handling of Wayne in the last three films seems nearly as insulting as the treatment meted out to him at Columbia, he was not the only contract player to suffer that way at the studio and it was probably not his choice to leave. At any rate, no lasting grudge resulted and Warners and Wayne were happily reunited in the Fifties for several years.

Wayne and Barbara Stanwyck in Baby Face *(1933)*.

8. The Lone Star Years (1933-35)

IT WAS Trem Carr, the production head at Monogram Studios (one of the principal companies on "Poverty Row"), who decided to star Wayne in a series of Westerns, made for little more than ten thousand dollars apiece on three-and-a-half-day schedules. Sixteen films were made in rapid succession, billed as "Lone Star" productions and released in the United States between October 1933 and July 1935, representing Wayne's only screen work during the period. Most were directed (and often written) by Robert North Bradbury (father of Western actor Bob Steele), photographed by Archie Stout (who was to work with Wayne again in the actor's better years), and featuring players George Hayes (prior to becoming the bearded comic "Gabby" Hayes), Earl Dwire, Lafe (Lafayette) McKee, and — most interestingly — Yakima Canutt.

Canutt was the man who performed the difficult stunts in these pictures (often doubling for Wayne) and generally appeared as a badman who had an inevitable set-to with Wayne as the hero. Working so often together, these two actors have been credited with developing much more convincing fistfights than were customary in such minor Westerns. They carefully rehearsed their action scenes together and took aim at each other's faces. Whereas, in other films, punches were often filmed from the side and patently missed the chins they were aimed at, Canutt saw that the camera was placed behind the punch so that the blow could appear to connect. Wayne demanded to be allowed to reply to his screen adversaries in kind: when they pitched chairs and tables at him, he was apt to sling them back. "Why does a cowboy star have to be so stupidly noble he can't give as good as he gets?", argued Wayne. In fact, just the use of objects to supplement mere fisticuffs was an advance on general practice. This was one of the ways in which this group of pictures compares very favourably with other independent action films of the time, if less well in comparison with the efforts of the larger studios.

Like the Warner Westerns earlier, these Lone Star productions made limited use of music: only the credits and the brief closing scene (generally a touch of romance or comedy) were backed by it, and the music chosen was usually not particularly suited to the mood of the film or sequence. Sound effects were limited: there is no sound attached to blows connecting in the fist fights of *Blue Steel* or *The Dawn Rider* and the later *The Star Packer* puts in some peculiar "clicks". These pictures generally offered rather drab scenery (they didn't stray far from the studio) and made heavy use of a fast pan to link up shots of two difference places or to cover the passage of time and distance on a journey.

Monogram initially broached the idea of making

John Wayne and Nancy Shubert
in Sagebrush Trail *(1933).*

Wayne a singing cowboy and created the character of "Singin' Sandy" Saunders for the first of the batch, *Riders of Destiny*. There had been songs in Westerns previously — in some of the early sound Ken Maynard pictures like *Sons of the Saddle* (1930) and also in such big-budget specials as *In Old Arizona* (1929) — but it was a novel addition for such cheap pictures as Monogram planned.

It presented one major difficulty. Wayne could not sing. His own limited baritone wouldn't do and so he merely mouthed the words of his songs while singer Smith Ballew loaned his voice out of camera range. Even Wayne's apparent guitar-playing was provided by an expert off-screen. The results, seen today, are somewhat hilarious as Wayne walks along facing the camera with a look of strained nonchalance on his features as a completely inappropriate voice mumbles a song about how "There'll be blood a-running in town before night" and a bystander mercifully interrupts the warbling to point him out as "Singin' Sandy — the most notorious gunman since Billy the Kid!" Wayne must have been much happier living up to that description in an archetypal main street shootout with the lean, mean figure of Slip Morgan (Earl Dwire), forcefully delivering the line "Make it fast, Slippery, this is your last draw!"

What finally put paid to Monogram's musical hopes was Wayne's acute embarrassment when he made some personal appearances only to be met with his fans' demands that he should regale them with a rendering of "The Desert Song" and other favourites. He protested to the studio and — apart from briefly "singing" at the start of the *The Man from Utah* and in *Westward Ho* — his days as a threat to the likes of Bing Crosby were over with the release of *Riders of Destiny*. (Shortly afterwards, the same studio recruited the leading hillbilly recording artist, Gene Autry, and made him into a cowboy singer with immensely profitable results.)

In *Riders of Destiny*, however "notorious" he seemed, Wayne was really a government man working undercover. He drifts into a small town where the local ranchers are being victimised by Kincaid (Forrest Taylor) who controls the water supply and is out to take over their land. Somewhat appropriately, Kincaid ends up being drowned and Wayne's Singin' Sandy is rewarded for his triumph over the villains by gaining the love of one of Kincaid's intended victims (Cecilia Parker).

The next film, *Sagebrush Trail,* presents Wayne as the cowboy wrongly imprisoned on a murder charge who escapes from jail and joins up with some desperadoes, hoping to run across the real killer. He befriends a member of the gang, Bob Jones (Lane Chandler), not knowing that Jones is the man he is seeking. Jones, however, suspects him and, being jealous of his interest in a girl (Nancy Shubert), decides to expose Wayne's John Brant to the gang. However, the girl

shows him how Wayne has been a loyal friend, and Jones saves Wayne at the cost of his own life.

The Lucky Texan starred Wayne as Jerry Mason, the man who comes West after leaving college and joins up with his late father's partner, Jake Benson (George Hayes, in a completely sympathetic part). The two men stumble across a creek rich in gold, but have to deal with two claimjumpers (played by Lloyd Whitlock and Yakima Canutt).

West of the Divide was the fourth of the series, and the best of several viewed in the writing of this book. It is revealing to find in Wayne's performance moments of the same intensity of feeling as he brought to later work. In a sequence near the start, he is seen hunkered at a camp, his eyes narrowed and fixed on the far distance, as he recalls for his sidekick (George Hayes) the time when he was left for dead as a youth alongside the body of his murdered father. It's a long monologue, delivered not flatly but with variations of tone, Wayne's voice

Wayne and unidentified player
in Sagebrush Trail *(1933).*

John Wayne, Barbara Sheldon and George Hayes in The Lucky Texan *(1934).*

38

hardening as he says: "And then somebody laughed . . . I'll never forget that laugh . . . it was the laugh of a crazy man." (Not unexpectedly, it is a laugh he is soon to hear again!) Later on, when Wayne says a quite ordinary line, "I've seen that fella somewhere . . . but I can't think when," he draws out the last five words a little as though searching his memory as he speaks, avoiding a straightforward reading that would have been sufficient. Still later, he fights a bully after witnessing his ill-treatment of a boy (who later turns out to be his long-lost brother), and a muscle twitches in his cheek as he concludes by warning: "If you ever whip that kid again, I'll break every bone in your carcase!" I don't mean to suggest that Wayne was giving a startlingly good performance, only that he was clearly a *working* actor, making the most of his lines instead of just reading them, and building up a useful reservoir of technique for later use.

In *West of the Divide* Wayne gains the confidence of the villain Gentry (Lloyd Whitlock) by assuming the identity of a wanted outlaw and joining his gang. After saving an elderly ranch owner (Lafe McKee) from the attentions of the badmen, he is able to confront Gentry as the murderer of his father. Repeating his grim memories of that childhood incident, he concludes ominously, ". . . but I *lived*, lived to even up the score!" And he does just that in an elaborate indoor fight, himself visibly performing a backward somersault, the fracas ending with Gentry being knocked right through a large paned window. Though strong in action, our hero is hesitant in love, and it takes his kid brother (Billy O'Brien) to propose for him to the rancher's daughter (Virginia Brown Faire).

The next, *Blue Steel*, is not so demanding of Wayne but it shows the same appealing sense of youthful sincerity that marked the less intense moments of *West of the Divide* — the likable, gauche manner, awkward but genuine, the sideways smile or open-mouthed grin, the sense of a largely unexplored but real strength of personality. Wayne played the U.S. marshal who sees a robbery and is suspected of being the thief by the sheriff (a tobacco-chewing George Hayes, working towards his later comedy image). The latter befriends him in the hope of uncovering evidence to use against him, not

Lafe McKee is the corpse being studied by George Hayes, Eleanor Hunt, John Wayne, Ed Peil and Yakima Canutt in this scene from Blue Steel *(1934).*

knowing his true identity. Eleanor Hunt, as Betty Mason, makes a most inept heroine whose father (an uncredited Lafe McKee) is killed off by the villains early in the film. Wayne is featured in some brisk action scenes, riding between two horses, scooping up the heroine after she's fallen off a horse, and taking on two men at a barn, suspending one by his feet from a rope and leaping down on the other — all in the process of dealing with a gang of bandits, organised by a leading citizen, who are trying to deprive a town's inhabitants of their property which extends over a valuable gold vein. Besides doubling for Wayne in some of the stunt-work, Yakima Canutt appeared as one of the heavies, the Polka Dot Bandit. The conclusion shows Wayne riding off towards the mountains with the girl.

The Man From Utah opened vigorously with Wayne's John Weston stepping into a fight on the side of the law in a small town but refusing the job of deputy sheriff as he is on his way to deal with a gang who are exploiting a rodeo. There he enters a horse-riding contest and, urged by the outlaws to lose the race to mutual benefit, he sets out to win after removing a needle coated with deadly snake poison and planted in his saddle. The rodeo background introduced some variety into the series but Wayne dealt predictably with the outlaws and won the hand of a judge's daughter (Polly Ann Young).

While Robert N. Bradbury had directed all but *Sagebrush Trail* to this point, Wayne's next, *Randy Rides Alone*, was entrusted to Harry Fraser and this may be the reason that he does deliver some of his lines clumsily in this one. As the lone rider called Randy Bowers, Wayne is accused of murder and attempted robbery but is released from jail by the trusting heroine, Sally Rogers (Alberta Vaughn), to sort out the real villains, a gang led by a mysterious figure who spends most of the time masquerading as one of the townsfolk, Matt the Mute. Played by George Hayes, this cunning character has padded his figure to pass himself off as a hunchback and is prone to impede the progress of the film no end by laboriously writing out messages that, except for his disguise, he could perfectly well speak.

The film is slackly shot and edited but I like the moment when Wayne stumbles into the secret lair of the villains behind a waterfall. They want to know how he got there. "I fell in!" snaps the soaking-wet Wayne, as though daring any of them to make something out of it. Who does he work for, they ask. "Nobody," he replies as brusquely, adding (to justify the film's title) "I ride alone." Wayne's walk in this film has a lazy air of increasing confidence, and he is seen twirling his six-shooter with professional ease before taking aim at the portrait on a wanted poster and shooting out the eyes to demonstrate his marksmanship (though earlier, in *West of the Divide*, Wayne is seen less expertly fluffing a first attempt to reholster his weapon).

Back under Bradbury's direction, Wayne is in better form generally in his next, *The Star Packer*, but finds it difficult when he has to pause to think out a point, his features overdoing the effort of thought and the dawning of the answer; he is also rather less than forceful

when, as sheriff, he issues orders to the townsmen. Wayne is first seen riding into town as John Travers and learning of the trouble caused by a gang working for a figure known only as The Shadow. Matlock, a leading citizen (played by George Hayes) in effect denounces himself when he complains of the gang's activities because he is in reality the criminal mastermind. Wayne, eyes narrowing to a squint, looks around and declares, "If it's just the same with you folks, I'll take the job of sheriff"; there are no objections and he sets about exposing the villains. The action climax is quite vigorously staged and lavish for this series with over twenty players on the screen at the same time. Quite apart from the double identity (more borrowed from the world of serials than a standard Western device), the villain also has a secret tunnel under main street which ends in a phoney-looking tree trunk most improbably located in the road. For a change, Yakima Canutt appears as Yak, a friendly Indian, who is seen at the fade-out teaching a young boy some native tricks watched by an amused Wayne and heroine (Verna Hillie).

All the preceding films were based on original scripts but *The Trail Beyond* was actually drawn from a novel "The Wolf Hunters" by a popular author of stories about the North-West, James Oliver Curwood, making this something of a special for the series with the increased costs of acquiring the novel's rights and other changes that result. The most noticeable is the more impressive background of timber country with snowy mountains in the far distance and vigorous winds. But the director is still Robert Bradbury and the plot creaks with the usual contrivances. Wayne plays Rod Drew who helps his half-breed college chum Wabi (Noah Beery Jr.) escape from the clutches of some cardsharps on a train journey. When they try to frame the death of one of the card players on Wabi, Wayne and the half-breed leap from the train into a river as it crosses a bridge. Wayne has been on his way to find a missing girl, and, while fleeing from a posse with Wabi, quickly (and coincidentally) stumbles on the trail that will eventually lead him to her when he discovers two skeletons in a shack and a map which shows a hidden gold mine. A bunch of villains try to get hold of the map, but Wayne pitches in to stop them kidnapping a girl who knows the combination of the safe in which it has been deposited at the store run by Newsome (Noah Beery Sr.). Captured by the gang, Wayne escapes when left alone by knocking a candle in a glass holder to the ground and cutting the ropes binding him with the broken glass. A canoe chase follows with Wayne dropping into the water to deal with the villains pursuing him, then rushing along the bank to pull a wounded Mountie clear of a canoe before it can crash over a waterfall. As the gang are massing to attack the Newsome store and gain the map, Wayne rides off to bring help from a Mountie post and returns in time to scatter the villains and go after their leader Jules LaRocque (Robert Frazer), dislodging him from a buckboard and rolling down a hillside. Just as La Rocque has a chance to knife Wayne in the back, the Mountie arrives to repay Wayne for saving his life earlier by shooting the villain. Wabi's innocence is

John Wayne, Polly Ann Young and Lafe McKee in The Man from Utah *(1934).*

Below, an appealing publicity shot for Randy Rides Alone (1934) *with Wayne and Alberta Vaughn.*

41

Wayne rescues Noah Beery Jr. from the cardsharps in The Trail Beyond *(1934).*

George Hayes, Lucille Brown and John Wayne in Rainbow Valley *(1935).*

now established and he is last seen waving as Wayne and Newsome's daughter Felice (Verna Hillie) take a canoe trip on a lake together, accompanied by the usual fadeout burst of music.

Besides the improvement over the usual nondescript scenery, the film offers the novelty of canoes being used in place of horses for transport and chases. The photography even aspires to one or two striking shots of sunlight streaming through the trees as LaRocque's men fire on the store at the climax, and clearly there was an extended schedule allowing more than the usual number of camera set-ups. There is a well above average number of extras riding in the climactic scenes and more stuntwork with horses than usual — a number of falls rather isolated from the rest of the action in the climax, and earlier two dives on horseback into a river from a height, one shown from above, the other from the side (perhaps the same stunt with two cameras). These benefits seemed to have impressed contemporary reviewers but *The Trail Beyond* is too underdeveloped in characterisation and too weakly plotted to rise more than marginally above the general standard of the series and whatever the reason for splashing out on this occasion, it was a once-only move and the series promptly settled down into its customary modest groove.

The next in release, *The Lawless Frontier*, cast Wayne as John Tobin with Robert Bradbury directing his own script. Here Wayne was out to avenge the death of his parents at the hands of a Mexican outlaw called Zanti (Earl Dwire, somewhat miscast). Wayne teams up with Dusty, an oldtimer played by George Hayes (a sympathetic part again) who has also suffered from Zanti's actions and, together with Dusty's daughter (Sheila Terry), they bring the bandit's career to an end.

'Neath Arizona Skies presented Wayne as Chris Morrell, the guardian of a half-caste girl, Nina (Shirley Ricketts). She is the heir to some land rich in oil. Wayne is helping her to locate her missing father and when bandits attack them Nina escapes and Wayne is left for dead, his clothes exchanged for those of a notorious bank robber. When heroine Clara Moore (Sheila Terry) discovers him, she believes in his story despite recognising the clothes as those of a wanted man. Eventually bandits capture both Clara and Nina but Wayne outwits the gang and calls in a posse to round them up. The bandit leader manages to take off with Nina leaving Wayne, in time-honoured fashion, to set out after him alone and overpower him following a battle in the middle of a river.

In *Texas Terror*, Wayne was the young sheriff who believes that he has killed his best friend by accident during a shootout with a band of bank robbers. Filled with remorse, he surrenders his badge to go and dedicate himself to the solitary life of the prospector. However, he comes across the dead man's sister (Lucille Brown) who has been in a stagecoach hold-up and rounds up the robbers. He then starts to help the girl run her ranch until she learns about his past and it takes Wayne's discovery that Joe Dickson (LeRoy Mason) was really responsible for her brother's death to set matters straight.

Rather unusually, all six of the players supporting Wayne in *Texas Terror* went on to appear with him in *Rainbow Valley*. This centered on a fight for possession of a valuable tract of land between the law-abiding inhabitants of a new gold-mining town and a bunch of bandits. Wayne was John Martin, the government agent who has been working undercover as a convict but who leaves to take on the job of protecting workers who are building a new road in the area. When Morgan (LeRoy Mason), a prominent citizen in league with the

Al Ferguson, John Wayne, Edward Chandler and Mary Kornman in The Desert Trail *(1935).*

Below, John Wayne and Dennie Meadows in The Dawn Rider *(1935).*

bandits, calls in a fast gun by the name of Galt (Buffalo Bill Jr.), the latter identifies Wayne as a former fellow convict. This forces Wayne to disclose his real identity and he disperses any doubts over his explanation by wiping out the bandits with liberal use of dynamite and capturing their leader. The conclusion found him courting the local postmistress (Lucille Brown) whose father (George Hayes, here providing bearded comedy relief) delivers the mail in a ramshackle Ford.

The Desert Trail presented Wayne as a star performer in rodeos called John Scott. With his gambler friend Kansas Charlie (Eddy Chandler, dispensing the light relief) he is wrongly suspected of having committed a hold-up. Local feeling against them runs so high that the pair quit town in haste. They suspect two others (Paul Fix, Al Ferguson) of having framed them and follow the two men to Poker City. A small complication arises when Wayne takes a shine to a girl (Mary Kornman) who works in a local store and who is the sister of one of the suspects, but Wayne manages to clear his

name and retain her affections.

The Dawn Rider introduced a similar catch to the romantic relationship: Wayne was John Mason, the Westerner seeking to settle a score with the bandit who robbed an express office and shot down his father. When Wayne stops a bullet, pretty Alice Gordon (Marion Burns) is on hand to nurse him back to health and she turns out to be the sister of the man (Denny Meadows) he is after.

With the last of the set, *Paradise Canyon*, Wayne was back to undercover work for the Federal government, playing John Wyatt who is assigned to ferret out a gang of counterfeiters working along the Mexican border. Doctor Carter (Earle Hodgins) is a prime suspect, so Wayne joins his travelling medicine show, and, along with developing an interest in Carter's daughter (Marion Burns), shows that Carter has been an innocent tool of the real villains, led by the notorious Curly Joe (Yakima Canutt). With the help of a group of Mexican rurales, Wayne soon brings the culprits to justice.

John Wayne has the drop on Yakima Canutt, Reed Howes, Tex Palmer and player in Paradise Canyon *(1935).*

9. Starting with Republic (1935-36)

IN 1935 Monogram and Lone Star Productions became part of the new Republic Pictures set-up along with Mascot and Consolidated Film Laboratories.* Wayne was the star of Republic's first release, *Westward Ho*, made at a cost of thirty-seven thousand dollars. This was released only a month later than the last of the Lone Stars handled by Monogram, and along with *The Lawless Range* (which had a delayed release) seems to have been one of the previous set simply turned over to Republic for distribution. The other films Wayne made for Republic have different directors and cameramen, more extensive casts, but their running times still never exceeded one hour and Wayne remained tied to exclusively starring in B Westerns.

Westward Ho presented Wayne as John Wyatt, a man nursing a deep hatred for outlaws from the time in childhood when he saw his parents killed by raiders on the trail to California and his young brother abducted. Fifteen years later, we find him leading a group of vigilantes dressed in black shirts and mounted on white horses. He joins a group of pioneers headed West, scenting trouble along the way, and doesn't recognise his brother (Frank McGlynn Jr.) when he also becomes one of the travellers. In fact, the brother is now one of the outlaw gang which kidnapped him as a child and is acting as their spy; he and Wayne form an attachment for the same girl (Sheila Manners) and the wayward brother eventually sacrifices his life to save her and

*Monogram emerged again as a separate concern in 1937. Although the company was then reported to have bought *DeLuxe*, a play by Louis Bromfield, as a starring vehicle for Wayne, they didn't in fact make any more films with the actor.

Frank McGlynn Jr. is comforted by Hank Bell, Sheila Manners and John Wayne in Westward Ho *(1935).*

John Wayne in The New Frontier *(1935).*

John Wayne confronts Warner Richmond in The New Frontier *(1935).*

Wayne, leaving Wayne to take care of his parents' murderers (Jack Curtis, Yakima Canutt). The film incorporated three songs, two sung by a cowboy group, the third by Wayne (presumably dubbed as before), called "The Girl I Loved Long Ago" and sung to the heroine under the moon.

The New Frontier (a 1935 release — often confused with Wayne's 1939 film of the same title) showed Wayne as John Dawson who follows in his old man's footsteps as a leader of pioneers' caravans. He arrives at a frontier town to find that his father, who has settled down to the job of sheriff, has been murdered at the instigation of the area's leading badman, the saloon keeper Ace Holmes, played by the splendid Warner Richmond, an actor once characterised as resembling Lon Chaney's Phantom of the Opera, here dressed very appropriately in a satanic black outfit with a razor-edged brim to his hat and two guns in his belt. It's no wonder Wayne enlists the aid of Kit (Al Bridge) and his gang, lesser outlaws he has befriended on his way into town, before confronting Holmes in his lair. The friendly badmen become Wayne's deputies and engage in a lengthy pitched battle with the Holmes crowd in which Kit kills Ace at the cost of his own life. The way is now clear for Wayne to become engaged to a settler's daughter (Muriel Evans). Musical relief was again a feature of the film with the good bandits singing nostalgic cowboy songs around the camp fire.

The Lawless Range found Wayne investigating some mysterious raids on cattle in an isolated valley; at one point he is captured by the rustlers and thrown into a cave with an old rancher (Earl Dwire) who has earlier disappeared; they manage to free each other and Wayne goes on to discover that a local banker is trying to scare away the inhabitants of the valley so that he can gain access to some secret gold mines there. Wayne leads a posse to round up the gang. Sheila Manners was again on hand for the film's romantic chores.

Wayne's first release of 1936 was another to recall the days of the covered wagon, in the period when California was still a Mexican possession. In *The Oregon Trail*, as it was titled, Wayne was the Army captain John Delmont who takes leave of absence to go in search of his father after the latter has disappeared while leading a supply train. It transpires that his father's guide and a renegade Major (Ben Hendricks) had made off with the supplies, abandoning the entire troop to starve to death in the snowy mountains. Aided by his friends Tom and Red (Yakima Canutt and Frank Rice, providing comedy touches) and by some Mexicans, Wayne is able to repulse an attack by the same band of renegades when he tries to pass through their stronghold with a wagon train headed for Oregon; he then launches a successful expedition against the villains' fort.

In *The Lawless Nineties*, Wayne portrayed John Tipton, the Federal agent dispatched from Washington to Wyoming with orders to ensure that there is no corruption in voting on a referendum concerning the

Left, Wayne with Muriel Evans in King of the Pecos
(1936) and, above, with unidentified
player in The Lonely Trail
(1936).

territory's proposed affiliation with the Union. This involves Wayne in busting up a gang terrorising the area, fighting a pitched battle from barricades at the edge of town, using sticks of dynamite, and exposing the chairman of the local law and order committee (Harry Woods) as the leader of the terrorists. George Hayes was reunited with Wayne on this film playing a slightly pompous newspaper editor who is killed by the badmen, leaving Wayne to be a solace to his daughter (Ann Rutherford).

In *King of the Pecos* — as in *Westward Ho* — Wayne played a figure seeking revenge for a tragedy in his childhood (with Bradley Metcalf Jr. playing Wayne as a child for flashbacks in both films). This time, however, the villain is known to Wayne from the start. It's the Texan cattle king Stiles (Cy Kendall) who ten years before murdered Wayne's homesteading parents when they refused to give up their property. Wayne has become a law student and first attempts legal means to break up Stiles's million acre empire with its hold on all the water holes and a profitable rustling sideline. But ultimately he has to rally the victimised landowners and lead them on an attack that disposes of Stiles and his men for good.

The Reconstruction period following the Civil War formed the background of *The Lonely Trail* but it was Wayne versus Cy Kendall all over again. Wayne appeared as the young ranch owner who is asked by the Governor of Texas (Sam Flint) to rid the State of plundering carpetbaggers. He has to overcome local prejudice because he fought on the Northern side in the war and also makes a mistake initially in recruiting the assistance of Cy Kendall's Holden, the man who as the adjutant general of a town is responsible for law and order. But he soon learns that Holden is filling his own pockets through iniquitous taxation and takes appropriate action.

The last Wayne picture in this series reunited him with Mack V. Wright, the director of three of his Warner Westerns. The film was called *Winds of the Wasteland* and Wayne's John Blair with his pal Smoky (Yakima Canutt) were former Pony Express riders who have lost their jobs with the arrival of the telegraph. They successfully compete for a new government mail-hauling contract, defeating the efforts of stageline owner Cal Drake (Douglas Cosgrove) to eliminate them from the race that decides who will get the job.

10. Six for Universal (1936-37)

AT THIS POINT, Wayne took a break both from Republic and from Western costume to make six action films for Universal. It would seem that Trem Carr, the producer of these films and the man who had started Wayne off on the Lone Star Westerns, lured him away from Republic. The films were certainly bigger — budgeted at about sixty thousand dollars apiece — and coming from a major studio tended to be shown in a better class of theatre. Some even had playdates on Broadway as part of a double-bill and were reviewed by the newspaper critics. Yet these films, going into release between September 1936 and the end of 1937, did not help Wayne break out of the B-film rut for good, despite improved supporting casts which meant that the leading villain in a couple of the Republic pictures, Cy Kendall, could be found playing a bit part in the first of these new productions. No doubt, Wayne's appeal had become too closely associated with Westerns, the type of film to which he promptly returned, and audiences didn't take too kindly to the different settings of these Universal releases.

The Sea Spoilers kicked off the series with Wayne portraying Bob Randall, the commander of a U.S. Coast Guard cutter, who goes to visit his actress *fiancée* (Nan Grey) on the yacht where she is supposed to be entertaining — and finds the yacht's owner shot, a contraband cargo of sealskins on board, and his girl nowhere to be seen. He sets out in a small fishing smack to look for her, taking along his old friend Hogan (Fuzzy Knight) whose pet seal Mabel provides some humorous asides. They eventually locate the pleasure yacht, a cover for smuggling operations, on which Wayne's girl is held captive, and round up the villains.

Conflict followed and was adapted from a strong Jack London story which had been the basis of a silent picture (the other five Universal films were all screen originals). Set at the turn of the century, it cast Wayne as the man who goes to work in the lumber camps and mining towns, gains a reputation as a fighter by licking a local trouble-maker and so becomes the obvious choice to take on a visiting battler (Ward Bond) who offers to fight all comers for a suitable purse. What Wayne's backers don't know is that he is in cahoots with the challenging prizefighter and the latter's manager (Frank Sheridan), and will lose the fight on purpose. However, once Wayne has become attached to a girl reporter

Left, Wayne with Jean Rogers in Conflict *(1936) and, right, in* Idol of the Crowds *(1937).*

I Cover the War (1937): Wayne with Don Barclay and Charles Brokaw tries to take his newsreel truck into an Arab camp.

Wayne with Jimmie Lucas (?) in Adventure's End *(1937).*

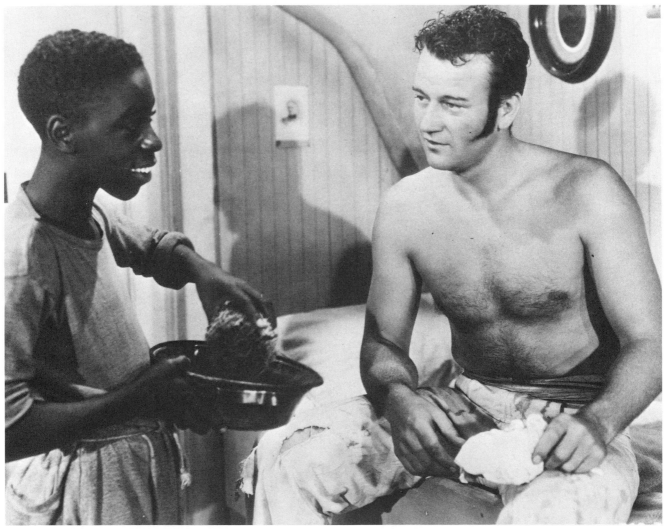

(Jean Rogers) and has saved a small boy from drowning (Tommy Bupp), his reformation is in sight and, in a wild brawl with no holds barred, he defeats his opponent and begins a new life.

Next came *California Straight Ahead,* a title that must have misled some of Wayne's old fans by not being a Western. Instead, it dealt with a race between a caravan of high-powered trucks and a freight train to deliver aviation parts to the Pacific coast before a labour strike can take place. Wayne starts out as a happy-go-lucky school bus driver who becomes the traffic manager of a big truck company and leads his vehicles across the prairies through blizzards and snowdrifts to beat the train despite its start of several hours.

In *I Cover the War,* Wayne was Bob Adams, a cameraman for the Atlas News Reel Company. After covering the Spanish Civil War, he is recalled to the London office and dispatched to North Africa with his pal Elmer Davis (Don Barclay) to cover an impending uprising against the British. There two gun runners (Jack Mack, Franklyn Parker) are posing as rival cameramen and have recruited Wayne's younger brother Don (James Bush) as an unwitting ally after Wayne has refused to help him become a cameraman. Wayne and his pal set out to locate and film the rebels' leader, become instead his captives, but escape in time to save a whole company of British lancers. Wayne also

Syd Saylor, John Wayne and Johnny Mack Brown in Born to the West *(1937).*

vies for the favours of a British commandant's niece (Gwen Gaze) who is engaged to a British officer.

In *Idol of the Crowds,* Wayne was Johnny Hanson who is signed up for a hockey team by talent scouts and becomes their outstanding player, piling up money with which he plans to extend his chicken farm. He refuses a bribe to throw the championship match and a girl (Sheila Bromley) who is sent to try and persuade him ends up falling in love with him. When a twelve-year-old boy is seriously injured in a taxi-cab crash in mistake for Wayne, the latter pretends to play along with the villains, and feigns injury during a game. He then stays under wraps to appear in the championship game and lead his team to victory, thus foiling the schemes of the gambler Jack Irwin (Charles Brokaw).

The last of the Universal batch was a seafaring drama, *Adventure's End,* based on a screen story by maritime author Ben Ames Williams. As Duke Slade, Wayne is the pearl diver in the Pacific who ventures into forbidden waters and, fleeing from the angered natives, seeks safety aboard a whaler. There the dying captain (Montagu Love) persuades Wayne to marry his daughter (Diana Gibson) to foil the plans of the first mate (Moroni Olsen). The two men quarrel but later make up their differences and Wayne is instrumental in quelling a mutiny by the crew. Stirred by Wayne's heroic deeds and the generous exposure of his rugged torso, the captain's daughter decides that she is happy with the marital arrangements made on her behalf earlier.

* * *

Just as an isolated Paramount film intervened at the end of Wayne's Columbia period before he settled down elsewhere, so here he made a single appearance for that studio in its Western *Born to the West* (subsequently reissued as *Hell Town*). Johnny Mack Brown, another Western star, was cast opposite Wayne in this Zane Grey story which Paramount had also filmed in the silent period.

Wayne was the roving Westerner, Dare Rudd, who arrives in town with his pal Dinkey Hooley (Syd Saylor) and takes an interest in Judith (Marsha Hunt), the girl friend of his cousin Tom Fillmore (Johnny Mack Brown), the town's leading citizen and owner of a large cattle ranch. Judith asks Tom to find a job for Wayne and he puts Wayne in charge of a cattle drive, believing that this will expose him as an irresponsible figure and so end Judith's interest in him. Wayne defeats the attempts made by a band of rustlers to steal the herd but loses the money the cattle bring in a crooked poker game. After Tom arrives to find out what has been detaining Wayne, he proves himself to be a more astute poker player able to expose the cardsharps but needing Wayne's intervention to save his life. As a result, the two men become firm friends, Wayne is offered a home and a job for keeps, and there are no hard feelings over Judith's preference for him. The action sequences of the cattle drive, the midnight raid by rustlers, and an episode with a runaway horse attracted most attention at the time and were almost certainly stock footage from earlier films.

11. A Third Mesquiteer (1938-39)

THE 3 MESQUITEERS were characters created directly for the screen by Western novelist William Colt MacDonald, lacking a D'Artagnan to lead them but putting wrongs right in the manner of Dumas's trio of stalwarts. They were taken up by Republic in *The 3 Mesquiteers* (1936) with Bob Livingston as Stony Brooke, Ray Corrigan as Tucson Smith and Syd Saylor as Lullaby Joslin.* Max Terhune took over from Saylor in the second of the series, accompanied by a dummy called Elmer with which he conversed from time to time. The series bubbled along without any further changes in the three leads until the seventeenth film when John Wayne returned to Republic to step into the boots of Stony Brooke. He stayed for eight films released between August 1938 and August 1939 before the success of *Stagecoach* enabled him to relinquish the part of Stony Brooke (it was given back to Bob Livingston) and go on to main features for good.

Although The 3 Mesquiteers series is highly regarded by most B Western enthusiasts, it required rather less of Wayne than his earlier work for there were three leading players instead of one in each adventure sharing screen time and requiring their own individual moments. While one Mesquiteer, Lullaby, was obviously in charge of comedy and bungling, the other two — played by Wayne and Corrigan — had less to distingush them although Wayne's Stony Brooke had a tendency to stand out as the leader by acting independently of the other two, and also had the visual prominence of a largely white outfit and the only white horse in the trio.

All eight of these films were directed by George Sherman, a Western specialist whose later, more ambitious work is of some interest; but here he was merely required to put the films through on schedule with unfussy competence.

One curiosity of these pictures is that they generally take place in modern times, seeming to argue in a naive way that traditional virtues and resources are more than enough to cope with complex contemporary situations.

The first, *Pals of the Saddle*, was "hot from the headlines" with America's security being threatened by the activities of foreign agents who are smuggling a chemical called monium — found in desert areas and used in making poison gas — across the border into Mexico. A condensation of the complicated plot will give the flavour of the series. The 3 Mesquiteers become involved by accident when they gallantly ride to the rescue of a girl (Doreen McKay) whose horse seems to have run away with her. She is in fact a government agent hoping to consolidate her friendship with her riding companion Hartman (George Douglas) by letting him save her. Her plans go further astray when a fellow

agent is forced to kill Hartman and flee, leaving Wayne's Stony Brooke to arrive on the scene and be suspected of the murder. Wayne manages to get away and goes after the girl and the other agent to clear his name. When the agent dies from gunshot wounds, the girl is forced to reveal her mission and ask for Wayne's help. He passes off the dead agent as himself, leaving him free to go to the spies' hideout, a dude ranch, and masquerade as Hartman. Meanwhile the other two Mesquiteers are nosing around, distressed that Wayne has apparently been killed and determined to find his murderer. When Wayne is exposed as a fake and taken prisoner, Tucson and Lullaby are on hand to rescue him from the wagon in which he is being transported across the border with a consignment of monium. After they have released Wayne they are all spotted and make off, hotly pursued by the rest of the convoy. When their wagon catches fire and crashes, the villains think they have been killed; but they have mounted the horses drawing them in time to ride off before the crash. They now ride on ahead to wait for the other wagons to arrive at the border, hold them back for as long as possible while the U.S. cavalry are being called out, then jump on the last one as it passes beneath them. Taking command of it, they overtake the others, leaping aboard, Wayne making a point of tackling their leader personally.

Despite its title, *Overland Stage Raiders* was again a modern story. The 3 Mesquiteers buy an aeroplane and a stake in an airport to fly out gold from a remote mining town after shipments by motor coach have been hijacked. The team have to contend with two gangsters brought in from the East to stop them by the villainous owner of the coach line (Gordon Hart) who has also blackmailed the 3 Mesquiteers' partner (Anthony Marsh) into helping him. What makes *Overland Stage Raiders* a more widely familiar title than any other in the series is its place in the history books through providing the last screen appearance of Louise Brooks, then barely into her thirties, as the blackmailed partner's daughter, Beth. (She has kindly provided the introduction to this book.)

Santa Fe Stampede featured another star whose career had seen better days: William Farnum. He played the miner who calls in The 3 Mesquiteers to share in the strike he has made since they had earlier grubstaked him. The trio capture a horse thief but he is acquitted in court after a farcical miscarriage of justice because the town's mayor (LeRoy Mason) has the judge in his pocket. The Mesquiteers collect signatures urging the governor to investigate and their miner friend sets out with the petition, only to be killed en route by the mayor's men. Wayne is accused of the crime and jailed; he almost perishes along with the heroine in a fire which breaks out after a dynamite explosion but his two pals rescue him in time and help him clear his name.

Red River Range also had a distinguished player in

*An independent company had previously introduced two of the characters in *Law of the 45's* (1935) and RKO had made a single feature with the trio called *Powdersmoke Range* that same year before Republic bought the rights.

Above, Max Terhune, John Wayne and Ray Corrigan as The 3 Mesquiteers in Santa Fe Stampede *(1938) with Tom London at left. Below, another scene from the film with William Farnum (black hat) and Ferris Taylor (bald head).*

Above, The 3 Mesquiteers *in*
Three Texas Steers *(1939).*

*Left, John Wayne face to face
with LeRoy Mason in* New Frontier
*(1939) with Bud Osborne behind
Wayne.*

the cast: veteran actress Polly Moran, frequent co-star of the late Marie Dressler. It further presented two young performers who would go on to make modest reputations for themselves as leading players: Adrian Booth and Kirby Grant. The story opened with ranchers appealing to the Governor to stop the activities of a band of highly organised cattle rustlers who are using portable slaughterhouse equipment and refrigerator vans to dispose of their spoils. The Governor enlists the aid of The 3 Mesquiteers. Wayne poses as an escaped convict and goes to the dude ranch which is suspected of being the rustlers' headquarters. Kirby Grant plays Wayne's stand-in as a Mesquiteer while he works undercover. Wayne pretends to kill two of the Mesquiteers and wins the trust of the rustlers' leader Payne (William Royle) in time to prevent his next raid.

It was at this point that Wayne took leave of absence to film *Stagecoach* for John Ford. He then returned to Republic to continue grinding out 3 Mesquiteers adventures. As series like this were usually filmed in packages of eight, Wayne was no doubt contractually obliged to make a further four; and he was probably keen to continue working as there was no guarantee that *Stagecoach* would make any lasting difference to his career, especially as his last big break, starring in *The Big Trail,* had worked out so badly. However, Republic was fully aware of the wave of interest that *Stagecoach* might stir up. While they usually pushed each 3 Mesquiteers picture into release little more than a month after shooting was completed, they held back the four that Wayne made after the Ford film until that had gone into release and must have benefitted considerably from the move. *Stagecoach* is discussed in the next chapter.

In *The Night Riders,* Wayne's Stony Brooke went to work unmasking a gambler (George Douglas) who is posing as the descendant of a Spanish don and, backed by a forged land grant, has made himself the dictator of thirteen million acres of the Southwest, evicting landowners who won't meet his tax demands. His victims include The 3 Mesquiteers who appeal to the authorities in vain and so put on capes and masks to become "night riders". In the best tradition of Robin Hood and Zorro, they rob his tax collectors to return the money to the farmers and eventually extract a written confession from the tyrant.

Three Texas Steers (released in Britain as *Danger Rides the Range*) was more modest in its scale. Nancy Evans (Carole Landis) is the girl who has inherited a ranch and a circus. Villains are after her ranch on which they want to build a dam to control the water supply, and so they cause a series of accidents at the circus. There is an impressive montage of tilted angles during a scene of the audience panicking after her crooked manager Ward (Ralph Graves) has started a fire. This was simply stock footage from Republic's earlier *Circus Girl* (1937) which was pressed into use again for the

studio's serial *King of the Carnival* (1955). By the time Nancy meets The 3 Mesquiteers, her circus has been reduced to one cage and a trailer (more within the budget of *this* film) and she is on her way to the ranch which the villains now hope she will have to sell since she is no longer making profits with the circus and has mortgage payments to meet on the property. The Mesquiteers rescue her from a spot of trouble on the road and escort her to their ranch which she mistakes for her own. The kind-hearted trio can't bear to reveal that her ranch is completely run-down and they set about raising the money to help her out. When Lullaby is robbed of this money, Wayne hits on the idea of entering the circus horse, Rajah, in a trotting race, having seen it perform a waltz on hearing some music. The Mesquiteers swing into action in a vigorous hotel room fight with the villains, are chased by a posse and caught, then let out by the stuttering sheriff (Roscoe Ates) in time for Lullaby to ride to victory in the race and claim the prize money, though not without one or two comic setbacks when the horse hears trumpet music and starts dancing. With so much going on (including the antics of a tame circus gorilla), Wayne doesn't have much chance to stand out, though he shows himself as the brains of the outfit.

With *Wyoming Outlaw,* Raymond Hatton took over from Max Terhune and Lullaby Joslin gave way to Rusty Joslin. This time The 3 Mesquiteers side with outlaw Will Parker (Don Barry) after he has stolen one of their cattle. He has been ruined by a crooked politician (LeRoy Mason) who runs the town, and steals to help feed his family. The politician's racket is making money out of selling state and federal work contracts to hard-up farmers trying to survive in dust bowl conditions: Though the Three Mesquiteers are jailed on trumped-up charges and witnesses are too scared to testify in their defence, they win through and their outlaw friend has the satisfaction of shooting the crooks' leader. Silent star Elmo Lincoln came out of retirement to play a small part as a U.S. marshal.

Wayne's final appearance in the series was in *New Frontier,* a film now retitled *Frontier Horizon* for American television release to distinguish it from Wayne's 1935 picture of the same name. Here The 3 Mesquiteers had to make up for mistakenly advising a group of settlers led by Major Broderick (Eddy Waller) to accept an offer of new land in exchange for their present property. Gilbert (LeRoy Mason) and Proctor (Harrison Greene) were the men who had persuaded the State legislature to agree to a scheme flooding the valley for a water reservoir. When the Mesquiteers discover that the new land is worthless, they are taken captive before they can warn the ranchers. However, they break loose and overcome the crooked band, winning much better land for the settlers to move to. The *ingénue* role on this occasion was taken by Phyllis Isley, an actress later to win fame as Jennifer Jones.

12. Stagecoach (1939)

AFTER HIS close association with John Ford in his first years of film work, Wayne must have been somewhat discouraged to have no part in the films Ford made in the middle Thirties. Ford just advised Wayne to keep on working and building up experience, and there were times, it is said, when the director would not even bother to stop and have a word with the young actor when their paths crossed. No doubt Ford in his characteristically evasive way was biding his time, for in 1937 he summoned Wayne to his yacht and showed him a story he had just purchased, Ernest Haycox's "Stage to Lordsburg" which had appeared in the April issue of "Collier's Magazine." Ford invited Wayne to sit down and read the story, which he did. The director then asked Wayne if he could recommend anyone for the part of the Ringo Kid. Wayne suggested Lloyd Nolan,

an actor scarcely more prominent than himself. Ford's reply is supposed to have been, "Oh, dern you, Duke, can't *you* do it?" But Wayne's surprise was echoed by that of the studios which were invited to finance the picture with him in the leading role!

Ford had initially interested David O. Selznick in making a film of the Haycox story and, when he resisted Selznick's proposal that Gary Cooper and Marlene Dietrich should be engaged for the leads, he formed a production company called Argosy Pictures to make it himself. Backing was still not forthcoming because distributors were afraid that any film starring Wayne would be regarded by the public as another of his B pictures and so would be ignored by the mass audience. It was also a lean period for big-budget Westerns in general as they were thought to lack popular appeal.

John Wayne travels to stardom as the Ringo Kid. With George Bancroft riding shotgun and Louise Platt.

Eventually, an enterprising independent producer, Walter Wanger, agreed to take on the project with Wayne. A certain amount of caution is evident in the fact that Wayne's leading lady, well known in main features, was billed ahead of him at the top of the cast.

The outcome is familiar history. The film, called *Stagecoach*, was Ford's first Western in twelve years and a smash hit, standing out from a year when Westerns flooded the market with *Union Pacific, Destry Rides Again* (in which Dietrich got her chance to go West), *Jesse James* and *Dodge City* all following it into release. It won the New York Critics' Award for Ford and Oscars for its composers and supporting actor Thomas Mitchell. But, like many Westerns that earned critical acclaim from the start — as opposed to those that have come to be regarded as masterpieces over the years — *Stagecoach* has dated. Its impact has been eroded by imitation, and its script is too polished and contrived to stand the test of time. Visually it is still magical (it was Ford's first use of the Monument Valley location) and its action scenes are as thrilling and well-staged as one could wish on seeing it today. And it could not have been better suited for the job of making John Wayne a major star.

Consider Wayne's first appearance in the film. All the other passengers travelling on the stagecoach are introduced in quick succession and we only hear of the Ringo Kid — that he has escaped from jail and is likely headed for Lordsburg to settle accounts with the men

Above, a shot that made a star: John Wayne halts the stage. Below, he talks to the driver (Andy Devine) and guard (George Bancroft).

who murdered his father and brother. A shot rings out as the stagecoach lurches along the trail, and the driver Buck (Andy Devine) recognises the Ringo Kid. Cut to a shot of Wayne, standing legs apart, facing the oncoming stage, rifle twirling in his right hand as he ejects the used shell, saddle on his other arm. Ford has the camera track in on him, momentarily losing focus before catching his youthful features in close-up. The director's very rare use of the track in this manner emphasises the shots it *is* used for, and the way Wayne "stands up" to the advancing camera adds an impression of rock-like strength. The delay in introducing him contributes dramatically to his stature.

Subsequent moments build on this initial vivid impression. We learn that Ringo's horse has gone lame and that he's seen signs of Indian activity in the neighbourhood. When Curly the marshal (George Bancroft) asks him to surrender his rifle, we see Wayne react with good-natured but firm resistance until the stage's cavalry escort appears and he realises that he has no choice. He climbs aboard and settles down, back against the door, in the crowded stage. Doc Boone (Thomas Mitchell) mistakes him for a patient of long ago, a boy who had his arm broken. Wayne says that it was his brother. Doc Boone asks after him. "He was murdered," replies Wayne, his friendly smile fading, his voice quiet with intense feeling. When the gambler Hatfield (John Carradine) is angered by Doc Boone's suggestion that he shot a man in the back, Ringo quietly intervenes to calm Hatfield, that half-smile which he fixes on the gambler putting a friendly front on his words of firm warning.

At the first stop on the journey, another side of Wayne's Ringo Kid emerges: the polite manners of a well-raised boy. The cavalry escort has to turn back and Curly starts taking a vote as to whether the journey should continue. When he asks Lucy Mallory, a lady passenger of aristocratic background (Louise Platt), and then turns to the whisky drummer (Donald Meek), Wayne interrupts to point out that he has overlooked the other lady present, Dallas (Claire Trevor). Though she is in fact a prostitute who has been run out of town, Curly accepts the rebuke and turns to her.

Wayne also intervenes at the meal when Dallas is uncertain whether she should sit with the others and he invites her to take a chair, quite unaware of the issue of propriety that is involved. He is amazed when Lucy Mallory moves away and they are left to eat on their own. "Looks like I've got the plague, don't it?" he suddenly figures, getting up to leave Dallas, only to be restrained by her.

Wayne's sense of chivalry again comes into play when the stage leaves to continue the journey and he makes Hatfield, having given a drink of water from the canteen to Mrs. Mallory, offer some to Dallas. Mrs. Mallory is on her way to join her soldier husband and at the next stage station she starts to give birth to her baby. Wayne's Ringo is there to rally Doc Boone from his customary state of inebriation, but it is Dallas who wins Wayne's approval by the devoted way she helps

deliver the baby. Soon, when the two social outcasts are standing by the corral, he very hesitantly and awkwardly proposes to Dallas, telling her of the ranch he has across the border. "... A man could live there...and a woman ... Will you go?" Dallas rushes off, embarrassed because he does not know of her past. Later she asks Doc Boone's advice and, encouraged by his best wishes, she urges Wayne to escape, promising that she'll come to him later. He rides off but promptly returns at the sight of Apache war smoke in the mountains.

The stage moves on, making an emergency crossing of the river when it is discovered that the ferry has been burned by the Indians. As the coach enters an open valley, the Apaches mount their attack, swarming off a slope to fall in behind the stage in wild pursuit. Here Wayne has his chance to go into action, climbing from the interior of the coach onto the roof, aiming his rifle down on the Apaches with deadly and rapid fire. As an adventurous Indian overtakes the stage and leaps on one of the lead horses, Buck yells out to Wayne who turns and picks off the rider. Then Buck is shot in the arm and he lets go of the leaders' reins which drag on the ground. We see Wayne (or rather his double, Yakima Canutt) clamber off the top of the stage onto the driver's seat and then onto the rear pair of horses, then forward, then forward again onto one of the lead pair, gathering up the trailing reins and whipping the horses on with the loose ends. These stirring images — like the other outstanding bits of stunt work performed by the Indians — have rarely been equalled and Wayne's association with them in the minds of the audience when he is in fact being doubled, as well as the shots of him firing earlier from the rooftop of the stage in front of the back-projection screen contribute immensely to the vivid picture of a Western hero that the film creates for Wayne.

The chase ends with the fortuitous arrival of the cavalry, and the stage proceeds into Lordsburg where one of the most pompous passengers, the banker Gatewood (Berton Churchill), is promptly arrested as an embezzler. So much, the film is saying, for appearances: a quite redundant proposition as Ringo, Dallas and the abused Doc have throughout enjoyed more audience esteem than the "respectable" figures.

Although very far from anti-climactic, the shootout between Wayne and the Plummer boys (who killed his father and brother and framed him for murder) has tended to be brushed aside as the Indian attack on the stage has become the classic chase sequence of its kind. And yet there is far more artistry, more delicacy of mood and staging in this following sequence than in the attack, which is constructed for sheer excitement. Rarely has the atmosphere of a town after dark with its pools of light in shadowy streets, of the tension in the air as Wayne sends his challenge to the saloon where the Plummer boys are spending the evening, been so skilfully evoked.

Howard Hawks has said that the art of making a film is to give the audience two or three scenes to remember

John Wayne and Claire Trevor.

George Bancroft and John Wayne fire at the attacking Indians.

and not annoy them the rest of the time. It seems to me that Ford refines this principle to demonstrate that the art of making a star out of John Wayne in *Stagecoach* lies in a couple of shots. One is the introductory track in on him; the other is that low-angled set-up of him diving to the ground firing his rifle towards the camera (and the Plummer boys behind it). The rest of Wayne's work does more than not annoy the audience: it builds on the impression these shots make, but it is these two images which to me shout that a star is born, indelibly fixing him as a man commanding attention and a man of action.

The second is made the more effective for being all that we see of the gunfight: Ford then cuts away to Claire Trevor's Dallas, left behind in the shabby quarter of town, hearing the four or five shots that ring out. Thus we are forced to feel for Wayne through her and Ford teases us with the sight of Luke Plummer (Tom Tyler) returning to the saloon, only the odd look on his face advising us that he is the loser before he falls down dead. The camera then tracks onto Dallas at this emotional highpoint as she looks around and cries "Kid!" on hearing Wayne approach, falling into his arms. All that remains is for the two of them to climb onto a buckboard and, with the blessing of Curly and Luke, be sent on their way to Wayne's spread over the border.

There could be no doubt about it: Wayne had finished his long journey to stardom aboard John Ford's stagecoach.

13. Allegheny Uprising (1939)

EVER ALERT to the obvious, the Hollywood studios noticed not only the success of *Stagecoach*, which they could hardly copy, but also the *rapport* the film demonstrated between Wayne and Claire Trevor. Consequently, both RKO Radio and Republic teamed them in new period adventures hoping that would be enough to draw the same audiences that had flocked to *Stagecoach*. To Republic's credit, they welcomed back their newly-found hot property with the best script they could muster and an accomplished action director, Raoul Walsh, borrowed from another studio. But first in line was RKO Radio's *Allegheny Uprising* which, like most films with awkward-looking American names

Above, Bud Osborne, John F. Hamilton, John Wayne, Wilfrid Lawson and Robert Barrat. Below, Moroni Olsen, Claire Trevor and John Wayne.

in their titles, was shown in England under a more immediately readable title of *The First Rebel*. This was as ponderous and dull a follow-up to *Stagecoach* as could be imagined, all the more of a disappointment after four routine 3 Mesquiteeers adventures had done little to enhance Wayne's new image in the months following the Ford film's appearance.

Nevertheless, it has handsome production values and is proficiently directed by William A. Seiter. Set in 1759 when America was a British colony, and apparently derived from fact, the film casts Wayne as Jim Smith, a man who loses patience with George Sanders's military commander, Captain Swanson. The latter's adherence to the rule book is allowing corrupt traders (led by Brian Donlevy as Callendar) to sell goods to the Indians under cover of a government permit, and threatening the peace of the valley.

Swanson speaks for old traditions, Wayne's Jim Smith stands for common sense and practical action. Swanson is the disengaged colonialist overlord, Smith the man concerned with the immediate problems of survival in what is his home country. When Swanson talks of observing the rules of civilised warfare, Wayne's reply is a terse "Tripe!" Backed by the local magistrate, who can identify with the settlers' fears for their future, Wayne defies the military and eventually gains the support of Swanson's superiors. When he is captured by Swanson's men, he refuses to be rescued from jail by the group that comes to his aid, standing by his acts as being backed by the local law if not by the British. He tells Swanson "You'll never learn, you'll never learn to know us," and the film shows the seeds of discontent that led to the Declaration of Independence.

It's curious that Wayne should recently have recalled this as the "one cautious role of my life" for he appears as a decisive and impetuous man of action through most of the film. Perhaps Wayne disliked the subterfuge of Smith and his men masquerading as Indians to burn Callendar's wagon train with which he is smuggling firearms and liquor to the tribes along with legitimate government supplies, and the need to avoid any bloodshed in confronting Swanson and his men. At any rate, Wayne casts aside the gauche, reticent aspects of his Ringo Kid characterisation, being pursued by Claire Trevor's stubborn, tomboyish Janie McDougle who is only kept from accompanying the men on two of their missions by the necessity to strip to the waist to masquerade as an Indian. At the end of the film, Wayne marches off without her. "If he had time for a girl, it'd be her," an onlooker observes, paying him that much of a romantic compliment, but Trevor won't take no for an answer and takes off after him. When someone bothers to ask where she's going, she declares "With my man!" and you couldn't ask for a more powerful impression of Wayne as a man's man that women love to follow, grateful for whatever scraps of attention he can spare.

14. The Dark Command (1940)

SEIZING its golden opportunity, Republic put seven hundred thousand dollars behind Claire Trevor and John Wayne to make *The Dark Command*. They brought in Raoul Walsh, who had of course directed Wayne's first big-budget picture *The Big Trail* and they even borrowed Walter Pidgeon from M-G-M to give their film a look of class. It was the studio's most expensive feature to that time. To keep their regular audience happy, Republic reunited Wayne with his old acting colleague, George Hayes, now in full whiskery bloom as "Gabby" Hayes, put in Roy Rogers, their rising B-feature star, and also such Western stalwarts as Harry Woods, Glenn Strange and Al Bridge. They bought a novel by W. R. Burnett and put four writers to work adapting it for the screen. But these writers' combined labours produced a rather awkwardly paced and plotted scenario, although Raoul Walsh's customarily brisk direction and alert use of camera movement keeps the film as lively as possible and Yakima Canutt (credited as the second unit director with Cliff Lyons) has the chance for some fine stuntwork. Somehow Republic never quite licked the problem of finding a clean narrative line for its A features: they always seemed to alternate between static dialogue scenes and bursts of wild action, lacking consistent mood and becoming cluttered and constipated. One feels that during the Forties Waynes saved most of their pictures in which he starred by his presence; they would not have been much without him.

Wayne's Bob Seton is the travelling companion of a dentist, Doc Grunch (George Hayes). His job is to drum up business by taking part in quarrels and letting loose well-judged blows that send his opponents into Doc's chair for treatment. There is plenty of hot feeling in Kansas where North and South meet in the pre-civil war period and Wayne finds one deserving victim of his attentions in the bully played by Harry Woods. Although already capable of such sterling sentiments as "A man born in this country is an American — it's his right to go where he pleases," as a justification for socking Woods and rescuing his victim, Wayne's cowboy is jolted out of his easy-going existence when he becomes enamoured of Claire Trevor's Mary McCloud, a well-bred lady of the town, on first sight.

He promptly corners her on the street and makes her very impatient when he starts relating his background as a clumsy preamble to a proposal of marriage. He sets out to make clear such attractive qualities as the fact that he's never murdered anyone and has difficulty reaching the point... "You got blue eyes, yessir, blue eyes — now let's see, where was I?" When she learns with surprise and irritation what's behind his approach and walks off haughtily, Wayne doesn't take much persuading from Doc Grunch that he should improve himself. Naive he may have been, but he is also thick-skinned, direct and now ambitious. He takes lessons in reading and writing and sets his sights on becoming

John Wayne and Claire Trevor.

town marshal. He promptly puts his foot in it again when he tells the schoolteacher Will Cantrell (Walter Pidgeon) about his plans to run for office, unaware that Cantrell has been until now the unopposed candidate for the job.

In a way, their opposing views foreshadow those to be contrasted more subtly twenty years later in *The Man Who Shot Liberty Valance*. Cantrell, making the more polished, thoughtful election address to the crowd, represents progress as James Stewart's Ranse Stoddard will, talking of the need to understand the increasing intricacies of the law and to respect them as a means of progress, of becoming more civilised. Here, as when playing Tom Doniphon in *Liberty Valance*, Wayne represents the old-fashioned viewpoint, having a straightforward, traditional notion of what the job entails. He says that there is too much law and what is wanted is someone like himself who can go out and bring in the bad men. When Wayne wins the election, Cantrell is understandably peeved by his rejection and the script rather slides over the process of change by which the man turns into a gun-runner and eventually leader of a guerilla band that terrorises the area. (Cantrell is clearly based on the real-life Charles Quantrill.) Though the film doesn't make a point of it, it is Wayne's action in standing for marshal, without the same dedication and interest as his opponent, that sets Cantrell off on his bloody path. But the film shows Wayne taking on the duties and responsibilities of his office with model dedication. Basically, the film mirrors what it believes to be mass-audience mistrust of deep thinkers (since most of the audience are non-intellectual) and supports the man who has the right feelings, the right instincts, rather than a thought-out position which may change as disastrously as Cantrell's does. In other words, Wayne's Bob Seton is a figure the audience can identify with and it is on such simple, upright figures that Wayne has built much of his popularity.

Here Wayne initially finds that his election success has done nothing to improve his standing with Mary McCloud who is annoyed when he even goes so far as to seize a kiss. But when he is forced to bring her kid brother, Fletch (Roy Rogers), to trial for killing a man, he finds that she is willing to give herself to him if he will release her brother. This he refuses to do, demonstrating his integrity, and Cantrell has the chance to step in. He acts in Fletch's defence and makes what seems a highly convincing case for acquittal — but he also intimidates the jury to make doubly sure. The outcome leaves Wayne standing in court with an open look of complete dismay and Mary agrees to marry Cantrell in gratitude although she does not love him. Fortunately, Cantrell is drawn away on urgent business on their wedding night and neglects to come back; as his raiders start pillaging the countryside, Wayne takes a posse out to deal with him but runs into an ambush (from which he escapes via a spectacular plunge with a wagon off a steep cliff into a river below). Though Wayne resigns from office after this *débâcle,* he is on hand to save Mary from being run out of town as the wife of hated Cantrell, and he takes her to within a short distance of Cantrell's camp, again professing his love for her and urging her to ride with him to a new life in Texas, then sitting astride his horse to say wistfully "Goodbye, Mary" as she insists on going to join her husband.

However, Wayne is caught by some of Cantrell's men and taken to his headquarters. Here Mary becomes dismayed at seeing for herself her husband's change of character, and tries to bargain for Wayne's life. He manages his own escape from Cantrell's clutches and alerts the town of Lawrence to an impending raid. He leaps astride the hastily erected barricades to lead the defence of the town and the citizens manage to ward off the attackers although the buildings are burned to the ground. Wayne confronts Cantrell in his home and shoots him. "All's well that ends well," Wayne is told at the fadeout. Informed that a guy called Shakespeare wrote the line, Wayne replies, "He must have come from Texas — we've been saying that for years."

Wayne a prisoner at Cantrell's headquarters. With Walter Pidgeon and Claire Trevor at right.

15. Three Faces West (1940)

IT WAS now time for Republic to test Wayne's popularity without Claire Trevor and the lavish trimmings of *The Dark Command*. Having been billed after Miss Trevor on their three pictures, he was now the main star with the Norwegian actress Sigrid Gurie and the character actor Charles Coburn in support. Republic also sought a stake in the interest that the release of John Ford's *The Grapes of Wrath* might arouse and put their picture through quickly enough to go on release in the same month as Ford's much more ambitious and painstaking film about the plight of the Dust Bowl. *Three Faces West* not only dealt with this but also worked in the problems of refugees escaping from Nazism in Europe.

Wayne's part of John Phillips is interesting because it develops two aspects of his screen personality: the leader of men and the man with a stubbornly-held narrow viewpoint, slow to accept change.

The film opens with an eminent Viennese surgeon, Dr. Braun (Charles Coburn), broadcasting a plea for work in the United States. It is Wayne who arranges for him to come to the farming community of Asheville Forks, North Dakota, where his uncle Nunk the veterinarian (Spencer Charters) has been the only source of medical assistance. When Dr. Braun, accompanied by his daughter Leni (Sigrid Gurie), is met at the train station by Wayne during a severe dust storm, he passes it off as "very unusual weather" and diverts the doctor to a round of visits on the way to his new home. Leni protests at this and is even less happy when they eventually reach their dust-laden new quarters. Soon the situation and the great burden of work awaiting Dr. Braun are apparent, but Wayne tries to instill a new purpose into Leni. "The way I figured it," he argues earnestly, "You stopped being a refugee when you came through Ellis Island. There's no reason why you can't start being a pioneer now — even in the Dust Bowl." Leni insists on leaving straight away and Wayne admits that he can't hold her, but Dr. Braun has become interested in one of his patients who needs a difficult operation.

The Department of Agriculture spell out to Wayne that Asheville Forks is doomed in its present location and the community should move to new land in Oregon just waiting to be farmed. This draws an angry retort from Wayne: "You can't shove us around...we're not licked yet." But he goes off to get drunk in a saloon. Wayne's heroes often turn to solitary drinking to console them in bitterness and despair. Drink is (within the conventions of the ultra-masculine screen hero) an acceptable and even admirable prop because it preserves independence of others, rejects a shoulder to cry on. Wayne angrily knocks over a bartender (Dewey Robinson) who finds his situation amusing and drunkenly drives his car into the barn doors of his house. He now agrees with Leni that she should leave but is not ready to move himself, and a fall of rain that settles the dust

brings such a mood of exhilaration and renewed hope that Leni agrees to marry him.

However, Wayne has a second burden to bear besides that posed by the dust and soil erosion. Leni's German *fiancé*, who helped her and her father escape to the United States, has turned up in San Francisco and, despite Wayne's entreaties that she should follow her emotions and marry him, she decides that she must honour her obligation to the man who saved them in Austria.

Wayne takes the positive step of organising the community's move to Oregon and has a sharp way with dissenters. "We can always stay here and go on relief," someone observes and Wayne replies with contempt, "That's right, you can do that." The convoy of battered trucks and run-down cars sets out. Before long, Clem Higgins (Trevor Bardette) is trying to persuade them to head instead for California and the sun. When Higgins wants to take over the money the community has collected, Wayne smartly knocks him to the ground. Leni and Dr. Braun are still with them and, as the prospect of their turning off to go to San Francisco becomes more immediate, so Wayne's strength of purpose fades and he agrees to let the group go to California even though he knows it has a surplus of refugees from the Dust Bowl. It takes Dr. Braun to persuade Wayne to do his duty to his fellow farmers and he intervenes in time to stop Higgins driving off. The film then switches for a hurried little scene in San Francisco (the kind that shows Republic's sense of plot construction up so badly) in which Leni's *fiancé* (Roland Varno) shows himself to be an ardent supporter of Hitler — which leaves Wayne and Leni to be reunited for a life of happiness in Oregon.

John Wayne, Charles Coburn, Sigrid Gurie.

The Duke at home in younger days.

A family gathering on June 20, 1962. Back row, starting at left: son Michael with granddaughter Teresa, son Patrick, Wayne himself, daughter Aissa, daughter Melinda, son-in-law Don La Cava, holding grandson Mark. Front row, left to right: granddaughters Anita and Alicia, daughter-in-law Gretchen with granddaughter Maria, wife Pilar with son John Ethan, daughter Toni with Granddaughter Brigid.

With son John Ethan Wayne in 1969 (left above), with daughter Marisa in 1976 (right above). Below at his Newport Beach home, Wayne welcomes Father Wasson of the Mexican orphanage to which Wayne contributed, and Alfredo, a Mexican youth from the orphanage who was scarred in a fire. With Wayne's support Father Wasson brought Alfredo to Los Angeles for plastic surgery.

Big John at home and on the range (above, in El Dorado, *1967.)*

Another shot of Wayne in El Dorado.

John Wayne's strong conservative leanings were well known, but he had won the professional and personal respect of people of all political persuasions. Above, President Gerald R. Ford presents him with a plaque at a Boy Scout ceremony in 1978. Below, he and Jane Fonda greet each other warmly at a Hollywood awards ceremony in 1977.

Young and old alike also loved the Duke. Above, he greets some admiring schoolgirls on the set of Hellfighters *(1968). Below, he addresses senior citizens and others, including James Caan, at Knotts Berry Farm.*

Photo by Frank Edwards/Fotos International.

Fording a stream in El Dorado, *and opposite page above, on the set in the same film. Opposite below, in* Hellfighters.

Above with Joanna Barnes in War Wagon, *below left, with Angie Dickenson in* Rio Bravo, *and below right with geishas in* The Barbarian and The Geisha.

Above, taken during the filming of Chisum *(1970). Below, left, leaning back in the saddle on location for* Sons of Katie Elder *(1965), and right, rehearsing a scene in* The Horse Soldiers *(1959).*

A pensive moment on the set of Chisum *(1970).*

Relaxing off-camera on location for Legend of the Lost *(1957).*

As Rooster Cogburn, doing a little drinking and shooting in the immortal True Grit *(1969).*

Oil-spattered and hardhatted in The Hellfighters *(1968); squinting down a rifle barrel in* The Sons of Katie Elder *(1965), and directing in* The Green Berets *(1968).*

John Wayne always cast a long shadow. It will be felt in American consciousness as long as movies and America exist.

16. The Long Voyage Home (1940)

JOHN FORD's *The Long Voyage Home* is a moody adaptation of three one-act plays by Eugene O'Neill, a study of a group of men aboard a tramp steamer for whom life drones on monotonously with only the solidarity of friendship, and the occasional few hours' leave at a port of call for drunken revelling, to sustain them. Although Wayne's name heads the cast list, his part is not predominant. It is a subsidiary role, although a key one — for Wayne's Ole Olsen (played with a passable Swedish accent) represents the possibility of escape. He alone has another place to call home, a farm to work in his native land, a family to rejoin. He is younger than the others, still innocent, still with his future ahead of him — good-looking, strong, and naive, at times so slow-witted as to be more of an overgrown child. He is warmly accepted by the men and yet is never quite one of them. Three times he has been paid off at the end of a voyage near his native Sweden but each time, as he ruefully recalls, "One drink with the boys and then —"

Wayne's Ole is always willing to help out, always ready with a friendly greeting, and prepared to take a joke. He is mainly useful for his strength — yanking straight the injured wrist of Drisc (Thomas Mitchell), stepping in to break up a fight, or carrying the drunken Smitty (Ian Hunter) down from the deck to his bunk. He looks happy when the men look happy; his eyes light up when the men are excited by the native girls at a Caribbean stopping point but he has no knowledge of women. He is noticeably absent from the intense scene when the men, suspecting that they may be harbouring a Nazi saboteur in their midst, grill their suspect, Smitty, and

John Qualen, Ward Bond, Jack Pennick, John Wayne, Thomas Mitchell.

probe his well-concealed private life. When Smitty is cleared and goes up on deck, Wayne is on watch and asks, polite as usual, "All's well, Smitty?", possibly discerning his strained appearance but content with the affirmative answer ("All's well, Ole") not to probe any deeper.

The others decide that they will make a determined effort to put Wayne aboard a ship for Sweden when they reach London. The other Swede in the crew, Alex (John Qualen), fusses over him as he has throughout the film, encouraging him to return home, and he now sews his back wages into the lining of his suit and fixes his ticket inside his jacket with a safety pin.

The men go ashore and leave Wayne to wait like an obedient pup outside a public house in Wapping while they partake of liquid refreshment. As they move from pub to pub, they allow Wayne a drink — a glass of ginger beer — and he continues to tag along, eventually being lost from sight long enough for a tawdry prostitute, Freda (Mildred Natwick), to take hold of him. He tries to get away but is drawn by natural politeness not to refuse her invitation to sit and take a drink. He relates to her his past history, courteously addressing her as "Miss Freda" as she feigns interest while waiting for the drugs she has slipped into his glass to take hold so that she can hand him over to the sailors anxious to shanghai him. He has no inkling of the trap being sprung and it takes the others to return and rescue him from his new ship in a fierce brawl that inadvertently results in Drisc being left as a subsitute for the reclaimed Swede. And so Wayne is safely dispatched and the others go back to sea, though part of them goes with Ole who represents their share in a better life.

Wayne's handling of the role of Ole completely effaces the usual strength and stubbornness of his screen personality. It may be that his carefully subdued manner makes Ole more of a simpleton that he might otherwise have been, but the character lives as a fine example of Wayne venturing outside his usual range and responding to careful guidance from a director who knows what he can give.

Top, John Wayne's Ole cheerfully allows John Qualen to sow his back wages into his suit. Below, the drugged Wayne is rescued from the shanghaiing attempt by Barry Fitzgerald and John Qualen.

17. Seven Sinners (1940)

SEVEN SINNERS was made by Universal and draws on Wayne's image in *Stagecoach* as a figure of simple gallantry and transparent honesty. The film was essentially a lively concoction designed to show off the talents of Marlene Dietrich following her spectacular comeback in *Destry Rides Again* after being branded as "box-office poison." There as here, she played an entertainer of dubious background. This time the setting was switched from the Old West to the South Sea Islands and she appears as Bijou, a torch singer who collects deportation orders as regularly as she draws pay when the menfolk riot over her café appearances. She is the woman of the world who is attracted by the naive charm and good manners of the spruce navy lieutenant Dan Brent (Wayne) as a relief from the eager lust she more commonly encounters. Having heard her perform at the Seven Sinners Café, he presents her with a bunch of orchids and invites her to sing aboard his ship. His superior officers are concerned by his passionate interest in the "lady" and, though she falls deeply in love with him, she knows that his navy record is in danger and gives him up just as he is ready to abandon the navy for her. She also makes the sacrifice to save him from the murderous jealousy of her knife-wielding admirer Antro (Oscar Homolka) but the film arranges a splendid fight with Wayne taking off his jacket and striding into the café to take on Antro and a dozen heavies, hugely enjoying himself with navy support arriving to give him a helping hand. When Wayne is knocked out at the end of the battle, this gives Bijou the chance to slip out of his life.

The film relates far more to Dietrich's career than it does to Wayne's, being built to the formula of Dietrich's total capitulation to a man — the right man — as established in *Morocco* and *Destry* among others, but here treated in much lighter fashion. Wayne's part was reportedly written for Tyrone Power though Wayne probably handles it in a lazier, more suitable manner than Power would have done.

Marlene Dietrich is the idol of the fleet in Seven Sinners.

18. A Man Betrayed (1941)

RELEASED in Britain as *Citadel of Crime*, this was another Republic starring vehicle. It is an odd mishmash combining some pleasant screwball comedy touches and romance between Wayne and the perky Frances Dee with the more serious business of Wayne as Lynn Hollister, the bright small-town lawyer, investigating the death of a friend found shot outside the town of Temple City's exotic and notorious nightclub, the Inferno. The script is cluttered with too much dialogue and explanation of legal technicalities, and it shows a distinct indication of strain at the conclusion when the town's crooked politician Tom Cameron (Edward Ellis), attempts to shed his ruthless past and appeal for sympathy. He claims that he became a crook to give his daughter the best things in life, and since she's the heroine, who has been blissfully unaware of his wicked ways, he has to try and redeem himself to smooth the way for Wayne to marry his daughter and bury the past.

Wayne's first encounter with the politician's daughter, Sabra, takes place when he calls at his mansion, seeking his help in the investigation. He takes Sabra off to visit the Club Inferno and picks up some evidence to suggest that his friend's death was not the suicide it was made out to be. He accepts an invitation to work for her father in the coming election, suspecting him by now and hoping to unearth evidence against him. Fortunately, Cameron's ally and owner of the Inferno, T. Amato (Alexander Granach), decides to depose the politician after being refused an appointment to public office, and the whole organisation splits apart in a confrontation between an army of illegal voters organised by Amato and a band of racketeers called in by Cameron to stop them swinging the election against him.

Wayne catches up with Amato's dim-witted brother Floyd (a choice role for Ward Bond) and forces him to admit that he murdered Wayne's friend. He also has the drafted voters and racketeers rounded up under an election law, and takes Sabra into his arms, her grief over her father's imprisonment assuaged by the thought that he will be able to come and live with her and Wayne when he has paid his debt to society.

Above, John Wayne and Frances Dee. Below, Wayne and Ward Bond at the Club Inferno.

19. Lady from Louisiana (1941)

HAVING FOUND a formula, Republic certainly liked to make good use of it. Released a month after *A Man Betrayed, Lady from Louisiana* has the same basic plot situation of Wayne as a lawyer busting apart a political racket and falling in love with the daughter of the man at the head of it. The similarity was disguised by transferring the story to a period New Orleans setting and making the father this time a dupe of his underlings.

Wayne appears as John Reynolds who exerts his simple, easy-going charm on the glamorous Southern belle (Ona Munson) he meets while travelling down the Mississippi on a river boat. After they have fallen in love, he discovers that she is Julie Mirbeau, daughter of General Mirbeau, who runs a lottery, and she learns that he is the lawyer engaged by an anti-lottery league to break it up. The rift that results from these revelations is exploited to the full by Mirbeau's lieutenant Blackie Williams (Ray Middleton) who wants Julie for himself. Julie sets about persuading Wayne that the lottery is a harmless affair. But the murder of a lottery winner by one of Blackie's men (Jack Pennick) reinforces his determination to expose the corruption behind it by which the profits are siphoned off for the personal benefit of Blackie instead of being put to useful purposes. When Mirbeau (Henry Stephenson) finds this out for himself, he is murdered by Blackie and Julie believes that Wayne's campaign has brought about his death. She takes over the operation of the lottery herself and, when Wayne uncovers evidence of Blackie's criminal activities, she is brought to trial along with the real conspirators. Wayne promises to try and help her but she doesn't believe him.

Scratching around for an action climax to enliven the proceedings, Republic decided on a bolt from the blue, a literal one that crumbles the courthouse during a raging storm while nearby a broken levee threatens to drown all and sundry. Fortunately, it discriminates by dispatching most of the minor villains from sight in a swirl of foaming water and merely leaves Julie stranded on the levee. Blackie gets away and buys passage aboard a departing steamer but Wayne catches up with him and persuades the captain to plug the gap in the levee with his ship. Blackie and Wayne fight it out and the former falls overboard to drown leaving Wayne to rescue Julie.

The period reconstruction and the flair of the special effects are still ultimately submerged by the weight of the plot and the familiarity of the situations, giving it a minor place in Wayne's career.

Ona Munson and John Wayne.

20. The Shepherd of the Hills (1941)

WAYNE's career took a healthy step forward with *The Shepherd of the Hills* although the film must have seemed an anachronism in the year that propelled the United States into the Second World War. To be hired by a really major studio, Paramount, as a leading man was progress indeed, a bonus being that he appeared in Technicolor for the first time. What's more, his role was a powerful one on the lines of *Stagecoach* but with greater depth involving the kind of intense, interior conflict that he could register powerfully. The drama is set among the superstitious mountain folk of the Ozarks, but Wayne's costume with its cowboy hat and suspenders when supplemented by a rifle is strikingly reminiscent of his appearance in *Stagecoach*. In Ford's Western, he was out to avenge the death of his brother with an exact focus for his revenge in knowledge of the killers' whereabouts; here he portrays young Matt

Matthews, the moonshiner obsessed with hatred of the father he has never seen who apparently deserted his mother, causing her early death and leaving a hex on the people of the region. He and his family have become increasingly ostracised by the community when a stranger (Harry Carey Sr.) drifts into the area, buys Matt's mother's old place, Moaning Meadow, against Matt's wishes, and instils new hope among the people with his good deeds and optimistic outlook. Of course the man, Daniel Howitt, is none other that Matt's father and it is Matt's girl, Sammy (appealingly played by Betty Field), who first spots the resemblance between the two but keeps it to herself. The truth comes to light in an eerie sequence when a woman (Marjorie Main) is given back her sight after a lifetime of blindness and the keenness of her vision leads her to remark on the facial similarities between the two men, whereupon there is a

Father and son: Harry Carey Sr. and John Wayne. Opposite: Wayne and Betty Field.

powerful image of Matt striding forward to pick up his rifle and kill Howitt. Their confrontation is briefly deferred and finally takes place in Moaning Meadow with Matt's tall figure approaching relentlessly, seen in extreme long shot, and Howitt going out to meet him. The pair come face to face separated by a fallen tree trunk. Matt takes aim with his rifle, the camera pans towards Howitt as a shot is heard, and picks up Howitt as the man who has fired and wounded Matt. Howitt himself has killed a man long ago and, sent to jail, was prevented from returning to Matt's mother; rather than see Matt go through a similar situation, he has fired the shot but the way is paved for a reconciliation as Matt finds the will to recover from a near fatal wound.

Despite the sentimental, melodramatic and dated nature of the story (compounded by Harry Carey's heavily indicative acting), the film has a powerful sense of atmosphere under director Henry Hathaway's handling, making the most of striking locations to fortify the drama and creating a genuinely disturbing and powerful sense of a people in the grip of primitive passions. Wayne's part is not unduly emphasised by his constant presence and he really comes into his own in the later scenes which drive him forward to seek revenge on Howitt and raise the curse, despite his liking for the man. In earlier scenes he is inarticulate if wordy, aware that his love for Sammy is handicapped by his thirst for vengeance but unaware of how to clear away the shadow over his life. There is real power to his handling of a scene at his mother's grave, his intensity of expression giving way to sorrow as he reaffirms his promise: "One of these days I'll find him — him that never came back to you." There is, however, a pleasant lightening of mood when Wayne intervenes to rescue Howitt from the attentions of Wash Gibbs (Ward Bond) who is angry at the decline Howitt has caused to sales of moonshine liquor. Wayne steps in to brawl with Wash amidst a flock of baaing sheep until Sammy intervenes and swings a flower sack, inadvertently felling Matt instead of Wash, and giving Wayne what was probably his first opportunity to put on that bemused, eye-focussing, what-hit-me? look that he does so well, as he sits sprawled on the ground. Later, his fierceness of resolve to kill Howitt foreshadows Ethan Edwards's seemingly implacable intent to kill Debbie in *The Searchers* years ahead, eyes glaring rock hard, locked under his eyebrows. But peace comes to Moaning Meadow. "I ain't lost from nobody no more," he is finally able to declare as he pulls out of danger after the shooting. Matt has grown up.

21. Lady for a Night (1942)

RETURNING to Republic, Wayne played second fiddle to Joan Blondell in *Lady for a Night*. She was Jenny Blake, the lady of the title, elected Queen of an annual Carnival Ball in the Tennessee of the 1880s but spurned by society because she is a gambling woman who operates a boat on the Mississippi. She develops an unshakeable desire to join the "quality folk" and so she marries Alan Alderson (Ray Middleton), a member of the Memphis aristocracy, in exchange for cancelling his gambling debts and promising to restore his family's fading influence and wealth. To do this she has to throw over her former beau, the gambler Jack Morgan (John Wayne), who had rigged the carnival to ensure her election as Queen of the Ball. Thereafter the film pushes Wayne to the sidelines and thrusts Jenny into an imitation *Rebecca* to face the implacable hostility of Alan's aunt (Blanche Yurka) who has taken lessons from Judith Anderson's Mrs. Danvers in the Hitchcock film. When the aunt serves up a poisoned drink and Alan swallows it instead of Jenny, it is Jenny who is put on trial for murder to be cleared by the evidence of another aunt (Edith Barrett). Wayne, who has been steadfastly loyal and understanding, now steps forward to welcome her back to the cleaner life of the gambling world.

Esssentially a "woman's picture" with its period trimmings and theme, it gave Wayne a bland but sympathetic part that must have done a bit to consolidate his appeal with the ladies without taking up much of his time.

John Wayne and Joan Blondell.

22. Reap the Wild Wind (1942)

AFTER small fry like *Lady for a Night,* Wayne's next film was a different kettle of fish altogether. *Reap the Wild Wind* was certainly the biggest, most expensive film Wayne had been in since *The Big Trail* and it turned out to be one of the best of Cecil B. DeMille's series of spectaculars for Paramount. However, Wayne had not yet established himself as a reliable box-office draw for an investment of this size and he had to be content with a second lead billing him beneath Ray Milland. (When the film was reissued in the Fifties, times had changed and Paramount's posters were re-designed to give Wayne and Susan Hayward — who had even more of a supporting role — pride of place before the film's actual stars, Milland and Paulette Goddard, whose popularity had slipped. Milland had ironically become the new

white hope of Republic by then after Wayne had left that studio for good.)

DeMille gave Wayne the role of Captain Jack Stuart, a well-drawn example of a character type that flourished particularly in Paramount pictures: the lusty, heroic figure who, through a weakness of character, turns bad and eventually atones for his mistake, usually by sacrificing his life to save the film's real hero, thereby releasing the girl both men have loved for the worthier man. (Other examples of the type that come to mind: George Raft in *Spawn of the North*, Robert Preston in *Whispering Smith*, Fred MacMurray in *Men with Wings*.)

Wayne's Jack Stuart is the most able captain of the Devereaux line, commanding the "Jubilee" in the 1840

At the inquiry into the loss of the "Jubilee", Wayne gazes hopefully at the model
of the "Southern Cross" which he has dreams of commanding. Ray Milland is standing at the window.

era just as the age of steam is about to open. He falls prey to a band of pirate wreckers off Key West when his mate knocks him unconscious and drives the ship onto some rocks during a hurricane. The wreckers, led by King Cutler (Raymond Massey), seize the cargo while another salvage ship, run by the impetuous, high spirited Loxi Claiborne (Paulette Goddard) and Captain Philpott (Lynne Overman), arrives in time to save Wayne and the crew. As she nurses Wayne back to health, Loxi falls in love with him and, learning of his fears that the loss of the ''Jubilee'' may cost him the captaincy of the line's new steamship ''The Southern Cross'', she determines to use her feminine wiles to ensure his appointment. She treats the company's foppish lawyer Steve Tolliver (Ray Milland) with contempt, making it clear that she regards Wayne as the real man of the pair but then tries to get round him when she learns that Tolliver has considerable influence over Wayne's future and would like to break him to put him out of the running for the eventual job of heading the company. Tolliver becomes keenly interested in Loxi

but doesn't allow personal feelings to warp his judgement and speaks up for Wayne's maritime skill. He volunteers to go to the Florida Keys and find evidence to convict Cutler. He takes with him papers appointing Wayne captain of the new steamship once he has been cleared of any complicity in the wrecking of the ''Jubilee''. In the meantime, Wayne has been reduced to mate of another ship and takes this demotion badly. His attempt to marry Loxi is thwarted by Tolliver which adds to the bad feeling between them.

But he postpones a second attempt to persuade her when he learns that Tolliver is about to be the victim of a shanghai attempt arranged by Cutler. He pitches in to help Tolliver ward off the men sent to collect him and is infuriated to discover by chance that Tolliver has the papers of appointment on him. He thinks Tolliver has maliciously withheld them and takes a sock at him. Conveniently, Tolliver refrains from explaining that he was forbidden to hand them over until Wayne's integrity had been confirmed.

Wayne goes off hotheadly charging into Cutler's lair

Wayne prepares to fight the giant squid.

and challenges him to fight it out man to man. But Cutler knows how to handle Wayne and is so sure of himself he even declares, "I've been looking for a long time for a man who's exactly your size of fool." He paints a vivid picture of the kind of life Wayne will be forced to lead when Tolliver bars him from work, revealing that Tolliver has just been appointed head of the company on the death of its owner. He plays on Wayne's pride and the life of poverty he will be giving Loxi: "You're slow in the head but you're more man than that." Wayne cannot hear the insults, only the appeal to his masculine pride, and this leads him into agreeing to pile up "The Southern Cross" for Cutler's benefit.

This tragic mistake is magnified by Loxi's shining faith in his integrity. When Wayne heads off with "The Southern Cross," Tolliver suspects the worst and takes Loxi's vessel in pursuit but Loxi disables the ship rather than allow Tolliver to humiliate her man. And so they watch, Loxi heartbroken, as "The Southern Cross" goes down.

Placed on trial with King Cutler acting as his defence lawyer, Wayne sits quietly as Cutler tries to persuade the court that bad seamanship rather than sabotage caused the wreck. But it is then discovered that there was a stowaway, now missing, on board and evidence suggests it was young Drusilla Alston (Susan Hayward), the sweetheart of Cutler's younger brother, Dan (Robert Preston). The sickened Wayne volunteers to go down with Tolliver into the wreck, sitting precariously on top of a reef, to see if Drusilla was aboard. The pair don diving suits and find the evidence which adds murder to the list of charges that Wayne faces. While underwater, a giant squid with thirty foot tentacles attacks them and takes hold of Tolliver. This presents Wayne with his moment of choice: to leave Tolliver and the damning evidence behind, or to rescue him and convict himself of murder. He regains his integrity by hacking Tolliver free from the tentacles of the squid and loses his own life in the creature's clutches. Safely above surface, Tolliver pays the final tribute: "He could have got away. He stayed down to save my life. It cost him his own."

Wayne's performance is excellent, despite DeMille's loose hold over actors. He makes an accomplished romantic figure, his husky voice caressing Loxi with the words, "Nights on watch I'll see you like this, Loxi, with your hair catching fire in the sunset and that look in your eyes, ten fathoms deep. You're in my blood, Loxi, same as the sea." We understand her devotion towards him. And Wayne's features evocatively catch Stuart as a broken man in court with a forlorn expression and narrow-eyed glazed look as he faces up to the knowledge of the death he has caused. Paulette Goddard's spunky, unladylike Loxi is a pleasure to watch, and Ray Milland's smooth portrayal of a man with quiet strength and less obvious virtues contrasts admirably with Wayne's more superficial and dashing Stuart. It is a happy teaming and *Reap the Wild Wind* must have done much to cement Wayne's appeal with audiences.

23. The Spoilers (1942)

THIS WAS the fourth film version of Rex Beach's 1906 novel and the second of three films in which Wayne's rising popularity was used to prop up Marlene Dietrich's wobbling film career (much of the European market was, of course, closed by the war). Here in an American period setting with two virile American stars competing for her (Wayne and Randolph Scott), her "foreignness" is minimised and never calls for mention.

The spoilers of the title are a group of villains horning in on the gold-mining boom at Nome, Alaska, at the turn of the century. They are led by the unscrupulous new gold commissioner for Nome, Alexander McNamara (Randolph Scott), and include a crooked judge (Samuel S. Hinds) and his attractive niece Helen (Margaret Lindsay). They attempt to swindle miner Roy Glennister — John Wayne — and his partner Dextry (Harry Carey Sr.) out of a valuable claim. Marlene Dietrich has the part of Cherry Malotte, the gambling lady who has grubstaked them and pitches in to help them foil McNamara's scheming.

She plays once again the seemingly self-assured, independent, impregnable woman of somewhat disreputable character whose defences crumble faced with the right man. As in *Seven Sinners*, Wayne is that man.

"No one else will do," she says simply and fully, explaining to her devoted friend Bronco (Richard Barthelmess), and at the start of the film we see her collecting together some of the hard-boiled eggs that are Wayne's particular weakness, deciding to wait in her room for him to arrive, and then throwing pride aside to go down to the boat to meet him on his return from business in Seattle. This, then, judging by Cherry's devotion towards him, is quite a man — and a sharp contrast with the likable but weak character Wayne had played in *Seven Sinners*. He was now stepping up in Hollywood's esteem to more virile roles.

Wayne does not return her warmth of feeling: he treats her rather frivolously, often calling her "sport," and is clearly not ready to be committed to any woman. He treats Helen, the judge's niece whom he has met as a fellow passenger on the boat, with much more courtesy and thereby upsets Cherry who sees in Helen just the kind of well-bred woman she has to fear.

When a rigged case brings Wayne's ownership of his mine into question, he falls out with his partner over how to handle the matter. Wayne wants to give the law a chance to sort it out and accepts the judge's promise of a quick hearing but warns him "Don't make any mistakes," clearly reserving his role of he-man hero.

*Above, Marlene Dietrich, Wayne
and players. Below, Wayne and
Margaret Lindsay.*

But Dextry calls him a "weak sister" and dissolves their partnership. When the judge double-crosses them, Wayne is still prepared to try a court of appeal in Seattle but finds that McNamara has had his funds frozen and the ship's captain has been warned off taking his lawyer as a passenger. So Wayne makes up with Dextry by agreeing to go about this his way. They black their faces and reclaim their money from the bank, only to be arrested through a slip-up in maintaining their alibi. McNamara plots to let Wayne escape from the jail to be shot down outside, but Helen and the judge rebel at adding murder to the list of their crimes. Helen packs her bags and warns Cherry of what McNamara has in mind. She visits Wayne to warn him and he is able to use the escape opportunity successfully. He now throws caution to the winds and organises a force of miners to take on the deputies stationed outside his claim, commandeering a train to crash through the barricades. Meanwhile, Cherry lures McNamara, a great admirer of her beauty, away while the raid is taking place, then delights in revealing how she has tricked him. She orders him out of her room over the saloon just as Wayne arrives at the door. McNamara sees the look on Wayne's face and says, "I haven't got a gun on me, Glennister." "No? Then we'll do it the hard way!" exclaims Wayne and pitches into him with his fists.

Ever since the first version of *The Spoilers* in 1914 created a sensation through its climactic brawl between William Farnum and Tom Santschi which carried screen fighting to new levels of realism, subsequent versions have been bound to try and make a similar impression. And the result in this 1942 version is probably the best remembered of all Wayne's screen battles. Slick, fast and impossible, the brawl smashes up a good part of the scenery, involves Eddie Parker and Alan Pomeroy in stunt-doubling for Scott and Wayne (who nevertheless put on a creditable performance in closer shots) and ends with McNamara laid out cold in the wreckage of the saloon.

Wayne restrains Harry Carey Sr. watched by Randolph Scott and Samuel S. Hinds.

24. In Old California (1942)

WAYNE reported back to Republic for *In Old California* to play Tom Craig, a young Bostonian who meets an attractive dance hall singer Lacey Miller (Binnie Barnes) en route to Sacramento where he plans to set up as a pharmacist. She is engaged to Britt Dawson (Albert Dekker), the boss of Sacramento politics who lives off tribute exacted from ranchers in the area. Dawson tries to make it impossible for Wayne to find a site for his pharmacy but is foiled when Lacey goes into partnership with him. Wayne becomes a popular fellow as he cures the local aches and pains but he remains aloof from Lacey because of her engagement to Dawson and instead takes an interest in Ellen (Helen Parrish), a girl of highly respectable background. When Wayne leads the ranchers in revolt against Dawson, the latter places poison in a tonic that Wayne prescribes and kills his patient Whitney (Emmett Lynn). The enraged locals are about to lynch Wayne when the news of the gold strike at Sutter's Mill distracts them. A despairing Wayne decides to head for San Francisco and Ellen, but Lacey intervenes to ask him to help fight an epidemic that has broken out at the mines. He breaks off his relationship with Ellen and leads supply wagons through opposition from Dawson and his men. Dawson is mortally wounded by his own brother (Dick Purcell) and as he dies he absolves Wayne from blame over the death of the patient.

By now the Republic banner was becoming a surefire guide to a more routine Wayne appearance, and this rather dreary picture is only enlivened by its action sequences. As in *The Spoilers*, but far less effectively, the film demonstrates the worth of a girl of dubious background over a lady with impeccable references (the pallid casting of the latter role always gives the outcome away from the start). Besides, what rugged figure like Wayne is going to want to spend the rest of his life sipping afternoon tea?

The film actually makes a rather subdued hero out of Wayne. It gives him an unusually respectable and potentially unexciting occupation as a pharmacist; it makes him an unwitting pawn of the villain to the extent of poisoning a patient; it has him almost strung up, saved only by the highly convenient discovery of gold; and it deprives him of the opportunity to settle his account with the villain.

John Wayne, Albert Dekker, Binnie Barnes.

25. Flying Tigers (1942)

FLYING TIGERS is significant only as Wayne's first appearance in a war film. Republic's tribute to an American volunteer group of flyers fighting for the Chinese against the Japanese invaders, it is also less obviously that studio's tribute to the artistry of director Howard Hawks in making *Only Angels Have Wings* (1939) about a group of mail pilots in South America. Here again, for those who missed the original, is the pilot with the failing eyesight (formerly Thomas Mitchell, here Paul Kelly) who refuses to be grounded and dies in the air; here also is the pilot with a blot on his record, desperate for another chance despite the contempt he will have to endure (formerly Richard Barthelmess, now Edmund MacDonald); here again is John Carroll, a member of the Hawks flying team this time promoted to co-star billing; and here is Wayne in the Cary Grant role as the sensitive commander who nurses his men through as best he can and mournfully surveys their belongings after they've cashed their chips.

There are moments that Wayne does well: an effective scene expressing bitter regret to himself for having allowed a young kid to fly to his death ("Should have stayed in college where he came from. But he begged for a chance — and I gave it to him!"). There is some tender romance with Wayne trading memories of back home, San Francisco, with those of Anna Lee as the Red Cross worker who remembers the steaks she ate in London. But John Carroll has the more colourful role as Woody Jason, the new flyer with a reckless, devil-may-care attitude, eager to get the $500 reward for every Jap knocked out of the sky. His disregard of orders enables Paul Kelly's Hap to take off in his place and die in action. This and the shocking news from Pearl Harbour straighten Woody out and he sneaks aboard a transport plane that Wayne is flying alone because his mission — to bomb a Japanese supply train — is so hazardous. Wayne recognises that Woody has now matured and lets him stay on board to drop the bombs. The plane is hit during the attack and Wayne decides they should both bail out but Woody stays behind to crash the aircraft into the train, the final atonement for his past mistakes.

Though one has to recall the propaganda motive behind the making of such films, *Flying Tigers* seems rather nauseating now in the way it relishes huge close-ups of enemy pilots with blood streaming from their mouths as they enter their last dives. The film makes a point of spelling out the nature of Japanese atrocities towards their prisoners, and the cockpit close-ups of Wayne's intently narrowed eyes zeroing in for the kill must have presented a reassuring picture of American determination in those worrying times.

John Wayne, Paul Kelly, Anna Lee.

26. Reunion in France (1942)

IT WAS WAR again in *Reunion in France,* released in Britain as *Mademoiselle France.* But the subject was treated in a much glossier fashion as one would expect from a film made at MGM, the aristocrats of film production. And Wayne's usefulness to the studio was that he represented new blood that could rejuvenate the image of their star Joan Crawford by being a youthful romantic partner for her as he had been to Dietrich at Universal. The film is very much a Crawford vehicle, Wayne's part is one of the most thankless he has ever been given, and the result is a dire attempt to combine romantic mush with war-time propaganda.

Crawford plays the Frenchwoman, Michèle de la Becque, whose *fiancé* is an apparent collaborator with the Nazi occupying forces of her country. Wayne is Pat Talbot, the downed pilot who takes a chance on her, as a complete stranger to him, by seeking her help in allaying the suspicions of two men watching him. His leg is hurt, he is suffering from exhaustion, and a state of near delirium would seem at this stage to account for his frivolous banter. So she pretends to be his girlfriend to put off the watching men and gives him refuge in her flat. As Wayne recovers and they talk to each other, he puts a lazy, seductive charm into his voice and expressions, but his abilities count for nothing when he has to keep up a tiresomely lighthearted front. Were you shot down? she asks. "My plane was," Wayne replies, "I couldn't figure out a way to stay up without it so I came down too." He was put into a concentration camp but became "bored" and escaped. Carefully delivered by a David Niven in the stiff upper lip fashion, this kind of bravado might get by, but on Wayne, as a brash American from Wilkes Barre, Pennsylvania, it is very wearying.

Michèle sets out to acquire some papers for him. His tactless contributions to her efforts include picking a fight with an obnoxious German officer she is playing up to on his behalf and recklessly venturing out of her flat into the open. All this earns only the mildest of protests — in fact more of a tribute — from her: "I wish you'd stop being so gay, so romantic and American about this"!

Eventually Michèle's influential *fiancé* (Philip Dorn) arranges a permit for her to leave the country and she passes Wayne off as her chauffeur. After some difficulties, they reach the border. En route Michèle learns that her *fiancé* is in fact secretly sabotaging the Nazi war effort at every opportunity, so she returns to his side, leaving Wayne to proceed to London and carry on flying against the Germans.

Joan Crawford and John Wayne.

27. Pittsburgh (1942)

THE THIRD FILM Wayne made with Marlene Dietrich also reunited him with Randolph Scott, a tribute to the successful collaboration between the three players on *The Spoilers*. As on that film, Wayne takes third billing to demonstrate that, outside of Republic, he was still not regarded as a sure-fire box-office name. Nevertheless Wayne has a more substantial role than Scott in both films, and *Pittsburgh* gives him a splendid opportunity to deepen his characterisations.

Here he plays a coal miner with ambitions, Pittsburgh ("a big name for a big guy") Markham. Someone says early on of him: "Who is he? Nobody. He seems awfully sure of himself, doesn't he?" This self-confidence manifests itself in a lack of consideration for others. He's usually friendly but he makes use of people: to promote a loan, to con a new suit out of a tailor, to raise some money for a boxing match — pushing his best friend, Cash Evans (Randolph Scott) into the ring to do the actual job of beating the challenger.

When he meets Josie Winters (Marlene Dietrich), he starts calling her "Countess" because of the impression she makes on him, although she reveals that she comes from the same kind of humble coal-mining background as himself. Wayne starts to think big. "I ain't always gonna be slinging a pick…I know there ain't a thing in the world I can't do once I set my mind to it. You're going to hear a lot about Pittsburgh Markham," he says. Josie remains somewhat unimpressed by his big ideas but when she dares him to actually quit his job he does so — and tenders Cash's resignation as well (without asking him). He then interests a banker in a supply of cut-price coke for a steel company and, needing the banker's signature on a contract to persuade the mine-owner to supply the coke, he forges it himself. Flushed with success, he starts talking of helping to improve the lot of the men he used to work with, but his first taste of big business goes to his head. He marries the banker's daughter (Louise Allbritton) much to Josie's dismay but soon feels out of his depth at the wedding reception, being asked how he likes opera by one of the guests. He tries to lure Cash into a corner to reminisce over old times and, being turned down, he goes off to look up Josie on his wedding night, telling her "It got a bit chilly up town — I thought I'd come

John Wayne, Frank Craven (as the research scientist), Marlene Dietrich and Randolph Scott.

Thomas Gomez, Marlene Dietrich, Randolph Scott and Wayne.

down here where it's warmer.'' He tries to explain away his new life: "Marriage with that crowd is business — I played my angles right and made a solid deal — but that's got nothing to do with you and me.'' Not surprisingly Wayne gets his face slapped. Josie tells him he could have married her but it's too late now.

As Wayne follows his lonely path to further heights of financial wizardry and big business success, his old ideals fall by the wayside. He puts his father-in-law out to pasture, he betrays the men over promises he made to them of new safety measures, a hospitalisation scheme and a chance to look over the company books. He refuses his wife the divorce she wants: he'll make any break, not her. He sums up his new outlook as "In my book, every time the clock strikes, it ought to ring like a cash register.'' He even puts a stop to research into a new medicine to be developed from coal tar to relieve world suffering because it doesn't show any profit, and here Cash draws the line and asks Wayne to buy out the stake he has had in Wayne's success. When the men stage a revolt against Wayne in the mines, he goes down to tackle them singlehanded, as bold and confident as ever, and Cash follows to intercede before trouble can break out, putting the dispute on a personal level between him and Wayne and turning it into a fistfight. Since the all-out brawl at the end of *The Spoilers* had been such a success, it had to be an ingredient of their second film together and, though I've never found the fights of Wayne's pictures as interesting as the details of characterisation, fights as skilfully and dynamically performed as this are a form of screen art which Wayne has always excelled at and based a good deal of his popularity on.

This marks the turning point of Wayne's career in *Pittsburgh*. His success goes sour. Cash abandons him, his wife walks out, Josie is badly hurt in an accident. He is all alone. He now goes into reverse gear and tries to win friends by putting right his past mistakes. "I'll make them like me — I'll cram it down their throats,'' he snarls as he puts into operation his scheme for a model city for his workers to live in. Cash and Josie marry and Wayne's business folds up under him. Only now does he feel genuinely repentant and as the Second World War engages America he goes to work for Cash's new company under an assumed name, starting at the bottom. Soon his ideas for improving output command Cash's attention and when the new employee comes to meet the boss only Josie prevents them quarrelling bitterly, giving the film a patriotic message that the important thing at this time of war is "devotion to our country.'' With the three united as friends again it remains for Wayne to make one small assertion of his old arrogance. Given the job of production manager by Cash, he upgrades himself to being his partner...

Now there is nothing particularly original about the film's development and there is no great profundity to any of the characters. *Pittsburgh* is simply the kind of glossy factory assembly job that Hollywood has always done so well — quickly forgettable but highly entertaining while it lasts. But it is important in Wayne's career because it gave him a chance to feel his way around the kind of character he was to play most memorably in *Red River* a few years later: the man who loses his humanity, who walks roughshod over people to achieve his ends but comes to see the folly of his ways in time to salvage a new future.

28. A Lady Takes a Chance (1943)

AFTER Dietrich and Crawford, it was Jean Arthur's turn to have Wayne as a leading man both insufficiently prominent to take top billing away from her and youthful-looking enough to reflect some of that youth onto her by his romantic interest. The film was an independent production by Miss Arthur's husband, Frank Ross, for RKO release and is much more her film than Wayne's but sadly no adequate vehicle for the delicious comedy talents of the actress after such gems as *The Devil and Miss Jones, Talk of the Town* and *The More the Merrier*. A conventional, shallow script lacking memorable highlights, it can have done her career little good. Here she plays Molly Truesdale, the kind of name that naturally suits the part of a somewhat defensive single woman in New York whose need of a coach tour promising "14 Breathless Days in the West" is

understandable when all she has in the way of beaux is the argumentative and pressing trio played by Hans Conried, Grady Sutton and Grant Withers.

Once out West the ideal man fall right into her lap. Literally. John Wayne as Duke Hudkins, rodeo rider, is tossed off a bronc right on top of Molly as she is about to take his photograph. Sprawling across her on the ground, he puts on that awkward, lazy, open-mouthed grin as he raises his head and they are soon off on a date.

Molly can't believe her luck and asks if she can feel his arm muscles. She goes with him drinking and gambling, sees Wayne exercise those muscles to telling effect in a brawl, and gets so carried away she misses her bus and accepts the offer of his hotel bedroom. When he tries to kiss her there, her maidenly self surfaces and she orders him out.

Wayne and Jean Arthur at the gambling tables.

Wayne makes his presence felt in a lively brawl.

Wayne plays a simple, easy-going fellow who prizes his independence. He doesn't believe in marriage and says of his settled friends, "They just make out they like it because they're ashamed to admit they made a mistake." He doesn't want to own a ranch and get tied down, and he cares more about his horse than he does about Molly Truesdale or any woman.

The latter point is demonstrated when he gives Molly a lift as he's driving his car and horse trailer so that she can rejoin her coach party at the next stop. They camp out for the night in the desert and she furtively steals a second blanket from Wayne's horse to ward off the cold of the desert night, going to asleep alongside him with a clenched rock in her hand. In the morning both Molly and horse start sneezing but Wayne only notices the animal and rushes it off to a vet. But Molly takes a constructive view of the situation: "Any fellow who can love a horse can love a girl."

The horse survives and Wayne doesn't turn up to see her off on the road to New York. She recoils at the bus station when the first of her old admirers (Grady Sutton) rushes up to welcome her back, followed hotly by the other two. But surprise! Wayne strides in and claims her for himself, administering a knockout blow to the burliest of her three suitors (Grant Withers) who makes the mistake of objecting. He tells Molly that he has divorced his old sidekick Waco (Charles Winninger) and manfully takes her off to the West.

Somehow, an amusing basic story is dissipated by a slackness of handling, a thinness of inventive detail, a poverty in production values to make this no more than a mild and dated success at best.

29. In Old Oklahoma (1943)

NO DOUBT from subsequent confusion with *In Old California*, *In Old Oklahoma*, which re-teamed Wayne with Albert Dekker, is these days better known by its reissue title of *War of the Wildcats*.

Here the background is the discovery of "black gold" on farmlands of Oklahoma in 1906. Wayne is Dan Somers, a cowboy friend of the farmers and Indians, and Albert Dekker is Jim Gardner, a prosperous oil-man. Both meet and are attracted to the schoolteacher authoress, Cathy Allen, played by Martha Scott, who has written a scandalous book.

Gardner wants to lease land from the Indians to drill for oil but the Indians trust their friend Wayne more and want him to work with them. As wards of the government they have to obtain Washington's approval, and Wayne is given the go-ahead providing that he delivers oil to a refinery in Tulsa on a set date.

Wayne has to contend with the obstructive tactics of his rival Gardner, a quarrel with Cathy, and lack of equipment. But he manages to have the oil ready to move with barely enough time to meet the deadline. Because Gardner has tied up the only pipeline, Wayne has to transport the oil in a convoy of wagons. All is set for the genuinely spectacular climax in which the wagons dash across the prairies, many being stopped by Gardner's men, and finally have to pass a raging brush fire that ignites many more of the vehicles. Wayne himself (or rather, his stunt double) just manages to unhitch the horses from one wagon and ride away before it plunges over a cliff and explodes. Needless to say, Wayne wins through in the nick of time.

It takes another of those rousing punch-ups for Wayne to knock the last ounce of resistance out of Gardner, and the latter unusually turns over a new leaf, abandoning his scheme to exploit the Indian land and joining with Wayne in developing it for the tribe's benefit.

Marsha Scott, John Wayne, "Gabby" Hayes, Marjorie Rambeau, Richard Graham, Grant Withers, Paul Fix.

30. The Fighting Seabees (1944)

REPUBLIC pitted Wayne against the Japanese again in *The Fighting Seabees,* casting him as Wedge Donovan, the construction boss who is drawn into the war to help organise special battalions of men who can set up front-line installations and also defend themselves against the enemy. It is an interesting role for Wayne, that of a man who is too hot-headed to heed instructions when his anger is aroused, too much of an individual to work within an organisation, a man whose ultimate death repelling the Japanese is both a form of expiation for past errors of judgement and a grand heroic gesture.

"He's a hotheaded ape with a hair-trigger temper. When he's nice, he's very very nice. When he's not, he's stinking." The words are those of news reporter Constance Chesley (Susan Hayward). We see him being very very nice with his men, we see him relaxing enough to take the floor for a spot of jitterbugging at a party, only to lose his balance. What maddens Wayne is the way some of the men he has dispatched to work at the front have been killed by the Japanese without a chance to fight back. He has little patience with the army point of view that they would be regarded as soldiers and not as civilians if they carried arms and have not been trained to fight well enough to keep from being captured. "You may as well teach 'em to drink," replies Wayne to the suggestion of their lacking fighting knowhow.

Lt. Commander Bob Yarrow (Dennis O'Keefe) develops the idea of forming special, properly trained battalions within the army and Constance, his girlfriend, sets about softening up Wayne to co-operate in putting the idea over in Washington.

While Washington deliberates, Wayne and his men go off on a job overseas, still as civilians working for the army, and Constance goes along to write it up as a story. One night on deck she and Wayne fall into conversation. She says,"Watching a ship's wake always makes me think of the things that time puts behind us for ever — hopes, dreams, illusions. What does it make you think about?" Wayne replies, "If they changed the pitch of that propeller, they'd get a couple or more knots out of this tub." Constance says, "I thought I'd caught you being human for once. Don't you have anything under that thick hide of yours but cylinders and a carburettor?" Wayne's amused reply: "A spark-plug maybe." This conversation, though lightly played, is a concise example of one of Wayne's great points of appeal — that he's a man's man with his thoughts firmly rooted in a man's world, with no time to be drawn into wishy-washy romantic philosophising. When he *is* a romantic figure, he decides the time and place, and takes the initiative, kissing Constance shortly afterwards while she waxes enthusiastic about his work and capabilities.

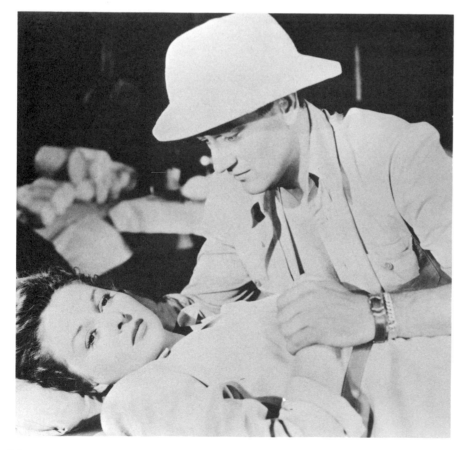

Susan Hayward and John Wayne.

Wayne and Dennis O'Keefe confer in front of the back projection screen.

Out on the island, Wayne quickly gets impatient with the red tape of filling out daily progress reports. And this impatience breaks out again when the Japanese start to strafe his position, killing some of his men. He hands out guns to his men and they go charging off to deal with what he somewhat contemptuously calls "Tojo and his bug-eyed monkeys." His men's intrusion stops Yarrow and the regular soldiers from ambushing the Japanese from behind cover and wiping them out. Wayne has to face Yarrow's charge that "Every civilian here was wounded or killed because a fool wouldn't obey orders." When Wayne admits his error ("I was wrong, rotten wrong"), all is forgiven.

The plan for setting up construction battalions gains Washington's approval and Wayne is appointed a Lt. Commander in the new force named the Seabees (from C.B. for Construction Battalion). After training in base camp, the men go out to set up an oil depot on an island to refuel the navy, but before long Wayne is boiling over again at Japanese harassment. Their snipers are as pro-vocative as possible: no sooner does a man say "Don't worry, there ain't any Japs here," than he is picked off by a bullet. And what with shooting up ambulances and picking off Wayne's best pal, Eddie Powers (William Frawley), just as he is completing the job by opening up the valve for the first oil to flow into the tanks, Wayne soon loses all discretion. He takes his men off to square accounts but the Japanese melt away into the jungle. Yarrow turns up to find that the situation has become critical through Wayne's disobedience with the Japanese surging forward and the oil tanks about to fall. Wayne devises a spectacular one-man solution, strapping dynamite to the front of a bulldozer and driving it forward to ram into one of the oil tanks, exploding it to spread a sheet of flame and engulf the enemy. On the way he is struck by an enemy bullet but the bulldozer goes right on, carrying him to his second screen death (the first was *Reap The Wild Wind*), with the element of heroic sacrifice more prominent than the expiation of past errors.

31. Tall in the Saddle (1944)

WAYNE'S name looked very much at home above the title of his next film, *Tall in the Saddle*. The film also marked Wayne's first positive step to determine the course of his career for it has been reported that he set about getting the film made, having taken a liking to the script which was partly written by his actor friend Paul Fix (who had most recently played with him in *In Old Oklahoma* and *The Fighting Seabees*). With the help of producer Robert Fellows, the film went into production at RKO Radio with Fix also appearing in the film as a shady deputy sheriff. Fellows's help and encouragement at this time must have had a part to play in the fact that he later became Wayne's partner in Wayne-Fellows Productions when the actor entered production in a big way.

Tall in the Saddle is an excessively complicated mystery Western more interesting for the way it is played by Wayne, female lead Ella Raines and villain Ward Bond, and for its touches of characterisation, than for the unravelling of its plot.

Wayne portrays the cowboy called Rocklin who arrives in the town of Santa Inez to become foreman of a ranch, only to discover that his prospective employer has been murdered. Burned perhaps by some past ex-perience, Wayne has a pronounced mistrust of women verging on misogynism and he therefore declines to work for the murdered man's successors, the young Clara (Audrey Long) and her guardian aunt (Elisabeth Risdon).

"I never feel sorry for anything that happens to a woman," he has been heard to observe earlier, and demonstrates as much when he has occasion to drive the stage into town and leaves the lady passengers holding their own baggage. But he does agree to help Clara when she is concerned about having her affairs turned over to Judge Garvey (Ward Bond) by her aunt. She believes that they are working together to suppress a letter which would establish her as being of age and able to run the ranch for herself.

Garvey has indeed had the letter and has just burned it when Wayne turns up to take a surreptitious look around his offices. Wayne fixes him with a sour look and goes about searching his desk anyway, finding a deck of marked cards. The scene explodes into a splendid fight between the two men, providing an indelible image when Ward Bond is smashed clean through a door as Wayne thuds into him. Certainly this fight, along with the ones between Wayne and Bond in *A Man*

John Wayne, Ella Raines and George "Gabby" Hayes.

Betrayed and *Shepherd of the Hills* previously, are
enough to rank Ward Bond alongside Wayne's other
principal adversaries in slugging matches like Yakima
Canutt, Randolph Scott, Forrest Tucker and Victor
McLaglen (*The Quiet Man*). At more composed moments in *Tall in the Saddle,* Bond's performance with
its suave, preacher-like smoothness and self-control
contrast admirably with Wayne's impatient style.

If Wayne is a match for Ward Bond, he is honourably
defeated in his attempts to deal with Ella Raines's Arly
Harolday. Her portrait of a Western woman is one of
spitfire independence and sultry aggression, making
her a far more vivid figure than Audrey Long's insipidly
well-bred Eastern lady. Dressed in Western costume,
Arly makes the sparks fly between herself and Wayne.
When he antagonises her on early acquaintance, she
sets out to get her own back by having her stepfather
hire him to work on his ranch so that she can have the
pleasure of sacking him. She even gets so mad that she
fires a pistol at him, leaving Wayne, looking visibly
scared, to down a glass of whisky to steady his nerves.
Later on, in the film's most tempestuous sequence, she
flings a knife at him when her temper boils over again,
and he seizes her in a fierce embrace. But he is soon
trying to ward her off, saying "You might as well know
no woman is going to get me hogtied and branded." She
is quite undeterred and knowingly comments, "I'm not
doing so badly."

Wayne has more problems that just Arly to contend

with. The plot thickens in a scene, more typical of a
Monogram B or Mascot serial, when he is questioning
Arly's step-brother. A hand reaches through the window of the hotel room, lifts Wayne's gun from its hols-
ter (handily within reach), and fires the weapon, killing
the man, before tossing it back into the room. Being an
upright figure, Wayne won't allow his pal Dave (George
"Gabby" Hayes) to lie to help him out of the fix, nor
plead the case of self-defence that Judge Garvey proposes when the townspeople think he has killed the
step-brother. Before long, he is on the run from the
sheriff and his posse, conveniently overhears a conversation between Clara's aunt and Garvey which lets him
know that he is the rightful heir to the ranch as the
nephew of the dead owner, and falls into the hands of
some other villains. It takes Arly to come and untie him
and this gives him the chance to exercise his fists again
in a brawl with George Clews, played by another familiar adversary, Harry Woods, who had fought Wayne in
Haunted Gold and *The Dark Command*. This time two
fences replace a door as objects to be busted through in
the *mêlée*. It turns out that Arly's stepfather (Don
Douglas) has been masterminding the complex conspi-
racy and Wayne is able to clear himself. Clara decides
that the East is a much safer place for a girl of her quiet
disposition, amd she instructs Wayne that Arly is the
girl for him. His resistance to women has now been so
completely eroded that he goes off to claim her.

Before and after the 'quake in Flame of the Barbary Coast. *Above, Joseph Schildkraut, Ann Dvorak and John Wayne. Below, Wayne rescues Dvorak from the debris.*

32. Flame of the Barbary Coast (1945)

WHEN REPUBLIC came to celebrate its tenth anniversary with the release of *Flame of the Barbary Coast*, it was doubly apt that the film should star Wayne, who had topped the cast of its first production back in 1935 and who was now its biggest star. The result was, as it turned out, an unremarkable period splurge, relying on lavish sets, agile camerawork and a reconstruction of the San Francisco earthquake of 1906 to enliven its constipated plot. Republic's action sequences were always pretty good thanks to their use of such stunt men as Yakima Canutt (as on *Angel and the Badman*) and here their regular special effects team of Howard and Theodore Lydecker, but it was asking too much of the latter pair to expect them to outdo M-G-M's celebrated reconstruction of the same catastrophe in *San Francisco* some nine years before and in fact the earthquake makes a surprisingly brief sequence, serving as a catalyst rather than a climax, leading to a solution of the characters' differences.

Wayne was cast as Duke Fergus, the cowboy from Montana who arrives in San Francisco, enjoying his first glimpse of the sea and a winning streak at the roulette tables under the expert guidance of Flaxen Terry (Ann Dvorak), a singer who knows how the gambling wheels turn. She is the *fiancée* of Tito Morell, black sheep of the Nob Hill aristocracy, owner of a riproaring gambling den called the El Dorado, and the king of the notorious Barbary Coast. Flaxen succeeds in annoying Tito by her interest in Wayne, and Tito cheats Wayne out of his winnings, sending him back to the Montana ranges.

Flaxen turns down Wayne's suggestion that she should accompany him home, and he finds that he can't get her out of his thoughts. He lays plans for a return visit to the Barbary Coast, engaging the professional gambler Wolf Wylie (William Frawley) to teach him the tricks of cardplay, and taking him along to safeguard his fortunes. No longer the naive, laconic Westerner, he uses his stake to win a fortune quickly from Morell at the tables and sets up a rival gambling establishment, the Silver Dollar, persuading Flaxen to appear in his opening show. Fans of *San Francisco* who remembered how Jeanette MacDonald's singing seemed to trigger off the earthquake there won't have been surprised when the first tremors occur just after Flaxen has completed a number. The ensuring devastation wipes out Wayne's business plans just as surely as it demolished Clark Gable's gambling establishment before, leaving Flaxen to make a slow recovery from a paralysing injury in the company of her man who turns his attention to helping clean up San Francisco's reputation before taking her off to the wilds of Montana.

33. Back to Bataan (1945)

CONTRACTED to RKO for a film a year, Wayne went off to war again in *Back to Bataan*, playing Colonel Joseph Madden who is fighting the Japanese on Bataan with the help of Captain Andres Bonifacio (Anthony Quinn) and his Philippino men. When Bataan falls to the enemy, Wayne stays behind in the general retreat to organise guerilla resistance among the stranded American troops and Philippino freedom fighters. His ragged entourage includes a refugee American teacher (Beulah Bondi) and one of her boy pupils ("Ducky" Louie). Wayne has to overcome Bonifacio's feelings of being let down by the Americans in their withdrawal from the islands, but the Captain is encouraged to fight on when he discovers that his girlfriend (Fely Franquelli) is not the traitor she seems but is playing up to the Japanese to extract information. A highlight of the film is the daring attack on the "independence" ceremony mounted by the invaders to try and combat the increasing effectiveness of the guerilla resistance.

This is basically a very routine war film, presenting sacrifice in cliche terms: the Philippino headmaster who is hanged because he wouldn't haul down the

Anthony Quinn and John Wayne.

American flag for the Japanese, the small boy for whom American freedom means a hotdog with relish and mustard and who, when his father is murdered, receives a comforting pat from Wayne and the quiet remark, ''War hurts everyone.'' The boy falls into enemy hands and dies heroically tricking them, and it seems that even Wayne is going to fall, to provide a flash of unexpected realism, when he strides out into a smoke-covered river to challenge the enemy on the other bank and machine-gun fire is heard — but he returns safely and it is left to *Sands of Iwo Jima* to put the sting of death into the tail of a Wayne performance a few years later. Nevertheless, *Back to Bataan* is lifted a notch above the average, regarded cinematically, by Edward Dmytryk's expert direction, seizing the most telling camera angles to put the action scenes vividly across and providing a moment when Wayne seems to be blown out of a hollow by an exploding shell. But with *They Were Expendable* following so closely after, and dealing with much the same incidents in the Pacific war, *Back to Bataan* is nudged onto the more forgettable side of Wayne's career.

Wayne himself remembers the making of the film with some bitterness. Though the finished picture is ultra-American in its patriotic regard for the American flag and the cause of freedom, Wayne found director Dmytryk and many of the cast too left wing for his tastes and maintains that they ridiculed the military adviser assigned to the picture, kidding him about his Catholic beliefs and having him turn to Wayne for support. Dmytryk and one of the scriptwriters, Ben Barzman, were leading victims of the Hollywood blacklist of later years.

34. They Were Expendable (1945)

IT TOOK John Ford to put Wayne into his first outstanding war film, *They Were Expendable*, starring beneath Robert Montgomery. The latter plays Lt. John Brickley, the calm, efficient commander of a squadron of motor torpedo boats in the grim days of the American retreat from the Philippines to Australia. Brickley is the one who is burdened with real responsibility, while Wayne as Lt. j. g. Rusty Ryan is the less stable character, expressing the frustrations of the situation in flashes of temper while Brickley absorbs and accepts them. As in *The Fighting Seabees*, Wayne reacts to the moment, doesn't look at things from a wider, long-term viewpoint. But the two men maintain a cordial relationship that allows Brickley to keep Wayne in line without antagonism developing and the film is another example of Ford's treatment of a close-knit community ob-

served with warmth and affection. Even when Wayne ventures outside the group to romance a girl (Donna Reed), she also is navy (a nurse) and he brings her into the den to be greeted and accepted as "Rusty's gal" before the others discreetly withdraw to leave the pair alone.

At the start of the film we find Wayne irritated by the lack of high-level enthusiasm over the potential of the PT boat in wartime. He is anxious to transfer to a destroyer for real action. He is annoyed again when the news of the Pearl Harbor attack comes through and the boats are assigned to messenger duty. His irritation vents itself with him kicking a bucket around. "Does that help?" inquires the watching Brickley and when Wayne yells "Yes!" and departs, Brickley takes a kick at the object himself — needing, in contrast to Wayne,

Jack Pennick, John Wayne, Robert Montgomery, Ward Bond.

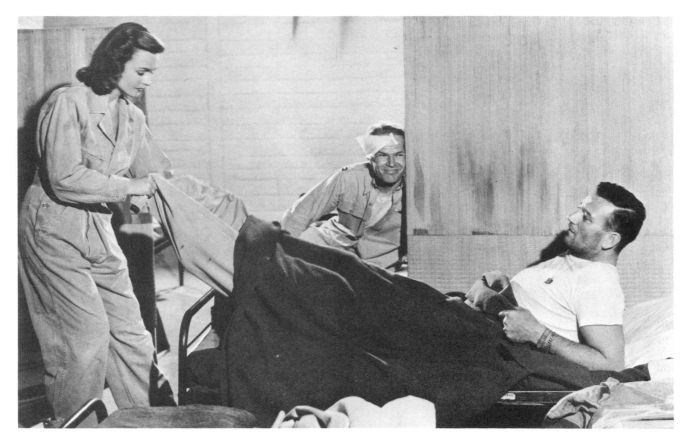

Donna Reed, Louis Jean Heydt, John Wayne.

both the suggestion and the privacy of being alone to do it himself.

When the PT boats get a chance to pursue a Japanese cruiser, Wayne is eager to go but Brickley spots his infected hand and orders him into hospital — proved right in the outcome because blood poisoning would have cost Wayne his entire arm had treatment been much delayed. Wayne arrives at the hospital, shouting to give vent to his frustration until quieted down by the nurse. When Sandy Davis (Donna Reed) suggests they might go to a dance together, Wayne is as impatient as ever replying, ''Listen, sister, I don't dance — and I can't take time out now to learn. All I want is to get out of here!'' But on calming down he does go and there is a warmly romantic scene in which he and Sandy discuss their home backgrounds (far better than the equivalent scene in *Flying Tigers*) and the distant flashes of war in the night sky can be momentarily likened to fireflies back home recalling a distant world of peaceful serenity...eloquently conveying, as few war films do, a sense of what is being fought for. Ford's sensitivity is seen in the discreet way that Brickley intrudes to bring Wayne back to the war.

When any kind of action is in the offing, Wayne is fully behind Brickley and he gets his chance to take a crack at a Jap cruiser. Here again the director's humanity rides over the bravura of war in a scene of a makeshift funeral in which Wayne has to substitute for a priest and reads a passage of poetry over a dead seaman, the very awkwardness of his delivery giving the words unusual sincerity.

The war goes badly and when Bataan has fallen and Sandy is somewhere on the island there is tenderness again in Wayne's performance as he wistfully remarks, ''The last time I talked to her was over the telephone ... her voice sounded swell, clear, brave, far away...'' It's because Wayne is so brash and insensitive at other times that such corny words have the ring of true emotion, making his Rusty Ryan a far more rounded and substantial figure than his other war heroes.

Wayne's final upsurge of spontaneous feeling and reluctant acceptance of his place in the scheme of operations comes after his boat has been sunk by the Japanese and he and Brickley are ordered to fly back to Washington to organise new PT boat squadrons for an active role in the fighting to come. Wayne is loath to leave the scene of the present struggle, with the rest of the men and boats turned over to the army. He has one of the few places available for leaving the battle zone and tries to get off the plane and give his seat to another officer lower on the list of priorities who is waiting to go. ''I got business *here*,'' Wayne declares and Brickley quietly asks, ''Rusty, who are you working for? Yourself?'', once again bringing him into line.

This scene was developed at Wayne's request to strengthen his part. It demonstrates how basic Wayne regarded this independent streak to his screen image.

35. Dakota (1945)

DAKOTA is an odd and unsuccessful film, but nowadays the oddest thing about it is noting the names of Carl Foreman, author of the film's story, and John Wayne on the same picture a few years before Hollywood's political storms put them at opposite extremes.

In *Dakota*, the inevitable happened sooner rather than later in that Wayne had Vera Hruba Ralston, to become Republic's most enduring leading lady, as his co-star. She was an addition to the number of foreign actresses Wayne had worked with (though names are sometimes deceptive: Ann Dvorak was American by birth). A Czech refugee from the Nazis (like the part Sigrid Gurie played in *Three Faces West*), she had been a champion ice skater and demonstrated as much in three films for Republic; she had slowed down for a couple of low-budget dramas but this was her first venture into the big league. She subsequently appeared opposite Wayne again in *The Fighting Kentuckian* (by which time she had dropped the Hruba from her name) and went on to marry Republic's boss, Herbert J. Yates, in 1952. Miss Ralston had all the advantages and it has often been queried how much she deserved them. Never outstandingly attractive, she was pleasant enough, high-spirited at times, especially when given the chances that *Dakota* provides to dictate to the male star rather than be dominated, but it's hard to be enormously enthusiastic about her presence in a film. Casting opposite so American a figure as Wayne must have helped submerge her "foreignness"(a quality never very appealing to audiences) and given her as good a career boost as possible.

Her Sandy Poli gets the film off to a brisk start when she escapes with her newly-wed husband, John Wayne's ex-soldier John Devlin, from the clutches of her irascible father (Hugo Haas), less concerned about retrieving his daughter than regaining the money she has obtained from selling one of his Gainsborough paintings. Sandy has plans to outwit her father, a railroad tycoon, by buying up land she knows his railroad will later need to extend their tracks into Dakota and she tricks Wayne out of his idea of settling in California. On the way to their new destination, Wayne is relieved of their capital when bandits board the riverboat on which they are passengers.

Reaching the town of Fargo, Wayne takes the side of the honest wheat farmers against Jim Bender (Ward Bond) and Bigtree Collins (Mike Mazurki), two villainous dandies who arranged Wayne's loss of his money and who have been terrorising the farmers into giving up their land. Wayne agrees to clear out if his money is returned to him at one point, but turns the tables on the villains, helped by Collins's murder of Bender after a quarrel. Wayne's moment of triumph is followed by another assertive action from Sandy who has invested their money in a new riverboat until the railroad comes along.

Dakota is singularly boring, hovering in an unresolved state between taking its complicated plot seriously and sending the whole thing up. The director, Joseph Kane, seems to muddle matters by allowing a bit of each. The hectic beginning sets a light tone, and Mike Mazurki and Ward Bond appear to enjoy themselves hugely as unorthodox and suave villains, pausing to attend to the heroine's welfare after a stray bullet hits her; but for too much of the time the film is bogged down in the faked exteriors of a studio sound stage, defying anyone to care what's happening.

Ward Bond, John Wayne, Vera Hruba Ralston, Mike Mazurki.

36. Without Reservations (1946)

BACK AT RKO, Wayne was pressed into duty as the male lead in a Claudette Colbert romantic comedy, *Without Reservations*. Unfortunately the film lacks both warmth and wit and Miss Colbert (though only four years past her glittering peak in *The Palm Beach Story*) is far too old for her part of an innocent — and seemingly young — intellectual called Kit Madden who writes a best-selling book but has little experience of life and love. She takes the train from the East to Hollywood where her book is to be filmed and en route meets a couple of marine flyers, Rusty Thomas (John Wayne) and Dink Watson (Don DeFore), who find her full of "yackety yak" but take an interest in her and invite her to have a drink.

Wayne, of course, represents the worldly figure who can show up the weaknesses in Kit's abstract theorising. She keeps her identity from Wayne so that he doesn't know she's the author of the book everybody is reading and has no reason to be polite about it. When she describes its analysis of the conflict between progressive and reactionary forces, he is quite scathing about it and lectures her on the values of self-reliance as opposed to the kind of co-operative society the book favours. The Wayne philosophy is summed up as

"Thanks, God, we'll take it from here." And he is no kinder to Kit personally who doesn't know her place in a man's world: "I want a woman who needs me, who's helpless and cute — not one who wants to put the world right."

Of course, such a limited notion of life and woman's place in it is endorsed by the film which shows Kit, after her several adventures with the two men, reaching Hollywood to tell her producers that she wants to revise many of the ideas in her book. (Another simple notion the film puts forward is that authors are generally invited to Hollywood to have a say in the films of their work.)

At this stage, Kit has lost sight of Wayne but the inevitable reunion is not far off. It would be more logical if she went to him as he has taught her so much and she had deceived him about her identity, which has upset him on learning about it. But since this is essentially a Colbert picture, it is Wayne who comes to her because he's been unable to put her out of his mind.

The anti-egghead approach of the film would be forgivable were it funny; but unfortunately the script is too linear and laborious, ultimately too insubstantial, to make the film anything but readily forgettable.

John Wayne, Claudette Colbert, Don DeFore.

37. Angel and the Badman (1947)

INDESTRUCTIBLE is the word that has attached itself to Wayne in recent years but as the actor entered his forties he began to see the day when he would no longer appeal as a leading man and decided to safeguard against it by moving into the production side of filmmaking. It was rare in 1947 for a leading man to be able to assert himself as a producer but then Wayne was so important to Republic that they were probably not very obstinate about it as a means of retaining his willing services as a star. And so *Angel and the Badman* came to the screen with a prominent credit, "A John Wayne Production," and no other identification of a producer. Republic also had to back Wayne in giving a chance to the film's writer, James Edward Grant, to direct his work. The result was surprising — but good. It is an unusual and impressive film, modest in size but most

effectively handled. And its message of opposition to violence made a refreshing change in the career of its star.

Wayne portrays Quirt Evans, a man that other men gossip about, recalling his days as Wyatt Earp's deputy in his fight against the Clantons and fearful of his subsequent reputation as a gunfighter. His name is enough to cause a change of heart in a rancher who has inconsiderately blocked the water supply of his neighbour; his presence is sufficient to draw the attention of Marshal McLintock (Harry Carey Sr.), waiting for the chance to take his man.

At the very start of the film we see Wayne's six guns blazing away past camera, then Wayne's flight on horseback from a band of pursuers in a hectic chase. He shakes them off but his wearied horse stumbles and

John Wayne as the recuperating badman with Gail Russell and Irene Rich.

throws him to the ground outside the home of a Quaker family, the Worths, who take him in and tend to his injuries sustained in the fall. The daughter of the house is Penny (Gail Russell), intrigued and attracted by this stranger who drapes his arm, still holding a six gun, around her, talks of other women in his sleep, and is such a handsome figure of a man. And the Wayne character is attracted to her, Gail Russell presenting what film historian Don Miller has aptly described as a "haunting mixture of sweetness and sex appeal." So the process of Wayne's reformation gets underway, conflicting with his desire to avenge the death of his foster father by killing Laredo Stevens (Bruce Cabot). The screenplay artfully contrives to deny Wayne any further use of his revolver. When Laredo Stevens and his men confront Wayne in the Worth home, Wayne bestrides a chair, half in shadow, his six-gun pointed at them, cautioning one man as he contemplates drawing his gun by asking "You nervous?" and controlling the situation; but little does he know that his gun has previously been emptied by Mr. Worth. Wayne still won't set aside his way of life as his interest in Penny deepens; "I've got places to go," he tells her, and instead of beating up a rival for her affections hauls the man off to encourage him to give her the kind of life she deserves. Wayne then takes the initiative in stealing a herd, helped by his friend Randy McCall (Lee Dixon), from Laredo (who has himself rustled it) and does the trick without firing a shot. And when action seems necessary to enliven the picture later on, the film introduces an exuberant saloon brawl that is all good knockabout fun.

Laredo renews Wayne's resolve to kill him when he ambushes Wayne and Penny while the pair are picnicking, Wayne having agreed to leave his gun behind and so forced to flee in the wagon they are using. When this ends up in a river, Penny becomes seriously ill after being rescued, and Wayne straps on his gun to ride into town. There is a splendid tracking shot of Wayne striding down main street; there is a *Stagecoach*-like moment of summoning Laredo from a saloon during which Penny arrives, having risen from her sickbed, and persuades Wayne to hand over his gun. At this very moment, Laredo emerges and prepares to shoot down his unarmed adversary. Marshal McLintock, still dogging Wayne's heels, is at hand to shoot down Laredo, making this the most unusual and unexpected outcome of any Wayne gunfight, enabling Wayne to hang up his weapon for good.

Though, as a writer, James Edward Grant gives excessive wordage to some of the supporting characters, he handles the drama with some flair, providing a good number of the kind of powerful images that mean so much in the cinema and enhance the appeal of the players they favour, Wayne and Gail Russell. The action scenes were delegated to Yakima Canutt and put over with considerable panache, yet smoothly integrating with the rest. The result is a distinct plus to Wayne's career as he obviously recognised in relying so much on James Edward Grant subsequently as a writer (if not director) of his later films.

38. Tycoon (1947)

FOR SHEER dreariness, Wayne's next film for RKO, *Tycoon*, takes some beating. In this vastly overlong (126 minutes) Technicolored romance-cum-adventure, he plays Johnny Munroe, a tunnel and bridge builder. Together with Pop Mathews (James Gleason), he has won a contract from the wealthy South American railroad owner Fredrick Alexander (Cedric Hardwicke) to drive a tunnel through a mountain to create a railroad link with some mines. Wayne has been in favour of a bridge by another route but agrees to construct the tunnel. The crew run into difficulties but the major obstacles are those placed by Alexander when Wayne courts and marries his daughter Maura (a lacklustre Laraine Day) against his wishes.

Wayne is drawn to Maura from his first glimpse of her and promptly follows her into church, though suffering the after-effects of a drunken binge, and sits there somewhat disrespectfully eyeing her during the service. She, having led a sheltered life, is intrigued by his attentions and invites him into the family house after he has extravagantly hired a band of musicians to serenade her. As in his first courting of Claire Trevor's Mary McCloud in *The Dark Command*, he hogs the conversation by talking about himself and his work, although he makes a less diffident and awkward figure here than in the earlier film. Alexander discovers them in his house and orders Wayne to leave. But they meet again secretly and are forced to spend the night in some remote ruins after they go for a ride in Wayne's jeep and Maura loses the way taking a shortcut through the jungle, with the jeep running out of petrol. Wayne has just got around to kissing the girl when her father turns up, having been alarmed by her absence, and Wayne puts on an expression of embarrassed alarm. Having gone this far, they are promptly married and Maura moves out to the construction camp with her new husband. He is too preoccupied with the problems of collapsing tunnel roofs and non-arrival of vital materials (withheld by Alexander) to find much time for her. The conflict between work and wife that has harassed so many Wayne heroes is fully evident.

Eventually, after a roof collapses on one of his best friends, Curley (Michael Harvey), Wayne blows up the entire mountainside with the remaining supply of dynamite and expresses bitter regret at having compromised and agreed to build the tunnel instead of a bridge. He tells Alexander he will build the bridge instead, still within the original cost estimate, and sets about cutting corners, disregarding safety precautions, refusing Alexander's offer of a ninety day extension,

Laraine Day and John Wayne listen to James Gleason at the construction camp.

Below, Wayne is exhausted by his efforts to save the bridge. Grant Withers, Paul Fix, Fernando Alvarado and James Gleason rally round him.

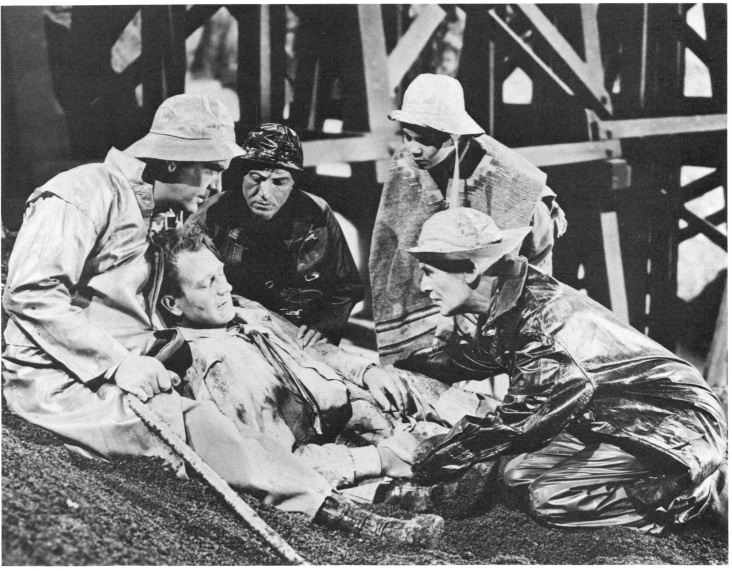

and seeing his friends and fellow workers quit in disgust. Maura, too, returns to her father, leaving Wayne to exclaim, "When I get enough money, I'll buy you back."

With newly recruited workers, Wayne has almost completed the bridge when a rainstorm further back in the mountains threatens to send down a torrent that will carry away the bridge. Wayne's crew are scared to continue working on the bridge and so he singlehandedly tries to set the missing centre span into place to give the structure more resistance to the impending barrage of water. His old colleagues now return to give him a helping hand and he then drives a train out on the completed bridge to give it added weight, scampering

across the top of the wagons to leap clear just before the weight of the arriving water dislodges the train although the bridge itself withstands the onslaught. Wayne now realises his past shortcomings — especially his betrayal of old friends — and wins back Maura.

The only really interesting feature of the film is the way the Wayne role hints at the part he was soon to play in *Red River* (as *Pittsburgh* had also done earlier). *Red River* was conceived by the writer Borden Chase who co-scripted *Tycoon* and in both films Chase gives Wayne the trait of an obstinancy that alienates his friends and supporters until he learns the hard way that he has been wrong. (Chase also wrote *Flame of the Barbary Coast* which doesn't fit into this pattern.)

39. Fort Apache (1948)

WITH *FORT APACHE,* Wayne entered a much richer phase of his career. This was the first of three films John Ford made over a two year period about the U.S. Cavalry. Wayne starred in all three of them, though his billing ahead of Henry Fonda on *Fort Apache* is misleading as the latter's Colonel Owen Thursday, styled on General George Custer, is the film's central figure. Order of billing reflects an estimate of box-office appeal, and so indicates that Wayne was more of an attraction than Fonda. In the later two films, *She Wore a Yellow Ribbon* and *Rio Grande*, Wayne dominates the story and far more is demanded of him. Here he is Captain Kirby York, an easy-going officer at Fort Apache, completely at home with his surroundings and popular with his fellow officers and men.

Fonda's Owen Thursday is the intruder from the North who comes to take over command of the fort, arriving during a regimental dance while Wayne is partnering Mrs. Collingwood (Anna Lee, his co-star of *Flying Tigers*). Thursday's interruption symbolises his later disturbance of the established ways of the community. An ambitious, glory-seeking man, Thursday is none too pleased to be sent to this remote outpost of Arizona and regards it as a temporary appointment. His arrogance and class-consciousness are seen in the way he is slow to master the names of his officers and in his actions to suppress the romantic attachment that springs up between his daughter Philadelphia (Shirley Temple) and young Lieutenant O'Rourke (John Agar), the son of a mere sergeant.

Thursday asserts himself by criticising the slack standards of dress that Wayne has allowed while temporarily in command, although these are far more practical and comfortable for the environment and it is Thursday in his kepi who looks ridiculous. Wayne's efforts to influence Thursday are all rebutted: he is stopped short when he tries to intervene in Thursday's dressing down of the amorous lieutenant; he is countermanded on every point when issuing instructions for a detail to go out, with the Colonel not deeming it necessary to inform Wayne as to the strategy he has

evolved until afterwards, and he is eventually encouraged to double-cross the Apaches and betray his word.

Respecting the rules, Wayne accepts Thursday's way but only at one point do their different outlooks mesh to good effect. This is when the pair visit Meacham, the crooked Indian agent (Grant Withers). Wayne is the impatient figure who has to be restrained from beating up the trader to gain answers to his questions, but Thursday is not above bending the rules himself to dispose of Meacham's stock of whisky and arms. It is Wayne who first draws attention to the cache of rifles but Thursday who puts his stylish signature on their destruction by observing that the rifles' pins are bent and need "straightening" with a mallet, thereby again taking the initiative away from Wayne in his sophisticated, self-asserting way.

As the Apaches under Cochise rebel at the ill-treatment that is meted out to them, it is Wayne who sympathises with their plight, hotly labelling the Indian Ring in Washington, who sent Meacham, as "the dirtiest, most corrupt political group in our history." Cochise has taken to hiding in Mexico and Wayne volunteers to go with a single companion, the Spanish-speaking interpreter Sergeant Beaufort (Pedro Armendariz), to parlay with the chief and persuade him to return to American jurisdiction. Even here Wayne's part in the film is reduced by eliminating all but the opening stage of his meeting with Cochise (Miguel Inclan) in favour of showing Thursday at the fort very reluctantly accepting a tradition by which he dances with the wife of the Sergeant Major at a regimental ball. Wayne persuades Cochise to meet an unarmed Thursday for a peace talk and returns during the dance to report. Thursday immediately calls the evening's entertainment to a halt, again showing his insensitivity to one of the strongest binding features of army life, and orders the regiment to prepare to march at dawn.

It is here that Wayne, so unnaturally subdued until this point (except for his attack on Meacham), has a chance to express some heated feeling. Thursday freely admits that he has had Wayne trick Cochise and Wayne

John Wayne and Henry Fonda as captain and fort commander in Fort Apache.

Left, Henry Fonda clashes with Ward Bond watched by Wayne and George O'Brien.

Below, the dance is interrupted as Wayne reports to Henry Fonda on his visit to Cochise. George O'Brien (centre) and Grant Withers (right) are among the listeners as the row develops.

protests, "Colonel Thursday, I gave my word to Cochise. No man is going to make a liar out of me, sir." The colonel replies sharply, "Your word to a breech-clouted savage! An illiterate, uncivilised murderer and treaty-breaker! There is no question of honour, sir, between an American officer and Cochise." And Wayne replies, with that firm integrity that is so much a part of his style, "There is to me, sir."

Nevertheless, Wayne accompanies Thursday and the men as they ride out, his anger showing in the way he drops the "sir" from his words with Thursday until the latter reminds him of the correct form of address. Everyone but Thursday has noticed that the Apache aren't where he thinks they are, and Wayne spells out to him that they outnumber the cavalry four to one. Thursday now finds it expedient to honour Wayne's word to Cochise and a meeting takes place at which Cochise issues warnings to Thursday that are taken by him as a threat. Despite Wayne's attempts to encourage restraint, Thursday issues a harsh ultimatum and the angered Cochise walks away.

Thursday now prepares to lead his men against the Apache, declining to believe that they are hidden from sight overlooking a narrow pass. He lines his troops up in column of fours to proceed. Here again Wayne protests, declaring that the formation is suicidal. Thursday relieves him of his command, accusing him of cowardice. This provokes in Wayne his strongest response in the film, his assertion of self after accepting his place for so long. He angrily spurs his horse forward, throws down his gauntlet, and wheels round to face Thursday: "At your service, sir!"

Thursday postpones answering the challenge and orders Wayne to stay with the supply train in safety, leaving him a grim, haggard-looking spectator to the massacre that ensues as Thursday goes forward, followed enthusiastically by his men. Wayne dispatches a rider to bring reinforcements and goes into the canyon to find Thursday, dismounted and bleeding from a head wound. Thursday commanders Wayne's horse and sabre and insists on rejoining his command further up the canyon, even though it means his certain death. And he gives Wayne these parting words of advice: "When you command this regiment — and you probably will — *command* it."

It is clear that Thursday's courage in continuing to his death wins him back some respect in Wayne's eyes — Thursday follows his convictions to the bitter end in the way that many a Wayne character of other films would endorse.

A short final scene takes place a good two years later. Wayne has become the new commander and is talking to newspapermen before he sets off to further the campaign against Cochise. On the wall is a painting of Thursday and a reporter eulogises over him and his celebrated charge — a defeat that has somehow turned into a triumph and made him "the hero of every schoolboy in America." Wayne comments "No man died more gallantly — or won more honour for his regiment," but the line is delivered by him in an emotionless, stiff manner as the narrow truth, the one constructive side of the incident. Again Wayne, hearing described a painting of Thursday's charge, comments with the same reserve, "Correct in every detail." Wayne only disagrees when one of the journalists observes that Thursday is remembered while his men are forgotten. "You're wrong there," says Wayne, warmth and feeling now entering his voice, "They aren't forgotten because they haven't died...they'll keep on living as long as the regiment lives...their faces may change, the names, but they're there, the regular army...they're better men than they used to be, Thursday did that, he made it a command to be proud of." And he leads his men out to the tune of a stirring song, Ford leaving us with another of his intensely romantic visions of the gallant horse soldiers.

As many writers have observed, this last scene fits the directive of *The Man Who Shot Liberty Valance*: "When the legend conflicts with the facts — print the legend." And the end of *Fort Apache* seems to argue that the army is never wrong, even if individual members are, and that for the sake of morale and faith in the future it is better to maintain the legend: Thursday made the regiment "a command to be proud of" not because of what he did but because of how others interpreted his action. For the more thoughtful observer, a nagging question remains unanswered: how much has Wayne become a new Thursday? He dresses like Thursday, has assumed Thursday's position, and is campaigning against Cochise, the same Indian who earlier spared his life and for whom he had great sympathy. It is only in the film's closing moments that this new aspect of complexity is introduced to what has otherwise been for Wayne a clearcut role, trading on that sense of open honesty and integrity in his screen *persona* and eschewing that aspect of stubborness and ruthlessness that his very next film was to draw from him so memorably. If Wayne had been inextricably involved with Thursday in *Fort Apache*, principally functioning as a commentator on the other man's actions, then in *Red River* he moved decisively to the centre of the screen for what was to be his most momentous role since the Ringo Kid in *Stagecoach*.

40. Red River (1948)

THOMAS DUNSON. When the name of the part is as readily remembered as the actor that played it — that's proof of its impact. It's also true of Wayne's playing Nathan Brittles (*She Wore a Yellow Ribbon*) and Ethan Edwards (*The Searchers*), John T. Chance (*Rio Bravo*) and Rooster Cogburn (*True Grit*). These are parts that measure up to the actor, that give him as much as he gives them, that are more than just Big John licking the yellow peril, the Indians, or the bad guys. And none was probably as astonishing at the time as Wayne's Thomas Dunson. Here was the actor, hardly renowned for his versatility and range, undertaking a part well beyond his own years: an ageing figure of granite-hard, single-minded stubbornness and determination, a man who is "wrong" and yet never loses audience sympathy and concern. It is not only one of Wayne's best performances: it is one of the most memorable in any Western.

A big budget picture costing nearly two million dollars, *Red River* gambled on Wayne even more than *The Big Trail* had done. An unconvincing Dunson would have wrecked the picture but director Howard Hawks, working for the first time with Wayne, knew what he was doing. Co-star Mongomery Clift was making his first picture and had uncertain appeal (although his second, *The Search*, was seen by American audiences a few weeks before *Red River*'s release). In the event it became one of the year's big hits, has been making money ever since, and the new wave of interest in Wayne ensured that a great many of his subsequent films were placed among their year's biggest grossers (*Wake of the Red Witch, She Wore a Yellow Ribbon, Sands of Iwo Jima, Operation Pacific, The Quiet Man*).

At the climax of the film, Wayne rides into Abilene determined to kill the man who has betrayed him: Matthew Garth (Montgomery Clift). Garth has rebelled at the way Wayne has been handling the men on a massive cattle drive, has taken over, and brought the cattle safely to the railroad on Wayne's behalf. Garth's success is intolerable to Wayne because it proves that Garth's way was right — treating the men as partners in the venture, relaxing the pace and even diverting the herd to visit a gambling train for a break, listening to two hearsay stories that the railway does extend to Abilene and taking the cattle there instead of the original destination. Wayne's way had been to act as a Captain Bligh of the prairie (one historian has called the film a re-make of *Mutiny on the Bounty*), expecting every bit as much from the men as he does from himself and stamping on any resistance to his own notions of what is fair and right.

Matt Garth has already been criticised by Wayne for his softness in leaving him alive after seizing command of the drive. Although the film has established that Garth is the faster on the draw, we are far from certain that his sensitive nature will allow him to shoot it out with Wayne. But we are sure that Wayne will try and kill Matt. Even the woman Tess Millay (Joanne Dru) who has fallen for Matt and tried to dissuade Wayne from his purpose, believes it; and Dunson's flaw of character is that he always follows through a line of action to the bitter end. The audience is also encouraged to accept a shootout as inevitable by the way that earlier all the hints of a stampede are followed by one taking place. This adherence to dramatic conventions leads us to suppose that Dunson will somehow die as a tragically flawed hero, true to himself to the end. Borden Chase, whose magazine story (later novel) and script were the basis of the film, saw it this way and had the gunfighter Cherry Valance (John Ireland) intervene because he knows his friend Matt won't defend himself, be shot down by Wayne, but wound him so badly that Wayne's shots at Matt go astray and he collapses to be carried off to Texas to die (this ending can be found in Chase's novel).

As Howard Hawks re-arranges the scene, we see Wayne marching through the herd of cattle, eyes intent on his destination, his body brushing aside the steers, the camera retreating to new setups to cover his steady advance. He is called by Cherry Valance who steps out behind him, turns and shoots him down, then continues, clutching his side where Cherry's bullet has struck him. When he comes face to face with Matt, the latter refuses to draw. Wayne looses some shots at him — past his head, at his feet and then closer still, grazing a cheek — but Matt stands firm. Wayne snarls, "You're soft! Won't anything make a man out of you?" He strides up to Matt and hits him three times, the third blow knocking him to the ground. Wayne goes to haul him up and suddenly Matt starts hitting back, sending Wayne sprawling in the dust. As Wayne sits there dazed, tongue exploring his damaged lip, the tone decisively changes, the film is almost comic. They battle on until Tess Millay fires a shot and verbally tears a strip off them. "I'm good and mad!" she bellows, letting out her nervous relief, "Anybody with half a mind would know you two love each other!" and then encourages them to fight on. But Wayne is now reconciled with Matt and fulfils a promise that he made when Matt was a kid, that he would share Wayne's brand, the Red River D, when he earned it. Thus Wayne, whose periodic funeral readings throughout the film have stated, "We brought nothing into this world and it is certain we take nothing out," has found a "son" to take on the benefits of his hard-earned success.

At the start of the film Wayne is briefly seen as a young man. Immediately, two fundamental aspects of his character are established. One is that his word is his bond: he stands by it and expects others to do the same. When he leaves a wagon train over the objections of its leader, he replies forcefully: "I signed nothing. If I had, I'd stay." The second is indicated by his companion Groot's words of advice to the wagonmaster: "He's a

Wayne is taken by surprise at the fast draw of Montgomery Clift.

Posed shot of Wayne with Joanne Dru as the strong-willed lady who carries a derringer to dissuade him from his urge for revenge.

John Wayne, Montgomery Clift and Walter Brennan contemplate the trail ahead.
Wayne shoots the quitters (Glenn Strange, Tom Tyler, Paul Fiero).

mighty set man. When his mind's made up, even you can't change it." And neither can his girl Fen (Coleen Gray) as she implores him to take her along.

She and Wayne are seen as small figures in the vast lonely landscape (wagons rolling past to emphasise the lack of time for discussion), then in powerful close-ups (the jump underlines the dramatic urgency). Wayne insists that "it's too much for a woman," but she tries to sway him from his decision, grasping him and caressing him with her flow of words, full of heated passion. "You'll need me. You'll need what a woman can give you to do what you have to do. Oh, listen to me, Tom, listen with your head or your heart too — the sun only shines half the time, Tom, the other half is night." I've made up my mind," Wayne replies. "Change your mind, Tom — for just once in your life, change your mind." "I'll send for you. Will you come?" "Of course I'll come. *But you're wrong.*" That last phrase keeps recurring through the film as Groot (Walter Brennan) has occasion to declare "You wus wrong, Mr. Dunson." And Wayne's unyielding response to the extraordinary fervour of Coleen Gray in her brief appearance gives us with tremendous economy the nature of the man.

Soon afterwards Wayne knows he was wrong and Fen was right. Indians waylay the wagon train and young Matthew Garth is the only survivor. Some Indians attack Wayne and Groot, leading to one vivid shot of Wayne struggling in a pool with a redskin, catching the knife thrown to him by Groot; he discovers on the Indian's wrist the bracelet that belonged to Fen, clinching her fate. (This contrived discovery is another touch that marks the film as being conventionally plotted, influencing one to expect a tragic resolution to the climax previously described.)

The following years see Wayne bury his mistake deep inside him and forge a cattle empire in the wilderness, fighting off opposition as a law unto himself. Fen's moderating influence has been denied him, and Matt even leaves to fight in the Civil War. Wayne makes his own decision to drive the entire herd of over nine thousand head to market in Missouri where there is money to pay for them in the hard times after the war. Matt's experiences before returning to join the cattle drive have no doubt broadened his outlook and developed a sense of independence that enables him to stand up to Wayne, who has retained the outlook of a self-sufficient pioneer in times that have changed without his noticing.

As the drive sets out, Wayne remains a sympathetic figure in many ways. He takes a keen interest in young Dan Latimer (Harry Carey Jr.), he good-naturedly gives in to Groot's indignant demands to come on the trip, and he makes his conditions very clear beforehand to the men who agree to go, spelling out the hazards of the journey and declaring "Every man that signs on for this trip finishes it — no one quits along the way."

The first real conflict arises when the sweet-toothed Bunk Kenneally (Ivan Parry) disturbs some pots and pans while stealing sugar and sets off a stampede in which Dan Latimer is killed. Wayne's grief has him

ensure that Dan's widow will be paid his wages in full and his anger makes him propose to whip Kenneally as he would a naughty kid. Harsh as this is, it doesn't seem that inappropriate but smacks more of the rough methods of earlier pioneering days, suggesting that Wayne's thinking is set in the past. (A whipping occurs, for example, in Ford's *Wagonmaster*, dealing with a pioneer wagon train, as retribution for a case of attempted rape on an Indian squaw though it is done to calm the angered Indians as much as for punishment.) At any rate, Wayne's proposal is taken as a sign of inhumanity and Kenneally's admission that "I was wrong, awful wrong" contrasts with Wayne's inability to admit he is ever in error although he invites Groot to deliver the ticking off he sees forming on his lips ("You wus wrong, Mr. Dunson"). Before this, the scene has been resolved by Kenneally drawing his gun rather than submit to the whipping and by Matt's fast shooting which saves Wayne from being killed.

As the hardships of the journey multiply, three of the men decide to quit, especially upset by Wayne's refusal to head the herd towards a reported railway link. Wayne, again backed by Matt, shoots down the quitters. Shortly after, three men disappear at night and Wayne sends the gunman Cherry Valance to bring them back dead or alive, going without sleep, spurring the men on to keep them too exhausted to contemplate quitting until Cherry comes back. When Cherry returns with two of the men, Wayne proposes to hang them as a lesson to the others and it is here that Matt rebels, taking over the herd with the men's enthusiastic support. As one of the men says to Wayne: "I signed a pledge but you're not the man I signed it with."

Even Groot abandons Wayne now, and he has to recruit a bunch of professional killers to follow Matt. He arrives at the camp where Matt has stopped earlier and won the heart of Tess Millay (Joanne Dru). She steps forward to offer hospitality to Wayne, having been denied a chance to go on ahead with Matt whose refusal "Nothing you can say or do..." echoes one of Wayne's standard sayings. Being left behind as Fen was earlier by Wayne, and wearing Fen's bracelet which Matt has given her (having worn it himself since Wayne gave it to him as a youth), marks her as a reincarnation of Fen, as does the high-spirited, aggressive manner both women have (in common with most other women in Howard Hawks's movies). Wayne is sufficiently impressed to look her over for breeding possibilities and invite her to give him a son to replace Matt; she loves Matt enough to agree if he will call off his pursuit. But nothing she can say or do will stop Wayne and he only gives way on the point of allowing her to come along with him.

And yet the final meeting between Matt and Wayne leads to a reconciliation, and the appropriateness of this ending has been debated ever since. Hawks simply declares that he liked the two men too much to kill either of them off.

Hawks has always been a consciously repetitive artist and he uses the opportunity provided here to repeat a scene that had appeared earlier in *The Outlaw* (which

he had left in mid-production). There Walter Huston's
Doc Holliday tries to goad Jack Buetel's Billy the Kid
into shooting it out with him while Jane Russell attempts to stop them. Then, when Doc has nicked Billy's
ears with bullets, Doc realises that he doesn't want to
go through with it after all. In *Red River* Hawks filmed
Wayne shooting nicks out of Matt's ears but Howard
Hughes, who had taken over *The Outlaw* from Hawks,
successfully intervened to have this particular bit of
"piracy" removed.*

So clearly Hawks couldn't resist adapting *Red River*
on the same lines and having this resolution appear on a
film bearing his name. Besides which, it *is* emotionally
satisfying, far more constructive than a tragic conclusion would have been in showing that a man *can* change
for the better no matter how late in the day. All that
seems wrong is that the film hasn't laid the ground for
this ending (which also seems rather rushed) but has at
this late point changed Borden Chase's script which
cues a different ending as it has accurately cued other
events earlier on.†

*Although Wayne is not involved, it's interesting to note that Hawks
lays claim to another scene in *The Outlaw*, where Jack Buetel wres-
tles in a barn with a hidden assailant who turns out to be a woman, by
having James Caan repeat it with Michele Carey in *El Dorado*.

†Charles Schnee is also credited with the script but in an interview
with Jim Kitses in "Film Comment" (Winter 1970/71) Chase seems to
limit Schnee's contribution to helping Hawks alter the ending.

Wayne and Clift slug it out at the climax.

41. Three Godfathers (1949)

AFTER *Red River*, Wayne reclaimed his youth starring
for John Ford in *Three Godfathers,* the director's re-
make of his 1919 *Marked Men.* Harry Carey Sr., who
had played in *Red River* just before his death, starred in
the original and this version, besides co-starring his
son, is dedicated to his memory as "the bright star of
the early Western sky." The popularity of this Peter B.
Kyne story is rather surprising — two other versions
came between the Ford ones — because it is a sentimental tale of three outlaws caring for a new-born baby
with some explicit Biblical parallels. Despite the obvious pitfalls of the subject, *Three Godfathers* emerges as
a remarkably fine picture, generally underestimated
alongside Ford's other great contributions to the *genre*
at this time. In particular, a warmth of feeling and good
humour keeps the potentially mawkish aspects in check
and this is a film in which Wayne's range is clearly
demonstrated to moving effect.

He plays Robert Marmaduke (Bob) Hightower, the
leader of the three outlaws who ride into Welcome,
Arizona, to rob the bank. The others are Pedro
Armendariz's Pedro and Harry Carey Jr.'s The Abilene
Kid. They are pleasant, likable people, misguided like
the cowboy in the song "Streets of Laredo" which
features in the film. Wayne is anxious that the Kid
shouldn't come to any harm and during the robbery he

stations him outside the bank to hold the getaway
horses. But first they swap pleasantries with Buck
Sweet (Ward Bond, in a sympathetic role for a change),
a townsman they find tending his garden, with Wayne
taken aback in mid-sentence as Buck pins his marshal's
badge to his shirt. Then, as they proceed down the
street, Wayne offers a gallant sweep of his hat to the
lady from the East (Dorothy Ford) who is delighted to
find three real Westerners. Next they commit the
hold-up and hightail it out of town hotly pursued by a
posse whose shots wound the Kid in the shoulder and
puncture their water bag. This is desert country and
they make for a watering halt on the railroad with
Wayne exhibiting youthful enthusiasm at the sight of
the water tower: "Boy, I'm gonna skin me down to the
hide, climb up that ladder and dive into that tank right to
the bottom!" But the marshal has anticipated their
move and arrives before they can get close and they
make off to another source of water, Terrapin Tanks.
Sheltering from a sandstorm (a fantastically vivid sequence, though only part of an always real sense of the
harsh environment), they find their horses have wandered from their tether and they walk the rest of the
way. Wayne goes ahead to take a look around and has a
virtuoso sequence reciting the catalogue of woes that
one "Mr. Tenderfoot" has imposed on them by his

John Wayne, Harry Carey Jr. and Pedro Armendariz take a fatherly interest in the newborn babe held by its mother (Mildred Natwick). A scene from Three Godfathers.

Pedro Armendariz, Harry Carey Jr., John Wayne.

prior arrival there, his speech building to the worst news of all. An emigrant has dynamited the hole in an attempt to get water from it and wrecked it for good. He has wandered off and not come back. His wife is still there in a wagon. "But that ain't the worst of it. No, sir! Not by a long shot. She's going to have a baby. She's going to have it right now." Wayne masters the odd construction of the speech splendidly and concludes "I'm a tough bird, an awful tough old bird, but I'm not going back in there!"

Pedro, who has had the benefit of marital experience, is dispatched to deliver the baby and later the three gather around the dying mother (Mildred Natwick) who fails to discern any villainy in their faces and asks Wayne if he will save the baby. "Yes, ma'am, I'll save him," Wayne replies without any hesitation, looking embarrassed as she goes on to express the hope that the infant boy will grow up to be like the fine men she has just appointed as godfathers. With the mother gone, the trio milk the gentle art of baby care for all its comic worth. There are unforgettable images of Wayne's tough hombre grinning with pleasure as he nurses the baby, patting its bottom and making it cry; expressing scepticism over the advice offered by a book on baby care; carrying on a hushed conversation over the word "toilette" for fear that it's one the baby shouldn't hear; applying axle grease to "slick him up a mite," laughing with the others as he does it; and growling "Say that again," when the Kid reads with great concentration from the manual that "the best and surest way of feeding the baby is the one which Nature has provided," commenting quickly, "Well, that's out."

Then the realisation of their predicament breaks through with Wayne momentarily giving way to anger. It is the Kid who first spots that it is divine intervention that has brought them to this spot and that they have an ordained role to fulfil, carrying the child to the town of New Jersualem with a bright star to guide them as three new wise men. They start across the salt flats with the Kid knowing that he isn't going to make it and putting in his share of the carrying before collapsing and dying. Pedro takes over and, when his foot goes into a hole and he falls sideways to avoid crushing the baby, he twists his ankle and Wayne has to leave him behind with a gun to shoot himself.

And so Wayne goes on alone, staggering forward, reaching higher ground, entering a gloomy narrow pass that mirrors his darkening frame of mind. He flings

110

away the Bible that has been passed on to him, then thinks better of it and picks it up. It has fallen open at a passage about finding a donkey. "You just try finding a burro in this country!" he yells to the air, moving on in a state of delirium and starting to sing "Streets of Laredo" to have the ghostly voice of the Kid take it up and Pedro join in to spur him on. Then he finds the promised burro waiting patiently ahead and so arrives in the town of New Jerusalem on Christmas Day, bursting in on the festivities in the saloon, crying "Merry Christmas to all!" and collapsing with total exhaustion.

The film then switches to some amiable bickering between marshal Buck Sweet, who wants to adopt the child, and his prisoner, Wayne, who refuses to sign the necessary papers in exchange for a suspended sentence, preferring to keep his word to the dying mother although agreeing to Buck looking after the infant while he's away. The judge (Guy Kibbee) is impressed and

gives Wayne the minimum sentence of a year and a day before (in typical Ford fashion) declaring the bar open for celebrations. When Wayne takes the train for the penitentiary, he is given a new responsibility of looking after Buck's dim-witted deputy (Hank Worden) and has the banker's daughter to wave farewell to him (in Dorothy Ford, he had an actress who, as one of Hollywood's tallest women, could really stand up to him). The festive ending of the train drawing out is an indelibly romantic image of the old West.

While it is Ford's genuine feeling for the subject that conquers its liabilities, the director draws on Wayne for those touches of dark despair and hard-bitten cynicism that he conveys so well to put the film on a realistic footing from time to time when it threatens to become saccharine or overly comic. *Three Godfathers* will never be to everybody's taste but is certainly among Wayne's better accomplishments.

42. Wake of the Red Witch (1949)

A STRANGE, stifled quality hangs over Republic's production of *Wake of the Red Witch*, due in part to the wordy, overlong script (involving two extensive flashbacks) and in part to the confining studio "exteriors" but at any rate giving an appropriate atmosphere to a story in which deep-seated hates and corruption together with the twists of fate choke the purity of a true love that has to look to the next world for its freedom.

The basic conflict is between Wayne's adventurer, Captain Ralls, and Luther Adler's Mayrant Ruysdaal Sidneye, powerful tyrannical head of a vast trading empire called Batjack. (Wayne fixed on the name, spelling it Batjac, for the production company he formed in the mid-Fifties but hasn't gained Sidneye's odious reputation as its head!) Sidneye is the hungry spider and Wayne the resisting fly from the moment Wayne comes aboard Sidneye's ship for safety, having (as in an earlier role in *Adventure's End)* upset some South Sea Islanders. Wayne boldly offers to guide Sidneye to a fortune in pearls and impudently demands the captaincy of the ship. Sidneye strikes a bargain, then has Wayne locked in the hold to teach him a lesson, releasing him when they reach the island where the pearls are kept by superstitious natives in a chest, guarded in a cavern by an octopus.

Here both men are attracted to the beautiful daughter of the French commissaire, Angélique Desaix (Gail Russell). She falls in love with Wayne and his romantic vision of the sea as an "empire of freedom" while Sidneye goes to her father and arranges her betrothal to him. When the enthusiastic Desaix (Henry Daniell) announces her impending marriage, Wayne is thrown into a deep fit of hateful despondency and, drinking himself into a frenzy, he brawls with the men on ship and advances menacingly on Angélique and grips her by the hair before she can reveal her own ignorance of the arrangement Sidneye had made. Out of bravado, he

goes after the pearls, defeating the octopus (unlike the one that claimed his life in *Reap the Wild Wind),* and is hero-worshipped by the admiring natives. He sees Angélique again and speaks of the new world of happiness she has opened up for him; but Desaix attempts to dispose of Wayne by having him arrested on a charge of stealing the pearls and Wayne accidentally kills the commissaire in self-defence, knocking him into the flames of a fire.

We learn how Angélique then marries Sidneye and Wayne comes back seven years later to find that her love for him has grown again. When the furious Sidneye sees the danger to his possession of her, he threatens to have Wayne beached for good and the latter retaliates by taking out Sidneye's ship "The Red Witch" and scuttling it at a secret position with five million dollars of gold bullion aboard, thus gaining a hold over a man whose property means everything to him. Wayne makes a second visit to Angélique when she has contracted a tropical disease and tries to take her away. But her illness is fatal and she looks on her death as a chance for a new beginning away from Sidneye. As in *Angel and the Badman*, Gail Russell's fragile beauty is most effective opposite Wayne's brute strength, and her suggestion of a gentle, sheltered innocence too frail to withstand the pressures of life is very moving.* She was quite the best of the actresses whose role it was to accept Wayne with shining faith rather than stand up to him in the manner of Maureen O'Hara from *Rio Grande* onwards.

Wayne's knowledge of the last resting place of the "Red Witch" causes Sidneye to lure him into an elaborate trap. Wayne bargains only for the freedom of his

---

* Sadly it was real enough. She died from alcoholism, aged thirty-six, in 1961. Wayne gave her a come-back role in *Seven Men from Now* which his company produced in 1956 with Randolph Scott as the star.

111

John Wayne and Gail Russell.

first mate (Gig Young) and Teleila (Adele Mara) whose love reminds him of his own for Angélique, and agrees to show Sidneye the site of the wreck, leaving their differences to be settled afterwards. The sunken vessel is sitting on the edge of a reef about to plunge into the depths; a storm is blowing up. Wayne is the only person bold enough to make the dive. It is all highly reminiscent of Wayne's last scene in *Reap the Wild Wind*. Beneath the waters, Wayne again loses his life, leaving Sidneye to contemplate both the loss of most of the fortune and (more importantly) his adversary — two of the things that gave distorted purpose to his life. The closing images of the film show Wayne and Angélique, side by side, sailing away on a ghostly Red Witch to a life of contentment in the next world...like Gary Cooper and Ann Harding reunited after death in *Peter Ibbetson*

and Laurence Olivier and Merle Oberon in *Wuthering Heights*.

Wayne's performance runs on sheer personal magnetism rather than any coherency of characterisation, drawing out the wild, impulsive nature of the man, his gift for commanding men, his gentle protectiveness towards Angélique and romantic hopes, his brooding over the bitter past, into a complex whole. But it is not as an artless adventurer nor as a romantic that we most remember this film's Wayne. Two of the most powerful close-ups Wayne has ever had stamp him foremost as a man of violence — the two shots when, in a drunken sweat, he advance on Sidneye's man Loring (Jeff Corey) in his cabin and beats the man up and when he advances on Angélique as his apparent betrayer and seems set to kill her.

43. The Fighting Kentuckian (1949)

LIKE *Angel and the Badman, The Fighting Kentuckian* was "A John Wayne Production" for Republic. It was one of his lesser pictures, reminiscent of *Dakota* in its repeat casting of a now Hruba-less Vera Ralston as his leading lady, Hugo Haas as her father, and the same mixture of moods — comic and serious — with an air of uncertainty as to which has the upper hand. It is distinguished visually by Lee Garmes's deep focus photography but otherwise gives little cause to stick in the mind.

It is set in Alabama in 1818 with Wayne as John Breen, a rifleman with the second Kentucky Regiment who falls for a French girl, Fleurette DeMarchand (Vera Ralston), and delays departing with his fellow men, using her to escape from the lumbering pursuit of his fat pal Willie Paine (Oliver Hardy in a rare appearance without Stan Laurel). "You're uncommon gracious," Wayne tells Fleurette, "I'd sure admire to meet you properly," and when she encourages his attentions and allows him to kiss her, he is a little put out but not at all put off, paying her a variation on the compliment

John Wayne and Vera Ralston.

usually reserved for Wayne heroines who are blowing their top: "You look beautiful when your eyes shine like that" (instead of "...when you're mad"). He finds that she is the daughter of General DeMarchand (Hugo Haas) who has brought a number of French exiles to settle in America, and he is glad to escape back to his regiment when her regular beau, Blake Randolph (John Howard), turns up with a few friends.

Wayne attempts to move in to Fleurette's aristocratic world, trading his coonskin cap for a topper (which he almost loses passing through a door). Dressed to the nines, he pauses to carefully wipe his boots on his trousers before knocking on the door of the DeMarchand mansion, only to be rebuffed by the butler who tells him that Fleurette is "not at home." Discovering otherwise, he deliberates with himself in an interior monologue about going back — a comic touch. He subsequently gatecrashes a party to see her and is pressed into performing with a group of fiddlers in front of the guests, consternation seizing him as each of the other musicians performs a little virtuoso turn and Wayne, who can't play a note, fluffs his moment...a terrible pause of silence followed by a round of applause for his and the others' efforts. Blake Randolph, wealthy, powerful, and clearly a shady character, corners Wayne and in a very curious exposition of the art of screen writing tells him, "You're a hero in the heroic tradition. You must wait for me to make the first move...the very thing that makes you a hero is the thing that makes you vulnerable." And when Wayne refuses a bribe to discontinue meddling in Randolph's plans, the latter comments, "I should have known you'd be heroically obstinate." Such candid analysis is both refreshing and disconcerting.

Fleurette is scheduled to marry Randolph the next day and Wayne decides to take her away in a buggy (rather as he eloped with Ralston at the start of *Dakota*). But her father intervenes to explain to him what is at stake with her marriage — the entire future of the French immigrants, who are being helped and protected by Randolph — and Wayne, being the hero and the *real* gentleman (unlike Randolph) has no option but to back down.

Instead, Wayne sets about exposing Randolph's real character and learns that he is planning to deprive the French of their land with the help of an impressive line up of villainous players: Grant Withers, Paul Fix and a deceitful Marie Windsor. Aided by his regiment, Wayne routs the motley band and claims Fleurette for himself before leaving with the Fighting Kentuckians for duties elsewhere.

114

44. She Wore a Yellow Ribbon (1949)

NOW AT LAST, perhaps in recognition of Wayne's great success as the ageing Dunson of *Red River*, John Ford gave him a real character part as taxing as any to be imagined. Under the director's guidance, Wayne rose to the occasion magnificently as the elderly Captain Nathan Brittles of *She Wore a Yellow Ribbon*. Ignominiously premiered as the top half of a double bill at one of London's least prestigious West End outlets, it has survived the years triumphantly, still playing in British cinemas, one of the films most often transmitted on television — a classic of the Western and one of John Ford's most enduring works, far richer than *Stagecoach*, far warmer than *The Searchers*, probably the most beautiful Western ever made and one in which the visual pleasure is constantly reinforced by the depth of feeling.

And there at the heart of it is Wayne's faultless study of Brittles. The film is primarily an emotional experience that rewards continued viewing and Wayne's performance withstands the closest scrutiny, showing how surefootedly he draws on fully justified sentiment and avoids risible mawkishness. There was full justice in Winton Hoch's Academy Award for his glorious Technicolor photography*; none at all in the failure to even nominate Wayne for his work (he was nominated instead that same year for his more typical performance in *Sands of Iwo Jima*).

Custer is dead, his men massacred with him at the

*Hoch was chosen by Wayne to photograph *The Green Berets*, and his work has been seen to memorable effect on these other Wayne films: *Three Godfathers*, *The Quiet Man* (another Academy Award), *The Searchers*, and *Jet Pilot*.

Victor McLaglen, Ben Johnson, George O'Brien, John Wayne.

Wayne beams on the romance between Joanne Dru and John Agar and mock-feuds with Victor McLaglen as his sergeant

Little Big Horn. The entire Western frontier is fraught with tension. A narrator sets the picture adding: "And wherever the flag rises over some lonely army post there may be one man — one captain — fated to wield the sword of destiny." *Yellow Ribbon* concerns that captain, a man who turned the tide in the army's favour against the hordes of Indians just minutes before his retirement.

In no other picture has the atmosphere of army life in those frontier days been so vividly evoked, the warmth of community living a buttress for the soldiers and their wives against the hard environment and demands of duty. We see the Sergeant, Quincannon (Victor McLaglen), come to Brittles' quarters at 5.41 a.m. relaying the latest news as the Captain dresses, answering queries that show his keen interest in what is happening to others. We see him step out into the open, breathing deeply, exhaling, rubbing his hands in the cold of morning, walking forward stiffly but briskly, shaking out his limbs. The way Wayne deports himself completely captures the sense of a man who has spent forty years in the army, going far beyond the superficial attributes of age — the white hair and old man's moustache. Throughout the film there are little touches that suggest a man who has become set in his ways with the sniffs, snorts, coughs, grunts, set mannerisms and phrases ("Never apologise — it's a sign of weakness") that never extend to caricature but leave Brittles warmly human. What is so difficult about playing the part is that he is an entirely admirable figure, an officer too close to his men and the heart of things to have risen to the remote heights of command. Despite the affection and respect he receives from all around him, Brittles is never dull because Wayne and Ford show him to us in the round instead of dictating his virtues to us.

His age is shown in his mistrust of youth, his reluctance to hand over command to young lieutenants like Flint Cohill (John Agar). He doesn't do this consciously — he knows he has more experience, better judgement — but it takes the wise Major Allshard (George O'Brien) to remind him that they have to learn the hard way as Brittles had once and to point out that "Every time Cohill gave an order, men would turn round and look at you — they'd wonder if he was doing the right thing." It is only when he is handing over command to Cohill that he comes to call the man by his christian name, for the first time in nine years of service.

There is Brittles's attachment to the past: the visits to the grave of his wife, dead for nine years, to water the flowers, report to her the latest news and talk out his plans for the future. He expresses his sadness at the news of an old friend's death at Custer's Last Stand, Wayne's voice softly saying "You remember Miles Kehoe. Happy-go-lucky Irishman…who used to waltz so well with you!", taking mock umbrage at the memory and making the dead soldier as vividly real in his warmth of recollection as any character we actually see.

From his lofty perch of old age, he can afford to look down with amusement on the ways of the young, especially the rivalry of the two lieutenants, Pennell (Harry Carey Jr.) and Cohill, for the hand of Olivia Dandridge (Joanne Dru). He takes pleasure in teasing Pennell over his attempts to take Olivia out for a ride. "*Pic - nic - ing!*", he exclaims, savouring the word and the situation as he overrules the jealous Cohill by allowing Pennell to leave the fort but then refuses Olivia permission to accompany him because of the danger from Indians. "You made a fool out of a couple of young lieutenants," he remarks to Olivia later and chortles "That's never against army regulations!" When she sports a yellow ribbon as a token of having a sweetheart, Wayne asks her who it's for. "Why, for you, of course, Captain Brittles," she replies and he laughs heartily. "For me! I'll make these young bucks jealous!" There is no malice in his teasing for he knows full well that Olivia and Cohill are destined for each other depite their constant bickering.

He also enjoys a boisterous relationship with Quincannon who has the disrespectful habit of addressing him as "Captain darling," and a weakness for liquor that Brittles tolerates with good humour, using it to have him thrown into the guardhouse to keep him out of trouble for his last few weeks of service, arranging with Allshard that the Sergeant will retire on a pension large enough to meet his alcoholic needs.

The richness of personal relationships is a necessary antidote to the bitter side of the film as well as the rigours of army life — the bunions from too much riding, the upheavals of transfer, the frustrations of restricting orders. When Brittles has to take the Major's wife and Olivia with him on his last mission to catch the stage to safer surroundings, he storms into the Major's quarters to protest, going through the rigmarole of filling out a complaint to join the others he has written over the years, scoffing at any idea that it will affect his care of the ladies, his resentment fully disposed of by his formal objection. But, as a result of the women's presence, he is forced to circle around some Indians instead of investigating their movements, and is late arriving at his rendezvous point with another patrol which has been attacked. When the corporal in charge bemoans his tardy arrival, all Wayne can say, his voice heavy, is: "I wanted to be there, Corporal." The Corporal is badly wounded and at first Wayne refuses the medic's request for a pause to perform an emergency operation, then quickly and humanly relents. At the stage station, he comes on the result of another Indian attack and murmurs despondently, "About time I did retire!" when he sees the mutilated bodies. There is one of Ford's moving funeral scenes as Wayne pays tribute to the dead Private Smith whose past as a Brigadier-General for the Confederacy is known to him. He then has to return to the fort, still escorting the women, his last mission a failure on all counts.

He has left Cohill to guard a river crossing and the Major refuses him permission to go back and take over since he retires the following day. On his last review of the troops, Lt. Pennell presents him with a solid silver watch bought by the men and refers him to the engraved sentiment. Wayne brings out his glasses, looks nervously around and sniffs back a tear as he reads the

117

words inside with a slight choke to his voice and more sniffs — a demanding moment delicately judged by the actor.

As Pennell rides out to relieve Cohill, the old soldier succumbs to nostalgic regret, telling Olivia he'll be glad if the blacksmith even asks him to shoe a horse. But he then rides out to join his men again and is given a rousing cheer of welcome. He cunningly points out that he still has four hours of service owing to the army and decides on a bold move against the massing Indians. He takes Sergeant Tyree (Ben Johnson) and rides straight into the Indian encampment to be warmly received by his old friend Pony-That-Walks, an Indian converted to Christianity and opposed to the warlike ways of the younger men. Behind the documentary-like impression of the Indian camp, there lies the point that both Pony-That-Walks and Wayne's Brittles are old men who can only chew over ancient memories and smoke a personal pipe of peace: the Indian has ceded all authority to the next generation as Brittles soon must do. There is no-thing for the soldier to do but ride back to the troops and lead them in a bold attack just before midnight that takes the Indians by surprise and routs them without the army suffering a single casualty. Having turned failure into triumph, Wayne takes his leave to ride off Westwards to his vague future in the new settlements, the setting sun a symbol of Wayne's own fading life.

It is a perfect ending, and yet not the one the film adheres to. Just as Howard Hawks didn't like to see Wayne killed at the end of *Red River*, so John Ford would have seemed moved to give Brittles a happier fate. He shows a despatch rider sent after Wayne to recall him for an appointment as the chief of scouts with the rank of Lieutenant Colonel. It is surely the nicest, most forgiveable of contrived happy endings.

How can anyone look at *Red River* and *She Wore a Yellow Ribbon* and not give Wayne credit for being a superb actor when he wants to be? Who else could one want to see playing Nathan Brittles? Performer and part have merged in the best tradition of great acting.

The last post: Ben Johnson, Wayne, and Frank McGrath (the bugler).

45. Sands of Iwo Jima (1949)

WITH THE obvious exception of John Ford's *They Were Expendable*, *Sands of Iwo Jima* is the only one of Wayne's war films to call for serious consideration as a thoughtful look at war in general rather than an enthusiastic endorsement of American participation in a particular conflict. For much of its footage it is stuck in a familiar rut with the usual rank-and-file humour and depiction of the enemy as numerically superior but otherwise dimwitted, one Japanese soldier rushing out to kill a marine only to be killed by the next marine in the line of men marching forward. But the marines' beach landings at Tarawa and Iwo Jima are brilliantly staged with the noise, the smoke, the fear, the suddenness of death from snipers' bullets vividly evoked, and a scene of a wounded soldier, crying out from a distant trench for help that has to be denied him, sticks in the memory. Though none of the characterisations of the men are subtle, Wayne's part is more deeply etched than usual in his war capers and Allan Dwan's dispassionate direction keeps the film on a sober footing. Unusually, the film allows the Wayne image to be challenged, thereby throwing it into sharp focus, even though the conflict of attitudes is rigged in Wayne's ultimate favour.

He is cast as Sergeant John M. Stryker, the hated martinet. "Stryker knows his business" — "So did Jack the Ripper!" While Corporal Thomas (Forrest Tucker) provides a conventional adversary, his hostility based on past grievances, with whom Wayne can have a punch-up in the woods, his principal critic is a new recruit, Peter Conway (John Agar), who despises him for his tough, insensitive methods of training and discipline. He spells out the difference in attitudes when he lectures Wayne on how he intends to bring up his newly-born son: "I won't insist that he'll be tough. Instead I'll try to see he's intelligent. And I won't insist he read the Marine Corps manual — instead I'll get him a set of Shakespeare. In short, I don't want him to be a Sergeant John M. Stryker — I want him to be intelligent, considerate, cultured, and a gentleman." Wayne doesn't listen to the argument and merely declares "He's got a right to dislike me", thereby reducing it to a personality clash rather than one of outlooks. And, since Shakespeare is a dirty word for the mass audience, there is no doubt of which way they were supposed to side; and besides they know that the Wayne character is really sensitive underneath, only he doesn't let it show, and his harsh discipline is for the men's own good. When, later, he hands over some bottles of saké for the men to enjoy after a battle, he tells his intermediary to say it came from a dead enemy soldier and rejects the suggestion that he should "break down a little" and own up to this good deed. And immediately after this verbal clash between Wayne and Conway, there is a scene that tends to prove Conway wrong.

During grenade practice, one of the men lets a live grenade slip and it falls at the feet of Conway who is dreamily reading a letter from his wife (Adele Mara). Stryker shouts out a warning and dives on top of him as the grenade explodes, sustaining wounds in the process of saving Conway's life. There is a clear suggestion that Conway's preoccupations with the other world of soft domesticity put him off guard while Wayne's standards of military alertness would not have done so. Before too long, Conway has an opportunity to save Wayne's life and then tries to apologise for his past attitude. Wayne helps him to do this, saying that everyone gets "out of line" at times and not admitting that Conway could have been in any way right. The only gesture towards Conway's position that the film makes is in employing him to use his educated mind to finish Wayne's half-written letter at the end of the film. But he quickly shows his adoption of Wayne's ways by sending the men to "saddle up" as Wayne always had.

But if the film seems to glorify Wayne as the professional soldier *par excellence*, even exerting a steadying influence on a panicking officer with the offer of a cigarette, he is far from the one-dimensional characters Wayne played in *Fighting Seabees* or more recently in *The Green Berets*. We see that his private life is in ruins and he is tormented by the demons of past mistakes. He was busted down from Sergeant-Major for reasons never made clear; his wife pulled out five years before, taking their son with her; and he is thrown into fits of depression when, as always, no mail turns up from his family, relying on drink to render himself insensible with one ambiguously loyal friend to watch out for him and cart him home.

There is a vivid little scene where Wayne is sitting in a bar in Hawaii and he buys a drink for a plain-looking prostitute who tries to interest him. Her hesitant, apologetic manner causes Wayne to accompany her back to her flat. He is left alone while she slips out to buy a bottle of whisky, hears a noise, and suspects he has been placed in a trap — but finds a baby in a cot. The mother returns and tells the baby that it must be quiet while she's "entertaining." Wayne sharply tells her to stop that kind of talk and questions her, learning that her husband has left her and this is the only way she can make ends meet. "You know about babies," she observes as he helps prepare the baby's food. "Yeah, I know about babies," Wayne replies with a husky tenderness in his voice. He gives her some money, refuses to stay, and she kisses him gratefully as he leaves. Through the director's detached handling, this isolated little episode never lapses into sentimentality and pinpoints the loneliness of both Wayne and the woman in an economical, telling fashion. It was also unusually realistic for a war film in bringing up the sordid side of off-duty recreation.

It was probably this and the closing scene that made the part stand out sufficiently for Wayne to gain an Oscar nomination (he lost out to Broderick Crawford

Wayne shouts out a warning as a grenade is about to explode.

for *All the King's Men,* a film he deplored and had indignantly refused an offer to appear in). At the end of the film Wayne is shot in the back by a sniper just after the battle has been won and the celebrated running-up of the flag on Iwo Jima is about to take place. Wayne is declaring he has never felt so good in his life and offers his cigarettes around when, without so much as a preparatory shot of the sniper taking aim, the bullet strikes. This absence of warning, this unremarkable form of death with no time for last words is quite shocking (and in complete contrast to his glorious demise in *The Fighting Seabees*): he's just plain dead when a moment before he was alive, a small hole in his broad back making all the difference. The scene is extended with the discovery of an unfinished letter on his body which Conway reads (a moment reminiscent of the ending of *The Ox Bow Incident)* and in which Wayne labels himself a failure in many ways (but not militarily), providing a downbeat ending in which Conway, taking over from Wayne in the dead man's style, rallies the others to move on. Though the closing image is a victorious one, the film has conveyed the price of war in human cost with far more than the token recognition written into most of Wayne's other war films.*

Wayne's next film work was shooting *Jet Pilot* for Howard Hughes at RKO. But the resulting picture was not finally released until 1957 and reappears in this commentary at that point.

*It seems more than likely that Harry Brown was the writer responsible for the more memorable aspects of the film: his other work includes the basis for *A Walk in the Sun,* perhaps the most distinguished film about the Second World War. James Edward Grant, who shares credit with Brown, was brought in by Wayne to doctor the script and presumably concentrated more on Wayne's image in it, contributing the familiar aspects of characterisation.

Wayne learns there is no whisky in the house when he goes back with a prostitute (Julie Bishop).

Richard Jaeckel lies wounded, being looked after by Wayne, Bill Murphy, and John Agar.

46. Rio Grande (1950)

RIO GRANDE was the third John Ford/John Wayne film about the U.S. cavalry, derived like its predecessors from stories by James Warner Bellah. The film puts Wayne in an age bracket between the youthful captain of *Fort Apache* and the veteran of *Yellow Ribbon* as the middle-aged Lieutenant-Colonel Kirby Yorke with moustache and a small pointed beard on his upper chin (the only beard Wayne has worn on screen*). Recurring character names provide cross-links between the three films — two have a Doctor Wilkins and a soldier named Tyree, all three have a Sergeant Quincannon — but these are not developed and there is no firm indication that Wayne is playing the Kirby York of *Fort Apache* in *Rio Grande*: the name is now spelt Yorke, there are no references back to the incidents in the earlier film and another event entirely, dating from the Civil War, is raised from this Yorke's past. They might as well be different men.

However, *Fort Apache*'s Owen Thursday does provide a useful contrast with Wayne as a commander of men in *Rio Grande*. He is all that Thursday was not, a stern figure but his bark is a token gesture of toughness and, when he addresses the new recruits with warnings of the hard life they have to expect, his voice has none of the intensity of a man who really means what he says: he is simply spelling out what the youngsters and tradition expect to hear said. And when he further tells his son Jeff (Claude Jarman Jr.) about army life — "Put out of your mind any romantic ideas that it's a way of glory. It's a life of suffering and hardship, an uncompromising devotion to your oath and your duty" — he contradicts the stirring, romantic tone of the film, in which duty certainly demands personal sacrifices but has its rewards in integrity upheld and duty accomplished. The very first image of Wayne riding back to the fort, emerging from a cloud of dust to salute the flag as he rides through the timbered gate, sets the tone of the film: he and his men may be worn out, some of them wounded, but they are figures of a historic glory — the distance of time helping to turn fact into legend even when the fact isn't distorted subsequently as in *Fort Apache* and *The Man Who Shot Liberty Valance*.

The film is particularly memorable for the first casting of Maureen O'Hara opposite Wayne. There is a powerful chemistry between them — both stubborn, she proud and aggressive, he strong, tender and reserved — that has made their five screen appearances together as memorably pleasurable as the more widely appreciated collaborations of Spencer Tracy with Katharine Hepburn. O'Hara is as much a woman's woman as Wayne is a man's man, both insisting on fulfilling their roles as they see them with inevitable conflict. Except in *The Quiet Man,* this conflict is one of career versus the home; and in every film it falls on

O'Hara to accept a woman's place in a man's world to effect a reconciliation.

In *Rio Grande*, Wayne has put duty before love and, back in the Civil War, he has followed orders to set fire to his wife's plantation. She has never forgiven him and they have been separated for fifteen years only to be brought together again when their son Jeff is posted to serve under his father.

Wayne is disappointed that his son has failed at West Point, and tells him that, having now enlisted, he can expect no special favours. But he hovers around protectively, watching with concern as his son attempts to ride two horses standing up and takes a fall; appearing at the hospital window to watch with amusement as castor oil is administered to the bruised youngster after a fight that he has allowed to continue; and he makes a point of checking his son's height against his own on the side of his tent when Jeff has gone.

Maureen O'Hara turns up at the camp to reclaim her son. She announces herself as "Trooper Jeff Yorke's mother" and not the wife of the commanding officer, and her arrival causes the Sergeant (Victor McLaglen), who helped Wayne burn her home, to cross himself fearfully. But her eyes moisten as Wayne comes forward to meet her and takes her arm to escort her back to his quarters. Wayne proves obstinate when she explains the purpose of her visit, declaring of Jeff: "Here he'll stay and here he'll serve." "Ramrod, wreckage and ruin! Still the same Kirby!" she exclaims, telling him that she'll buy Jeff's release. Wayne then refuses his signature and turns to complimenting her on being "a fine figure of a woman," coming close to her. The sense of an underlying yearning for each other is very apparent but attitudes overrule emotions, if not always predictably. When their comfortable silence after dinner is broken by the arrival of the regimental singers to serenade Kathleen by singing "I'll take you home again, Kathleen," the choice seems an unfortunate one, reminding them of the past. Here one can see on Wayne's features a real actor at work: his brow stiffening, his discomfiture made obvious, his expression turning to sadness and regret as he looks down, telling Kathleen stiffly "This music...is not of my choosing." "I wish it had been," she says gently.

That night while Wayne leaves her to settle down furtively in an empty wagon, the Sergeant thoughtfully offers to take her to Jeff. Kathleen speaks to Jeff of his father, "He's a lonely man...a very lonely man." "They say he's a great soldier," replies Jeff. "What makes soldiers great is hateful to me," she declares. She tells Jeff that she has come to take him away and he refuses to go. "You're stubborn proud, Jeff, just like he is." "Just like you, mother," observes her son.

She tries to bargain with Wayne. When he returns from an abortive mission trying to capture some Indians who have crossed over into Mexico and safety, he finds Kathleen waiting in his tent. They embrace warmly and

---

* Apart from appearing heavily unshaven as in *Texas Terror* and *Back to Bataan.*

Maureen O'Hara has cleaned and ironed Wayne's uniform for the winter campaign. Looking his "elegant" best, Wayne comes to bid her farewell.

talk over the past: she has rebuilt the house he burned down, perhaps they can rebuild their marriage. She suggests that Wayne should make a gesture in that direction by releasing Jeff. Wayne replies sensitively: "I could say yes very easily but I owe Jeff something." And at dinner with General Sheridan (J. Carrol Naish) and the other officers, it falls to her to propose a toast: "To my only rival, the United States cavalry."

Wayne's devotion to his job makes him agree to Sheridan's suggestion that he should breach the international treaty and take his men over the border to solve the Indian problem once and for all. He puts his personal loyalty to Sheridan, his old commander from Civil War days, over and above the illegality of the mission, prepared to risk court martial afterwards. In relieving his frustration over the unchecked raids by the enemy, this is a characteristic example of Wayne as a figure of independence, answerable to himself rather than a book of rules (only in *They Were Expendable* does he reluctantly knuckle under).

He does, however, relent a little where Kathleen is concerned. When it comes time to send her and the other women and children away to a safer area while he takes his men out on the campaign, he assigns Jeff to be one of the escort. "He'll hate you for it, Kirby," she says, adding warmly, "But I'll love you for it." "Aren't you going to kiss me goodbye?" she adds, giving Wayne his cue for one of those lines he can handle better than anyone: "I never want to kiss you goodbye, Kathy."

However, the party of women and children are attacked *en route* and a wagonload of children are abducted. Jeff breaks through the ranks of the attacking Indians and rides off to bring help. Wayne and his men come to the rescue and plan an attack on the Indians' refuge in Mexico with Wayne accepting the suggestion of Tyree (Ben Johnson) that he and two other men should creep into the village beforehand and join the children to protect them during the raid. Tyree picks Jeff as one of his team and Wayne agrees. The children

123

Wayne with J. Carrol Naish as General Philip Sheridan.

Wayne leads the attack on the Indian stronghold at the climax of the film.

are held in an old church at the back of the village and — when the three soldiers are safely in position — Wayne leads his men in a fierce charge through the encampment up to the church, receiving an arrow in the chest as the Indians are roundly defeated. He has Jeff pull it out and is brought home on a travois.

Kathleen has by now joined the other women waiting anxiously, praying for their men's safe return, thus completing her adaptation to army life from having taken her place in the laundry line after simply fainting like an outsider during an Indian raid shortly after her arrival. As the weary soldiers come in, she falls in alongside Jeff, then takes Wayne's hand, expressing to them her submission to their way of life, taking pleasure in Wayne's report that "*Our* boy did well." A final scene points up their reconciliation in happier circumstances, Wayne having fully recovered, as the soldiers parade past General Sheridan and the other officers, with Kathleen twirling her parasol in time to the music and smiling at her husband.*

*A synopsis of the film indicates that another scene was originally planned to follow with Wayne being dispatched to London as military adviser as a "punishment" for his illegal action against the Indians, the trip turning into a second honeymoon for him and Kathleen. But it would have been anti-climactic and was wisely deleted. The last shots sum up the important outcome of the film and a change of setting away from the army — and to London, of all places — would have been disruptive. Ford has always been more interested in characters than plot, hence the untidy resolution of the latter aspect of the film.

47. Operation Pacific (1951)

WAYNE'S first film for Warner Bros. since the Thirties, this was his second film for writer-director George Waggner, following *The Fighting Kentuckian*. Just as that film was curiously, even refreshingly specific about the roles of hero and villain, so this film's dialogue is unusually precise in pinpointing the customary difficulties of Wayne's strong-willed leading women in accepting him for what he is. The film is otherwise a thoroughly routine submarines exercise and it was a good break for Wayne if a bad one for Patricia Neal when she was assigned to the picture under a studio contract.

Patricia Neal is an exceptional actress, strikingly feminine but conveying obvious intelligence behind her slyly husky voice, and just the kind of strong figure to spark off Wayne's deeper responses as an actor. He is "Duke" Gifford, submarine officer; she is Mary Stuart, navy nurse and ex-wife who divorced him four years earlier after the death of their son in infancy. The film opens with Wayne bringing an orphaned baby out of the jungle back to the base hospital where Mary Stuart works. She arranges to run into him as if by chance to test her feelings about him and calls him a "big ape" by way of friendly greeting before they kiss. Wayne is still keen on her and wants to make a fresh start, taking the blame for their break-up in a Hollywood-primitive analysis of what happened: "We had something — I guess I kicked it around." However, she backs away and takes up a date with a young navy flyer (Phil Carey) who is pressing her to marry him and by coincidence (alias contrivance) is the kid brother of Wayne's commanding officer, "Pop" Perry (Ward Bond).

John Wayne and Ward Bond.

In an action scene, the submarine is forced to dive at high speed on Pop's orders after a freighter flying a white flag opens up on them — a subplot has to do with dud torpedos that make the submarine defenceless. The wounded Pop has to be abandoned on the bridge, and kid brother feels bitter towards Wayne for leaving him up there; but that "ol' debbil coincidence" turns up again to balance things out when Wayne's submarine is the one to pick up the younger Perry after his plane has gone down in the ocean.

Nevertheless, Wayne feels Pop's death and it enables Mary to analyse the difficulty between them. She didn't mind his absences at sea, but the trouble was she couldn't cry with him, comfort him when their son died, or now that Pop has gone. "You went off into some corner alone," she accuses, "never realising that by comforting you I could have helped my own grief," and she concludes "You don't need anybody but yourself" — pointing to that egocentrism that is part and parcel of the Wayne *persona*, the flaw that makes the hero human.

But the film sides with Wayne as he is, having Mary's superior at the hospital (Virginia Brissac) tear a strip off her: "You married him for what he is, and then tried to make something else out of him, but you couldn't." Thus deprived of the role of a woman to modify and complete a man's personality, to give him some need of her to make their relationship a two-way affair, Mary quickly gives in and she and Wayne are reunited by the end of the film.

The rest of the footage is routine heroics with Wayne sitting in the middle of the Japanese fleet and firing off all torpedos at once, with them now working properly to maximum devastating effect; indulging in a spot of American imperialism, alias blackmail, to bail out his rowdy crew from a Hawaiian jail after they've enjoyed shore leave; and otherwise showing resolute, resourceful American spirit. Pop's death masquerades as a maturer element for a postwar analysis of armed conflict and the notion was contagious enough for William Holden to suffer Wayne's kind of self-doubt about a past decision in another drama released later that year, *Submarine Command*.

Ward Bond, Philip Carey, Patricia Neal and John Wayne.

48. Flying Leathernecks (1951)

WAR AGAIN was the subject of RKO's *Flying Leathernecks* which can be seen as an attempt to emulate the success of *Sands of Iwo Jima* by casting Wayne as another unpopular officer and having one of that film's two scenarists, James Edward Grant, write the script. Howard Hughes, boss of RKO, reportedly paid Wayne a record $301,000 for making the picture and also arranged for the artistic sensitivity of co-star Robert Ryan and director Nicholas Ray to be as thoroughly annihilated as the enemy in the film.

Wayne plays Major Dan Kirby, commander of a marine fighter squadron in the South Pacific in 1942. He has just been appointed to head the squadron and faces immediate resentment because the men had supposed that the popular executive officer, Captain Carl Griffin (Robert Ryan), would be promoted to the job. The film abounds with the *cliché*s of the *genre*: the careful allocation of deaths among the team in action; the old "watchmaker of civilian life losing his hands" routine taking the form of a pilot who's a bronc-buster in ordinary life and loses a leg; the appearance of a scrounger (Jay C. Flippen) who can conjure up spare parts by diverting them from their intended destination (without ever a thought as to how badly needed they might be where they were supposed to go); and the usual tactical problem over and above defeating the enemy, here one of winning approval for close air support for ground troops despite the risk of hitting them in error.

The film also purports to examine the stresses of command, a subject touched on in Wayne's *Flying Tigers* but most thoughtfully examined in *Twelve O'Clock High* two years before *Flying Leathernecks*.

Wayne watches an argument between Robert Ryan and Adam Williams.

John Wayne as the squadron commander in Flying Leathernecks.

Wayne is more suited to command than Griffin because he's the one tough enough to quickly decide on who should face near certain death; Wayne can accept the tactical objective and force the men to meet it, not worry about whether any of them are fit enough to do so. But Griffin, while rallying the men behind Wayne, criticises him for his hardness and even quotes Donne's line "No man is an island" at him in a scene that nearly leads to a fistfight. As with Private Conway's call on Shakespeare as an ally in *Sands of Iwo Jima,* Griffin's knowledge of a line of poetry is enough to betray him as unsuited to the job — that is, until he comes round to Wayne's point of view and models himself on Wayne when it is his turn to take over command, the pair burying the hatchet by getting drunk together.

It's no surprise when Wayne's toughness proves to be a *façade* and he takes it on himself to write the letters of condolence to next of kin; and there is another image-softening episode of Wayne's return home to visit his wife. Unlike the scene with the prostitute in *Iwo Jima*, this domestic sequence is totally unreal with a poor set, weak actress, and flat handling. Wayne gives his son a sword as a souvenir and, reticent as ever, has to be asked before he'll tell his wife he loves her.

The tough *façade* is still presented for audience endorsement and is necessary for films made during the war for propaganda purposes when the torture and anguish behind difficult decisions is better left unemphasised. But, with the Second World War left behind, films like *Flying Leathernecks* seem obnoxious in making war glamorous rather than tragic. Griffin's greater humanity and concern seem more praiseworthy than the attitude Wayne represents. At least Wayne represents it better than, say, Victor Mature or Alan Ladd would have done.

49. The Quiet Man (1952)

AFTER these two undemanding war pictures, Wayne thankfully heeded the call of John Ford again and went to Ireland to film *The Quiet Man*, his one straight love story. Paired again with Maureen O'Hara, their romance is the entire subject of the film without the kind of dramatic relief afforded by the Indians in *Rio Grande* although a massive fistfight between Wayne and Victor McLaglen has a fully justified place in the film.

Here it is Irish tradition that puts O'Hara at her usual disadvantage as Mary Kate Dannaher, while Wayne, as Sean Thornton, is burdened by his prize-fighting past in which he has accidentally killed a man in the ring. He returns to the land of his father to start a new life and first spots Mary Kate as a barefoot shepherdess in the woods, unable to stop herself staring at the handsome stranger — a mixture of shyness and sensuality, her mouth moving hungrily before she turns and disappears from frame. Her wild red hair, her refreshingly natural good looks, her strong features and exciting firm body make an image (stunningly well photographed, like the rest of the film, by Winton Hoch and Archie Stout) that enables us instantly to understand the effect she has on the watching Wayne, thoughtfully blowing out a stream of cigarette smoke. She looks like some wild but beautiful forest creature, momentarily transfixed before flight, and Wayne is the big white hunter who has invaded her territory, sizing her up and noting her for future pursuit. "Only a mirage brought on by your terrible thirst!" comments Wayne's driver Michaeleen Flynn (Barry Fitzgerald), eyes set on the nearest pub; but Ford's handling of this scene does make Mary Kate such a vision of ripe loveliness that mirage is almost the word for it.

The image of a frightened animal is maintained when, after she has eyed Wayne in church and he has waited for her outside, cupping holy water in his hands for her to cross herself, she scurries off wordlessly only to look back at him from the concealment and distance of a gate. Wayne moves into the old cottage that is his birthplace and catches her there putting the place in order for his arrival. He frightens her out of hiding by yelling. As the frightened girl rushes for the door, Wayne seizes her and swings her back into the room. He draws her close for a kiss and she swings a slap at his face, then gives him a quick kiss of encouragement before running off.

After this moment of vivid, primitive passion, their romance takes more orderly lines. She watches with interest from afar the arrival of the double bed Wayne buys for the cottage and, when Michaeleen comes to read the formal proposal of marriage, she listens eagerly taking momentary umbrage at Wayne's lack of concern over her dowry but smiling while her back is turned on her visitor before saying that she "goes for the idea."

But earlier Wayne has upset her brother, the massive Red Will Dannaher (Victor McLaglen), by outbidding him for the cottage. Subsequently, he has bested Will in a handshake which becomes a trial of strength that has Will's face screwed up in pain. Now, observing the formalities of Irish courtship, he accompanies Michaeleen, acting as his marriage broker, to put the proposal to Red Will, Wayne seen praying for patience as the long-winded Michaeleen gets underway. There is Red Will's inevitable opposition which totally blocks the marriage and a sharp little scene follows when Wayne and Mary Kate accidentally run across each other and he speaks a few words, his voice hard with bitterness, his brow stiffening before he goes on his way.

The locals, led by the mischievous Michaeleen, work out a plot to persuade Red Will to agree to the marriage by telling him that he will land the wealthy widow woman he fancies if only he can get Mary Kate out of

Wayne catches the fleeing Maureen O'Hara in his cottage and gives Victor McLaglen as the rumbustious Red Will Dannaher a handshake to remember (most immediately watching are Barry Fitzgerald, Sean McClory, Ward Bond, and Jack MacGowran).

Barry Fitzgerald as the marriage broker cautions Wayne on his conduct and formally greets Maureen O'Hara inside the house.

Wayne drags Maureen O'Hara across five miles of countryside and seizes the switch handed him to beat his lady, much to his wife's fury. Below, Wayne lays into Victor McLaglen watched by an eager crowd.

the house. So Red Will softens and Wayne is subjected to the next stage of formal courtship. This is the chaperoned outing with he and Mary Kate seated back to back and Michaeleen driving, Wayne's arms crossed in resignation until the pair can escape on a tandem bicycle to the hills. Here the motif of hunter and hunted reasserts itself with Mary Kate slipping a few steps ahead and turning to throw away her bonnet, then Wayne similarly abandoning his gloves and bowler to run and catch her up. They shelter from a rainstorm in a graveyard, their rainsoaked embrace reviving the passion of their early encounter in the cottage.

No sooner have they completed the marriage ceremony than Red Will discovers the deception and he takes out his anger on Wayne, who has not been a party to the scheme, by knocking him to the floor. At this point as Wayne lies dazed, John Ford inserts an expressionistic montage of Wayne's past as a boxer with one unforgettable close-up of his sweat-stained features staring down in wide-eyed horror at the body of the man he has killed, conveying more than adequately the nightmare quality of the experience that has driven him so far to a new life and makes him so reluctant to fight Red Will. With Mary Kate losing the dowry she sets such store by (although Wayne dismisses it as unimportant) and lacking the personal possessions from her old home, she doesn't consider herself properly married and bolts the door to the bedroom to keep him out. Wayne angrily kicks his way in, seizes her by the hair and kisses her, bringing her to the point of submission. He then flings her on the bed which breaks under the impact, and storms out to settle down in a sleeping bag. This scene cleverly maintains the Wayne image by allowing him to choose the outcome and, in backing down, to show his customary respect for the other sex. This latter point is also seen in the way he covers up the situation in front of their visitors the next morning, with Michaeleen impressed by the ardour implicit in the broken bed.

Their life continues in a friendly enough fashion, Wayne applying a jovial slap to Mary Kate's rump as she clambers over a wall to fetch her shoes for a walk. But, for her, the absence of a dowry is still humiliating and at one point she almost strikes Wayne with a horse whip for not taking it up with her brother. Wayne is soon venting his frustration by kicking stones and flinging boulders across the countryside. Then Mary Kate brings matters to a head when she runs off to catch a train to Dublin.

Wayne turns up at the station and drags her off the train, ducking a haymaker and kneeing her in the rump to speed her progress on the five-mile walk back. The driver deserts his train to follow (trains are always running late anyway in Ford films) and, along with an ever increasing crowd of locals, falls in behind the pair. A woman hands Wayne a switch to use on Mary Kate,

expressing popular sympathy with his tough action, leaving her to glower helplessly. Wayne brings her to Red Will, working in a field, and throws her back as an unsuitable wife for lack of a dowry. Red Will peels off some money and hands it over to Wayne who puts it into a boiler nearby with Mary Kate enthusiastically opening the door. The dowry disposed of, the stage is set for Wayne and Red Will to fight it out with Mary Kate setting off jauntily for home. A spectacularly exaggerated brawl takes place. Buckets of water are applied to revive the two contestants and there is a break for a spot of refreshment in the pub after which the fight is concluded by Wayne knocking Red Will clear through the entrance door. The two men now have respect and affection for each other and they stagger home for dinner with Mary Kate. It remains for a final scene to show Wayne and Mary Kate making up for lost time as she comes up to him sitting outside and whispers a suggestion in his ear, making off towards the house. He gets up and waits while she runs ahead and then pauses to look enticingly back at him as he catches up and takes her arm.

In the hands of an artist as sensitive and resourceful as John Ford, *The Quiet Man* is able to deal with sexual attraction in an honest yet indirect way without ever lapsing into bad taste. For Wayne, the part of Sean Thornton has its aggressive side in the final fight but otherwise calls for unusual restraint in the face of Irish customs and Red Will Dannaher (with resultant expressions of comic frustration). He can occasionally break out into a dark, repressed rage, but the film draws most on his gentlemanly reserve, allowing him enough decisive moments to affirm his masculine brute strength. The only contrived aspect of the characterisation, if an essential one, is his withholding the secret of his past from Mary Kate. The film never raises this as an issue and so it is never made to seem a devious action on Wayne's part.

Although *The Quiet Man* was only indirectly a Republic picture (it was part-filmed on the studio's soundstages and released by the company, but made by Ford's Argosy Pictures), it was Wayne's final association with the organisation whose boss, Herbert J. Yates, had incurred his displeasure by backing out of a deal for Wayne to film the story of the Alamo (Yates's only recorded — and happily frustrated — contribution to the making of *The Quiet Man* was to try and have its title changed to *The Prizefighter and the Colleen*). Had Wayne remained an occasional star of Republic Pictures, it would have probably kept the studio in business much longer than the six or seven years it managed with the loss of its major star. As it was, Wayne had now aligned himself with Warner Bros. under a comprehensive deal that allowed him to also produce pictures without starring in them.

50. Big Jim McLain (1952)

THIS WAS Wayne's first undertaking as a producer-star for Warner Bros., having formed Wayne-Fellows Productions with Robert M. Fellows, a former producer at RKO and Paramount. Their collaboration lasted until after *The High and the Mighty* when Wayne bought out his partner's interest and re-named the company Batjac. Since, then, he has used his younger brother Robert E. Morrison, former assistant director Andrew V. (son of Victor) McLaglen and latterly his son Michael to produce the pictures made for the company.

The new producing arrangement allowed Wayne in *Big Jim McLain* to put forward his political beliefs forcefully. James Edward Grant, who was becoming Wayne's most trusted writer, was one of the three authors of the film. Edward Ludwig, who had directed *Wake of the Red Witch*, was given the same function here.

The film does not mince words. After invoking the spirit of Daniel Webster, the film shows us the hearing room of the House of Representatives Committee on Un-American Activities and a narrator declares: "We, the citizens of the United States of America, owe these,

our elected representatives a great debt. Undaunted by the vicious campaign of slander launched against them as a group and as individuals, they have staunchly continued their investigations pursuing their stated belief that anyone who continued to be a Communist after 1945 is guilty of high treason."

We see witnesses taking the Fifth Amendment, refusing to answer the Committee's questions on the grounds that it might tend to incriminate them. Quickly we are given the case of an economics professor who is — the investigators know — responsible for sending no less than 1,500 microfilms to the Communist and whose beliefs are contaminating the kids he teaches. Much later in the film, Wayne, as Big Jim McLain, HUAC investigator, has these lines: "There are a lot of wonderful things written into our constitution but they're meant for honest decent citizens and I resent the fact that it can be used and abused by the very people that want to destroy it."

The film depicts the efforts of Wayne and fellow investigator Mal Baxter (James Arness), former war hero, to expose a Communist spy ring in Hawaii. They meet a labour leader who was a former Commie and

The Commies put the boot in.....

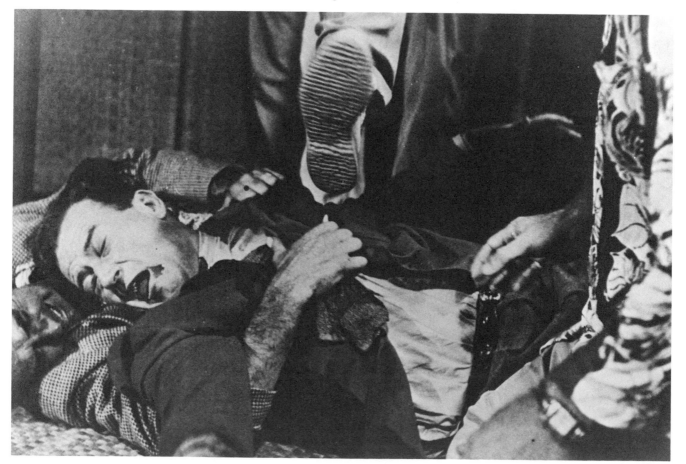

saw the light: "After a while you get it through your skull that all this party line is a lot of con." The unrepentant Communists are headed by the suave Sturak (Alan Napier) and are waiting for their big day to take over, with plans laid to cause an epidemic, bring labour out on strike, etc. They murder Mal Baxter, leaving Wayne to carry on forcefully but with some restraint, declining to sock one Commie because he's too small: Wayne believes in "fair play and all that stuff." Wayne himself is barely rescued in time from the hands of the Communists and the film ends on an embittered note as Sturak takes the Fifth Amendment, there apparently being no evidence on which to convict him other than the self-incrimination he has denied them. All that Wayne ends up with for consolation is the nurse (Nancy Olson) he has met in Hawaii, and the picture concludes with an implicit call for the revoking of the Amendment.

The astonishingly crude presentation of the Communist menace makes the film a shallow propaganda piece. Wayne's character name of Big Jim McLain has an emotive similarity to that of Joe McCarthy; the Reds act like a bunch of ruthless gangsters, betraying members to the investigators when it suits their purposes and indulging in all manner of criminal offences, making their activities more suited to FBI rather than political investigation. By likening the film to an ordinary gangster picture, it was presumably hoped to make it more acceptable to the mass audience, but *Big Jim McLain* was not successful at the box-office.

The film is most deplorable for side-stepping the very real arguments against the form of investigation used by HUAC and its parallel Senate committee which has now caused their activities to be almost universally regarded as a dismal blot on recent American history. It seems exceedingly irresponsible to have introduced HUAC into the film — other anti-Communist pictures of the period used the FBI — and to praise it so extravagantly without finding space for the criticisms made against it — the way it put people on trial without the right of defence, with power to jail them for "contempt," and ruined the careers of many people who challenged its right to probe their private beliefs in a free country.

The film's one reference to an intellectual Communist, the college professor, also very conveniently makes him in the same breath an active spy. Consequently, there is no consideration of Communism as an ideological force and no reflection whatsoever on the more controversial aspects of HUAC's work, despite Hollywood's close familiarity with it. By equating Communism with terrorism, the film underestimates its enemy and *Big Jim McLain* can have only reinforced the beliefs of the very simple-minded.

....but Wayne is rescued in the nick of time.

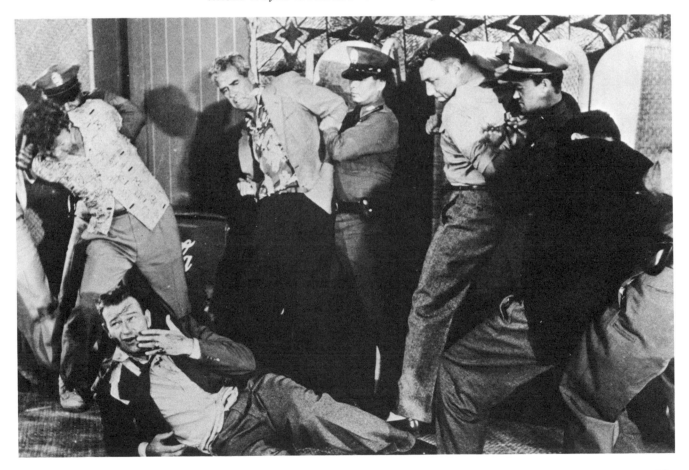

51. Trouble Along the Way (1953)

THIS WAS Hollywood's idea of a sure-fire formula picture, the kind that shows what the "studio system" meant. Give an audience a man and a boy, football *and* religion, and you've got a strong spread of appeal for all ages and both sexes. Casting Wayne as the man with the boy and as the football coach, though not as a man of the cloth, is an offbeat touch as this kind of part more usually went to a performer with a lighter style like Bing Crosby. But Wayne acquits himself with ease, and thanks to the polish of Michael Curtiz's direction and the slick dialogue of the Melville Shavelson-Jack Rose writing team, the picture turns out quite passably if not the kind of film you'd want to stay up late to watch on television.

Wayne plays Steve Williams, the former big-time football coach who has been kicked out of the game and has gone to pieces, his marriage broken up with his young daughter (Sherry Jackson) the only thing he cares about. Alice Singleton (Donna Reed) is the woman from the Probation Bureau who comes to inves-tigate his child's welfare and sees the rough environment in which she lives but misses the genuine affection she has from her father. Wayne, using his background of worldly experience, chips away at the lady's defences, telling her she has nice legs and diagnosing her as a young old maid who's afraid of love.

But he starts to shape up and takes a job as coach to a rundown college needing a financial miracle to stay open. Cynically, he feels that the college head, Father Burke (Charles Coburn), is wasting his money but he won't lose any sleep over it. Wayne investigates the job on hand and asks how the team did last season. "We turned up for every game," he is told. On further acquaintance with the problems he would face, he hands in his notice. "We're giving you an absolutely free hand," says Father Burke. "Then you'd better shake it. Because I'm leaving right now," replies Wayne.

We learn that Wayne is afraid of the ridicule to which he will be exposed if he fails to lick the team into winning shape, but he then hits on a way of getting the

Wayne pauses during a practice session to listen to Tom Tully.

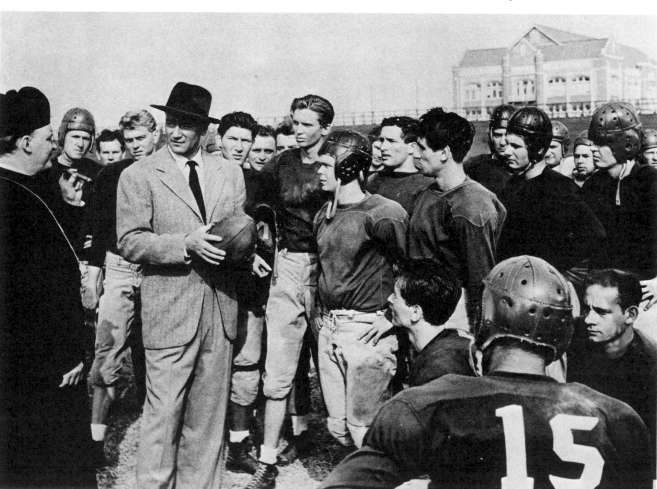

136

job done by various unethical means behind Father Burke's back, and goes to work. He resorts to blackmail to get uniforms and good playing dates at the grounds, fakes academic standards to get promising talent enrolled at the college, and wins players' cooperation by promising a share in the money to be raised from various subsidiary angles like parking, selling of pennants, etc. that Father Burke knows nothing of.

The ruses are obvious to everyone but the good Father and when he is told about it he cancels the rest of the season. Wayne refuses to admit to any shame over his actions but he turns to drink. Meanwhile the lady from the Probation Bureau has withdrawn her unfavourable assessment of Wayne as a father but still insists his daughter is being brought up with the wrong values. It looks as though Wayne's ex-wife (Marie Windsor) will gain custody of the child.

But it's always darkest before the last reel in this kind of picture. Father Burke claims responsibility for Wayne's actions as a coach, declaring that it was his way of doing what was demanded of him; the college's future is suddenly assured and Wayne given the job of coaching the team again. With the Probation Bureau and Father Burke behind him, Wayne has nothing to fear from the custody proceedings and he hasn't forgotten that Miss Singleton has nice legs. The world isn't such a bad place to live in after all when Hollywood's running it.

Sherry Jackson, as Wayne's daughter, brings him a tomato juice.

Wayne questions Donna Reed as the woman from the Probation Bureau. Richard Garrick is the judge in the background.

52. Island in the Sky (1953)

UNDER his own production banner, Wayne next starred in the long, dreary, talkative *Island in the Sky*. Written by Ernest K. Gann from his novel and directed by aviation specialist William A. Wellman, the film was virtually a try-out for *The High and the Mighty*, made by the same team almost immediately afterwards and also dealing with a crippled aeroplane, suspense, and character stress. *Island in the Sky* is the first film on which the cinematographer William H. Clothier seems to have worked with Wayne: here he did the aerial photography with Archie Stout handling the rest.

Set in war-time, the film casts Wayne as Captain Dooley, the chief pilot of a four-engined transport plane that breaks down over the frozen wastes north of Labrabor. He heads the plane towards uncharted terrain where he is able to "ride the ship down" onto the flat surface of a frozen lake. A veteran of some twenty years' flying experience, he shows his maturity by licking his crew into shape to endure the six days their food supplies will last, cajoling co-operation, slapping one of

the crew out of a state of hysteria, and generally keeping up spirits while rescue planes search for them and their radio transmits a weak signal giving their position. Unfortunately, the film has all the standard *clichés* of characterisation: the immature, gum-chewing, wisecracking younger crew members whose thoughts of their wives, childrens and mothers intrude as flashbacks — men who bare their heads and say the Lord's Prayer, and who have only to look at the sky to prompt a celestial choir to fill in the silence of their hopeful gazing. Falling prey to sentimentalism and excesses of self-pity and tears, script and direction undermine the chilly realism of the black-and-white photography, but there is a fair measure of suspense from crosscutting between the elaborate rescue operations and the worsening situation on the ground with such dramatic highlights as the moment a plane flies over without spotting the men on the ground. The demands on Wayne are slight and routine, artistically speaking, the kind of part he could play in his sleep.

John Wayne slaps an hysterical James Lydon.

53. Hondo (1953)

IMMEDIATELY following completion of *Island in the Sky,* Wayne had to fly to a remote location in Mexico to star in *Hondo.* Not for the last time, he found himself in difficulties attempting to function solely as a producer. Star Glenn Ford and director John Farrow had made *Plunder in the Sun* for his production company and were set to continue the association on *Hondo.* But Ford had not enjoyed working with Farrow and, since Wayne liked the script James Edward Grant had written for *Hondo,* he took on the leading role himself. He was not wrong in his judgement. Although almost every critic at the time compared it unfavourably to *Shane,* the film is an excellent Western by any standards — and one of the films to be really enhanced by the use of 3-D though coming too late to dispel the impression that it was a gimmick to bolster exploitation pictures. As in Roy Baker's *Inferno,* 3-D was able to bring out the vastness of desert country tremendously well but CinemaScope quickly came along to dislodge it for good.

Comparisons with *Shane* occurred because Wayne plays an ex-gunfighter, Hondo Lane, who turns up at a ranch occupied by a woman, Angie Lowe (Geraldine Page), and her small son Johnny (Lee Aaker), much as Alan Ladd's gunfighter arrived at the homestead of Jean Arthur and young Brandon De Wilde in George Stevens' film. But there the similarities really end. Wayne's first appearance is a memorable one as he walks out of the desert with a saddle over his shoulders, followed by his dog, Sam. He is a dispatch rider and scout for the U.S. cavalry (the year is 1874) and he soon spots from the state of the place that it has been without male attention for some time and that Angie is lying when she says her husband is expected back at any moment. As the abandoned wife, Geraldine Page sensitively depicts the affection she develops for the tall and capable figure who helps her restore the ranch to good order. He breaks in a horse and buys it from her, preparing to leave. He warns her that trouble with the Apaches is imminent but she declares that the Indians are her friends and refuses to leave with him. He tells her that she reminds him of his dead Indian wife and rides off after kissing her fiercely. In town, he runs across Angie's husband, Ed Lowe (Leo Gordon), find-

John Wayne and Geraldine Page.

John Wayne and Geraldine Page.

ing him in a poker game; the two men fall foul of each other and twice brawl, with Wayne eventually obliged to kill Lowe after the latter ambushes him on his way back to Angie and the boy. He then falls into Apache hands and is tortured with hot coals placed in his palms. His courage in withstanding the pain earns him the respect of the Apache leader Vittoro (Michael Pate), and the discovery that he is carrying a tintype of Angie's boy on him decides the chief to spare his life, since the boy has become Vittoro's blood brother. However, Vittoro's second-in-command, Silva (Rodolfo Acosta), is incensed at this decision and challenges Wayne to a knife duel. 3-D enhances the resulting fight, staged with great vigour, the combatants kicking sand into the camera, and Wayne overcomes his opponent, sparing his life.

When Vittoro and his men escort Wayne to the ranch, Angie quickwittedly identifies Wayne as her husband and thereby avoids marriage to one of Vittoro's braves since the chief thinks his young blood brother needs a father. Wayne awkwardly admits to Angie that he has killed her husband but she accepts his explanation and agrees to move on with him to land he owns in California.

But Silva has become the Apache leader following Vittoro's death and is conducting merciless raids. Eventually, when he attacks the wagon train Wayne is leading, there is a pitched battle which enables Wayne to gut Silva with a lance much as the blackhearted Indian had earlier speared his dog Sam. Wayne is thus free to continue his journey to a new life in California with Angie and Tommy.

The film is interesting for its sympathetic depiction of Vittoro as a chief justly angered by treaty violations, but it is otherwise simply a superior version of a routine story. The casting of Broadway actress Geraldine Page in her first film role pays off well, giving Wayne not only a fresh face to respond to but also a strong performance that supports his own work, showing it to better advantage. (The part of Angie Lowe had first been offered to Katharine Hepburn, but I suspect that she would have been too overpowering for it.) *Hondo* lacks the extra depth that John Ford brought to the slightly similar *The Searchers* (though the director did some odds and ends of second unit work when he paid a visit to the *Hondo* location), but it remains a distinct plus in Wayne's career and one of the best of his producing ventures.

54. The High and the Mighty (1954)

DEALING with the way in which the crew and passengers of an aircraft cope with an emergency situation, and being based on a best-selling novel, *The High and the Mighty* was very much the *Airport* of the Fifties, not only in subject but also in terms of commercial success (it grossed over six million dollars in the U.S. and Canada alone). It reminded British reviewers at the time of *Outward Bound* and *Grand Hotel* in its method of placing assorted types within a confined situation but the obvious parallel within Wayne's own career seems to have passed unnoticed — not so much his recent *Island in the Sky* but *Stagecoach*, especially since its leading lady Claire Trevor was back again with Wayne in a part that earned her an Oscar nomination (as did Jan Sterling's performance, though neither actress won).

Wayne's role was originally written with Spencer Tracy in mind but the actor belatedly declined to play it. As with *Hondo,* Wayne had one obvious solution to such casting setbacks on his own productions and he again substituted himself. The role is of quite modest dimensions but suited to the Wayne image. He plays the veteran flyer Dan Roman whose career, we are told, ranges back to pioneering days, daredevil and endurance flying, and bombing raids in the Second World War. He is now reduced to acting as co-pilot of a commercial aircraft, never having got over a plane crash from which he was the only survivor with his wife and child among the victims. As a ground engineer admiringly comments: "Dan's the only guy I ever knew who had guts enough not to commit suicide." However, the past preys on him and memory flashbacks show him struggling away from the burning wreck, while his limp is a permanent souvenir of the tragedy.

Wayne's part is established early in the film which then goes on to introduce most of the passengers as they arrive for the flight. Curiously, Claire Trevor's character isn't given a detailed introduction and, although she is billed second to Wayne, it is little elaborated upon with she and Wayne not given an opening for any kind of relationship.

Wayne is unusually quiet in the early scenes in the cockpit, whistling occasionally and taking note of the disturbing tremors that presage the later difficulties of the flight. But he predictably proves to be the tower of strength when the crisis develops, levelling with the passengers in a typically direct, encouraging fashion

Flashback – Wayne survives the crash that claims his wife and child.

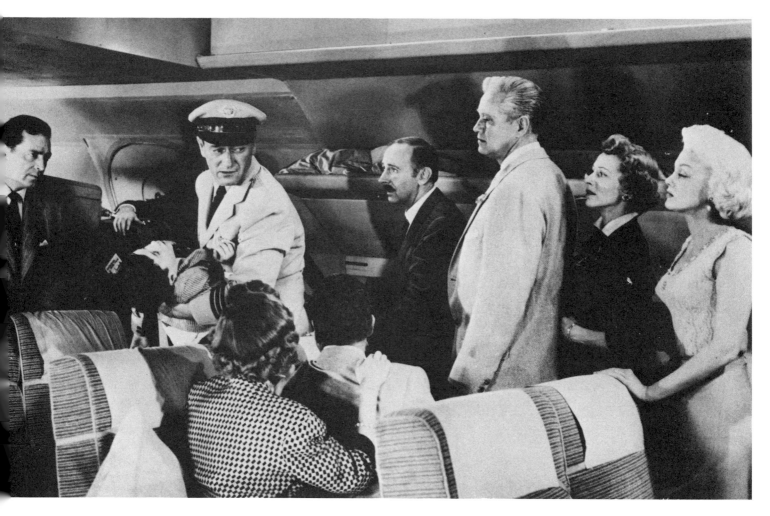

Wayne calms the passengers: John Howard, John Qualen, David Brian, Julie Bishop,
Jan Sterling. He's holding Michael Wellman.

about the near certainty of a crash landing at sea, and making the necessary preparations, including carefully enclosing his picture of his wife and child in a water-proof wrapping. When calculations reveal that the plane has a chance of reaching San Francisco airport, Wayne exerts his greater experience and calm nerve to insist that they make the attempt to go all the way and takes over from the chief pilot Sullivan (Robert Stack) who has lost his composure. When Sullivan comes round and thanks Wayne for taking the initiative, Wayne returns the controls to him to make the landing successfully and limps away whistling into the night with only the fond murmur of an airline official, "So long, you ancient pelican," to accompany him.

This long (147 minutes) picture is too attenuated to develop real suspense and too contrived in its charac-terisations to cause much concern over the fate of the passengers whose flashbacks are particular phoney in their handling. It was Wayne's first venture into CinemaScope, a process that tended to make the audi-ence feel drawn into the setting in its novelty days while dissipating the sense of confinement. But the way films about ailing aircraft strike a ready chord of fearful iden-tification in audiences ensures that *The High and the Mighty* at least intermittently exerts a grip, and its great commercial success must have been encouraging to Wayne in his early days as a busy actor-producer.

55. The Sea Chase (1955)

EVEN Wayne's most stalwart fans must have found it hard to sit through *The Sea Chase* without a sinking sense of disappointment. After *Hondo*, it was a dismal second association of Wayne with director John Farrow (who was something of a specialist in sea pictures, having made *Two Years before the Mast* and *Botany Bay* and been a sailor in real life). The film makes little headway against a poor script and the foolish central casting of Wayne as a German (without resolving the problem of accent).

Wayne's Karl Ehrlich is a good German of the Second World War. He has opposed Hitler and been relegated to command of a mere freighter. But he is a patriot and wants to return to his homeland. The film deals with the battle of wits between him and the pursuing British war ship captained by his pal Napier (David Farrar). As Napier comments in his voice-over narration, Wayne's Ehrlich has integrity and this is "a man's supreme obligation to himself." Wayne's integrity shows itself when he saves Napier from the clutches of a German spy, Elsa (Lana Turner), by threatening to expose her to him if she doesn't leave the British officer alone. Wayne cannot tell a lie: he later levels with a wounded man on ship about his condition and he doesn't answer Napier when the latter asks if he's said anything to Elsa to make her go off him.

By way of contrast, Lyle Bettger plays a bad German, Kirchner, a ruthless Nazi who murders six fishermen sheltering at a shipwreck station on an island the fleeing freighter visits. This is done without Wayne's knowledge, and when he finds out he socks the German and ensures that Kirchner goes down with the ship at the climax.

Wayne is forced to take Elsa on as a passenger by the German consul in Sydney; he is annoyed about it, having brushed with her in the past. But when later she explains how she was forced into her way of life, Wayne offers her this thought for consolation: "Did anyone ever tell you you're beautiful when you're angry? You're quite a woman, Elsa!" Before long, the compassionate side of Elsa's nature is spilling out and she criticises Wayne for some of the tough measures he is taking to keep up speed. He retorts, referring back to an earlier conversation, "I forgot to mention why I never married — I like to run my own ship." The old theme, of Wayne trying to do his job with women intruding, is there but the German setting undermines it hopelessly and Lana Turner performs better lounging in doorways and striding around than she ever does trying to develop her role. They pretend to a torrid passion for each other and in one of those legend-of-the-sea endings are left living happily ever after in Norway after British shells finally sink the ship.

The same sort of story was repeated in the British *Battle of the River Plate*, a more realistic telling of the pursuit of the Graf Spee, but, for an object lesson in how *The Sea Chase* could have been handled, Hollywood's *The Enemy Below* serves admirably.

Lana Turner, John Wayne and John Doucette.

Above, Wayne and Lana Turner. Below, Wayne and Tab Hunter.

56. Blood Alley (1955)

THIS was the first Wayne-starring venture under the Batjac set-up which replaced Wayne-Fellows Productions. No producer is actually credited. Like *Hondo* and *The High and the Mighty*, Wayne's participation in front of the camera was forced on him — under rather dramatic circumstances. The film went into production in early January, 1955, with Robert Mitchum starring under William Wellman's direction. The star and director had worked together amicably on another production of Wayne's, *Track of the Cat*, but trouble blew up after less than a week's shooting on *Blood Alley*. Wellman became annoyed at one of the actor's practical jokes and described it as "detrimental to the making of our film." Mitchum called his prank of pushing the unit's transportation manager into San Francisco Bay "just a bit of horseplay." Wellman insisted that Mitchum should be removed from the film and Wayne agreed. Jack Warner, whose company was distributing the film, demanded a replacement star of equivalent stature and gave Wayne a short list of possibilities including himself, Gregory Peck and Humphrey Bogart, the husband of the film's leading lady, Lauren Bacall. Bogart wanted half a million dollars, too large a salary to suit Wayne, and so the latter abandoned some holiday plans and took the role himself. He soon found

himself acting as director for a while so that William Wellman could recover from a bout of flu. Whatever the immediate feeling Wayne had for Mitchum, it didn't stop them co-starring in *El Dorado* some ten years later.

Blood Alley was both adventure film and Commie-bashing propaganda, dealing with the escape of a whole village of 180 people from Red China to freedom in Hong Kong by taking a ferry boat down the Formosa Straits, the 300-mile "blood alley" of the title. An undistinguished film by most standards, it is given firm drive by Wellman's handling and he and cameraman William Clothier bring a pictorial flair to the images, creating with art director Al Ybarra a convincing representation of China on Californian coast locations with shots of great beauty and atmosphere, especially in the sequence at the graveyard of sunken ships. It hangs together much better than *The Sea Chase*.

Wayne is first seen languishing in a Red jail, "a guest of the Commies" who resists the effects of brainwashing not by talking to God but to a composite picture of all the girls he has known, looking up and addressing comments to "Babe," a figure he somewhat regretfully dismisses when doctor's daughter Cathy Grainger (Lauren Bacall) has a firm enough grip on his emotions. Wayne is rescued from jail by the efforts of a village

Wearing his escape uniform, Wayne talks to "Babe" watched by Lauren Bacall.

who want to use his knowledge of the local waters as a merchant marine captain to guide them to freedom in the local ferry. As this flat-bottomed paddle-wheeler was made in the good old U.S.A., albeit in 1887, it can hardly fail to do the job. Wayne, busily talking to himself from habit, likes the idea — "A whole village scratched off the Red map and put down in Hong Kong!" — but he disclaims any ideological motives at this point for aiding the villagers. He tells Cathy, who is working in the village with her father, "Somebody pinned the bleeding heart of China on your sleeve, baby, but they never got around to me." To him, the Reds are merely a nuisance because they closed down the ports he used to visit and kept him away from the girls he used to see. He is on hand to bayonet a Chinese soldier who attempts to rape Cathy, then kicks himself for not having responded to Cathy's attractiveness himself. But the village elders summon him away before he can make a call on her bedroom late at night. He is asked to tell her that her father, who has failed to save the life of a stricken Communist official, has been put on trial and stoned to death; and in his rough-and-ready way he does the job as delicately as possible by slapping her to make her good and angry and put her in a better mood to receive the bad news!

As the riverboat moves along, unconfirmed reports of the village's escape reach the free world to be dismissed as malicious propaganda by the angry Communists. Out of the generosity of their hearts, the villagers have taken along the one (very large) family with pro-Communist views rather than leave them to suffer reprisals, and this makes for some mischief en route. Two of the family attack Wayne in the pilot house leaving him to complete the journey with a bandaged head and leg wound. Suspicion falls on them of having poisoned the food supply, a problem that Wayne gets to grips with by starting to force-feed one of the family's children until her mother anxiously snatches her away.

Parallels with *The Sea Chase* crop up. Whereas in that film Wayne bore down on the German sailors who

Wayne rescues Lauren Bacall from the unwelcome attentions of Victor Sen Yung.

resisted his order to break up the lifeboats for fuel, here he relaxes a mite in the same situation of fuel crisis when an elder (Paul Fix) shows him some pieces of wood bearing ten years' worth of carving on them. "Hide them some place," he says quietly, almost as though not letting himself hear his concession. And there is ingenuity in dodging pursuit in both films. Here it takes the form of attracting a flock of seagulls to settle on the ferry and cover it so thoroughly that it looks indistinguishable from the nearby reefs to a passing Communist plane (this sequence was inexplicably deleted for the film's British release).

As in the episode of sparing the carved wood, Wayne is unusually considerate with the pro-Communist family despite the poisoning attempt. When they are put ashore at the graveyard of sunken ships, Wayne takes the time and trouble to address them through an interpreter telling them "Your China is misguided" and giving them the opportunity to continue to Hong Kong. All but one elder (Berry Kroeger) take the opportunity, leaving him to retreat foaming abuse and to be promptly blown up by a shell from a Chinese destroyer which has arrived. How's that for tidy plotting?

Cathy has also left to stay in China but the ferryboat makes an exciting return run to pick her up when the destroyer materialises. By now Wayne has really come around to the cause and starts talking to himself through his old ally of "Babe" or "Baby." "Look at them, baby!" he says, gazing on his passengers, "Let them make it, they gotta make it!" and, as the doughty Chinese haul the vessel through shallow water by rope from a bank, he goes even further: "The bleeding heart of China — you can pin one on my sleeve, babe." Eventually the battered company reach Hong Kong to admiring comments from officers aboard a British war ship (one sees Lowell Gilmore speaking here in what looks very much like anticipatory footage shot during production of *The Sea Chase*). Oddly, the view of Hong Kong looks very like the view Wayne had from his cell deep in Red China, conjuring up a momentary thought that the whole story might have been an illusion inside Wayne's head, but the film is too conventional for stimulating twists of this sort. It is rather a good comic-strip adventure and incidentally far more effective anti-Communist propaganda than *Big Jim McLain*.

57. The Conquerer (1956)

WAYNE's next in release was a $5 million fiasco called *The Conqueror* in which he played Temujin, better known by his later name of Genghis Khan. Studio releases stated that Wayne had demanded the part after seeing the script lying around at RKO; it would be more charitable to think that he took it on to fulfil a contract. Some kind of loyalty to the studio or its boss, Howard Hughes, for whom he had made the still unreleased *Jet Pilot*, seemingly impelled him to make a rare visit to London for the world *première* — a man of courage in real life as well as on the screen! It was his last substantial work for RKO — he had in fact made the film before *The Sea Chase* — but there was still *Jet Pilot* and a cameo bit in support of a George Gobel comedy to come in the studio's floundering years before it quit production altogether like Republic.

Commercially if not artistically, *The Conqueror* must have seemed a reasonable proposition with Wayne ensuring the attendance of Western fans and several pitched battles between Mongols and Tartars the equivalent of the cavalry versus the Indians. Wayne's Napoleon of the steppes is costumed in a fur hat and spiked helment, his eyes slightly taped up and his mouth adorned with two wisps of downturned walrus-like moustache; but his voice is so quintessentially American that his interpretation is doomed from the start, especially when called on to utter the stilted *clichés* of Oscar Millard's script. Beyond that, Wayne is not basically suited to the part because, when he hasn't been completely independent, he has always played the leader of men within a limited framework, a man doing a particular job. He cannot convey a figure with unlimited ambitions of empire, good as he is at squinting at far horizons; nor does he look happy acting ferocious and following barbaric impulses.

Always impressive visually with its Utah desert locations spread across the CinemaScope screen, and backed up by splendid 2nd unit action staged by Cliff Lyons, *The Conqueror* is otherwise sheer camp. It opens with Wayne on horseback sitting atop a hill silhouetted against the skyline (a publicity handout declares that one of his three horses in the film is the bay mare he rode in *Tall in the Saddle*). He is observing a wagon train passing by below with the daughter of a Tartar chief, Bortai (Susan Hayward), reclining on a pile of cushions in a contraption that has been likened to a moving section of the Albert Memorial and Brighton Pier. It doesn't take long for someone to observe "She is a woman — much woman!" and for Wayne to conclude "I feel this Tartar woman is for me. My blood says: Take her." He rides down with some men and after a few minutes of battle, in line with his other purpose of killing Tartars in revenge for his father's death, he reaches her and leans over to tear her silver gown by way of making his thoughts clear. "Know this, woman," he tells her, "I take you for wife." Bortai subsequently offers some lively resistance while in his hands, even swinging a sword at his head, and snarls, "For me there is no ease while you live, Mongol!" Wayne's admiring comment is second nature: "You're bewdiful in your wrath!", the period paraphrase of "You look beautiful when you're mad," as used in so many other films.

Wayne has the advantage of knowing female ways

Wayne and the woman (Susan Hayward).
Above, Agnes Moorehead is the peeved spectator.

and tells Bortai, "Your hatred will kindle into passion," himself kindling it along with such choice flattery as "All other women are like the second pressing of the grape." All this, plus the opposition of his blood brother Jamuga (Pedro Armendariz) to his interest in Bortai, rather distracts him from his military objectives and causes him to fall into Tartar hands which promptly place him on the torture rack. Bortai abandons her cycle of peevish, bad-tempered and bored reactions to Wayne's enthusiasm for her, deciding "I am consumed with want of him," and rescues him from the thumbscrews. After a memorable shot of Wayne on top of a mountain bellowing "Eternal skies, send me men!" (promptly supplied), the stage is set for an epic battle between Mongols and Tartars before Wayne can be dispatched by Bortai to write his chapter in the history books.

58. The Searchers (1956)

NOT SINCE *The Quiet Man* had Wayne taken on a part which really displayed his acting abilities, and it was John Ford again who drew from him a truly outstanding performance. Wayne liked his part of Ethan Edwards so much that he has named one of his sons Ethan, and his affection is fully understandable. It was an extremely difficult assignment to fully realise the character: it goes beyond Wayne's basically powerful screen presence, beyond what he says, the way he looks and acts most of the time, and demands a communication of interior feelings that have to be sensed burning inside the man even while he appears open and relaxed. The result is unforgettable: as far from Nathan Brittles and Sean Thornton as it is possible for an actor to get.

Wayne's Ethan is a loner of the old West, a man who unlike his brother Aaron (Walter Coy) has never been "civilised" by the process of marriage, children and settling down. He has fought on the losing side in the Civil War but doesn't believe in surrenders and has kept his sabre ("Didn't turn it into no ploughshare either!"); it has taken him three years to come back to his brother's ranch and he has clearly been carrying on the war in his own way by at least one bank robbery. But it is more than the defeat of the South that has made Ethan a lonely, withdrawn figure for all his expansiveness on returning home: we learn that he had toyed with the idea of leaving his brother's ranch before the hostilities broke out but stayed around, as his brother puts it, "beyond any real reason", and Ford subtly conveys that it was his love for his brother's wife Martha (Dorothy Jordan) that kept him there. As Martha welcomes Wayne back, the warm music touches on Ford's favourite "Ann Rutledge" theme from *Young Mr. Lincoln,* which conveyed there (and will do so again in *The Man Who Shot Liberty Valance*) the poignancy of lost love, and we see that Martha reciprocates Wayne's affection in a telling moment of her stroking the army coat he has been wearing. Nothing has come of these feelings, out of respect for Aaron, but it is clear that a mistake has been made. Ethan is the strong brother while Aaron is a weak figure who has only kept his ranch going because of Martha ("She just wouldn't let a man quit," Aaron remarks); and, beyond the glamorous image Wayne represents to the children, there is a child's recognition of Wayne's greater strength and dependability in the son's line "I wish Uncle Ethan were here, don't you, ma?" when the family faces an Indian attack without his support.

After his initial warmth of welcome, Aaron may not be entirely casual in enquiring how long his brother intends to stay but the question is sufficient for Wayne to snap "I expect to pay my way" and place money on the table, assuming that there is pettiness in the remark and showing that he is ill at ease. When the Texas Rangers, led by Reverend Sam Clayton (Ward Bond), come by to recruit help in investigating some cattle rustling, Wayne intervenes to snatch his brother's place. It is not long before Wayne realises that they've been lured away so that the Comanches can conduct a murder raid, and that he is powerless to return in time to protect his brother's family. When he does return, it is to find that his worst fears were justified. As Wayne looks on the mutilated bodies of all but two nieces the Indians have taken away, he absorbs its impact without releasing it in open grief while Martin Pawley (Jeffrey Hunter), who lived with the family, becomes distraught without even being allowed close to the grim sight. It is at this moment that the figure we are to live with for the rest of the film takes shape: a man burdened with an error of judgement in being away when he was needed, obsessed with seeking revenge on the Comanches who have destroyed Martha and with recovering the nieces in whom she lives on. Given a new purpose to his existence, Wayne strides impatiently away from the funeral in a striking image of irresistible determination.

Martin Pawley and another boy, Brad Jorgensen (Harry Carey Jr.), tag along as Wayne starts his search. Shortly after, he alone discovers the ravaged body of Lucy, reverently buries her in his army coat (the one that Martha had fondled), and bottles up the incident until Brad's questioning drives him into revealing it. When Brad probes for details, Wayne's fury erupts with frightening force: "What do you want me to do? Draw you a picture? Spell it out? Don't ever ask me! Long as you live, don't ever ask me more!" Then the deranged Brad charges into an Indian trap and loses his life, leaving Wayne and Martin to continue alone.

"We'll find 'em just as sure as the turning of the earth," says Wayne, and the search for the remaining niece, Debbie, takes five years, the passage of time imaginatively conveyed by changes of costume and season and by such details as the letter of information that waits a year for Wayne to return and read it.

Martin Pawley's presence at Wayne's side gives us a sounding board to his real feelings and also explanations for such actions as Wayne's slaughtering of buffalo (to deprive the Comanches of meat for the winter). Martin brings to the surface Wayne's racial hatred of the Indian in his cutting observation at the start of the film, "Fellow could mistake you for a half-breed" (he is one eighth Cherokee), and voices the fear that Wayne will kill Debbie now that time has allowed her to become a Comanche squaw fully integrated into Indian life. Martin is also involved in some of the film's lighter moments as when he has to endure Wayne's cruel amusement at accidentally acquiring a fat Indian wife while bartering at a village; but even such moments give way to the film's more darkly dramatic side as when Wayne builds up the camp fire and Martin protests at the heat to be left as a decoy while Wayne slips way to deal with three ambushers hiding in the dark.

Eventually they locate Debbie at the camp of her family's murderer, Chief Scar (Henry Brandon). That night she sneaks out to tell them she doesn't want to

Martha's funeral. "There's no more time for praying. Amen!" Wayne strides away, anxious to go after the abducted girls.

Wayne and Jeffrey Hunter spot Debbie (Natalie Wood) in Chief Scar's tent as she displays his collection of scalps.

Wayne warns Jeffrey Hunter to get out of the way so that he can shoot Natalie Wood as Debbie.

153

leave. In a chilling moment, Wayne draws his gun on her and Martin moves to shield her, this moment of decision put off by the need to break away and retreat from attacking Indians. Back home, Wayne's determination to put a bullet in Debbie's skull receives the support of Martin's girl, Laurie Jergensen (Vera Miles), who says "It's too late. She's a woman full grown now. I tell you Martha would want him to." But Martin persists in trying to save Debbie and, when Clayton organises an attack on Scar's camp, he protests: "We go charging in there, they'll kill her and you know it." "That's what I'm counting on," comments Wayne. But Clayton gives Martin the chance to slip in ahead of the attack and he finds Debbie now anxious to be taken back.

The climax of the film occurs when the fighting is more or less over and the running Debbie comes face to face with Wayne, Martin being too far away to intervene. Martin cries out in alarm. There is a pause. Then Wayne says softly, "Let's go home, Debbie," and

Wayne brings Debbie (Natalie Wood) safely home again.

scoops her up to envelop her in his massive arms.

A last scene shows Wayne delivering Debbie to her old friends. He steps aside to let the others enter through a ranch door and is left there standing in the blazing sun. He makes no move to follow. There is an agonisingly sustained shot through the doorway which concludes with the door swinging shut, blacking out the image as its cuts Wayne off to wander away.

The moment that Wayne spares Debbie is one of the great, enduring moments of cinema. It works despite all the pointers to suggest that Wayne will attempt to kill her: Martin's fears, Laurie's support of the idea, Debbie's initial disowning of her past and her mother in wanting to be left with Scar, and perhaps most powerful of all the shot of Wayne's eyes staring in black-shadowed close-up at other captives rescued from the Comanches and hopelessly beyond readjustment to their former lives. But there is none of the uneasy stirring that Wayne's climactic change of heart as Thomas Dunson in *Red River* brings about.

The moment works initially because it is impossible to resist so affirmative a gesture of Wayne's humanity asserting itself over the demons of hate and destruction. Martin might have intervened to shoot Wayne, or Wayne might have gone ahead and killed Debbie, but these alternatives are intolerably bleak. Further, the whole film centres on Wayne's interior feelings and these have to be resolved from within. The sheer complexity of Wayne's feelings is far advanced from the simple *idée fixe* of Dunson in *Red River*, and this complexity makes for unpredictability. Five years worth of thoughts have ranged through Ethan Edwards's mind. Ultimately, of course, Ford is a poet and Hawks is a superb storyteller. For a poet who builds on emotions, unlike a storyteller working through logic and plot construction, anything is possible; and what Ford makes work, in *The Searchers* through Wayne, is indelibly moving. *The Searchers* is a great film by a great director — and Wayne becomes a great actor to fulfil his key place in it.

John Wayne as Ethan Edwards, the searcher.

59. The Wings of Eagles (1957)

WAYNE AND FORD teamed up again for *The Wings of Eagles*. It is certainly one of the director's lesser pictures, but that leaves it reels ahead of most other directors' work and, as always, Wayne is shown off at his best working for Ford. The film is an affectionate biography of Frank "Spig" Wead, an outstanding navy flyer who was crippled in a domestic accident and turned to writing before making a contribution to the Second World War effort. Among Wead's screenplays was Ford's *They Were Expendable* in which Wayne had appeared. Wead died in 1947 and Wayne plays him from a youthful flyer to the end of his war service. Maureen O'Hara plays Wead's wife, Min.

As a Wayne-O'Hara relationship, it is a typically "difficult" one with O'Hara resenting the demands made on Wayne by his navy career and his willing acquiescence to them. We are introduced to Wayne as a member of the navy's first regular flying class in 1919, already married with one child and in debt. He's an impulsive figure responding to the gibes of army flyers about one of the navy planes — "This pile of junk — can anybody get it up in the air?" — by taking an army man up on a daredevil flight for his first time in solo command of an aircraft. He buzzes the spectators on the ground, flies through a hangar, and when he runs out of

gas puts the plane down alongside the admiral's lawn tea party. Min watches helplessly from the ground and hopes he'll be kicked out of the navy but to no avail. As the years pass, they have two more children and keep on the move until Min finally rebels at one more change of house and they separate.

For the first time Wayne actually has a part in the knockabout comedy routines that Ford so enjoys inserting in his films. Previously, such scenes in *She Wore A Yellow Ribbon* and *The Searchers* served as light relief from the more serious story carried by Wayne. Here the low humour is based on army versus navy, the two sides competing in races to try and build up the country's air force. When the army are celebrating a victory in advance, Wayne and his team invade the dinner. We see Wayne delighting in excessively polite dialogue with the army leader (Kenneth Tobey) as a prelude to a cake-flinging punch-up that turns into a riot until the MPs make an appearance. Later when Wayne and his fellow flyers have taken the Schneider Cup in a seaplane race, it is the army's return to invade the celebrations and set off a return fracas.

Meanwhile Wayne has become a stranger to his two daughters. When he turns up unexpectedly to see them and his wife, the pair fail to recognise him. Min weeps to

Dan Dailey, Maureen O'Hara, John Wayne.

156

Convalescing in his wheelchair, Wayne is wheeled out by Dan Dailey for his first look at a real aircraft carrier, describes it as "a beautiful lady" and becomes angry with frustration.

see him again and willingly accepts his suggestion that they should grow up before their kids do and live together again. Here Ford draws on that strong sense of rapport between Wayne and O'Hara to make us believe in their frenzied embrace and feel the emotional warmth of them stretched out on a settee with one of the children innocently suggesting that they should go to bed. Ford then cuts discreetly to Wayne smoking contentedly in bed, establishing the success of their reconciliation. When one of his daughters cries out, he rushes to her and accidentally tumbles down the stairs, breaking his neck and losing all feeling in his back. As Min looks down anxiously, he tells her to call the hospital, then makes a small correction — call the *naval* hospital. That's the Ford hero, the Wayne figure, speaking most clearly.

There he willingly accepts a risky operation but is left stretched out on his stomach, largely paralysed. Ford draws comedy from the selection of old-maid nurses in attendance, and from the supply of forbidden liquor all

and sundry smuggle in. But, as the months go by, Wayne becomes increasingly irritated by his confinement, and it takes his old pal Carson (Dan Dailey), a mechanic, to instil some small hope of recovery. They start by trying to force life into Wayne's big toe by sheer brain power, the pair reciting "I'm gonna move that toe" to fever pitch. When the toe ultimately responds, Carson falls to the ground in a faint.

Wayne is still bedridden and turns to writing, piling up rejection slips. Carson brings him a wheelchair and takes him out into the open to see the navy's first big carrier in the harbour. "Take me back," Wayne asks sharply. Carson keeps up the rehabilitation programme and another pal (Ken Curtis) wangles an introduction to a film director seeking a writer for a picture about the navy's new carriers. The director is John Dodge (Ward Bond), made up to look and act as a mirror image of Ford himself, and installing Wayne in an office with the simple instructions, "Write about people — navy people." By this point, Spig Wead is ageing and Wayne has

157

Wayne discusses the possibility of becoming a scriptwriter with Ward Bond as the film director, John Dodge, made up to look and act like John Ford himself. Below, Bond and Ford are seen at a script conference (Bond at left) with Wayne (sans toupee) between them and cameraman Paul C. Vogel and producer Charles Schnee standing behind.

shed, for the first time, his toupee to become a balding figure. It's an unusual move for a star to make (Ray Milland caused quite a stir doing it in *Love Story*) but it fits in with Wayne's often-expressed devotion to Ford's every command. While Wayne is unavoidably less than convincing as the young trainee earlier on, he makes up for it in the later stages of the picture, and is even jovially labelled "fat" and "bald headed" to rub in the point when he has a reunion with Carson.

Wayne writes the picture for Dodge and we see footage of *Hell Divers* (1932) to represent it, with Clark Gable and Wallace Berry starring (Wead did contribute that film's story while George Hill, rather than Ford, directed). After authoring a successful play, Wayne returns to Min but immediately Pearl Harbour comes up and Min accepts the inevitable: "If they won't have you, Spig, I will," she says. The Navy take him on as an instructor and he struggles with a vague idea of what takes shape as "jeep" carriers when a friend plants the right word in his mind and then leaves him immersed in drawing up the scheme. He goes aboard one of the big carriers to see in operation his scheme for supporting "jeeps" to bring up replacements for aircraft lost in action. But the stress of war tells on him and he collapses after three days of tiring duty to be told by a doctor that he has only a short time to live. As he walks off the ship, his friends line up in farewell tribute, and Ford plays the scene with all the emotional stops out, Wayne moist-eyed and steeling his features to conceal his feelings at their goodbyes.

It is a warm, touching, humorous picture, expanded beyond its formula biography approach by Ford to encompass the broad humour and rich emotions that mean so much to the director. But the inevitably episodic nature of the film, its wide time span, its cocooning of Wead in fond memory, make too slight a basis for Ford's responses and for Wayne to register really memorably.

An American in Russia: John Wayne with Janet Leigh as the ace Soviet airwoman in Jet Pilot *(see overleaf).*

60. Jet Pilot (1957)

WHEN *Jet Pilot* finally blazed across the screen nearly eight years after principal shooting, it lingered barely long enough to be recognized. In Britain, it bypassed the West End to take a quick spin through the Gaumont circuit and shortly after disappeared. In America, too, it has not been seen for some years. Both this film and *The Conqueror* have become the personal property of Howard Hughes who initially sold them along with the rest of RKO Radio Pictures and then bought them back for a reputed incredible figure of twelve million dollars.

The Conqueror was absurd enough but *Jet Pilot* caps it as the most ludicrous film of Wayne's career. The British distributors must have thought much the same in keeping it back from the newspaper critics. Audiences can only have rubbed their eyes at Wayne's apparently rejuvenated appearance, at the twenty-two-year-old Janet Leigh as an ace pilot of the Russian Air Force, and at the delectable lunacy of the storyline. The film has a perfection of sorts to show from its long period of gestation with continual technical updating; but it's an isolated perfection that no other film would seek to rival.

John Wayne is called on to represent the American way of life and Janet Leigh's Russian just naturally defects to him at the end, leaving a repressive Russia that seems to have been borrowed from *Ninotchka*. Wayne is Colonel Shannon of the Air Force and he's delegated to show Janet Leigh's Anna around when she turns up at an Alaskan air base with a story of wanting political asylum. He is allowed to show her some of the secrets of the new American planes and the pair demonstrate their flying skill to each other. From mutual admiration comes mutual affection with Wayne marrying her to ensure her acceptance into his country. The Secret Service establishes that Anna was sent to lure Wayne back to Russia, and when he falls in with the scheme it is part of a counterplot he has concocted with the authorities. It is not long before Anna sees her homeland in a new light and is soon hankering to get back to the U.S.A. She escapes with Wayne and they end up in Palm Springs sinking their teeth into oversized steaks (symbolising the goodness and generosity of American life), Wayne pausing to tell her to wipe the gravy off her chin before administering a fadeout kiss.

Among the more risible moments in the film are the scene where Wayne attempts to search Anna in the chartroom after her first arrival (echoed later in *Rio Bravo*, part scripted by *Jet Pilot's* writer Jules Furthman, when Angie Dickinson challenges Wayne to search her), and a scene where Anna emerges from a bath clad in a towel to warm up in front of a stove — both ludicrous because they raise erotic possibilities the film cannot develop. But most memorable of all is the moment when Anna delivers a knock-out blow to Wayne's chin! The film just had to be laughed *at*, not laughed *with* — if it was envisaged as a hilarious comedy it does too good a job of concealing its hand.

61. Legend of the Lost (1957)

WHILE Wayne was merely acting in *Jet Pilot* and *The Conqueror*, he has less excuse for being seen in *Legend of the Lost* as his own company, Batjac, co-produced it with a leading Italian outfit. This ridiculous desert melodrama has the benefit of Jack Cardiff's magnificent Technirama—Technicolor photography and an eerie, echoing score by A.F. Lavagnino, while Sophia Loren must have seemed powerful box-office bait alongside Wayne (he was here getting the same kind of help from a younger generation of star as he had provided for long-established leading ladies after *Stagecoach*). Unfortunately, Miss Loren's efforts count for little in the face of the feeble script and her curiously scraggy appearance. Wayne relaxes into his role, never one to betray any dissatisfaction with a shallow part, and Rossano Brazzi is lumbered with the most idiotic aspects of the film.

Wayne portrays Joe January, an American derelict trapped in Timbuktu and first seen cooling off in jail after rather too exuberant a celebration of the Fourth of July. He is recommended by the corrupt Prefect of Police (Kurt Kasznar) as the ideal guide for Paul Bonnard (Rossano Brazzi) who wants to make an expedition into the desert. Guaranteed enough money to escape for good from Timbuktu, Wayne takes the job. Bonnard is beseeched by a local chippie, Dita (Sophia Loren), to take her along after he has sympathised with her plight. He refuses but she follows them on foot and gains acceptance. At camp one night Bonnard reveals that his purpose is to locate a hoard of riches found by his father years before. Wayne roars with laughter at the idea of being taken on a treasure hunt. "We're out in the middle of nowhere looking for nothing in the wrong season," he cries, turns to his mule to add "Damn it, you have a pal on this trip, a fellow jackass — that's me!" and heehaws. It's a good job this analysis of the situation comes before the real absurdities of the film are apparent, otherwise a chorus of heehaws could have been expected from the audience.

The whole film falls apart in Bonnard's Jekyll-and-Hyde transformation from a sympathetic idealist, dreaming of building a medical centre to the memory of his doctor father, into a raving lunatic when he discovers some sordid truths about his father's weakness of character. Just as his father and his guide fought over a

Left, John Wayne as the cowboy in Africa. Above, Wayne examines the skeletons from a previous doomed expedition. Below, a passionate moment with Sophia Loren.

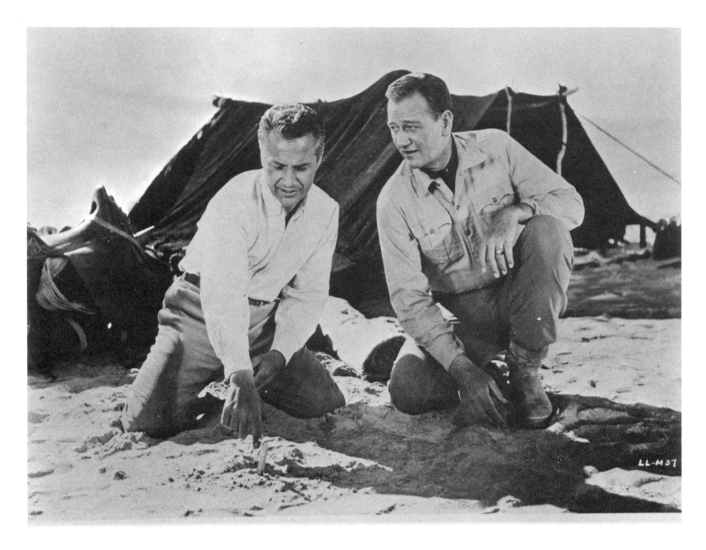

Rossano Brazzi as the idealist conferring with Wayne.

girl they had taken along on their trip (a deduction Wayne makes from the skeletons they discover), so Bonnard suspects that history is repeating itself and Wayne and Dita will steal the riches they have (to Wayne's surprise) discovered. Bonnard takes all the supplies and abandons the other two. They trudge after him and find him still barely alive, clutching the treasure. When he attempts to kill Wayne, Dita shoots him dead, and the pair make amends for the film's previously unsympathetic attitude towards Bonnard's distress by Wayne speaking of him as having been a good guy really. And since he has brought Wayne and Dita together, Wayne thanks him for "a good finish" as the pair settle down to die only to be rescued by a passing caravan immediately afterwards in the last of the film's shameless contrivances.

Wayne's part, built on cynicism and jealousy, is too one-dimensionally boorish and uncouth to be very interesting. Sophia Loren puts up a lively performance against Wayne, even taking a kick from his boot but conking him with a frying pan and wading in with her fists — but her energies are wasted in the context of so dismal a picture.

62. I Married a Woman (1958)

WAYNE next cropped up as a guest star playing himself in a dreary George Gobel — Diana Dors comedy, *I Married a Woman*. Gobel plays the advertising man whose career gets in the way of his marriage to the model played by Dors. Her favourite movie star and idea of a man is John Wayne. There is a sequence in which she goes to the cinema and watches Wayne and Angie Dickinson playing in an imaginary film called *Forever and Forever and Forever* in very wide screen and colour (the rest of the film is in black-and-white RKO-Scope). Then at the end of the film Wayne appears as a passenger aboard a ship, being tracked down by his wife who has been looking everywhere for him. She accuses him of never thinking of anything but making pictures. Dors' disillusionment with her hero is completed when he falls in behind his wife with unexpected docility, saying "O.K., honey" rather than arguing with her. The idea of Wayne guying his image falls as flat as the rest of this weak undertaking — the kind of picture that put an end to RKO Radio.

George Gobel talks to Wayne as their wives wait (Diana Dors at left).

Above, John Wayne as Townsend Har and Eiko Ando as the geisha.

Left, Wayne organises the burning of a village to stamp out an epidemic.

63. The Barbarian and the Geisha (1958)

HERE was a distinctly offbeat undertaking by both Wayne and 20th Century-Fox. It has most to do with director John Huston's liking for challenges in subject matter and methods of production. Known initially as *The Townsend Harris Story,* it was the story of the American sent by President Pierce on a five thousand mile journey to enter Japan as the first Consul-General in 1856 under a treaty forced on that country by American military might. Japan was then totally isolated from world trade and hostile to all foreigners. The film also depicts Harris's legendary (and fictional) association with a geisha — a more promising selling angle for the film as recognised by its final title. Fox allowed Huston to shoot the picture entirely in Japan, assigning their remote locations specialist, Charles G. Clarke, as cameraman. Through it does not look a particularly

expensive undertaking, there were many difficulties in giving the settings a proper period look and it cost a million dollars just to pay Wayne and Huston (the actor was guaranteed almost $700,000 for fourteen weeks work, the director got $300,000). The project finally cost over three and a half million, the greatest amount ever spent on a film in Japan to that time. The resulting picture caused barely a ripple and has become one of the more obscure films of Wayne's career.

To Huston, Wayne was ideal casting for Townsend Harris: "I want to send Duke's gigantic form into the exotic world that was the Japanese empire in the 1880s. Imagine! — this massive figure, with his bluff innocence and *naiveté*, with his edges rough, moving among these minute people. Who better to symbolise the big, awkward United States of one hundred years ago?" To

Wayne looks uncomfortable amid the film's picturesque trappings.

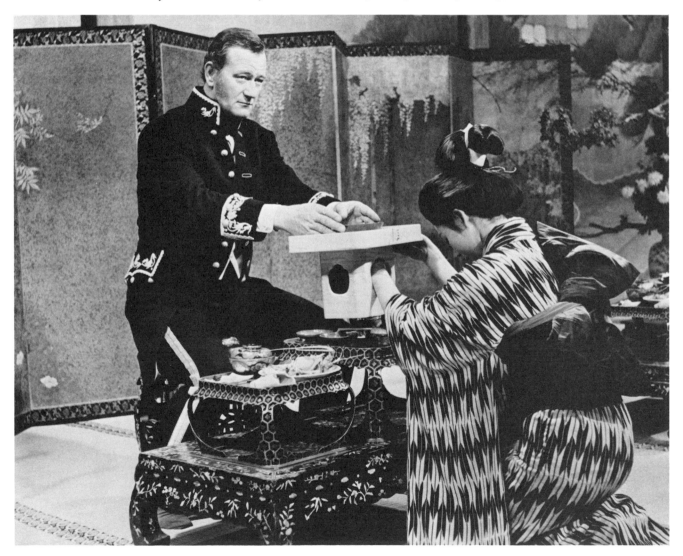

A lighter moment between Wayne and Eiko Ando.

reinforce the contrast that Huston saw, he cast 5'7'' tall Eiko Ando opposite the 6'4'' of Wayne and had a line in the script from Wayne's interpreter, "I think, Mr. Harris, we had better raise the doorways or cut off your legs."

As detailed earlier in the chapter "Working With Wayne," the relationship between Wayne and the dogmatic, tough, quirky Huston was a strained one with the actor feeling that his image was being destroyed. The resulting film certainly did not attract his fans in their usual numbers, and it is indeed one to disappoint audiences wanting the traditional strong, action-laden type of narrative. It is a quiet, leisurely attempt to evoke the period, a film of considerable pictorial beauty, superficial in its handling of the subject but drawing respect for its integrity and unusual story.

The film very largely rests on Wayne's capacious shoulders as, apart from Sam Jaffe's Henry Heusken as his interpreter and adviser, he is the only Western player in the cast — an anchor of familiarity in the strange world of Japanese feudalism and its strict code of honour. Wayne's dialogue is often couched in the rather stilted language of diplomacy. When questioned by the Japanese lords on slavery in the United States, he says "There are men in my country who would die to end that evil. It cannot long endure." Now it would be idle to pretend that such lines just roll off Wayne's tongue but the actor's inherent sense of honesty and sincerity does much to overcome their awkwardness and there is no reason to suppose that Harris should have been at ease with the conversational aspect of his mission (we are really told very little about his background qualifications). But such is the strength of Wayne's image that we expect him to be at home with his dialogue and not decked out in such costumes as close-fitting breeches, and it is undoubtedly true that more stereotype casting would have meant an actor like Gregory Peck taking the part.

One of the film's most unusual scenes concerns Wayne taking on some Japanese warriors, battering down a giant samurai with his fists but being thrown about with ease by a tiny Judo expert and left sitting on the ground with a nonplussed look at the surprise and indignity of his defeat. Wayne was troubled by how his fans would take this but it doesn't seem at all destructive of what Wayne stands for, given the circumstances.

The way in which Harris has to bide his time also opposes the traditional Wayne image of a man who forces events, or at least has events to react to. He is given accommodation in a derelict temple, ignored by the townspeople on orders from the local governor, instructed to take down the American flag he has raised, and becomes increasingly irritable at the five months' delay in hoping that his papers will be forwarded to the capital instead of being held by Tamura (So Yamamura), who provides one of his geishas, Okichi (Eiko Ando), to help him and also spy on him.

The Japanese suspicion of foreigners seems justified when men from a cholera-infested ship swim ashore, despite Wayne's efforts to stop them, and spread the disease before they can be rounded up. Many of the villagers die and Wayne burns down infected houses to stamp out the cholera. When his action is explained, Tamura responds by allowing Wayne to proceed to the capital, Yedo, just as he is about to give up. Here he finds the lords divided on the proposals he brings with him but, after a miscalculated assassination of one of the principal supporters, the others vote in his favour. By now, Wayne and Okichi have fallen in love and she helps prevent Tamura from killing him after he has reluctantly been ordered to make a last attempt to stop Wayne from completing his mission. Now that she has betrayed her lord and master, she has to leave Wayne for ever and can only watch from a distance his triumphant progress through the crowds to gain the Emperor's signature on the treaty.

64. Rio Bravo (1959)

RIO BRAVO was only Wayne's second film for Howard Hawks. But like the first, *Red River*, it stands out from Wayne's crowded career. A long, leisurely-seeming Western, it eschews suspense in favour of developing its team of heroes and heroine, exploring the way they relate to each other. The bad guys are an undistinguished lot who pose a threat largely by their number. The film seems stereotyped with the players donning custom-made roles that they can relax in; the one relative unknown, Angie Dickinson, fits in with a long line of Hawks heroines; the basic situation is from page one of the Western plot book. But there is a rare warmth and subtlety about the picture. It never seizes you emotionally, Hawks employing his customary detached style; it never strives for effect and never overwhelms. But it leaves one thinking back on it with quiet pleasure; and it is this lingering delight in a job so immaculately done that has given *Rio Bravo* its place as one of the classic Westerns.

It is well known that *Rio Bravo* partly originated in rebuttal of *High Noon*. There the marshal (Gary Cooper) begged the community for help to carry out the job they paid him to do, failed to get assistance (except for one timely intervention by the heroine) and found he was up to handling the situation by himself. Here the sheriff, John T. Chance (Wayne), refuses all but selected help, gets more than he expects (including one timely intervention by the heroine), and finds he needs it to get the job done. The tortured sensitivity of Cooper's Will Kane is unimaginable from Wayne who replaces it with Chance's stubborn independence and unwavering courage.

Wayne's introduction is a memorable one — a rare subjective shot, showing him looking down on his former deputy and stopping him from humiliating himself by recovering a dollar piece from a spittoon to buy a drink. The deputy is Dean Martin's Dude, an alcoholic laughing stock, who pulls himself together to help Wayne arrest Joe Burdette (Claude Akins) for murder and gets another crack at his old job.

Joe's influential brother, Nathan (John Russell), bottles the town up tight while he tries to figure a way to spring his brother from jail knowing that Wayne's garrulous, cantankerous jailkeeper Stumpy (Walter Brennan) is ready to shoot Joe if any rescue attempt is made.

Wayne waits for the arrival of the circuit judge and watches over Dude, suggesting a turn around the town when his nerves are telling on him in the sheriff's office. On the patrol, Wayne asserts his powerful presence on one of Burdette's watchers and stares him into an embarrassed retreat. His old friend Pat Wheeler (Ward Bond) arrives in town and asks incredulously whether a game-legged old jailkeeper and a drunk are all he's got on his side. "That's *what* I've got," replies Wayne, emphasising the positive. He turns down Wheeler's own offer of help because he's not good enough and would cause worry, but he agrees that he could use Wheeler's young gunhand, Colorado Ryan (Ricky Nelson), and compliments the lad on his good sense in declining to take part in somebody else's business.

Angie Dickinson's Feathers initially appears as a diversion from the main story. She is splendidly introduced catching Wayne holding his Mexican friend Carlos's gift for his young wife, a pair of red pants, against his figure, causing her to observe: "Those things have great possibilities — but not for you." She

Wayne discusses his problems with old friend Ward Bond.

Wayne in a shootout with Ricky Nelson and talking with Dean Martin.

again disconcerts Wayne by challenging him to search her for some missing aces after she has played in a rigged card game, transferring her embarrassment at the situation on to him. When her innocence is established, Wayne refuses to apologise ("Never apologise — it's a sign of weakness," he might have said) and it is she who expresses regret for causing him bother on top of his troubles with Burdette. She continues to stand up to Wayne, however, guarding him without his knowledge while he takes some rest, refusing to leave town, and co-operating with Colorado to get Wayne out of a tight spot when he is caught unprepared by some of Burdette's men outside Carlos's saloon. She flings a flowerpot through a window to distract the men while Colorado throws a weapon to Wayne and the pair dispose of the bunch. Colorado now joins the team as an official deputy.

Burdette's men manage a second time to catch Wayne, and Dude, unawares. Dude's quick thinking rescues Wayne but leaves him a hostage for Joe. Wayne owes Dude too much not to agree to trade Joe for his deputy at Burdette's warehouse (near where earlier Pat Wheeler has stowed away a consignment of dynamite). Wayne intends to manage the trade alone but Colorado insists on accompanying him and Stumpy takes unkindly to being left behind because he's crippled.

But all the men join together to defeat Burdette during the trade. Dude leaps on Joe as they pass each other and knocks him cold, taking refuge behind an adobe wall. Stumpy turns up anyway to fire his shotgun into

some of Burdette's men creeping round behind Wayne and Colorado. Carlos arrives with an extra supply of shells and Colorado starts looking for the girl with another flowerpot. Using Wheeler's sticks of dynamite, they soon blast Nathan Burdette into submission.

Wayne's John T. Chance is the head of a team, the one whose strength and leadership binds the rest together. He takes pride in *what* he's got, looking on with a benevolent smile in the song sequence where Dean Martin and Ricky Nelson perform with Walter Brennan playing a mouth organ accompaniment — the group expressing a happy unity. He's there to rally Dude when he starts to get the shakes, and he is only cruel to be kind, taking Dude down a notch when he becomes over-confident in a hurry and reminding Stumpy he's a cripple to stop him taking undue risks. Wayne repays Stumpy for his support by planting a kiss of gratitude on the old man's forehead after the latter demands some respect — the kind of exaggerated comical touch that contrasts with Wayne's small gestures of warm affection and shows, as they do, that he finds it difficult to display his feelings openly. This is even more true with Feathers who has to fight through this emotional reticence.

It is she who first kisses him rather than the reverse, and observes after a further try: "I'm glad we tried it a second time. It's better when two people do it." He does eventually admit that he's glad she stayed on but goes no further. So she dresses up in a revealing costume for a job she's taken as a hostess in Carlos's

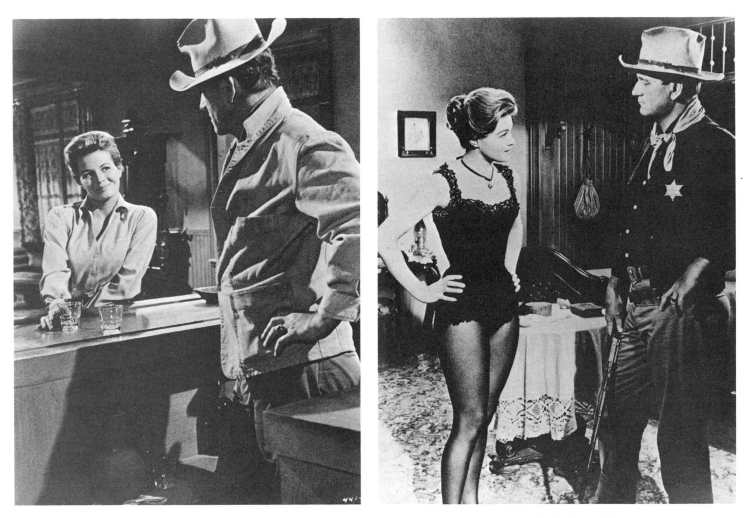

Wayne is provoked by Angie Dickinson as Feathers, seen at right in the costume which draws his roundabout confession of love for her.

saloon. She tells him, "I'm hard to get, John T., you're gonna have to say you want me." She prepares to go downstairs in her scanty outfit and Wayne tells her "You'd better not." She presses him for a reason. "You wear those things and I'll arrest you" is the best he can manage. She turns back, tears streaming down her face, saying "I thought you were never going to say it." "Say what?" asks Wayne. "That you love me." "I said I'd arrest you," replies Wayne. "It means the same thing," she declares. "You know that, you just won't say it."

Angie Dickinson's provocative manner makes her an ideal romantic partner for Wayne who had recommended her to Hawks, and subsequently employed her on one of his company's productions, *Gun the Man Down*. Here Hawks realises her potential in a stunning

way and her relationship with Wayne gives his part an extra dimension outside his more confined role within the main plot.

It remains to observe one small development in Wayne's combative style: the way he hits a Burdette man in the face with a rifle, telling an alarmed Dude, "Aw, I'm not gonna hurt him!" This — a relatively gentle precursor of the increasing violence in the Western — has become a familiar aspect of Wayne's fighting repertoire, applied to guest actor George Plimpton in *Rio Lobo* and extended to kicking Strother Martin in the face in *The Man Who Shot Liberty Valance*, among other examples. By the time of *Big Jake* and *The Cowboys*, violence in the Wayne Western has become gruesome and painful but *Rio Bravo* keeps it stylised in the old tradition.

65. The Horse Soldiers (1959)

THOUGH it reunited Ford and Wayne in a near-Western Civil War subject, *The Horse Soldiers* is one of their weaker collaborations. Here Ford was working solely as a contract director sandwiched between John Lee Mahin and Martin Rackin as writers and producers and he may not have been quite as free to elaborate on his basic material as he would have been making the film for his own production company. He certainly finds opportunities to handle scenes with his characteristic warmth and tenderness (no one will forget the sad yet splendid march by the youngsters of the Military Academy against the Union forces), but he is saddled with a rather superficial script and set of characters. Though visually the film is superb, it is too closely tied to its weak story.

John Wayne plays Colonel John Marlowe, who is assigned to lead a mission deep into Confederate territory during the Civil War to destroy the enemy's line of railroad communication through Newton Station. Here Wayne is not a career officer but a former railroad worker, so the mission is not an appetising one for him. William Holden is Major Hank Kendall, the medical officer who is part of Wayne's band and constantly clashes with him. Wayne worries about losing time

while Holden demands it to care for his wounded. This makes Wayne seem rather stern and unyielding (he is called "Old Ironhead" at one point by Holden) but he is also a gentleman who displays great gallantry when he has to take over the home of a Southern lady, Hannah Hunter (Constance Towers). After she spies on an officers' meeting, Wayne is forced to take her along to prevent her revealing his plans. She resents his orders that she should be watched at all times and shows her mettle by taking a sock at him.

Wayne has his sympathetic side. In the battle at Newton Station, he cries almost hysterically, "I didn't want this, I tried to avoid a fight," as his men decimate an advancing line of Confederate troops pouring off a train. He comforts the dying soldier Hoskins and he hits two excessively co-operative Confederate deserters in disgust. And, in a scene in a bar at Newton Station, we belatedly learn the reason for his hostility towards Kendall when, much the worse for drink, he reveals that two doctors operated on his wife for a suspected but non-existent tumour and killed her while he had to force a leather strap into her mouth to stop her screams. This experience causes him to believe that Kendall is more concerned with his own reputation than helping

170

Above left, Wayne and William Holden slug it out in the forest. Right, Althea Gibson as ''Lukey'' lies dying from a Confederate bullet. Wayne talks with Holden as William Leslie comforts her and Constance Towers watches.

Wayne discusses strategy with Willis Bouchey.

A drunken Wayne angrily explains his hatred of doctors to Constance Towers.

his fellow men. Wayne brings all that intense, pent-up bitterness he can so ably convey to this scene, yet it is an awkward one — misplaced in the film as an explanation for Wayne's feelings toward Kendall after we have already accepted it as a conflict between military and medical demands, and over dramatised by having Wayne drunk to say it when a quiet, calm statement of Wayne's reason for disliking all doctors to Kendall at the start would have worked better.

Wayne and the doctor first endeavour to settle their differences by a fist fight after Wayne has flung a cup of water into the other's face. Their fracas is broken up by an enemy attack during which Wayne is shot in the leg and therefore forced to submit to Kendall's care (much to the latter's delight) but carries on issuing orders while on the operating table, showing his measure as a man. Hannah is on hand to carefully cut away his twenty-dollar boot while he stares at her in recognition of her tender care and refuses whisky, preferring to grimace with pain as the bullet is removed from his leg. As he hobbles off, he stops to try a conciliatory word of thanks but Kendall hurriedly orders him out to get on with his job. Later, when Kendall decides to stay behind with the wounded in Confederate territory and risk

imprisonment in the notorious prison at Andersonville, Wayne offers a farewell handshake which is accepted and the two men part. "So long, croaker," says Wayne warmly. "So long, sectionhand," responds Kendall.

There are also farewell scenes between Wayne and Hannah. While the role of so fiery, stubborn and independent a Southern woman would have far better suited Maureen O'Hara, Ford uses Constance Towers well in the two parting scenes. In one Wayne takes off his hat, the gentleman again, and says his goodbye, apologising for the hardships she has suffered, and has her briefly cling to him for protection when there is a sudden outburst of enemy artillery fire; in the other, Wayne admits to the hold she has gained over him, though in a slightly but characteristically roundabout way, by telling her "It so happens [i.e. he didn't cause it] that I'm in love with you," and taking her headscarf as a souvenir. Then, when he has blown a bridge to thwart the Southern troops and ridden off, we see her looking at him and then into the distance. These scenes are backed by the use of the "Ann Rutledge" theme from *Young Mr. Lincoln* again, with its moving sense of bitter-sweet poignancy.

66. The Alamo (1960)

WAYNE produced, directed and took a leading role in *The Alamo* as the realisation of a cherished dream. To Wayne, the heroic defence of a crumbling fortress in 1836 against overwhelming Mexican opposition represented one of the most glorious episodes in American history; it was a moment when, as the opening titles put it, Americans had to choose between accepting oppression and making a stand for liberty. It was a defeat that contained the seeds of victory as the men who died at the Alamo gained valuable time for the Americans to consolidate their forces and overthrow the dictator Santa Anna at San Jacinto a few weeks later.

As has been mentioned, Wayne almost made the film some ten years before. He had found a site in Panama that ideally represented the San Antonio area of Texas and gained Republic's support for the project, only to be let down when the studio chief, Herbert J. Yates, got cold feet over the expense of the picture. Wayne continued to explore the possibilities of making the film. A few years later he was in Peru, looking for suitable locations, and met his present wife Pilar who was starring in a local film production. Shortly after, Republic went ahead with a film on the subject after all, but without Wayne. It was directed by veteran Frank Lloyd and called *The Last Command* with Sterling Hayden as Jim Bowie, Arthur Hunnicutt as Davy Crockett and Richard Carlson as Col. Travis. It was a proficient, sometimes exciting film but a far cry from the epic Wayne was to make. Nevertheless, it must have ruled out a second film on the same subject for a while. (Republic, incidentally, had made the other major talkie about the Alamo, *Man of Conquest*, back in 1939.)

During the Fifties, Wayne had largely worked at Warner Bros. as producer and star, but his relationship with the company was deteriorating and he moved to United Artists. Part of his new deal involved that company financing *The Alamo* and from early 1959 Wayne was busy setting it up to be filmed around Brackettville, Texas. He assigned the script to his close friend and most trusted writer, James Edward Grant, who was

John Wayne as Davy Crockett.

173

also to function as associate producer during filming.

The production cost six and a half million dollars to make and when it overran its original budget Wayne was compelled to mortgage Batjac, his production company, and put over a million dollars of his own money into it to ensure completion. The film was not a great sucess critically or commercially on first release but has proved a strong attraction on subsequent cinema reissues and TV screenings. Wayne, however, sold out his interest in the picture to United Artists soon after its first run and it was the latter company that benefited when the film finally showed a profit. Wayne has said that he eventually recouped his financial stake but gained nothing for his work as producer, director and star.

The screenwriter Borden Chase (*Red River*) has expressed the view that Wayne's efforts were decried in advance by people out to get their own back on Wayne for his strong support of blacklisting (Wayne feels there is a little truth in this assertion). John Ford came down to work on the film directing a second unit (the book "Ford on Ford" quotes him saying "We got some wonderful scenes — guys swimming rivers, that sort of thing — but they were all cut out") and he later announced "It's the greatest picture I've ever seen. It will last for ever, run for ever..." One reviewer, John Cutts in "Films and Filming," quoted that last sentence of Ford's and added "May I humbly suggest to Mr. Ford...that...the film only *seems* to last forever." Clearly United Artists agreed that the film was overlong and, like most epics of its time, it was gradually cut down, losing some fifty-two minutes for its mass release version. Among scenes usually absent now is a knife-fight sequence featuring Richard Widmark's Jim Bowie.

The Alamo does have its adherents: British writer Douglas McVay found it one of the few films to have the essential qualities of the epic and bracketed it with *The Battleship Potemkin, Alexander Nevsky* and *The Seven Samurai* in this respect concluding (in issue 6 of "Motion") that it was "a tale of bold endeavour in the great poetic tradition of 'Maldon' or the 'Chanson de Roland'."

Speaking for myself, I must take a middle road. *The Alamo* has, to my mind, one of the great screen battles for its climax (perhaps largely the work of the official second unit director, Cliff Lyons) but most of what precedes it is dull though watchable. It is by no means the worst of Hollywood's epics but both as a commercial and artistic venture it does have serious flaws.

Commercially speaking, it has the problem of being most immediately about a *defeat*, regardless of how it ultimately ensured victory. The film's heroes meet vivid deaths at the hands of the Mexicans — Wayne's Davy Crockett is bayoneted to a door, at least managing to ignite the powder store as he falls, Jim Bowie dies gruesomely while being stabbed by a horde of Santa Anna's men. While the film tells us that the Mexicans are oppressors and we hear a little in support of this, we don't respond to them as real villains and they are portrayed as chivalrous opponents, perhaps from con-siderations of not damaging present-day American-Mexican relations and obtaining playing time for the film in Mexico. As a result the film seems rather to portray a local squabble down Texas way than a great fight for freedom from unendurable oppression.

Wayne understandably chose to play a subsidiary role to relieve the pressure on him as director and producer. The film's central figure is Col. Travis, the commander, and he is portrayed as a rather tiresome boor. Laurence Harvey's performance brings out strongly the cutting, cynical, conceited side of the character but hardly makes him the most winning advocate of the fight for freedom even though he gains respect for his strength of purpose, dedication to his task, and his sense of chivalry and honour. Neither Wayne as Davy Crockett nor Richard Widmark as Jim Bowie are much developed as characters and Wayne would have been better off in the latter part (fine though Widmark is). Davy Crockett is represented as a shrewd and loquacious ex-politician, a Tennesseean renowned for his wit and masquerading as a simple figure. Wayne is too direct and laconic for this kind of role: though acting friendly enough, he is not the right man to suggest a fund of tall stories and a natural talent for mixing with people. Arthur Hunnicutt's casting in *The Last Command* or Fess Parker's portrayal in Disney's *Davy Crockett, King of the Wild Frontier* seem much nearer the mark and, had the film's script done a better job of developing Crockett as a born wit, I can visualise Andy Griffith fitting the role well with an admittedly offbeat opportunity.

Wayne does a very proficient job of direction but it requires a bit more than this to maintain sharp interest on a film of this length. Most epics fall down in this department with only a director of the technical resourcefulness and analytical command of an Anthony Mann (*El Cid, The Fall of the Roman Empire*) or Stanley Kubrick (*Spartacus*) able to fight off tedium. Wayne is weakest in the comedy interludes, especially that concerning his own rescue of Linda Cristal's Flaca from the unwelcome attentions of a landgrabber (Wesley Lau) which is handled in a very heavy, plodding manner. Wayne's camera style is straightforward and he rarely if ever moves it dramatically so that an isolated shot from high up a massive tree, looking down on himself and Flaca, rather jars. No doubt, Wayne was influenced by the unshowy styles of Ford and Hawks but they have usually ensured that their scripts were stronger than that of *The Alamo*.

Frankly, James Edward Grant's script is just not imaginative enough. It's cluttered and woolly, making nonsense of the claim in the film's souvenir brochure that Grant is "one of the few who realise that a good screen writer must be a 'miser with words'." It's debatable whether dialogue is ever an adequate means of evoking the point of a film — actions speak louder than words. Certainly, Grant's words are inadequate where the film's key speeches are concerned.

There is one in which Wayne is discussing with Travis the plan to declare Texas a republic free of Mexican rule. "Republic," says Wayne thoughtfully,

Above, Richard Widmark as Jim Bowie, Laurence Harvey as Colonel Travis, Wayne as Davy Crockett. Below, Wayne's farewell scene with Linda Cristal and his death at the Alamo.

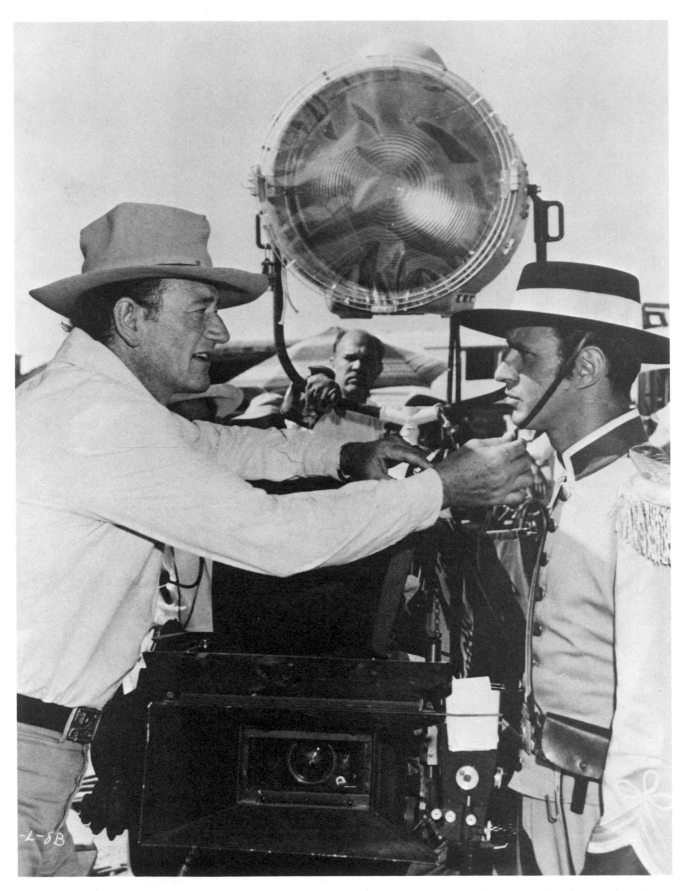

Wayne makes some small adjustments to the appearance of a Mexican soldier during production of The Alamo.

176

"I like the sound of the word. Means people can live free, talk free, go or come, buy or sell, be drunk or sober, however they choose. Some words give you a feeling. Republic is one of those words that makes me tight in the throat." As though unable to choose how to express the point, Grant even has Wayne make another stab at it a couple of sentences later, declaring that the word "gives you a feeling that makes your heart warm." The word in itself is hardly one that sounds attractive enough to produce any such feeling and seems a poor basis for the argument while the definition is hardly inspired either.

Later, in a scene with Flaca, Wayne has another passage that is clearly vital to the film in which he talks about the need to feel useful and do right in this world. In case the words aren't riveting enough (and they're not), Wayne asks Flaca to "listen tight" (i.e. the audience should too) and then tells her "As a matter of fact, I'm talking about all people everywhere" (to ensure that the audience realises that the message is aimed at them) and even heads off criticism by admitting "I may sound like a preacher yelling up a revival meeting but that don't change the truth none." The message is so simplistic and wrapped up in such awful phrases as having Wayne refer to a lifetime that hasn't seemed "worth the pain of the mother that bore me," that the scene doesn't seem worth the trouble of the man that wrote it. As Sam Goldwyn is supposed to have said, "Leave the messages to Western Union." The old cliché, "There are some things a man's just got to do,"

has a lot to commend it, leaving the actions to speak for themselves. Wayne should breathe the cause, not drum it up in words.

When Wayne does dispatch Flaca to safety before the final confrontation, he tells her "That's what's written, that's what's written. When it's time it's time." At moments like this, the film does seem to be running forever. But there is, just after Flaca has gone, a small example of Wayne's strength as a performer. The Parson (Hank Worden) asks Wayne, "You never pray, do you?" "I never found the time," he replies, speaking the line with a husky heaviness that doesn't so much answer the question as convey his bitter feeling at losing Flaca.

Apart from the powerful battle, *The Alamo* does have some impressive moments and it again reflects adversely on the script that these are based on silence. There is the aftermath of an earlier battle when women are seen on the battlefield looking for their men, wounded soldiers are being helped away, and a line of injured men are being bathed and helped at the riverbank. And on the night before the last fight, there is a short sequence of close-ups of many of the men inside the fort quietly reflecting and Wayne then being asked what he's thinking and softly replying "Just rememb'ring, that's all." This line gives the audience something to work on instead of spelling it out, and these scenes momentarily catch the kind of poetry that was second nature to John Ford.

67. North to Alaska (1960)

THIS is a bouncy, richly enjoyable comedy that set a pattern for most of Wayne's films since, showing him fully at ease with humorous material and marking the beginning of a much broader style to his playing. It was conceived as an old-fashioned adventure but director Henry Hathaway opted for a lighter treatment and with an excellent cast produced a small gem of lighthearted entertainment at a time when Hollywood seemed to have all but lost its flair for that kind of thing.

It casts Wayne as Sam McCord who, with his partner George Pratt (Stewart Granger), has struck it rich in the goldfields around Nome. He is dispatched to bring back the latter's French *fiancée* from Seattle while George builds a honeymoon cabin for the girl he hasn't seen in three years. Wayne's Sam is a genial, fun-loving figure with a deep mistrust of women, having been almost trapped into matrimony twice. He tells his partner, "The wonderful thing about Alaska is that matrimony hasn't hit up here yet — let's keep it a free country!" but he dutifully sets out to fulfil his errand only to find that George's girl has married someone else. While relaxing with some of the "ladies" in a honky tonk and declaring that "Any woman who devotes herself to making one man miserable instead of a lot of men happy don't get my vote," he is struck by the somewhat aloof

Michelle (Capucine) and engages her, being French and classy, to substitute for George's disloyal flame. "A Frenchie broke his heart, a Frenchie can fix it," he reasons, but forgets to explain that he's taking her along for George's benefit and not his own. She warms to Wayne at a logger's picnic where he wins a pole-climbing contest and is too drunk to reply to a toast in the celebrations, waking up on his way back to Nome with Michelle taking care of him. She has a fit of depression when Wayne's scheme becomes clear to her, and the hardy old woman-hater can't understand why a game of cards won't snap her out of it. "Women — peculiar," he mutters. By the time they have reached Nome, he has begun to appreciate her a bit more and tries to call off his deal, but she decides to revert to her old way of life and provide George with the necessary comforts, learning that he is both rich and good-looking. Though George first flies off the handle at Wayne's letting him down, he starts to warm to Michelle and soon realises that she isn't really interested in him but loves Wayne. He hatches a plot to bring them together and takes her to the honeymoon cabin, leaving Wayne and George's kid brother (Fabian) to keep each other company. Wayne takes to drink and counts the minutes, becoming increasingly

177

Wayne and Stewart Granger involved in a boisterous brawl.

irritable as time passes and the pangs of jealousy bite home when the sounds of merriment from across the way reach his ears. Wayne starts fomenting about women in general, takes a bath to cool down, and George comes out briefly to take a look at him, reporting back to Michelle: "It won't be long now. He's in his silent period. I saw him once like this before when somebody had stolen his favourite horse." By now Wayne is turning green and when George coaxes a laugh out of the despairing Michelle, Wayne finally boils over, sweeping the bottles from the table in front of him, standing up, uttering a war whoop, and charging across to the other cabin like a maddened bull to plunge though the door that George has thoughtfully opened before his shoulder can break it. When Wayne recovers, he decides to clear out, not realising the ruse that has been played on him. But after she has helped him sort out a cross-claim on his mine concocted by the smooth-talking confidence trickster Frankie Canon

(Ernie Kovacs), he steps in to prevent her leaving on the next boat back to Seattle. She walks off down the muddy main street of Nome and he pursues her followed by a large crowd. "You've got to stay, Angel," he argues. "Because you have to, that's why," he says by way of amplification. "Because I want you to," he concedes when she remains dissatisfied with his answers. "I don't understand," she replies obstinately, "Come on, tell me, Sam!" The townsfolk chip in with cries of "Come on, Sam!" "Tell her!" and the great misogynist finally gives in with a yell, "Because I love you, that's why!", drawing cheers and whistles from the observers as he kisses her.

Besides the romantic banter, the film has a couple of splendid mass brawls handled in silent comedy style with great gusto and Wayne in the thick of them. It's as jolly a blend of disarming entertainment as could be asked for, and Wayne's performance was happily infected with much of its good humour.

Wayne is forced into a public confession of his love for Capucine's Angel in the muddy main street of Nome, Alaska.

68. The Comancheros (1961)

THOUGH *The Comancheros* has the polish and pace that were second nature to director Michael Curtiz, credit for staging this lively, very pleasing picture is somewhat more dispersed. Wayne himself stood in for Curtiz at times as the director weakened from the ill health that led to his death soon after the film's completion; Cliff Lyons's second unit handled the big action sequences; and producer George Sherman, who had directed Wayne's 3 Mesquiteers pictures, may well have taken a hand.

Wayne was very much the film's big attraction, billed as "Big John" in the advertising with his name as large as the title. But the supporting cast was an excellent one, helping to show off Wayne to best advantage. Big John is Jake Cutter, a captain in the Texas Rangers since his wife died and he left his ranch in the hands of some former employees. His commanding shadow precedes his first appearance in the film, falling on the wall of the cabin occupied by Paul Regret (Stuart Whitman) aboard a riverboat as Wayne arrests him for extradition to answer a murder charge in Louisana, the result of a duel in which Regret killed a judge's son.

Stuart Whitman plays the happy-go-lucky adventurer, Paul Regret, with brash charm and insolence. He takes to calling Wayne "friend," despite the latter's attempts to correct him. He tries offering a bribe but Wayne good-naturedly replies: "I've got what you might consider a weakness...I'm honest" and advises Regret: "I wouldn't try any city-slicker stuff on this poor old country boy." Regret tries to outsmart Wayne at every opportunity on the ride to the rangers' headquarters. He ventures the suggestion, "I don't suppose you'd take my word of honour I won't escape," and it's hard to communicate the rich savour of Wayne's beaming reply, "Monsewer! You *are* a lulu!" But in such moments as this lie much of the satisfaction of the film (for which the plot is really little more than an excuse). When they make camp, Regret draws a derringer from his fancy outfit while Wayne's back is turned. Wayne sees it and patiently puts down a frying pan he is holding, wipes his hands, and delivers a knockout punch. Regret perseveres and eventually lays Wayne out cold with a shovel, reducing the proud Texas Ranger to shuffling back to headquarters on a mule past the derisory comments of the men.

The film develops its main plot here and allows Guinn "Big Boy" Williams to contribute a brilliant cameo as Ed McBain, a gun-runner hopefully professing to see the error of his wicked ways. Wayne is assigned to take McBain's place and turn up at a hotel where the man was going to arrange the sale of a cargo of weapons.

The hard-drinking, eagle-eyed, half-scalped Tully Crow, played to the hilt by Lee Marvin, enters the story as a kind of preview of Marvin's Liberty Valance in

Wayne in disguise as a gunrunner.

Wayne and Stuart Whitman are escorted into the stronghold of the Comancheros and there talk to Ina Balin who knows they are really Texas Rangers.

Wayne's next film. The two go on the town together, each expressing a wary cordiality, and Wayne is forced to shoot Crow during a card game. Sitting at the table is Paul Regret who has kept Wayne's real identity from Crow and is somewhat put out to be placed under arrest again. On their second trek to headquarters, Wayne stops off at the ranch of a friend Schofield (Bob Steele) and chains Regret to an anvil before they enter the house. Schofield's wife Martha whispers in Wayne's ear: "Jake, that young fellow with you — what's he carrying under his arm?" "Well, that's an anvil, Martha, he's carrying an anvil," Wayne replies conspiratorially. "Why ever would he want to do that?" asks Martha. "Well, he's become attached to it, sort of," replies Wayne. This kind of genial playing with a situation suits Wayne's comedic abilities to the ground, teasingly withholding any further explanation from Martha. Having criticised James Edward Grant's writing of *The Alamo*, it is only fair to acknowledge him as the co-writer of this excellent script.

A big Indian attack takes place on the Schofield ranch during which Paul Regret takes off but brings back a detachment of rangers to save the day. Even now Regret can't coax Wayne into releasing him. Wayne reminds him of the oath he swore and says, "Monsewer, words are what men live by — words they say and mean. You must have had a real careless upbringing!" Further along on their travels, they pause for a meal with a glamorous young widow friend of Wayne's (Joan O'Brien) and Regret calls him "simple minded" for not having married her. "Well, don't make a point of saying it too often," says the simple-minded Wayne, "and once more'll be too often."

However, Wayne speaks up for Regret and a bit of legal corruption sees the Frenchman enlisted as a ranger and given an alibi for the murder charge. Before he knows it, Wayne has volunteered him for a hazardous trip carrying the consignment of rifles into the stronghold of the comancheros, white men working with the Indians. They are given a warm welcome — stretched out to bake in the sun — until Pilar (Ina Balin) arrives and recognises Regret as the man she fell in love with on the riverboat before his arrest. She has them cut down and turns out to be the daughter of the comancheros' leader, Graile (Nehemiah Persoff), a wheelchair-ridden tyrant reminiscent of the shipping magnate in *Wake of the Red Witch*. Graile receives them with cautious hospitality until they are revealed as rangers, forcing them to swing into action, ignite the stronghold's powder supply and stave off capture until the rest of the rangers can ride in and finish off the comancheros. Regret is given his freedom to leave with Pilar whose father has been killed in the fighting.

The Comancheros marks Wayne's acceptance of being an older leading man. We learn that he has become a bit of a windbag about his past exploits as a pioneer, bending the ears of the other rangers, and we find him leaving the principal romance to younger players. (He is given the consolation of the busty blonde widow at the fadeout.) There is also some gentle mocking of Wayne's appearance when Graile criticises his daughter's choice of Regret as a future husband, saying that she should have ignored the handsome one and chosen "the big, ugly one" whose broken nose suggests a man who puts up a fight for what he wants. These small points, taken with those in *North to Alaska,* introduce a more relaxed Wayne, mocking his own image while preserving its underlying strength.

69. The Man Who Shot Liberty Valance (1962)

AGEING though Wayne may have been, it did not deter John Ford from calling on him to play a part far younger than his years in *The Man Who Shot Liberty Valance*. It is rather disconcerting at first sight to find not only Wayne but James Stewart playing young roles (though Stewart also appears as an old man). Ford must have been more comfortable working with two actors he knew so well rather than less experienced players he would have had to whip into shape, but Wayne and Stewart are also cast to take advantage of what they stand for. Stewart, as Ranse Stoddard, is the tenderfoot lawyer out West and he quite naturally embodies qualities of fundamental decency and altruism and the same respect for the law as he did, for example, in *Mr. Smith Goes to Washington*. As Tom Doniphon, Wayne just as ideally symbolises dogged individualism, playing the simple, old-fashioned kind of Westerner who can pat his gun and say "Out here a man settles his own problems," and who replaces community spirit with personal loyalties and friendships. Another difficulty at first sight is the stark sets, which give an air of unusual realism yet clash with the gargantuan meals served by the film's restaurant that belong to the West of fictional elaboration. But the clash between the West of fact and the West of legend is central to the film. On repeated viewings, it shapes up as one of Ford's most heartfelt and moving pictures. No other film has so poignantly confronted the real West of slow and difficult progess with the colourful West of legend. No other film has so hauntingly conveyed the transition between the old and new West in making Wayne's Tom Doniphon both the instrument and victim of its evolution.

The framing story shows Ranse Stoddard, a celebrated politician, returning with his wife Hallie to the small town of Shinbone to attend the funeral of Tom Doniphon who has died in complete obscurity. The town's newspaper presses him to give the reason for his interest in this apparent nonentity and, with a consenting smile from Hallie, he cues the flashback that forms the bulk of the film.

We see Ranse on his way out West as a young man hoping to set up as a lawyer and being involved in a

Andy Devine, Wayne, Jeannette Nolan, John Qualen and Vera Miles are concerned for the tenderfoot lawyer played by James Stewart.

Below left, Wayne advises Stewart to pack a gun in order to deal with Liberty Valance. Right, Wayne intervenes to challenge Lee Marvin as Liberty Valance while James Stewart seethes with humiliation after Valance has tripped him up in the restaurant.

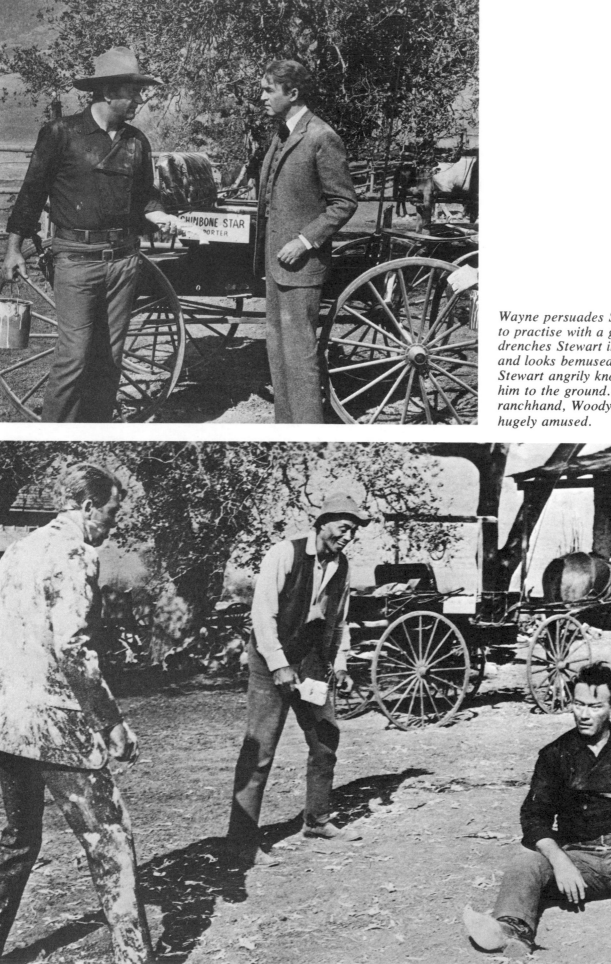

Wayne persuades Stewart
to practise with a gun,
drenches Stewart in paint,
and looks bemused after
Stewart angrily knocks
him to the ground. It's Wayne's
ranchhand, Woody Strode, looking
hugely amused.

Wayne pours himself a drink after killing Liberty Valance while Liberty's henchman Strother Martin tries to stir up a lynching party, backed by Lee Van Cleef. A moment later Wayne explodes with rage at their antics.

stage hold-up and brutally beaten by the leader of the robbers, Liberty Valance (Lee Marvin), when he tries to protect a lady. He is found by Wayne and his hired hand Pompey (Woody Strode) and brought into town to be nursed by Wayne's girlfriend Hallie (Vera Miles) and the Swedish couple (John Qualen, Jeanette Nolan) who run a restaurant. Wayne is amused at Ranse's determination to bring Valance to justice, knowing that the tubby town marshal (Andy Devine) is scared stiff of the notorious badman. "Liberty Valance is the toughest man south of the picket wire — next to me," Wayne declares, and advises Ranse to pack a gun. But Ranse rejects this crude counsel and his quiet determination appeals to Hallie as does his enthusiasm for teaching her to read and write. While Ranse looks to the future, Wayne clings to the present. All he can offer Hallie is old-fashioned gallantry, bringing her cactus roses, saying twice she looks awful pretty when she's mad, and prolonging their courtship indefinitely. He even hauls Pompey out of one of Ranse's reading classes, showing how his mind is shut to the future.

Ranse is goodnaturedly helping out as a waiter in the restaurant when Liberty Valance tries to provoke him by tripping him up. Wayne intervenes to order Valance to retrieve the steak that has fallen on the floor but Ranse steps in to do it instead and stop the two men shooting it out. However, Ranse secretly starts to accept Wayne's belief in force to meet force and practises firing a revolver. The worried Hallie asks Wayne to help him. Concerned over Hallie's fears for Ranse, Wayne makes a point of telling him that Hallie is his girl,

gives him a rather sharp lesson in shooting and makes a fool out him, puncturing paint tins as Ranse is putting them up as targets. Ranse angrily knocks Wayne to the ground, giving the actor an opportunity to put on one of those cross-eyed expressions of muddled amazement.

Ranse starts to organise the people to use their voting strength to defeat the territory's big cattle interests who are resisting Statehood to protect their own power and keep open range. Ranse proposes Wayne as a delegate to a territorial convention but Wayne refuses, planning to concentrate on his personal plans which include finally marrying Hallie. He seconds a proposal that Ranse should be the town's delegate along with the local newspaper editor (Edmond O'Brien). A third, self-nominated candidate is Liberty Valance, who is in the employ of the big ranchers. He is roundly rejected and promises to kill Ranse. Wayne urges Ranse to slip out of town but Ranse's resolve to stay is strengthened when Valance murders the newpaper editor. Hallie calls on Wayne to protect Ranse from Valance.

Liberty and Ranse confront each other on the street. The gunman fires three shots around Ranse to tease him. When Ranse returns a single shot, Valance falls dead. Hallie is so overwhelmed to see Ranse safe and so proud of his courage that she transfers her affections to him. A surly Wayne turns up to apologise for arriving too late, then walks away. He starts drinking heavily in a local saloon and turns angrily on two of Valance's men (Lee Van Cleef, Strother Martin) who are hopefully trying to stir up a lynch mob to avenge their leader's death. Pompey collects him and takes him back

Vera Miles as Hallie expresses her concern for Stewart's safety when he goes off to challenge Liberty to a gunfight.

to his ranch where he expresses his deep hurt at losing Hallie by setting fire to the extension to his ranch that he was building for Hallie's benefit.

Now that Liberty has been killed, the way is clear for Ranse to further his campaign but he wilts under the accusation of being a killer. He walks out of the territorial convention to be stopped by Wayne who explains that Ranse didn't kill Liberty Valance; he did. He had arrived on the scene as Ranse was facing Liberty and had fired his rifle from the shadows to coincide with Ranse's shot. With his conscience cleared, Ranse is able to return to the convention and lead the territory to Statehood, Hallie by his side.

As Ranse rises to the heights in politics, Wayne is left behind, an understandably bitter loser whose time is past. We don't see (or need to see) what becomes of him: his obscurity at the time of his death tells us enough.

The part of Tom Doniphon shows both the virtues and limitations of the Wayne image. Wayne has done all the right things. Though a rancher, he has aligned himself with the townspeople. He has proved his point about needing to deal with Liberty Valance on his own terms with a shootout. He has taken on the job himself and only revealed his part in Liberty's death when it was necessary. But he has had a reluctant role in shaping progress. He is too stubborn and self-centred to

change his ways. He believes in the individual, in the ''liberty'' expressed in Valance's first name as long as it doesn't harm others, and he responds to Hallie's demands on him, to Valance's acts of provocation, rather than to general issues. He can assert Pompey's right, as a coloured man, to drink in a saloon because drinking is part of a way of life he believes in and Pompey is his friend, yet deny Pompey the chance to educate himself and disturb the relationship between them. Like Ethan Edwards in *The Searchers,* he has to live with himself and it is a lonely business for such unadaptable types.

At the end of the film, the Western wilderness has become a cultivated garden as Hallie had foreseen. She places a cactus rose, symbol of an unirrigated past, on Wayne's coffin. The shadows of history have claimed him — the newsman refuses to disturb the legend of Valance's death — as at various points in the film Wayne has stood in the dark outside the mainstream of events. He had shot Valance from a dark passageway while the spotlight was on the gunman and Ranse Stoddard in the brightly illuminated street. He had walked away from the lit door to leave Hallie with Ranse and disappear into the darkness of the night. He has walked away again as Ranse re-entered the convention hall to rousing cheers, stepping into the public eye as Wayne disappears from it. It is impossible not be moved by this figure: the hero drowned by the tide of history.

70. Hatari! (1962)

WAYNE's only African wildlife picture is *Hatari!*, filmed in Tanganyika by Howard Hawks with an international supporting cast of players from Italy, France, Germany and Spain, giving it a boost in almost every major market. No doubt Wayne was considered enough for the English-speaking world.

Hatari! is a lightweight picture but a highly pleasurable one, a signal accomplishment being the way it banishes any hint of tedium for 159 minutes of running time. It deals with a bunch of big game catchers rounding up animals under contract for zoos during a three months' season. It gains immeasurably from the fact that the actors themselves caught the animals without the use of doubles...and are clearly seen to be doing so. Shooting was improvised around the action as it developed in these scenes and there is considerable excitement as rhinos batter the vehicles driven by the men. The part may be very undemanding for Wayne after the intenseness of *Liberty Valance* from an acting point of view, but he has to exert himself physically to

handle wildbeeste and rhino which seems no mean accomplishment for a man well into his fifties.

In the manner of many other Hawks films, *Hatari!* explores the relationships between a group of people working together, all of them judged by their behaviour as professionals and needing to earn and keep the respect of the others. Wayne, as Sean Mercer, the Irish-American, is the undisputed leader of the group who work for young Brandy (Michele Girardon), with Kurt Mueller (Hardy Kruger), Pockets (Red Buttons), Luis (Valentin de Vargas) and the Indian (Bruce Cabot) as established members of the team. Two newcomers are the Frenchman (Gerard Blain) who proves his worth after a bad start, and Anna Maria D'Allesandro (Elsa Martinelli), a girl photographer who has inadvertently misled the men by not revealing her sex in advance and who first relies on a letter of authority from a zoo to force their acceptance of her but then decides to earn her place or leave.

Anna Maria, nicknamed Dallas for no particular

Wayne and Gérard Blain rope a baby elephant.

reason that comes to mind, takes up residence in Wayne's bed while he and the others are away. It seems a handy place for a nap, but is quite a surprise for the drunken Wayne when he returns from celebrating the Indian's survival of a bad accident. Dallas is thus perfectly introduced as the aggressor in typical Hawks style with Wayne as the resistent male to be eventually won over by her charm and sincerity. He first reacts against her as being unsuited for a man's world but she reasonably replies: "Why don't you find out what kind of a girl I am before you make up your mind?" She soon falls for Wayne and asks his close friend Pockets what he has against women. "Oh, he thinks they're trouble," replies Pockets, telling her of the *fiancée* he once brought out to the camp who didn't like their world and left. Pockets gives a rationale of Wayne's behaviour (which would apply to other Wayne characters as well): "If a man falls for a woman and gets his fingers burned, what does he do? If he doesn't like you, he doesn't care and he can be nice to you. But if he does like you, he doesn't want to get in any deeper so he acts mean. The more he likes you, the meaner he acts."

Dallas shows the affectionate side of her nature by adopting an abandoned baby elephant Wayne was going to shoot to save it further distress, with the other men rallying round to dismiss Wayne's objections. Dallas has soon adopted two more to keep the first company and arranged a supply of goats' milk to feed them. Discouraged by Wayne's continuing coolness towards her, she takes further advice from Pockets who suggests she should make a positive move. This brings about the amusing scene where Dallas advances on Wayne and boldly asks, "Sean, how do you like to kiss?" Wayne finds the question rather baffling and as she pursues it ends up declaring "It's silly to stand around and talk about it," giving her the perfect cue to try out some ways on him.

At the end of the season, when even the reluctant rhinos have been rounded up, Dallas is no nearer capturing Wayne and after a fit of tears she packs her bags and leaves overnight with only a note of thanks to the men for their hospitality. As with Feathers in *Rio Bravo*, Wayne won't admit outright that he loves her but he does declare that he's going to find her and stop

Wayne is amused as Gérard Blain teases Hardy Kruger (others watching: Eduard Franz, Red Buttons, Michele Girardon, Valentin De Vargas) but (next page) steps in to break up the fight that develops.

her; not being sheriff in this movie, he can't arrest her but he does try and have the police do it instead by saying that she has stolen something. The men ride into town looking for her and give the scent to the baby elephants who create chaos in the streets, finally cornering her in a hotel.

To conclude, there is a repeat of the first scene with Dallas, re-establishing her in Wayne's bed — only this time they have married. Pockets does his usual act of butting in (as he had in the first bedroom scene and the kissing sequence) and is being turfed out by Wayne when the three baby elephants intrude to clamber up on the bed and create a riotous closing image.

Like Wayne, Pockets has been reticent about revealing his affections for the other girl in the group, Brandy, and he too gets his girl when pushed into it. But Pockets lacks Wayne's personal magnetism and the excuse of past hurtful experiences. With Pockets, it becomes part of his comical make-up (emphasised by Red Buttons' small stature); with Wayne, his reluctance in love always enhances his masculine image.

Hatari! is a welcome change from the usual run of safari adventures: no animals and no humans are killed, and a genial atmosphere of affection and give-and-take is established. The film remains a pleasing mixture of adventure, comedy and romance.

Wayne and Elsa Martinelli. Below, the invasion of baby elephants into the nuptial chamber.

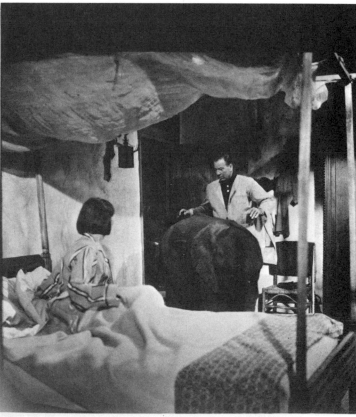

189

71. The Longest Day (1962)

WAYNE next appeared on the roster of stars assembled by Darryl F. Zanuck for his production of *The Longest Day*. The film was an epic reconstruction of the events on June 6, 1944 when the Allied invasion of German-occupied Europe took place. Wayne's role was that of Lt. Col. Benjamin Vandervoort of the Eighty-Second Airborne; he took it over from William Holden who was originally announced to play it. He was one of the American paratroopers who dropped on the town of Ste. Mère Eglise at night, broke his ankle but kept on fighting, helping to make this ancient town the first to fall into Allied hands on D-Day. Though Wayne's part was small, it was linked to one of the most memorable episodes of the film where the paratroopers drift down to be illuminated by the flames from an incendiary bomb and suffer heavy casualties from German marksmen.

Wayne's name was a great asset to the picture at the box-office and, while the rest of the cast was listed alphabetically, there was a small displacement at the end to give Wayne the prominence of being last. This entailed moving Stuart Whitman, earlier his co-star in *The Comancheros,* ahead of him and when by error reissue posters reverted to alphabetical order throughout, stickers later went up to correct the "correction."

Wayne as Lt. Col. Benjamin Vandervoort, seen below resting his sprained ankle and listening to Stuart Whitman. Tom Tryon is between them.

Wayne as General William Tecumsah Sherman in How the West Was Won *(see overleaf).*

72. How the West Was Won (1962)

BULLDOZING a place in film history for itself as the first fictional picture to be made in Cinerama, this fourteen and a half million dollar epic had a genuinely starstudded cast but Wayne's footage was very limited. If most of the film seemed to demonstrate that the West was won rather boringly, a clear exception would have to be made for John Ford's Civil War sequence in which the great director characteristically plumped for an intimate story, not in the least deterred by the vastness of the screen. The real star of this episode is George Peppard as Zeb Rawlings, the country boy who enlists with the North and goes off to find glory, only to be shocked by his side's bloody defeat at Shiloh. Joined by a young Confederate deserter (Russ Tamblyn), he welcomes the chance to share his disillusionment with the war.

Nearby, in a clearing in a wood, two Northern generals are deep in discussion: Harry Morgan's Ulysses S. Grant and John Wayne's William T. Sherman. Grant is wearied by his side's defeat at Shiloh and by adverse comments about his character. Wayne's dishevelled Sherman, whose arrival had stopped total disarray, tries to revive Grant's spirits, recalling, "A month ago they were saying I was crazy, *in*-sane. Now they're calling me a hero. Hero or crazy, I'm the same man. Doesn't matter what the people think. It's what you think, Grant." Sherman encourages Grant to see that wars are not fought for the politicians but for a cause, in this case freedom and America's greatness.

While the onlooking Zeb is heartened by this insight into the thoughts of the Generals, his new-found friend the Southerner is overcome by this chance opportuntiy to intervene in the course of history and raises his gun to shoot Grant. Zeb has to choose sides again and bayonets the would-be assassin to death.

This small and barely consequential episode gives one the sense of eavesdropping between the pages of history, of turning back time to the quiet moment rather than the big event, and makes a reflective pause in the film's sweep through frontier history in generally comic-strip terms. It is Wayne's most effective cameo appearance in an all-star picture, requiring little more than a single note of calm reassurance but allowing him to flesh out a character given substance by Ford's masterly touch in decisive, personal strokes.

Wayne as Sherman, Henry ("Harry") Morgan as Grant with the two privates (Russ Tamblyn, George Peppard) eavesdropping in left background.

73. Donovan's Reef (1963)

WHEN it first appeared, *Donovan's Reef* was widely regarded as marking a new low in John Ford's career. Even now, its worth is being hotly debated by Ford's admirers. And if it was a bad John Ford film, then it could hardly be a good John Wayne one. But I like it more than enough to reclaim it from the lower depths of both star and director's careers.

In some ways it is more a Wayne picture than a Ford one, continuing the line of broad humour from the actor's preceding films like *North to Alaska* and *The Comancheros*. Subtle, it is not. We find, for the first time, Wayne's writer James Edward Grant working on a Ford script (along with Ford's favourite, Frank Nugent) and Grant no doubt contributed most of its crude humour. But Ford has always been at home with lashings of horseplay and he adds his own inimitable touch, his sense of pleasure and affection in the rowdy goings-on, to fill out what is for him an unusually thin story basis. Only the sticky religious aspects fail to harmonise with the rest.

It is, I suppose, a "holiday film" (like *Hatari!*): everyone had a good time in Hawaii and they haven't forgotten to show it on the screen. Just because Ford isn't being profound (and is enjoying his old age), it's silly to criticise the film instead of relaxing with it. It is true that the film invites consideration in terms of Ford's disenchantment with modern civilised life and that living on the island of Haleakahola is a rather artificial and strained alternative beneath the surface, but these aspects are outside the scope of this book.

It is only necessary to comment that for Wayne's Michael Donovan, as for his pal Doc Dedham (Jack Warden), the island has become a comfortable refuge since they served there during the war. But whereas Doc has proved a valuable asset to the local people and has accepted their way of life, marrying a princess and raising a family, Wayne has remained Wayne, an expatriate American who has surrounded himself with the Western way of life, running the bar that gives the film its title, driving a jeep at great speed, and brawling

Wayne and Lee Marvin as partners in deception.

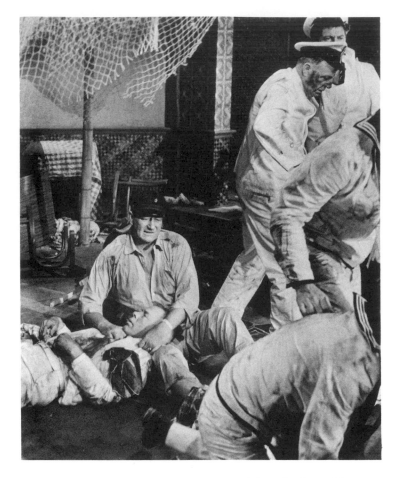

After the brawl is over.... Wayne and Lee Marvin.

lustily with a fellow American, Boats Gilhooley, and any other willing outsiders (like the group of Australian sailors taking shore leave). It seems rather incidental to the Wayne character that he is given a college background and can distinguish Mozart from Chopin, and far more appropriate that he should have been a gunner's mate in the war.

The real curiosity of *Donovan's Reef* is that Wayne is deeply involved in a deception. He had tricked Father Burke in *Trouble along the Way* but it was a natural response from the kind of person he portrayed, not something that left him feeling awkward as he does here. The trickery arises when Doc's daughter by an earlier marriage, Amelia Dedham (Elizabeth Allen), comes out from Boston to see her father for the first time. He is absent visiting a patient and his friends are worried about her reaction to his three half-caste children. Wayne poses as their father in his place. It should be observed that the ruse is suggested by an Oriental, that the other islanders connive at it willingly, that (as it turns out) Amelia is looking for an excuse to disinherit her father from the family shipping concern, and that she does unconsciously look down on the children in a patronising fashion at first. Wayne starts to worry when she turns out to be partly human after shedding some of her prim Boston ways, and in the end the children's charm (plus the fact that one is a princess?) win her over.

In Amelia Dedham, Wayne is provided with yet another Eastern shrew waiting to be tamed. And a boisterous business it naturally proves to be with actress Elizabeth Allen being soaked and spanked in public, among other humiliations, before coming to enjoy the island's uninhibited ways and responding to the coarse charm of Wayne. She is not above flaunting herself before him in a swimming costume and showing him a trick or two; but for the woman who's never been really kissed before and the man who may just have loved his mother ("She's dead," comments Wayne to stop that avenue of investigation), true love is entertainingly inevitable.

Wayne's other sparring partner is Lee Marvin's Gilhooley and the two seasoned professionals make the most of their boisterous relationship, Marvin being promoted to Wayne's equal after his supporting stints in *The Comancheros* and *The Man Who Shot Liberty Valance*. The brawl with which they annually celebrate their joint birthday is a cherished event and has developed its rituals, notably the cautious handshake and the crooked smile on Wayne's face before he lands the first blow on the other's chin. Though Wayne's eyes narrow with exasperation at the first mention of Gilhooley in the film, he loves his pal enough to give him Donovan's Reef at the end of the film where he can play with his giant train set while Wayne plays with Amelia Dedham.

194

Stages in the hectic romance between Wayne and Elizabeth Allen.

Comedy highlights: Wayne and Maureen O'Hara celebrate a good mudbath; Wayne tweaks the nose of "Big John" Hamilton; and charges like a maddened bull through the McLintock residence.

74. McLintock! (1963)

WAYNE's first venture back into production after the financial upset of *The Alamo* was the broad Western comedy *McLintock!*, a screen original by James Edward Grant. It was a close-knit enterprise with Wayne's son Michael functioning as producer, his brother Robert working as the production supervisor, his son Patrick heading the supporting cast and daughter Aissa featured lower down. William Clothier handled the camerawork as he had on *The Alamo* and Wayne's recent Ford pictures. The players also included some old working partners: Maureen O'Hara, Chuck Roberson (a skilled stuntman rider and bit player), Edgar Buchanan, and Hank Worden. The gamble in an otherwise safe commercial bet was the entrusting of the direction to Victor McLaglen's son, Andrew, who had first worked for Wayne's production companies as the assistant director of *Big Jim McLain, Island in the Sky, The High and the Mighty, Blood Alley*, later co-produced *Seven Men from Now* and directed *Gun the Man Down* and *Man in the Vault* for Wayne, and had then directed some small pictures elsewhere. *McLintock!* put McLaglen in the big league, although it was his next film *Shenandoah* that enabled him to make his mark with the critics. Here his handling is rather too slack and broad although the script hardly calls for great discipline.

McLintock! is much too long for its own good (127 minutes) but passably entertaining and interesting for the way it expresses the Wayne philosophy. Wayne's

George Washington McLintock is the man who carved an empire out of a wilderness, fighting off Indians and earning their respect. Miner, timber baron, cattle king, he has had the town named after him and he more or less rules it, dispensing a helping hand to those who need it and poking fun (and fists) at those who don't measure up to his standards of conduct. He plans to leave almost all his property to the nation to become a national park and in effect defends the possession of wealth as long as it is in the hands of responsible people imbued with good neighbourliness. Nothing comes free, though: when Wayne gives a badly needed job to Dev Warren (Patrick Wayne), he cuts off the latter's expression of gratitude by telling him he'll *earn* his wages, they're not a hand-out. The film realises Wayne's position may seem a little old-fashioned and even allows him to be labelled a "reactionary" which is defined as a person "who wants to sell at a profit." As this label of "reactionary" comes from the college-educated son of a feeble politican, it can be readily dismissed. Wayne here stands in favour of Statehood as a means of disposing of the political appointees who run the Territory neither wisely nor well and it is hard not to see in the name of the Territory's ineffectual Governor, Cuthbert H. Humphrey, a dig at Hubert Humphrey who was far from being one of Wayne's contemporary heroes, out on the left-hand side of the political spectrum. Thus there is really behind the comedy of this film a clear expression of a right-wing *laissez-faire* viewpoint.

Wayne and Yvonne De Carlo (as his housekeeper) take a drunken tumble down the stairs.

In other respects, the film repeats the succesful formulas of past Wayne pictures. First there is *Rio Grande*. Wayne has become estranged from his wife Katherine (Maureen O'Hara) who returns to claim her daughter (as opposed to a son in the Ford film) and take her back East to become a society belle rather than be corrupted by life out West. Then there's *The Quiet Man*, invoked by the finale when Wayne finally loses all patience with his wife and pursues her all over town, causing the same kind of public humiliation as O'Hara's forced walk in the earlier film. This time she suffers that added indignity of having lost her dress and being spanked on her exposed pantaloons to everyone's amusement, as a result of which she surrenders completely to Wayne's way of life. Male dominance rather than sex equality is another old-fashioned viewpoint of the film (as of most of Wayne's pictures). Given no subtleties of motivation, Maureen O'Hara contributes a rather exaggerated performance that tends to invite Wayne's strong-arm treatment.

The humour has all the lusty relish of Ford's knock-about scenes with added slapstick angles. There is a memorable mass fight at the top of a slope leading down to a mudhole. It starts with Wayne handling a hotheaded troublemaker (Leo Gordon), gritting his teeth to say, "Now we'll all calm down," and adding, "I'm going to use good judgement. I haven't lost my temper in forty years. But, pilgrim, someone ought to belt you in the mouth. But I won't. I won't. The *hell* I won't!" Everyone around (including Katherine) is successfully engineered into sliding down to the mud below. There is also Wayne returning home in a drunken state and sharing a few glasses with his attractive cook (Yvonne De Carlo) to stagger up the stairs with her and tumble back down. Before long, the highly suspicious Katherine has taken a further tumble down the stairs with them and in the belief that nothing succeeds like excess the stunt gets a third airing. All the players seem so happy in their work that there's nothing to do but enjoy it with them.

Wayne pursues his wife (Maureen O'Hara) all over town and beats some sense into her (next page).

75. The Magnificent Showman (Circus World) (1964)

NO CLEARER demonstration of Wayne's standing as a box-office star exists than the circumstances behind the making of this film. Without him it would never have been made, as Paramount would have withdrawn its financial participation. And because Wayne set a date when production would have to get underway, it was shot without its many script problems being adequately resolved. Originally, the film was to have been directed by Frank Capra who quit when Wayne's trusted writer, James Edward Grant, turned up to take a hand in the script (Wayne was away holidaying on his boat). Paramount (who had the American distribution rights) approached Henry Hathaway, who had just completed *Nevada Smith* for the studio, and asked him to take over, knowing he was on good terms with Wayne. The star apparently agreed to wait an extra two months for the script to be straightened out. In businesslike fashion, Hathaway disposed of James Edward Grant, whom he found no more helpful than Capra had, and went away with writer Ben Hecht to knock the script into some sort of shape. Wayne gave his approval to their plans and the film got underway. As Hathaway has since observed, "The fundamental story material was weak," and he regards the picture as a "mistake." It is certainly not a great picture but with a substantial budget and presentation in Cinerama it passes muster as an adequate spectacular.

Wayne's role is that of Matt Masters, the circus owner who takes his company to Europe and has a disastrous setback when the ship they are using sinks in the harbour at Barcelona. He goes to work for another circus outfit and slowly builds up a new team of performers to go back into business for himself.

Wayne himself participates in Wild West acts and is seen sharpshooting from on top of a stagecoach under attack from Indians and later, in a publicity drive along the Champs-Elysées, leaping onto the lead horse in the stagecoach team to bring it to a halt after it has taken off.

Besides his friendship with Cap Carson (Lloyd Nolan), Wayne is attached to Toni Alfredo (Claudia Cardinale) whom he has brought up as a daughter since the death of her trapeze artist father and the disappearance of her mother, Lili. Humour is derived from Wayne's attempts to deal with Toni whom he still sees as a child rather than a grown woman. When he tries to have a serious talk with her over her morbid belief in circus superstitions, the bed he sits on collapses, sending her into a fit of laughter. And when Toni takes a romantic interest in the rider Steve McCabe (John Smith), Wayne gets in his two cents' worth. Steve is brash and conceited but strong and confident: he even apes Big John by exaggeratedly copying a wink that Wayne gives Toni. She asserts herself by exercising on

John Wayne, Rita Hayworth, Lloyd Nolan.

*Wayne's attempts to have
a serious chat with Claudia
Cardinale are undermined by
a collapsing bed.*

*Wayne is staggered to find
Claudia Cardinale and
John Smith kissing and demands
a talk with the young man.*

*Wayne fights the fire in
the big top.*

a trapeze bar, Wayne looking comically wild up at her, getting angry with the onlooking Steve and quickly covering up her scanty costume from his gaze, gruffly telling Steve "Go ride your horse!" and "She's just a kid!" Then when he catches them kissing, he grunts, his eyes pop, his arms go out, and he bawls at Steve, "You — I want to talk with you!" choking on the words. To him, no circus performer is good enough for Toni, but she persists and Steve eventually wins acceptance as husband material for her and Wayne's new partner in the circus.

Wayne's gruff manner, as a man laden with responsibilities and worries, makes his speech of thanks to the team who have made his new circus possible sound like he's ticking them off. But, as usual, the surly exterior fails to conceal his warm heart, and in another scene his voice slips to become soft and husky when he tells Toni of all the happiness she has given him.

A motive behind Wayne's trip to Europe is the hope of finding Toni's mother, Lili (Rita Hayworth), whom he had loved. He eventually tracks her down in a sleazy waterfront joint in Hamburg and sternly accuses her of "hocking her soul," indulging in self-pity, and taking the easy way out in abdicating her responsibilities to Toni. He tells her to make herself look decent enough to see her daughter again (she has been dressing like an old flowerseller). He eventually allows her to join the circus as a trapeze performer under an assumed name. She and Toni become close friends and, after suspicions of the circumstances of her father's death have been dispelled, Wayne is forgiven for his part in the deception.

The film's big climax is a fire under the big top that breaks out for no clearly explained reason, and involves Wayne battling the flames, visibly falling through a plank amidst them. Disaster is averted and the film ends on a happy note on all-round reconciliation.

All-round reconciliation: John Smith, Claudia Cardinale, Wayne, Rita Hayworth.

76. The Greatest Story Ever Told (1965)

WAYNE next misguidedly allowed himself to be involved in George Stevens's life of Jesus, *The Greatest Story Ever Told*. Having courageously opted for an actor without mass appeal to portray Jesus — namely, Max von Sydow — Stevens then retreated to enlist the services of many well-known stars like Wayne to enact the smaller roles. No doubt, the argument was that these would ensure good audience support without which the massive endeavour would be pointless — the more people who could be persuaded to see so worthwhile a story the better. And then it must have been flattering for an actor to be asked to appear in the film, to demonstrate that star billing and size of part didn't matter when so important a subject was involved. Nevertheless, it was a calamitous mistake, encouraging audiences to count off the stars as they appeared and inflating small parts at the expense of the main one. When Wayne clanks along as the Centurion accompanying Jesus to the cross, who are the audience watching? And Wayne is very ill-equipped to speak the line "Truly this man was a son of God": it is against everything his image has represented for him to be awed in any way and his quintessentially American voice has never been convincing in non-American contexts.

Accompanying Jesus (Max von Sydow) to the Cross.

77. In Harm's Way (1965)

WITH a great cast, Otto Preminger's polished handling, and an incisive script, *In Harm's Way* could hardly be anything but highly watchable through its 165 minutes of screen time even though it is not an outstanding achievement. It's one of the few dramas to keep a whole gallery of characters in check and not allow the main stars' roles to develop out of proportion to the rest. The story dominates the people and thereby accommodates a wide range of characters. Even Wayne fits in rather than standing out and his performance is the better for it, giving him more substantial figures to react against. He is Captain Rockwell Torrey, in charge of a cruiser on the fateful Sunday morning of December 7, 1941. He is nicknamed "The Rock" and not without reason for he is the one figure of unshakable steadfastness in the period of trial and confusion following the Japanese sneak attack on Pearl Harbor.

But he is part of a chain, not the isolated leader with the near freedom of action usually granted to war film heroes. He suffers under the indecisive leadership of Admiral Broderick (Dana Andrews). When he has to lead the battered remnants of the attack in a completely hopeless counter-action against the Japanese, he deliberately violates his orders and charts a straight course for the enemy to conserve fuel instead of zigzagging. As a result, he is beached and brought before a court of inquiry after a torpedo splits his ship in two and his arm is fractured. He has to submit to the frustration of desk work until the higher command suddenly look on him with new favour and give him tactical command of an operation called Skyhook to capture enemy-occupied islands as well as the means to circumvent the interference of Broderick. The next battle with the Japanese fleet is no easy victory and Wayne's ship is again struck by the enemy. This time it sinks and shellshock puts Wayne in a three weeks' coma while his injuries neces-

Wayne in command. Right, with Kirk Douglas as his executive officer.

Wayne with Patricia Neal as a navy nurse and Brandon De Wilde as his son.

sitate the amputation of his left leg. At the film's conclusion, he has been promised an artificial leg and the command of a new task force to carry on the fight. Wayne, then, is no invincible hero: the only certainty is that he'll do his best, not that he'll succeed.

Still, Wayne is again portraying the complete serviceman at the expense of a troubled private life. The familiar opting for devotion to the job above all else has cost him a broken marriage and kept him apart from his son, Jere, for eighteen years. His wife came from a Boston society background and her influence has apparently corrupted their son (Brandon De Wilde) for when Wayne comes across him as a naval officer in a PT boat squadron he discovers that Jere is contemptuous of him and has become an opportunist angling for a plush job with the very admiral that Wayne heartily despises, Broderick. In his disappointment, Wayne rejects his son until it falls to him to pass on the news that Jere's girlfriend (Jill Haworth) has committed suicide after being raped by Wayne's executive officer (Kirk Douglas). The tragedy brings them closer together and Jere returns to the PT boats to become a casualty of the operation that Wayne leads against the enemy but a son in whom he can take pride.

Wayne finds a suitable romantic partner in a navy nurse who understands the calls of duty: she's played by Patricia Neal who was also a navy nurse (and Wayne's ex-wife) in *Operation Pacific*. She is here the nurse who X-rays Wayne's fractured arm and meets him subsequently at a party he is bullied into attending by his pal Egan Powell (Burgess Meredith). They strike an immediate rapport and she is ultimately at his side to comfort him as he comes out of the coma and faces up to the loss of his leg. Patricia Neal's warm yet reserved manner works as well opposite Wayne as it had an unbelievable fifteen years before in the other film and the durability of both players is emphasised.

The real contrast to Wayne's dedicated outlook occurs in the character of Kirk Douglas's Paul Eddington. Whereas Wayne has buried his marital disappointments beneath that leathery, reserved exterior, Eddington takes to bouts of drinking to compensate for the promiscuous activities of his wife and has to be ticked off by Wayne for indulging in self-pity. Whereas Wayne always acts honourably, Eddington is a typical Kirk Douglas character given to wild impulses that lead to self-destruction. After he has caused the suicide of Jere's girl, he cannot live with himself and commits suicide in a suitably bravura fashion by commandeering a plane and sending back valuable information before being shot down, the flawed hero who pays the price. The intriguing contrast between two powerful styles of acting and star images did not wait long before being mined again in *The War Wagon* and *Cast a Giant Shadow*.

78. The Sons of Katie Elder (1965)

WHEN Wayne saddled up for *The Sons of Katie Elder,* he had barely finished playing the leading role in a real-life drama of "Big John versus the Big C." "The Big C" was Wayne's term for cancer, which was found to have invaded his left lung; the odds were that he would not survive the operation for its removal. His stay in hospital was initially passed off as a routine operation, but Wayne subsequently insisted on revealling the truth, figuring that it would give courage and hope to others. Calling cancer the Big C gave it the dimensions it deserved as a formidable adversary and, in effect, enhanced Wayne's image as one who had vanquished it.

The film itself is a lazy exercise, plodding along for an excessive 122 minutes but professionally handled by director Henry Hathaway. It was an ideal film for looking at Wayne anew: the role was devoid of any underlying complexities and it gave plenty of time to appreciate the commanding strength of the man and his strange topheavy look of a giant Sequoia ensuring that it doesn't topple. This is archetypal Wayne, catered for with brawling comedy, cutting verbal encounters with villains, and moments of action both in partnership and for himself alone. Without Wayne, it would have been a corny, forgettable affair; with Wayne, it becomes a Western with a claim on the memory (if only just).

The first half of the film rings to the praises of the late Katie Elder who would seem to have been insufferably noble and brave, dying in poverty without the comfort of her sons' company. Wayne plays John Elder, gunslinger and oldest son; Dean Martin is Tom, cardsharp and con-man; Earl Holliman, Matt the quiet one; and Michael Anderson Jr. young Bud, the hope of the family. (Ma evidently believed in spacing out her children: there's some thirty-five years between the birthdates of Wayne and Anderson.) Her funeral comes at the start of the picture. Wayne watches the burial from high above in some rocks, at home in surroundings as enduring and upright as himself. This also emphasises Wayne as something of a loner, set apart from his brothers by age and nature; even when all are together, he tends to stand slightly apart or at the edge rather than in the middle. The star asserts himself.

The film's idea of a family get-together is for the brothers to sock each other silly for the sheer joy of it. But soon they are putting their heads together to investigate belatedly the death of their father (another unseen figure) who had died on the night he supposedly gambled away his ranch to the town's boss, Morgan Hastings (James Gregory), reducing their mother to near poverty.

The sheriff (Paul Fix) warns the brothers to stay out of trouble, knowing their reputation as hell raisers. But Morgan Hastings is still afraid of them and kills the

My biggest fight wasn't in pictures.

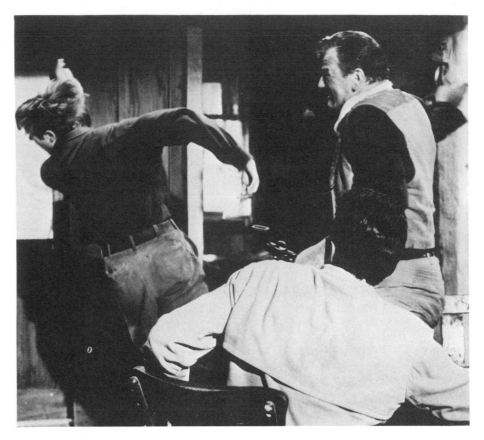

Left, Wayne puts his weight behind the work of the American Cancer Society. His operation took place just before he made The Sons of Katie Elder *in which – above and below – he was fit enough to indulge in some Elder family horseplay.*

It happened in real life. I was just finishing my 99th ridin', jumpin', fightin', picture. Never felt better in my life.

But my family nagged me into getting a medical checkup. And it turned out I had lung cancer. If I'd waited a few more weeks, I'd be kicking up daisies now.

So, friend, I know what I'm talking about when I tell you, get a checkup. Talk someone you like into getting a checkup. Nag someone you love into getting a checkup.

And when the lady from the American Cancer Society rings your doorbell, dig deep in your pocket. They're working to rid this world of cancer once and for all.

American Cancer Society

We want to wipe out cancer in your lifetime.

Earl Holliman has been killed by a wood splinter but Wayne and Dean Martin fight on.
Below, Wayne watches anxiously as the doctor (Karl Swenson) tends the wounded Michael Anderson Jr.

sheriff, pinning the blame on the foursome. The deputy sheriff (Jeremy Slate) arrests them and, to avoid a possible lynching, swears in a posse to escort them to another town. The posse members turn out to be in Hastings's employ and overcome the deputy: the Elders manage to hole up under a wooden bridge and shoot it out but Matt is killed by an exploding stick of dynamite and Bud wounded before the other two can get away, taking Bud to town for medical treatment. They hide in a barn and bring the doctor to treat Bud. Tom does his bit, creeping out to capture Hastings's son Dave (Dennis Hopper); and when Morgan Hastings comes a-shooting to rescue his son, he wounds the lad by mistake prompting him to confess that his father killed the Elders' father. Tom now expires from a gunshot wound and with Bud still badly hurt it is left to Wayne to go it alone: "This is something I have to do for myself," he tells the deputy sheriff as he loads his revolver. And so Wayne emerges from the group to take on Hastings who hides in his gunshop to be blown to smithereens.

Nothing is taken too seriously — or can be with such an elementary plot. Wayne can viciously whack a Hastings man in the face with a rifle early on and it doesn't seem particularly painful. Two brothers are dead but the family name is cleared of shame, with Bud destined to go to college and their mother's rocking chair set in motion as though the old lady were once again resting in it contentedly. The film did great business at the box-office.

John Wayne as the General in Cast a Giant Shadow, *seen below with Kirk Douglas as Mickey Marcus.*

79. Cast a Giant Shadow (1966)

WAYNE's role in *Cast a Giant Shadow* was a subsidiary one, as was that of Frank Sinatra. But Wayne's early enthusiasm for the film as a depiction of a popular American involvement in another country's affairs (at a time when Vietnam policies were arousing controversy) had helped get studios interested in the idea of making a Jewish story: that of Colonel David Marcus, the American Jew who licked the Israeli army into shape to face the threat of Arab attack at the end of the British Mandate. Wayne's name and Sinatra's seemed to promise the attendance of a wide audience. By the time Wayne flew to Rome for his few scenes, shooting of most of the picture had been completed in Israel with Wayne's son Michael co-producing and his company Batjac partnered in the venture with Melville Shavelson's Llenroc company.

Wayne appears as General Mike Randolph, a composite of all the American officers the real Marcus had served under as a colourful, rule-breaking hero of the Second World War. Marcus is played by Kirk Douglas, again setting his flashy, impulsive style against the Wayne reserve. In one scene, introduced as a flashback, Wayne (representing here General George Patton) is being taken by Marcus to see conditions in the Dachau concentration camp. A huge Panavision close-up of Wayne's sky-blue eyes registers the horror of what he sees and he immediately accedes to Marcus's demands for supplies to help the pitiful survivors, barking to one of his officers in a typically grumpy snarl, "Give this insubordinate son of a bitch every blanket and truck you can lay your hands on!"

In another scene where Wayne and Marcus are both in Washington to receive medals, the latter takes the opportunity of pressing Wayne for the official American attitude towards a declaration of independence by Israel to become a new state. Wayne at first replies with the offical view that fear of upsetting the Arabs with their vital oil supplies must cause the Americans to oppose it. But, as always, Wayne's allegiances are not dictated by the book but by his own feelings. He promises his support. "Stand up and be counted, Mickey," he says, "And a lot of us'll stand up with you." Even with Wayne's participation, the story of Mickey Marcus failed to draw large audiences, perhaps from the downbeat conclusion of the story in which Marcus is accidentally shot by an Israeli sentry, perhaps because comedy specialist Melville Shavelson was out of his depth as the writer-director of a drama (he did at least draw a hilarious, best-selling book from the experience, "How to Make a Jewish Movie," with a fascinating portrait of Wayne that is entirely complimentary). The film's American gross was less than half that of *The Sons of Katie Elder*, but Wayne had a couple of Westerns up his sleeve to draw in the crowds again.

80. The War Wagon (1967)

UNIVERSAL had their first opportunity to handle a Wayne picture since the early Forties when they contracted for *The War Wagon*, a co-production of Wayne's Batjac company with producer Marvin Schwartz. There was a slight gamble behind the camera. The direction was entrusted to Burt Kennedy who had begun his film career as a writer under contract to Wayne, scripting some of the lesser pictures that his company made (*Man in the Vault, Gun the Man Down* and the Western *Seven Men from Now* that turned out so well Wayne regretted not having starred in it himself, according to director Budd Boetticher). Kennedy had done a few modest, generally well received pictures and now had his big break (as Andrew V. McLaglen had in similar circumstances making Wayne's *McLintock!*). The writer was not Kennedy but Clair Huffaker, adapting his own novel. Huffaker had done an excellent job with James Edward Grant in writing the screenplay of *The Comancheros* and, since Grant had died in 1966, Wayne had to turn to new writers. With two such bright hopes for the future of the Western (Kennedy had made *West of Montana* and *The Rounders* as writer-director and both were excellent), the result was unexpectedly disappointing. Huffaker's original novel, called "Badman," is serious and good, but his screen adaptation is angled to develop a considerable amount of humour (to which Kennedy added touches of his own). Many of these comedy moments are excellent but the film seems to have been pressed too much into a routine mould of safe entertainment; there is a certain slackness about it (the result of Kennedy's rather stolid visual style) and it loses much of the dramatic effectiveness of the novel. What might have been a good Western becomes a rather forgettable one, losing its hold on the attention at a second viewing.

Wayne's role is that of Taw Jackson who is not quite the customary Wayne hero as for once he is on the wrong side of the law — though with justification. The local lawman is in the pocket of the villain Pierce (Bruce Cabot) who has cheated Wayne out of his land, had him put away in jail on a trumped-up charge, and made himself rich by mining the gold on Wayne's property.

Kirk Douglas makes his third appearance opposite Wayne, this time playing a character called Lomax and partnered with Wayne in a scheme to relieve Pierce of some of the gold which he periodically transports in the

An edgy partnership: Douglas cautions Wayne watched by Howard Keel.

war wagon of the title, an armour-plated coach heavily guarded *en route* by a bunch of riders. Again the steadiness of Wayne contrasts with the volatile temperament of the not-too-trustworthy Douglas, much as Gary Cooper contrasted with Burt Lancaster in *Vera Cruz* (the best example of an uneasy partnership) or Stuart Whitman with Wayne in *The Comancheros*. Lomax has in fact been offered a contract by Pierce to kill Wayne, an old enemy who is the only man he ever shot and didn't kill, merely putting him in hospital for six months. The two men lead cautious lives: both are seen, for humorous effect, in their long johns early one morning, guns securely strapped around their middles. Their professional competitiveness is brought out when they outdraw two of Pierce's men who foolishly decide to try for the price their boss has put on Wayne's head. "Mine hit the ground first," announces Lomax with satisfaction. "Mine was taller," replies Wayne, not to be outdone. Its succinct humour makes this the best exchange in the picture, better than such other attempts as when Wayne collects a weapon belonging to him from one of Pierce's men. Pierce observes that the shells in it belong to his man, leading Wayne to reply,

"Tell him he can come and get them anytime."

Given the relaxed nature of the film, no final confrontation is necessary between Wayne and Lomax although they kick the notion around, and the bulk of the gold they seize from the war wagon in the elaborate hold-up goes ironically out of reach, solving the moral problem of not allowing crime to pay even for these more than usually justified badmen.

There is a new degree of moral relaxation for a Wayne-shaped picture in another sphere with Lomax displaying a keen appetite for women's company overnight. Wayne observes this without criticism but his own standards remain as high as ever (he has never been known to misconduct himself with a woman in his pictures beyond spanking them for their own good). Kirk Douglas was even reported to have been filmed in a rear nude shot but this never reached the screen (at least not until Douglas did it again in *There Was a Crooked Man*). For Wayne, then, there is a slow acceptance of changing standards in what the screen can actually show of sex — as of violence — in his kind of family entertainment — as long as it's not a nude Kirk Douglas.

Making plans: Wayne, Robert Walker, Howard Keel, Keenan Wynn, Kirk Douglas.

*Kirk Douglas and John Wayne shoot down two foolish adversaries.
"Mine hit the ground first," says Douglas. "Mine was taller," replies Wayne.*

81. El Dorado (1967)

WAYNE's role in Howard Hawks's *El Dorado* is in one respect a considerable departure from his usual screen image. He plays Cole Thornton, a wandering gunfighter picking up assignments, one of the three fastest shots around (the other two are also in the picture). He is still the hero and incorruptible but he is no longer self-sufficient and invulnerable. He is twice shot by accident, leaving in one case a bullet lodged near his spine to bring on bouts of paralysis affecting his gun hand and even causing total collapse, and in the other a spray of buckshot reducing him to hobbling around on a crutch at the close of the picture. He only makes the final shootout by taking a wagon, he has to pre-arrange a diversion to trick his opponent, and has to be saved from death from another of the villains by a quick-shooting female.

Beyond the story level of sheriff and friends versus a greedy land baron, the film concerns itself with professional standards and the fear of declining abilities. When Wayne rides into town and takes a wash, he fails to see the sheriff, Robert Mitchum's J. P. Harrah, enter the room with a rifle levelled on him. Fortunately, the two are old friends but Harrah has been playing it safe until he knows which side Wayne is taking in a local feud. Wayne wanders close to his gunbelt and Harrah cautions him away. Wayne remarks, "I just wanted to see if you'd slowed down any." "Not that much," says Harrah, the conversation betraying an awareness of the inroads of time on old abilities and loyalties (Harrah believing that Wayne might now be reduced to going against a former pal). This stress on knowledge of present capabilities and limitations is taken up by other characters and seems to become an index of a man's worth. The doctor (Paul Fix) refuses to take the bullet from Wayne's side, saying "I'm not good enough." James Caan's Mississippi relies on a knife to deal with the murderers of a gambling friend because he knows he's no good with a gun. However, he is willing to learn the use of a gun from Wayne because he's good enough to teach him, being the best (and Wayne takes him to a gunsmith who's good enough to know what weapon Mississppi should use to make up for his deficiencies). When Mississippi defends his dead friend from the charge of being a cheat at cards by declaring "He was good — he didn't have to," he indicates the alternative to not being good enough — to cheat. And this is what Wayne has to resort to at the end of the film.

Another aspect of the film goes by the label of "professional courtesy" and is what the hired killer Nelse McLeod (an excellent portrayal by Christopher George) keeps extending to Wayne. It is a mark of respect between two men who, though on opposite sides, have in common a way of life at which both excel. McLeod criticises one of his own men for having used help to kill an old man (Mississippi's friend) and when Wayne ultimately arrives to take up "a little question unanswered between us," that of which one of them is best, McLeod dispenses with any help and gives his opponent time to clamber down from his wagon. McLeod admits to being curious as to how Wayne will make up for the loss of his regular gun hand and he should be alert to trickery, but the diversion behind McLeod that distracts his attention is an unprofessional solution to a personal challenge. Wayne shoots McLeod down, not cleanly but several times, firing his rifle with his left hand. As he lies dying, Nelse McLeod says — partly in recrimination, partly seeking an excuse for his defeat — "You didn't given me any chance at all, did you?" "No, I didn't," replies Wayne, "You were too good to give a chance to."

Here as elsewhere, Wayne is that much more ruthless and cautious in his responses. He backs his horse a considerable distance away from Bart Jason (Edward Asner) and his men after refusing to work for him against the MacDonalds whose spread he is after. Then, riding on, he is fired at unexpectedly and he shoots first, asking questions later, discovering that he has gut-wounded a young MacDonald who panicked while on look-out duty. Being shot here (as with McLeod) is a

Wayne watches James Caan's Mississippi prove what a bad shot he is. Right, the two cripples: "Can you hit anything that way?" asks Mitchum. "If I can get close enough," replies Wayne. "Load it, will you?"

215

Above, Wayne (with Robert Mitchum at right) invades a church pursuing villains.
Below, Wayne and Charlene Holt enjoy the spectacle of Mitchum taking a bath;
and Wayne argues with Michele Carey, watched by Arthur Hunnicutt.

messy, prolonged affair rather than instant painless death and the boy commits suicide rather than endure the agony of the wound any longer. When Wayne is shot by the boy's sister (Michele Carey), her marksmanship is no more accurate but then she is an amateur. Later on in the film, he collapses while riding as the lodged bullet causes paralysis, and he has to scramble for cover under some rocks — in a most undignified way for a Wayne hero — as another rider approaches. Later still, Wayne impatiently shoots one of Jason's men in the arm and leg to persuade him to go through a door into a suspected ambush, and the terrified man is duly shot to pieces. When a moment later, just before he can force the same fate on a second villain, he collapses again, this comes almost as a retribution for his impatient action. It is only as an observer that Wayne shows restraint, and this is when he intervenes to stop Harrah shooting Bart Jason after smashing a rifle barrel into his face.

It is often observed that *El Dorado* reprises the basic situations of the same director's *Rio Bravo* and the same characters in all but name. Mitchum's J. P. Harrah is the equivalent of Dean Martin's Dude, turning to drink after tangling with "some wandering petticoat" and being coerced into taking a bath after he straightens out; James Caan's Mississippi is a less skilled but more inventive equivalent of Ricky Nelson's Colorado Ryan; Arthur Hunnicutt's bewhiskered deputy is Walter Brennan's Stumpy all over again, down to hating his boss to be nice to him; and Charlene Holt's Maudie is Angie Dickinson's Feathers once more with the same past history but much less screen time. (She becomes Wayne's girl for keeps at the end after Harrah has pushed him to her by advising him to leave her alone, playing on Wayne's standard trait of ornery resistance

to advice.) The small details of both films are often similar, an object thrown through a window serving as a diversion in each one. And there is the same trade of prisoners (this time Wayne for Jason) as well as a church shootout that matches *Rio Bravo's* one in a barn, with Harrah, like Dude, following a trail of blood to the enemy's saloon and regaining his dignity inside.

But as Hawks repeats the situations he seems to examine them in the light of the eight years that have elapsed between the two films, to see how older men, now past their prime, would make out. When Harrah, himself wounded in the leg, looks at what he's got to fight the villains and sums it up as "Two cripples, a green kid, and a noisy old Indian fighter," there is no-one to contradict his assessment by saying "That's *what* you've got"; the old confidence has evaporated and all Harrah can do is promise the MacDonalds that he will *try* and handle Jason at the climax of the film. When Wayne is delivered bound and gagged for exchange with the imprisoned Jason, his helplessness is the furthest he has ever got from his usual command of things. And the final shootout is a far cry from the traditional form of open confrontation in *Rio Bravo*.

Wayne's frailty does not, of course, stem from weakness of character as does that of Harrah in lapsing into self-pity (though Wayne confesses he has been through Harrah's situation himself in the past). He often does assert his old sense of dependability, rallying Harrah from his drunken stupor (an element of high comedy for the picture) and watching out for him, reloading his gun as he rolled cigarettes for Dude in *Rio Bravo*. Wayne's physical difficulties are a piece of bad luck but they do serve to deprive him of his total dominance of a film and to make him part and parcel of the doubts and anxieties it expresses.

82. The Green Berets (1968)

FOR the first time since *The Alamo*, John Wayne went out on a limb to make *The Green Berets*. It wasn't so much a matter of money this time as a controversial subject. The film is virtually the only Hollywood production to portray the Vietnam conflict, and certainly the only major one to date. Two studios declined to back the picture but it is a reflection of Wayne's box-office drawing power and his personal enthusiasm for the project that it should not only have gone ahead (for Warner Bros.-Seven Arts) but have cost six to eight million dollars. Wayne's participation extended well beyond taking the leading role (it has no other major stars): his production company was behind it (son Michael producing) and he was the film's principal director. Ray Kellogg is credited as co-director but he had never directed a feature before and had a long record as a special effects man and occasional second unit director, indicating that he was more concerned with the technical aspects rather than the dramatic ones. Cliff Lyons was the actual second unit director and an old

colleague of Wayne's. Veteran director Mervyn LeRoy was sent over by the studio to watch progress and help out if the film fell behind schedule. John Ford was a visitor to the location (Fort Benning, Georgia). But reports of the film in production make it clear that Wayne was fully in command of the picture.

As in his statements about *The Alamo*, Wayne indicated that, as a good businessman, his purpose was primarily to entertain audiences; but one imagines that Wayne would consider it almost un-American to make a film without the profit motive uppermost. Yet other statements indicate that Wayne was as much concerned to make a point. He had been to Vietnam and met the American troops there and his film was "to show what those lads are going through." He has denied that his film glorified an unpopular war and his contempt for the "doves" stemmed from his belief that they were undermining the American position and helping the enemy. To Wayne, as a patriot, there is no choice but to stand by his government's decisions and back them up.

*Battle scene and briefing of
a war correspondent (David Janssen).*

218

Wayne and his men repulse the enemy's attack on "Dodge City"

Subsequently, he accepted with reluctance the evidence of atrocities at My Lai, telling reporter Gerald Pratley, "...as the courtmartial found Lt. Calley guilty then he *must be* guilty, and I loathe what he did." (My italics.) One sees then in Wayne a man emotionally committed to his country's prestige and this is a honest motivation for what seems to me a dishonest film. *The Green Berets* owes more to Hollywood *cliché* and past war films than it does to the particular event of the Vietnam war.

Some critics even labelled it a Western in disguise with the Vietcong playing the Indians. This view is encouraged by the nickname of "Dodge City" for the American base in the film, while a line like Wayne's "Due process is a bullet" is another way of saying "The only good Vietcong is a dead one." The modesty of the pin-ups on the wall where Peterson (Jim Hutton) is billeted place it in the Second World War before the advent of "Playboy" nude spreads. The film's only gesture towards contemporary doubters is the inclusion of an uncommitted American reporter (David Janssen) who represents a newspaper opposed to American par-

ticipation in Vietnam. But the film quickly disposes of this line of potential resistance by exposing the reporter to the atrocities committed by the Vietcong and so thoroughly shocking him that he is soon lending a helping hand in killing the enemy ("What can I do?", he asks anxiously during an attack). The film implicitly accuses those who oppose the war of not knowing anything about it: "Pretty hard to talk to anyone who hasn't visited this country and seen it," says Wayne, admiring its beauty one calm evening. No one reminds the audience that the opponents of the war, including those who have experienced it, are just as shocked by the horror of it all and simply hope for a better solution than adding to the devastation by continuing the fight. The Vietcong are represented as an anonymous horde of barbarians for most of the film but the last sequence deals with a raid on a house occupied by a leading North Vietnamese general who is only too ready to bed the glamorous spy dangled in front of him and whose life style seems to be one of wealthy if arid Western decadence rather than Communist self-deprivation. There is, on the other hand, no discreditable action on the part

Wayne on the kidnapping raid and comforting Hamchunk (Craig Jue).

of an American soldier within the standards of behaviour deemed honourable by the film. Even the familiar figure of the scrounger who makes off with supplies that might be badly needed elsewhere is accepted as a demonstration of American resourcefulness and humour. How the South Vietnamese conduct themselves is little elaborated upon. Captain Nim's record of enemy killed is seen as an indication of his zeal to free his country rather than Vietcong-like "enjoyment" of the war. The reporter is shocked by the brutality Nim (George Takei) inflicts on an enemy agent who has infiltrated his forces and Wayne does intervene to calm him but Nim's anger is seen as understandable. When the newsman complains about the absence of "due process" in handling the spy, Wayne uses that line "Due process out here is a bullet" — which is not at all what it has been shown to be and indicates the film's eagerness to include a smart line rather than elaborate on a point. Wayne recalls that the general they are assigned to kidnap had been freed by the South Vietnamese for lack of evidence against him although his guilt was well enough known, indicating his impatience with but ultimate acceptance of "due process" of law.

Some of the American actions in the film are as shocking as those of the Vietcong, although they are not intended to be and no point is made about the way the Americans are almost reduced to fighting in the same manner as the enemy. It is not so much the use of such crude terminology as "killing zone" or the array of

spiked sticks awaiting enemy soldiers clambering over a barbed wire fence (the Americans decently refrain from poisoning the ends, unlike the Vietcong) but the wholesale slaughter of the enemy, machine-gunned from the air once they have overrun "Dodge City" or frying in an inferno of flame on the barbed wire. This second image is followed by a small boy's mourning the death of his dog (but the dog was on our side, of course). Even the kidnapping raid on the general has its discreditable aspect, tricking the general into bed with a female spy and catching him with his trousers down.

War only becomes appalling when American lives are lost. Captain Coleman (Jason Evers) is seemingly the only casualty of a shell barrage on the very last day of his service before returning home; the reporter can't comprehend the complete disappearance of the man he was talking to just a moment before the shell landed. The likable Peterson (Jim Hutton) is caught in a booby trap and rammed to death on an upright bed of spikes; but the tough Sgt. Kowalski (Mike Henry) can impale an attacking soldier on a spiked branch from a tree that just happens to be at hand (the form of death is the same as Peterson's but unpremeditated) and he takes four of the enemy with him when he dies. But death has its compensations when you have a privy named after you as the case of Sgt. Provo (Luke Askew) proves (his concern for a suitable monument earmarks him for death sooner or later.) Though these deaths bring momentary pauses for regret, there is no doubt that in

220

effect these dead Americans are less to be mourned than gloried over.

The purpose of it all, the film shows, is to free the next generation of Vietnamese. Two children are introduced for maximum emotive effect: the young daughter of a village elder whose foot has been poisoned by a pungi stick laid down by the enemy and who is on her way to recovery thanks to American medical aid when she is murdered by the Vietcong; and the small boy Hamchunk (Craig Jue) who befriends the camp scrounger, Peterson, and finds comfort in sleeping alongside him with a hand draped around the American's waist for protection. When Peterson is killed, Wayne has to break the news: "Peterson was very brave. Are you going to be?" Wayne puts the dead man's green beret on the lad's head and assumes responsibility for him. "You're what this is all about," declares Wayne. The pair set off along a beach backed by the setting sun as the rousing "Ballad of the Green Berets" swells up on the soundtrack and the film ends.

Thus the picture operates on the most primitive levels of identification, showing good and bad as absolutes and using a small boy to carry its message. It is set back in 1963 when the war was more clear-cut and less controversial, which may form an excuse for avoiding its later complexities but hardly a valid one as this is not emphasised and the audience had no reason to suppose from the film that its argument was not fully valid when it came out. The picture essentially reassures Americans than they can take pride in their country's involvement in Vietnam and it naturally aroused the ire of those who found it complacent and evasive. In London and elsewhere, the film was picketed but it seems to have found a ready audience nonetheless: only *True Grit* among Wayne's regular starring vehicles has taken more money in North America.

83. Hellfighters (1968)

HELLFIGHTERS may look a bit different by not being a Western but it really is the kind of Wayne film put together by numbers. Though not made by Wayne's production company, it surrounds him with reliable and familiar colleagues. The script is an original by Clair Huffaker, consolidating his position as an expert on catering to the Wayne image after his work on *The Comancheros* and *The War Wagon* (surprisingly, Wayne has not made use of him since *Hellfighters*). The director is Andrew V. McLaglen, easy-going and compliant. The director of photography is again William H. Clothier. Vera Miles, who had handled the romance with Jeffrey Hunter in *The Searchers* and been youthful again as the "young" Wayne's girl in *The Man Who Shot Liberty Valance,* steps into the mature bracket as a suitable partner for the admittedly ageing Wayne in this film.* Old friend Bruce Cabot has a good part while Jim Hutton (from *The Green Berets)* and an uninspiring actor called Edward Faulkner, whom Wayne was making a habit of using, are featuring in the supporting cast. The only fresh blood for the young audience is Katharine Ross who had attracted attention just beforehand in *The Graduate.*

Unadventurous casting, behind and in front of the camera, is the first element. The second is the script itself, lacking any spark of inspiration to light up the film as effectively as its spectacular oil-well fires. The third is technically competent but artistically uncreative direction. The stock components, as written, cast and played, can be itemised as follows.

1) The Wayne character. Here it's Chance Buckman (styled on the real-life Red Adair). Head of an outfit specialising in fighting oil fires wherever they occur, he is described by his faithful friend Lomax (Jay C. Flip-pen) as "one of a kind, the best there is at his kind of job." Wayne then is again the complete professional, excusing his shortcomings in the domestic field. And typically he is also secretive, a loner, with Lomax the only man in the company who knows about the wife who left him long ago and the daughter he hasn't seen for years.

2) The "senior" romance. Wayne's marriage has foundered on the familiar reefs between career and home life with Madelyn Buckman (Vera Miles) unable to take the stress of the recurring danger to her husband's life. Vera Miles thus has a typical Maureen O'Hara role, turning up in his life again and enabling Wayne to try and patch up their differences. He pays her the usual warm compliments, telling her of the effect she has on him just walking down a restaurant towards him and gently hinting that she might spend the night with him by not using the key to her hotel room. Like O'Hara, she wavers, old feelings stirred but says "I won't if you ask me not to and you know it. Please don't." Wayne, the perfect gentleman in such matters, lets the suggestion drop. Soon after, he even agrees to retire from action to a desk job, delighting Madelyn so much that she wants to return to him; but we know that this resolve of his won't last for long.

3) Moral laxity (by Wayne standards). Moving with the times, as in *The War Wagon,* the film has a firefighter called Greg Parker (Jim Hutton) who makes a habit of recruiting girls to witness his work and takes advantage of the circumstances to bed them. This merely causes Wayne to comment indulgently, "Well, I can't say I blame you. Fella as ugly as you are couldn't get to first base without a fire."

4) The "junior" romance. This is between Parker and Wayne's daughter Tish (Katharine Ross) who comes to her father's hospital bed after he has been injured. She is so precious to him that he swallows with emotion at

---

*She had in fact, played his wife in *The Green Berets* for one scene set in the States but her appearance was cut from the film because of length problems.

Wayne settling down to desk work (Jay C. Flippen at left); and in action as a firefighter.

Wayne fears the worst when he sees his daughter's friendship with Jim Hutton. Katharine Ross is the girl; Vera Miles at rear plays Wayne's wife.

the sight of her — the kind of response that Wayne carries off so well, affirming the kind heart beneath the rough exterior. Once Wayne sees the friendly interest Greg has taken in Tish and learns that she has seen him in action at a fire, he fears that Greg has been up to his usual tricks and starts to boil over but Greg manages to establish that they were properly married beforehand in a whirlwind courtship — which makes it all right.

5) The lusty brawl. When Wayne's team meet up with a crew of Australian drillers, it's not long before a friendly, furniture-smashing fight is underway.

6) Vivid action. Wayne has always had a keen regard for the value of rousing action scenes and been willing to pitch in himself to add realism. Here we see him actually capping oil fires with black oil spurting in his face and can believe he's taking a risk, just as he was visibly in the thick of the circus fire in *The Magnificent Showman* or personally catching the wild animals in *Hatari!* These are some of the scenes that have made Wayne the screen's most convincing action hero. Here,

using Red Adair as consultant, the various fires are most impressive and the methods of handling them clearly and educatively shown. But the value of this approach is limited by the plot cliches that surround their appearances.

7) Resolving the plot on Wayne's terms. There is a particularly difficult job in Venezuela where three wells are burning in close proximity and rebel guerillas are sniping away from the surrounding hills. Wayne comes out of retirement after Tish has pleaded with her mother to ask him to help Greg handle the situation. Both wives watch as their men go to work. Madelyn throws a fit over the danger Wayne is exposed to by the inefficient protection of the Venezuelan army. Wayne responds by telling her "You'll do," and that she'll need a tin hat to watch him in future. So both wives become reconciled to the danger of their men's work. Once again, the male viewpoint triumphs, giving Wayne the best of both worlds.

84. True Grit (1969)

LIKE *Stagecoach, Red River, The Searchers* and *Rio Bravo, True Grit* was one of those rare opportunities for an actor to pump new vitality into his career. Wayne's playing of the one-eyed deputy U.S. marshal Reuben J. "Rooster" Cogburn won him unstinting praise from American critics who tipped him for the Oscar he duly won — the first of his career. Wayne had tried to buy the film rights after reading the galley proofs of the Charles Portis novel but Hal Wallis beat him to it and then offered him the part. Wallis, who had brought Wayne and Henry Hathaway together for *The Sons of Katie Elder*, repeated the combination here and the result was a picture that has become the fifth highest grossing Western, a short way behind *Paint Your Wagon* and *Little Big Man* and only thoroughly eclipsed by *Butch Cassidy and the Sundance Kid* and

How the West Was Won (in which Wayne, of course, had been a principal attraction). (These comparisons are based on figures from "Variety" for the North American market; world wide, *True Grit* may well have edged ahead of its closest rivals.)

Kim Darby plays the girl Mattie Ross, out to hire a lawman to bring to justice Tom Chaney (Jeff Corey), the murderer of her father. She seeks out the advice of the sheriff (John Doucette) on possible choices and hears Cogburn summed up as "a pitiless man, double tough, fear don't enter into his thinking" while a land-lady adds that he "loves to pull a cork." (The novel provides the film with many unfamiliar and authentic-seeming turns of phrase which have a refreshing effect.)

We first see Wayne from afar bringing in prisoners from the badlands, then closer to in court being irked by

Wayne shows Kim Darby as Mattie Ross his "immediate family": a Chinaman (H.W. Gim) and a cat.

As Rooster J. Cogburn, Wayne brings in the prisoners, sits tall in the saddle preparing to do battle with Ned Pepper, and falls drunkenly off his horse on the trail, carefully keeping his whisky bottle upright.

At nightcamp, Wayne falls into reminiscing over his past to Kim Darby as young Mattie Ross.

the criticism of his habit of shooting first and not taking unnecessary risks with badmen. "You can't serve papers on a rat," the disgruntled Wayne later demonstrates with the help of a genuine rodent, this attitude causing the film to be regarded in some circles as an argument for a tougher line on law and order in contemporary times (but the situations are so different that the transposition is not really applicable).

Wayne makes Cogburn, a former outlaw, into a boozy, smelly, cantankerous figure, indifferent about his appearance and the impression he makes on others, lining his pockets with rewards for doing his job and confiscating much of his whisky supply from the men he captures. This is Wayne openly playing his real age in a role that is both dominating lead and colourful character part. He is at first amused by Mattie's proposition but takes more of an interest when he hears of the financial offer she is making. "I'm giving you my children's rates," he comments when she tries to bargain with him over the price, and the deal is set.

A handsome Texas Ranger, La Boeuf (Glen Campbell), also has an interest in catching Chaney and joins up as Wayne sets out into the untamed badlands. Mattie doggedly insists on coming along and the pair attempt to leave her behind at a ferry crossing only to observe her swimming across the river on horseback. Here Wayne begins to admire her pluck: "My God, she reminds me of me!" He takes to trading insults with the Texan who taunts him over his Civil War association with Quantrill, a man Wayne unexpectedly defends. It's intriguing to find him, after having so often glorified Texas (as in *The Alamo*), hitting back by running down everything to do with the place. He exhibits the fondness for alcohol that the landlady had observed and at one point falls off his horse, keeping the whisky bottle upright and brightly suggesting the place as a good one to rest up for the night.

Wayne settles comfortably into reminiscing with Mattie over his past — a broken marriage, a son who didn't like him — then turning to brighter memories of the occasion from his law-breaking past when he turned around on a pursuing posse and charged, causing them to scatter in terror of their lives. Soon after, faced by the outlaw Ned Pepper (Robert Duvall) and some of his men, Wayne can't resist repeating his proud exploit, despite his greater age and the more determined opposition. Ned Pepper, a practical man, gives Wayne the chance to back down: "Well, Rooster, will you give us the road? We got business elsewhere." Wayne's stubborn response causes Ned to label him "a one-eyed fat man" and this leads directly to one of the most unforgettable images of Wayne as he draws back on his horse at the words of insult and yells "Fill your hand, you sonuvabitch!", filling both his own with a cocked rifle and six-gun, gripping the reins between his teeth, and spurring his animal forward. Like a medieval jouster armed with lance, he charges forward, guns ablazing, and passes through the Pepper mob to wheel around. His shots take their toll but a bullet from the other side brings his horse down and, as an indication of the character's advancing age, he doesn't leap clear as a younger Wayne hero might have done but lies trapped under the animal. With a mortally wounded Ned Pepper slowly advancing on him, it takes the help of the quick-shooting Texan from afar off to enable him to survive.

Tom Chaney is small fry compared to the likes of Ned Pepper. But Chaney proves dangerous in his sneaky way, delivering a head blow to the Texan who has captured him, and being the cause of Mattie tumbling into a snake pit while firing a shot at him. Wayne turns

227

up to put a finish to Chaney and needs the aid of the dying Texan to haul Mattie up to the surface.

With La Boeuf dead and Mattie seriously ill from a snake bite, Wayne comes into his own, riding a horse into the ground while rushing her to the nearest source of medical aid, pushing on by foot and commandeering a wagon at gunpoint from some resting cowboys to complete the journey.

After making a complete recovery, Mattie expresses her gratitude to Wayne by a sentimental gesture, offering him a place in her family's graveyard when his time comes to "meet eternity," knowing that his only friends are a Chinaman and a cat. The snow-covered landscape, following the autumn of earlier scenes, points up the prospect of death but Wayne stoutly declares that he'll put off the day for as long as possible and rides off inviting her to "Come and see a fat old man sometime." He jumps his horse over a four foot fence to show off and waves his hat, arm outstretched...the film freezing on him in a blurry image as a man receding into the vague mist of legend and history.

Some writers have accused Wayne of hamming up the part. He certainly exploits it for all it is worth, like W. C. Fields as Mr. Micawber (and nobody complains about that). His one eye glaring and glinting from his puffy face, his arm making expansive gestures, his body swaying under the effects of alcohol, he is a perfectly believable image of an old man who has gone to seed but is still capable of showing "true grit." Wayne had already played old men "straight" to prove he could do it, and this part calls for none of the strength of character and self-control of Thomas Dunson (*Red River*) or Nathan Brittles (*She Wore a Yellow Ribbon*). Although both are more finely observed and demanding portrayals (hence more deserving of that Academy Award), his Rooster Cogburn coheres because Wayne is at home in the part and knows how to give it substance rather than a display of superficial tricks.

Despite the torrents of praise, Wayne evidently had no intention of being retired into old men parts. His next picture, *The Undefeated*, cast aside all the trimmings of *True Grit* and it wasn't until *The Cowboys* that Wayne again took a chance on varying his set image.

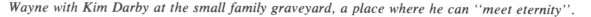

Wayne with Kim Darby at the small family graveyard, a place where he can "meet eternity".

85. The Undefeated (1969)

WRITTEN, produced and directed by the same team that made the slightly superior *Bandolero!*, i.e. James Lee Barrett (also the writer of *The Green Berets*), Robert Jacks and Andrew V. McLaglen, *The Undefeated* strikes me as Wayne's least interesting film of the Sixties, redeemed only by the occasional moments that he can handle really well and by one or two pictorial splendours from William Clothier's camera. Rock Hudson is unhappily cast as James Langdon, a Southerner leading his defeated people to a new future in Mexico. There are a number of dreadful supporting performances that clearly slipped away from directorial control, especially that of Marion McCargo as Wayne's romantic interest, her eyebrows jumping up and down like typewriter keys in one scene, and Roman Gabriel as Wayne's adopted son, very much like Jeffrey Hunter in his Wooden Indian period before John Ford unearthed surprising potential from him. That these two

key relationships are so weakly played undermines Wayne's own performance as John Henry Thomas, the ex-Union officer leading his men on a horse drive south of the border.

McLaglen pays his usual "homage by imitation" to John Ford, introducing a Fourth of July fracas between Northerners and Southerners that is all surface knockabout with no sense of the shape and delight Ford brought to his equivalent mass fights. The early scene with Paul Fix as a general accepting Wayne's resignation from the army is deep in Ford territory and as one looks on its nondescript handling, one begins to think of how richly Ford would have elaborated upon it.

The action scenes — a shootout with bandits, a charge using the mass of wild horses — are lavishly enough staged to be momentarily impressive and one can salvage odd moments of pleasure from Wayne's scenes: his confident posture amidst the milling horses

John Wayne and Rock Hudson.

and the clouds of dust; the cracked grin before Wayne launches into two thieving horse buyers, they asking ''You calling us thieves?'' and Wayne replying with his usual candour, ''Why, yes, that's a pretty accurate description''; his encouraging words to Anne Langdon (Marion McCargo) when she's about to use a rifle, ''Windage and elevation!'', the gift of his wealth of experience; the careful conversation between Wayne and Langdon on the one hand and the bandit leader (Pedro Armendariz Jr.) on the other, when the two sides sound each other out at a parlay.

With its message of reconciliation between North and South, *The Undefeated* seeks to attain some significance. With such touches as giving Wayne a wife who didn't take to him going off hunting or wherever he pleased (and left him to teach piano in Philadelphia), it knows how to cater for its star. But its slack grip on the narrative, its tired handling and its dreary colour make one hard put to care. Wayne's next, *Chisum*, is more conventional in script, again directed by Andrew V. McLaglen, but works out much better.

Left, Wayne hands in his resignation to Paul Fix as an army general, and below takes a sock at Bruce Cabot during a friendly fracas.

Above, Wayne fights off Mexican bandits attacking the wagon train. Below,
Wayne and Hudson discuss selling the horses to Tony Aguilar as General Rojas.

*Above, Wayne with Geoffrey Deuel
as Billy the Kid.*

*Wayne with Pamela McMyler
playing his niece from Baltimore.*

86. Chisum (1970)

CHISUM, like *The Sons of Katie Elder*, has the air of having been made twenty years earlier; but since Westerns of the late Forties and early Fifties were often engaging in their simplicity, that's no bad period to recall. Introducing several real-life figures, it tells the story of the Lincoln County War in the New Mexico of 1878 which made a folk hero out of the nineteen-year-old William Bonney, "Billy the Kid." The first screen representation of Bonney since Paul Newman's in Arthur Penn's psychologically-orientated *The Left Handed Gun*, it settles for showing Billy as a quick-tempered but essentially likable boy, loyal to his friends. The performance of Geoffrey Deuel is so shallow that the possibility of stealing the film from Wayne never arises.

Wayne appears as John Simpson Chisum, cattle king, seen in the opening shot of the film sitting on a hillside in a simple and poetic shot, surveying his domain, looking back on the past, gently puffing on a cigar*: a man, a horse and a tree on a slope. Later there's another quiet scene on a porch as dusk approaches with Wayne and

*Though Wayne gave up smoking after his cancer operation, he still uses a cigar as part of his screen image, even taking a tentative puff on one in an early scene on the courthouse stairs in *True Grit* before discarding it.

his niece from Baltimore (Pamela McMyler), which again suggests Wayne as a man who is well satisfied with what he has achieved. But the film turns into one of those "this town ain't big enough for the both of us" kind of Westerns with Wayne battling it out with Forrest Tucker, an excellent heavy who had last appeared with him in *Sands of Iwo Jima*. Tucker plays Lawrence Murphy, a corrupt businessman buying up the area to bring it under his control (cf. James Gregory's Morgan Hastings in *The Sons of Katie Elder*).

As in *McLintock!*, Wayne is the kind of man who knows that wealth and power place a responsibility on him to lend a helping hand to folks less well off than himself; and when the law is corrupt and the Governor in the villain's pocket, it takes a man of Wayne's unselfish determination to straighten things out. We also see him stepping in to restore some dignity to an old Indian chum held at a fort, White Buffalo (Abraham Sofaer), by having a few firm words with the sergeant in charge of him.

Much of the action is precipitated by Bonney, out to avenge the death of his employer (Patric Knowles), but Wayne has a pleasing bit to himself riding up with some men to a riverbank and confronting a Mexican bandit whose gang have made off with some of his cattle. The Mexican, played in the traditional image of toothy-smiled mock reasonableness perfected by the late Alfonso Bedoya, starts off by offering Wayne the thought that "There must be some mistake here." "You made it," replies Wayne curtly. The Mexican tries to sell him back his cows and asks "Did you bring some gold with you?" "No," says Wayne. "Silver?" "No. Just lead." And the shooting starts. Such a patently rigged conversation nevertheless allows Wayne to shine so well that it is immensely enjoyable. Unfortunately, most of Andrew J. Fenady's dialogue isn't this sharp and the film drags a bit through its 110 minutes length but it can be forgiven much for its climactic fistfight between Wayne and Tucker, a splendidly protracted free-for-all that recaptures the spirit of such encounters as that of *The Spoilers* in its aggressive exuberance and concludes with Tucker being knocked out of a window to fall to his death on the points of an antler.

An exuberant showdown between hero Wayne and villain Forrest Tucker.

233

Wayne, above with Jack Elam, below being "comfortable" for Jennifer O'Neill.

87. Rio Lobo (1970)

THIS FILM cruelly pinpoints Wayne's dilemma as an actor used to working from time to time with the best directors in the business. With John Ford in retirement and with Howard Hawks losing his grip as badly as he does here, he could no longer turn to the two directors who have served him best (though it is premature, on the basis of *Rio Lobo*, to entirely write off the possibility of another really good Hawks-Wayne film.) Wayne has admitted to not liking *Rio Lobo*, and its deficiencies are made only too apparent by the way it demands comparison with *Rio Bravo* and *El Dorado* as a second variation on the earlier film. *El Dorado* was a coarser, more violent version of *Rio Bravo* but one felt that Hawks was on top of the entire film. One small lapse — where a sultry girl ineptly whispered to Robert Mitchum's J. P. Harrah that some men were hiding in a church — proves to have been the thin end of a wedge that rams into *Rio Lobo*, making all the female performances distressingly shallow with Hawks missing the potential in Jennifer O'Neill that other directors have uncovered. The tight quartet of Wayne/Dean Martin/Ricky Nelson/Walter Brennan in *Rio Bravo* and Wayne/Robert Mitchum/James Caan/Arthur Hunnicutt in *El Dorado* has here become the loose combination of Wayne/Jorge Rivero/James Mitchum/Jack Elam. The plot is no longer an integral part of the picture but a pretext for arriving at particular confrontations; it rambles so much as to dissipate tension and concern; and the male performances, apart from Wayne and Jack Elam, both of whom can look after themselves, are undistinguished. It is not a matter of denying Hawks and writer Leigh Brackett the chance to work over *Rio Bravo* again but the way they did it. *Rio Lobo* is no different from the obviously routine films of this period in giving satisfaction from isolated moments, from small reflections on the Wayne image rather than from Wayne's place in the overall picture. Many of the Wayne touches turn him into a good-natured butt for moments of callous humour directed at his figure and age.

Wayne is given a tight-fitting Army uniform for the opening Civil War sequence, denying him any disguise for his widening shape. This and the way he struggles when a Confederate leaps on him, dislodging him from his horse into a river, lead him to be described as like "a small baby whale," the first time Wayne has ever been called small. This capture takes place when Wayne, as Colonel Cord McNally, improbably separates himself from the men he is leading in pursuit of some Confederate troops who have taken a gold shipment from a train and killed an officer whom Wayne had regarded as like a son (a relationship baldly stated rather than demonstrated). Wayne is intent on settling the score with the traitor who leaked the news of the shipment to the other side; the two leading Confederates, Cordona (Jorge Rivero) and Tuscarora (Chris Mitchum), know only what the man looks like, not his name, but at the end of the war they promise to keep their eyes open for him.

They are eventually able to summon Wayne to Rio Lobo where the man he seeks, Ketcham (Victor French), is now the land baron who controls the law and is victimising locals who resist his attempts to buy them out, notably the fiery old-timer Phillips (Jack Elam). Tuscarora is put in jail on a trumped-up charge and Wayne, together with Cordona and Phillips, seizes Ketcham, terrorising him into signing over all the properties he has stolen to their original owners. They then take over the jail, freeing Tuscarora, with Cordona sent to bring back troops to take Ketcham into legal custody. However, Cordona is captured and Ketcham's ally Sheriff Hendricks (Mike Henry) proposes an exchange of prisioners, bringing about the "trade" situation previously seen in *Rio Bravo* and *El Dorado*.

This time Ketcham is caught in the middle when Cordona leaps into a stream. Wayne lets Hendricks know that his boss has signed away his stolen wealth thereby signing Ketcham's death warrant. In the ensuing shootout, Wayne takes a bullet in the leg but the badmen are routed, Hendricks accidentally shooting himself in the face. This sequence is even more graphically violent and painful than anything in *El Dorado*.

At the end of the film, Cordona and Tuscarora go off with their respective girlfriends. Wayne, left alone, turns to Amelita (Sherry Lansing) whose face was disfigured earlier by the villains. They are simply company for each other, or at best two people who will settle for each other because nobody else will have them. To a really attractive young woman like Shasta (Jennifer O'Neill), Wayne has merely become "comfortable" while the younger Cordona attracts her sexually. There is a scene at a night camp where she snuggles up against Wayne for security and when the flustered Wayne suggests she might do better with Cordona, she replies with innocent cruelty, "He's too young but you're older, more...comfortable." As the scarred girl leans on Wayne at the end of the film and starts to tell him, "You feel awfully...", he cuts in to plead, "Please don't say comfortable!" Wayne's insecurity with young women is also brought out when one faints into his arms and he asks helplessly, bewilderment seizing his features in a comic fashion, "What do I do with her?"

While Wayne has become "a comfortable old man" to the fair sex, he has become an even more ruthless adversary where the bad guys are concerned. He almost lets flames engulf Ketcham when he meets his enemy at last and when he pleads with Hendricks to make a move so that he can shoot him, there is as much relish in the prospect as there is anger. As in *El Dorado*, this can be interpreted as the increasing impatience of old age, but it also conveniently fits in with the callousness of many contemporary Westerns.

There was something of an inside joke neatly integrated into *The Searchers* when Wayne ridiculed his son Patrick's efforts as a green lieutenant in pompously delivering a message; and *Rio Lobo* belatedly pays him back by mocking his own thespian abilities. Wayne goes to talk with the town's dentist, who opposes Ketcham's take-over, and is made to play a patient to allay the suspicions of some watching villains. The dentist gives Wayne some real treatment, answering his protests with "If you'd been a good enough actor, I wouldn't have done it."

In truth, Wayne is too good an actor to be wasting his time on such a feeble *pot-pourri* as this. But Wayne's faith in Howard Hawks that led him to accept the role, script unseen, and to merely ask knowingly, "Do I get to play the drunk this time?" is fully understandable in the light of their past accomplishments together.

Left, the comic tooth-yanking episode with David Huddleston. Above, Wayne and Jack Elam keep a close grip on Victor French while Chris Mitchum keeps an eye on the rear.

88. Big Jake (1971)

WHILE Wayne has always been Duke to his friends, he is Big John to publicists and so it is not surprising that the title of the film should have been changed before release from *Million Dollar Kidnapping*, hardly suggestive of a Western (although an accurate summary of the plot situation), to *Big Jake*, centering fair and square on the main character of the film and approximating its performer's popular nickname. The film has a couple of pleasant reunions: Maureen O'Hara again, and (making a change from Andrew V. McLaglen) George Sherman as the director, the man who directed Wayne in all his 3 Mesquiteers adventures in the late Thirties and popped up subsequently as the producer of *The Comancheros*. Sherman's direction is easy on the eye though rather too slack to make the most of the opening and climactic

scenes, and William Clothier takes yet another opportunity to enhance a Wayne film with some splendid views.

The time is 1909. The East is watching *The Great Train Robbery* and its successors, but the West is still the West playing the games for real and proving more than a match for the trappings of Twentieth century progress. Wayne's Jake McCandles is, like his George Washington McLintock of *McLintock!*, a man with a town named after him (the railways stations look suspiciously similar in both films), the pioneer who built the biggest spread around. But he is an absentee from McCandles and his wife Martha (Maureen O'Hara) who does live there insists that she has no husband — until she needs him. It's never made clear whether he de-

As Big Jake, Wayne has just taught his screen (and real life) son Patrick Wayne
not to be insolent while Maureen O'Hara watches in the background.

John Wayne and Maureen O'Hara at the station.

Wayne's real life son John Ethan Wayne (playing Big Jake's grandson) makes deadly use of the derringer during the film's climax.

serted her or was booted out but there's talk of Martha's past resentment at his interest in other women. One day a band of vicious outlaws led by John Fain (Richard Boone) ride up to the McCandles ranch-house, coldbloodedly murder ten people, abduct Martha's eight-year-old grandson, Little Jake (John Ethan Wayne), and leave a ransom note demanding one million dollars. Martha has no problem raising the money but she declines the help of the Texas Rangers and the military in delivering it. This, she declares, is "going to be an extremely harsh and unpleasant kind of business and will require an extremely harsh and unpleasant kind of man to see to it!"

On this splendid introduction, the film cuts to a giant close-up of Wayne's eye squinting down the barrel of his rifle. He is about to break up a small lynching party down below, thinks better of it (muttering to his dog, called Dog, "No, sir, I ain't"), then thinks again when he sees one of the lynchers kick a small boy trying to rescue his sheepherder father from the noose. Wayne rides up to the hanging tree in his pink shirt and braces (pink is his favourite colour to judge by its frequent appearance), looking dangerously amiable, agreeing most readily that sheep bring a terrible odour to the land, but buying the herd from their unfortunate owner and transferring the cowboys' grievances to himself. He has only to mention his name for the men to back down from their threatening stance and hastily release their victim. "I thought you were dead," their leader (Jim Davis) comments.

This little good deed accomplished, Wayne gets the message from Martha, puts on his best clothes and turns up at McCandles station where she is waiting. "You're as young, as lovely as ever," Wayne tells her, always ready with a warm compliment for his screen reunions with wives. He also shows his deep attachment to her by knowing to the year and month (if not the day) how long it has been since he saw her last (a familiar device from earlier films with the same situation). O'Hara's Martha is as headstrong as one would expect, assuring Wayne that their son (shot in Fain's raid) will recover because "I would not contemplate otherwise." He agrees to deliver the ransom money after learning for the first time that he even has a grandson. She decides to let the Texas Rangers try and ambush the kidnappers but Wayne prefers to deal with them alone, allowing her to accuse him of being as stubborn as ever, of not having changed. "Not a bit," he readily agrees, and once again we see the two players refusing to bend to each other. Though Martha never reappears in the picture once Wayne has set out on his mission, the small part is so effectively conceived that it gets the film off to a bright start and is a worthwhile addition to O'Hara's line of appearances opposite Wayne.

Wayne displays his undiminished capabilities by singlehandedly carrying off the chest of ransom money that *two* men have lugged in, but he is eventually joined by his two sons, James (Patrick Wayne) and Michael (Chris Mitchum), as well as by an old Indian friend, Sam Sharpnose (Bruce Cabot). There is a lot of the usual horseplay between father and sons, Wayne socking each of them at least a couple of times; there is also a scene where Wayne specially seeks out the orneriest man in a town to start a brawl as a cover for a scheme elsewhere. Fain rides into Wayne's camp one night to conduct an edgy conversation with him, neither revealing their true identities but making their positions clear, and they finally meet at a "trade" to set beside those in the Hawks films. Wayne hands over the ransom chest and allows Fain to discover that it merely contains ordinary paper, then *sotto voce* warns the man that he'll be dead the moment he allows one of his sharpshooters to pick off Wayne's waiting grandson. A moment of stalemate is succeeded by a bloody shootout in which Wayne is hit at least twice, his Indian friend and dog killed, and his grandson (played by Wayne's youngest real-life son) has to fire a bullet from a derringer into the largest member of Fain's gang. Here, as in the opening raid on the ranchhouse, each little incident tends to be handled in isolation, dissipating tension: when the small boy helps put a tourniquet on Wayne's bleeding leg, there is no sound of continuing gunfire elsewhere with the rest of Wayne's team to keep up the suspense. The

brutality, too, seems somewhat excessive — the most violent climax in a Wayne film to this point, and a regrettable genuflection towards trends in Westerns generally.

The most interesting aspect of the film is the contrast between progress and traditional ways — with the latter, as expressed in Wayne, winning hands down. Texas Rangers set out in their motorised convoy with all the confidence of the Twentieth century, steaming across a bridge and deflecting Wayne and his horse to take the river alongside, but soon their vehicles have been shot to pieces and they are left to nurse their wounded and wait for help as Wayne rides by and leaves them behind. His horse also outlasts the motorbike that his son Michael rides with youthful enthusiasm, unsettling Wayne's steed to tip him into a muddy puddle, hairing among the rocks to distract the men ambushing the Rangers, but wrecking it in a crash. It is Wayne who symbolises dependability and stamina.

He has *almost* become a man of the past. Four times people see him and declare "I thought you were dead," but Wayne proves himself to be very much alive. After the third person makes the remark, Wayne warns "The next man says that I'm gonna shoot, so help me." The next man is Fain. We find Wayne donning spectacles to read the ransom note, an idea borrowed from Joel McCrea's ageing Westerner of *Guns in the Afternoon* (*Ride the High Country*), and old Sam Sharpnose confessing his sight isn't what it used to be, but Big John at least is still sharp-eyed enough to observe that his son James is favouring one leg owing to a concealed bullet wound.

It's Big Jake, alias John Wayne, who carries off the film, like the ransom chest, on his broad shoulders. Without him, it would have been in a minor bracket.

89. The Cowboys (1972)

AFTER becoming set in his ways again following *True Grit*, Wayne was at last ready to break out of formula film-making by undertaking *The Cowboys*. It isolated him from his usual colleagues, working solely as an actor with new writers, director, cameraman, fellow players, etc. The result could not help but be considerably refreshing given the proven capabilities of writers Irving Ravetch and Harriet Frank Jr. (whose sparkling dialogue enhanced *Hud* among other films) and the youthful outlook of a rising director, Mark Rydell, whose best known picture, *The Fox,* was hardly the kind to endear him to Wayne.

The film has an interesting concept, thrusting Wayne as a sixty-year-old rancher, Wil Petersen, into a working partnership with a bunch of green kids on a trail drive after his regular hands have deserted him because there is a gold strike nearby. "In my day, a man stayed with you on a handshake," mutters Wayne, a man of old-fashioned strength of character as well as an old

man's suspicion of youth's capabilities. He turns down the offer of help from Long Hair (Bruce Dern), not because the man is an ex-convict, but because he tells a lie. He won't put off the drive until next year because it would mean owing people money and he won't live "on tick" even though everyone else does. And it takes the insistent probing of his old friend Anse (Slim Pickens) to remind him of what it is like to be young. "How old were *you* when you went on your first drive?" Anse asks as Wayne doubts the kids' stamina for the job in mind. "What's that got to do with it?" asks Wayne. "How old, Wil?" "Thirteen!", Wayne snaps, "And I already had a beard."

Wayne's part is reminiscent of that of Thomas Dunson in *Red River* and he is intended to be something of the same kind of tyrant, whipping the kids into shape and maintaining iron discipline. However, Wayne is virtually all bark and no bite: he makes threats but his worst action is to push a dozing boy off his horse.

*Above, Wayne discusses his problems
with an old friend (Slim Pickens).
Below, Wayne and his young
team on the trail.*

*John Wayne beats badman Bruce Dern in a gruelling fistfight, is shot in the back,
and dies being comforted by the cook (Roscoe Lee Browne).*

When, for example, he berates a boy whose stuttering prevents him uttering a vital message, his angry remarks are clearly justified and have the beneficial and intended effect of curing the impediment as the lad cries "You sonovabitch!" and develops it under Wayne's coaxing into a fluent "You goddam, dirty sonovabitch!", leaving Wayne to dispel the bitter mood by saying good-naturedly "I wouldn't make a habit of calling me that, son," and the boy to share with his pals his delight in gaining fluency of speech. The weakness of this is that we don't feel the boys being moulded under intense, unrelenting pressure as they would have to be to learn their jobs from scratch. (Possibly scenes developing this were trimmed out, as a sequence involving Indians seems to have been, but the synopsis

conjures up a much more biting relationship between Wayne and the boys.) One might observe here that the sunny colour photography, as opposed to the gritty black and white of *Red River*, helps make the trip seem a fairly pleasant outing in its early stages.

One of the boys is killed in a plausible accident as a gesture towards realism, but this does strike a jarring note, detracting from the basic strength of the Wayne character who ought to bring them all through safe and sound to justify the bold idea of using them.

The most important drawback of Wayne's fairly soft handling of the youngsters is that, when his death suddenly occurs, we don't feel that he is dispensable, that the boys have matured enough to get along without him. The script maintains this is so, giving the boys lines that were Wayne's to show them acting in his image, yelling "We're burning daylight," to urge an early start to the day's work and declaring , "It ain't how you're buried — it's how you're remembered," as they have to place his tombstone only roughly in the area where he died. But one doesn't *feel* their development, and the way the boys avenge Wayne's death owes nothing to Wayne's instruction and everything to the imagination of the writers, pitching the film into implausible high adventure rather than stern drama. To have made Wayne the kind of man the boys hated while he was alive but came to respect for what he had made of them *after* his death would have been the most challenging way of handling Wayne's part and the film; but such a high-budgeted production seemingly lacked the nerve to veer too far towards a more rigorous and less cosy approach.

Wayne's death is, of course, quite shocking, stemming from one of those situations any Western hero usually survives quite comfortably, but it still leaves him with a certain dignity. When he and the boys fall into the hands of the rustlers, he is unable to prevent this because they are an unequal match for Long Hair and his men. But he cuts through the devious pleasure Long Hair takes from playing with him. "Do I look the kind of man that would harm an innocent child?" Long Hair asks. "You look the vermin-ridden sonovabitch you are!" replies Wayne, issuing his defiant challenge : "I'm thirty years older than you are. I've had my back busted once, my hip twice, and on my worst day I could beat the hell out of you." The ensuing fight is a punishing affair for both men but Long Hair comes off conclusively worst and takes his beating badly, reaching for his gun. Wayne looks down contemptuously. "It'll have to be in the back," he snarls and strides off to be shot viciously in the arms and legs, surviving only long enough to command his trail cook (Roscoe Lee Browne), the only other adult in his party, to see the boys back home. Normal scripting procedure would have Long Hair defer killing Wayne on some pretext, perhaps binding him up so that he can escape, but the film scores in being more realistic about it.

In the manner of Wayne's death, as in the subsequent killing of the remarkably stupid rustlers, there is an unsettling degree of brutality not exactly healthy for the children in the film or those in the audience watching it. Granted that the film needs to put Wayne out of action to let the kids take over, it does seem debatable whether Wayne should have been killed rather than just immobilised. Since so much of the film falls short of the stark realism of Wayne's death scene, it seems something of a gimmick (it was a major point of exploitation for the picture) and one is reminded of Howard Hawks's view (apropos *Red River*) that it's silly to kill characters the audience likes.

Wayne's serene home life with Sarah Cunningham as his devoted wife.

And then the film omits to tie up Wayne's home life, so carefully established earlier. The real loser from Wayne's death is his devoted wife, Annie (who, played by Sarah Cunningham, is the oldest screen wife Wayne has ever had). There is no scene to show her receiving the news of his death, although we know the boys will see she gets the proceeds of selling the cattle. The quiet scenes of Wayne at his ranch are among the best in the film, with Wayne expressing his concern that Annie shouldn't end up a fry cook in somebody else's kitchen and she reminding him affectionately, "I've been a fry cook in yours for forty years" and being quietly on hand to offer him a cup of coffee as he stands outside one evening contemplating his problems.

Despite these reservations, *The Cowboys* is both an interesting and creditable addition to the Wayne *oeuvre*, not only from the way Wayne so reliably breathes life into his part but from the sharp realisation of the other adult characters and the expert casting of the boys.

90. The Train Robbers (1973)

THE TRAIN ROBBERS typifies Wayne's present career inclinations in providing the sort of undemanding entertainment that will please his regular fans but hardly augment their number. It harkens back to the kind of Western that Randolph Scott was making in the late Fifties — those written by Burt Kennedy and directed by Budd Boetticher such as *Comanche Station* and *Ride Lonesome*. There can be little doubt that Wayne makes a more commanding and intrinsically interesting figure that Scott did, but against this advantage must be set the slackness of Burt Kennedy's work as the writer and director of *The Train Robbers*, betraying the promise of his earlier work on the Scott pictures and lacking the rigour of Boetticher's treatment of them. Now his amiable dawdling in *The Train Robbers* is pleasant enough at the time but his plot inevitably lacks great interest — the recovery of a half-million in gold from its desert hiding place is basically a less interesting subject that tales keyed to powerful enmities between individuals or conflicts contained within the personality of a leading man — and the story breaks down into isolated scenes instead of building a sense of urgency and accumulating tension.

Wayne appears as Lane, the man who has agreed to help a beautiful widow, Mrs. Lowe (Ann-Margret), recover the gold her late husband stole so that it can be returned. She hopes this will help her child's future; Wayne is working for the 10% reward.* He calls on his two pals, Grady (Rod Taylor) and Jesse (Ben Johnson), to round up some help and await his arrival by train at the town of Liberty, Texas. "Long time since I seen that Lane," remarks Grady, "He as bull-headed as ever?" "He ain't changed," replies Jesse. After this build-up, Wayne is seen alighting from the train in long shot with Mrs. Lowe, giving him the kind of carefully calculated grand entrance to the picture that his stature demands. He soon punches Grady to the ground for having brought along too temperamental a helper (Christopher George) and otherwise asserts himself. "Bullheaded!" Jesse is soon declaring, leaving Grady to pick up Jesse's earlier remark: "He ain't changed!"

Two characteristics stands out in the Wayne figure. First, he's incorrigibly honest. Second, he's prone to mistakes, most notably when he asserts that a mysterious band of pursuers that follows them into the desert won't open fire, whereupon they do. In this respect, Wayne's image *has* changed, but what causes his fallibility is never explored. As in the Boetticher Westerns that Kennedy scripted, we are presented with characters that have no real purpose in life and are eager to seize on any mission that gives them temporary fulfilment and companionship. Wayne is a self-admitted drifter, a widower, a man who fought in the Civil War, a man whose sad reply to Mrs. Lowe's romantic interest in him is: "I've got a saddle that's older than you are." Grady and Jesse have a melancholy discussion about death and old age; Christopher George's Calhoun is anxious to stay on with Grady once the job is done. But these points are rather baldly made and never worked into the weave of the film, seeming more to pad it out than contribute depth. Similarly, the scene in which Wayne, Grady and Jesse decide to forego their share of the reward so that Mrs. Lowe can use the money to help bring up her son is a surprise rather than an inevitable outcome of characterisation.

Another surprise is a legitimate twist to the tale: Mrs. Lowe is revealed as a cool deceiver with no child and no marriage. But the question of how far she was ruthlessly using Wayne and his men and how far she may have come to regret the deception is beyond answering because earlier scenes have not shown us enough about her. Still, it's very nice to see Wayne, learning the truth after her departure, leaping into the saddle to pursue her and hold up the train she has taken, giving Grady the chance to tag along and welcome it as "something to do."

Wayne's band exist in a curious void during the film: the townspeople of Liberty are conspicuously unseen with the notable exception of one old character awkwardly cut in so that we recognise him later as a bloody corpse. The anonymous group of riders who so hotly pursue Wayne into the desert is an obvious imitation of the eerie posse in *Butch Cassidy and the Sundance Kid* and seems as much of a gimmick here as before. One can see in this an attempt to lend fashionable, modern trimmings to an old-fashioned Western, but essentially one is left feeling that the film is utterly reliant on Wayne's presence and would not have been a viable box-office proposition without the appeal of his name or that of one or two other big stars like Clint Eastwood. Though the idea of three comrades as presented by Wayne, Rod Taylor and Ben Johnson might seem promising — and reminiscent of *Three Godfathers* or even the 3 Mesquiteers — the sense of friendship between Wayne and the other two is handled in a very superficial manner, with Wayne standing apart and less explored as a character. *The Train Robbers* is most disappointing for just using Wayne for what he stands for and not really making him work at a part. This neglect of Wayne's potential leaves him wasting time at an age when time is precious if we are to have further opportunities to relish what Wayne can do when real dramatic demands are made on him.

*It seems no more than coincidence that Wayne used the same character name, Lane, in *Hondo* which also had a feminine lead playing a Mrs. Lowe with a young son.

Above, Wayne with his two pals, Ben Johnson and Rod Taylor.
Below, Wayne with the widow (Ann-Margret) who's younger than his saddle.

91. Cahill, United States Marshal (1973)

TEDIOUS though the film is, *Cahill* is not that much of a step down from *The Train Robbers*. Rather, it is more of the same self-satisfied formula film-making for people presumed to be content enough to see Wayne shuffling through familiar situations and pay for the opportunity. I don't mean to be cruel: there *is* a certain amount of satisfaction in seeing Big John in command of things, brushing aside or shooting down the opposition, and in noting that Wayne hasn't lost his ability to say lines with profound feeling, whether explaining to his oldest son his reasons for being a bad parent or issuing warnings like that to a black to submit to being handcuffed or else. But are such moments enough? Do they excuse a rambling narrative with far too many lines that should have been pruned out, or direction that too often complies with the weaknesses of the script? There are warning signs that Wayne's box-office pull is falling away. In Britain, there are enough West End showcases to give *The Train Robbers* and this a solo opening run but for general release both were delegated to support films with more modern appeal: *The Thief Who Came to Dinner* and *The Mackintosh Man*. In so far as old booking patterns persist, this is little better than the kind of treatment that Randolph Scott films were receiving in the late Fifties and they became uneconomic propositions by the early Sixties.

Cahill was obviously made with one eye on the children's market as *The Cowboys* had been. In fact, the film should really belong to Wayne's two sons in the film: twelve-year-old Billy Joe and seventeen-year-old Danny who, neglected by a father who is all too often away rounding up outlaws, help Abe Fraser (George Kennedy) and his men commit a bank robbery during one of their father's absences. Director McLaglen obviously recalled the famous graveyard scene from *Great Expectations* in a scene he directs with relish in which the grown-up robbers corner their youngest ally in the rainy dark and terrify him; and another scene with Wayne and his Indian sidekick (Neville Brand) deliberately frightening the boys in this film's graveyard also attempts to be powerfully subjective.

But the film's focus is split. It looks at Wayne head on

246

Above, Wayne with Marie Windsor and Clay O'Brien and Gary Grimes as his two sons.
Below, Wayne gets another shoulder wound watched by Gary Grimes.

John Wayne in the opening scene at some outlaws' nightcamp.

instead of approaching him from the boys' point of view which might have reduced his footage but added considerably to his overall impact. Instead, there are typical moments for Wayne to establish himself as the invincible stuff of legend. We don't actually see villains quake at the very mention of his name but the effect is the same. In the opening, Wayne rides boldly up to a night-camp to arrest some men. Well aware of the two gunmen deployed to cover him from each side, he nevertheless shoots it out and manages to survive, an unusually sharp frozen frame catching him in a memorable shot from behind, his six-shooter blazing white flame, and serving as a background for the main title. Later, Wayne is bringing in some other prisoners and some stolen loot when he is confronted by a huge bunch of men on the trail who want to relieve him of the money he's carrying; his conversation with their leader (Chuck Roberson) makes him realise their lack of determina-

tion and he rides straight through them with an "Aw, hell, get out of the way!" Such moments are incredible, of course, as is Wayne's recognition of badman Abe Fraser's bluff when the latter pretends to be dead at the climax. The fact that Wayne usually ends up shot in the shoulder hardly affects his image of basic invulnerability. Yet this image is not reconciled with that of the bad father, nor are the more dramatic aspects of the film tellingly advanced.

During production, *Cahill* was known as *Wednesday Morning,* the title referring to the time when a band of robbers will be hung in error unless Wayne can catch the real villains. The film so clearly dissipates tension that the title was no longer apposite once it had been edited, and the change enables the advertising to make use of a familiar treatment — "John Wayne IS *Cahill*" — which emphasises that the film has to fall back on Wayne as its most effective element.

248

92. McQ (1974)

WITH THIS FILM, even Wayne acknowledged the staggering decline in popular interest in the Western and joined the cop cycle, ruefully confessing that he had once been offered the title role in *Dirty Harry* by writer Harry Julian Fink and had turned it down (Frank Sinatra was then going to do it but had to bow out when he injured his hand; finally Clint Eastwood took it on and scored a huge hit). Wayne is reported as saying: "I felt like a bit of a change myself. I had to stick to action movies, of course, and the tough cop thriller is where a lot of the action is these days. So that's what I went for." It *is* quite a change, too, for Wayne had never played a cop or detective before, surprising as this does seem. And *McQ* brought Wayne into collaboration with new people both in front of the camera and behind,

including a director, John Sturges, who has some first-rate work to his credit (though little dating from recent years). *McQ* also gained a fresh look by being shot (seemingly in its entirety) on location in Seattle.

McQ is certainly a notch above Wayne's other recent work, not at all bad on a first viewing though distinctly dreary on a second. Wayne is police lieutenant Lon McQ (his full surname is never mentioned). He sets about investigating the murder of his closest buddy, a fellow cop, and resigns when his efforts are impeded, eventually exposing corruption within the police force itself that involves the theft of vast quantities of confiscated drugs from the property department.

The film should have arrived at an extraordinarily bleak ending but it sticks to a level of superficial action

Wayne does some forceful questioning of drug king Al Lettieri in the men's room and, below, shoots it out with the villains during the beach climax with the scheming widow (played by Diana Muldaur) behind the windscreen.

instead of emphasising the effect of the film's numerous revelations on Wayne.

For Wayne's McQ is a man who ends up utterly alone, betrayed by almost everyone he knows and deprived of his one major consolation, a warm-hearted bar waitress. At the end of the film, he takes back his badge because there's nothing else for him to do but go back to being a cop, and he goes off for a drink with his superior officer, Captain Kosterman (Eddie Albert), whom he dislikes and has wrongly suspected of being corrupt. They are accompanied by a black cop, J. C. (Jim Watkins), whom he had trusted to help him but who was in fact working for internal security and had kept Kosterman informed of Wayne's activities.

Wayne's best friend, the murdered cop, is shown as a cold-blooded killer and drug trafficker. After a close-up of a photograph of Wayne and his pal together, the phone rings on Wayne's boat, his hand reaches up into frame to pick it up, then his voice is heard and he blearily staggers to his feet and learns of his buddy's demise during the night. This thoughtfully arranged introduction to Wayne is reminiscent of the way an initially unseen Humphrey Bogart received a night-time call about his partner's death in *The Maltese Falcon*. There is a further parallel in the deceitful lady of each film. Here it's the dead cop's wife, Lois (Diana Muldaur), who fools Wayne with her display of grief and tempts him into going away with her (a chance interruption puts the idea in abeyance). She tells him that she and her late husband had been talking of divorce: Wayne's surprise at this, though it is probably a fabrication, must make him feel that his friendship with the dead man wasn't as close as he had supposed. In fact, Lois is in cahoots with another cop (Clu Gulager) who is also a fairly good friend of Wayne's, and she needs Wayne only because a fortune in drugs has been hidden in his car, making him the unwitting carrier.

Wayne himself has been divorced from a still beautiful wife (Julia Adams) whose wealthy, philanthropic but mousey-looking new husband rubs in the lack of security that he had given her while her words to him on a visit clearly indicate that he could have resigned from the force and kept her: it was only the lonely nights and the worry about his safety that forced them apart. So, for once, the familiar conflict between work and marriage is resolved to Wayne's lasting disadvantage. His teenage daughter, whose company he has enjoyed every Sunday, can no longer find time to fit him in to her crowded life of social engagements. Wayne's only genuine feminine comfort comes from the faded, lonely cocktail waitress (a marvellous performance by Colleen Dewhurst) who provides him with information after luring him, not too reluctantly, into her bed for the night. Believing that Wayne is at the front door, she later opens it and is killed, leaving Wayne with the burden of wishing he had come to see her instead of driving off.

So Wayne is really a tragic figure. "Feel kinda silly acting like an avenging angel all that time," he tells Lois when the truth is out. And of not having suspected her: "Feel kinda silly about that, too." But Wayne's response is no more complicated than that.

Wayne is really a simple figure: his integrity and loyalty are unshakable if misplaced. He threatens to kill the informant who first tells him his dead pal was crooked if he ever says that again, and he is never tempted by the two million dollars' worth of drugs. In parallel circumstances in *The Maltese Falcon*, Bogart was tempted by both the treasure and the woman, but here when Wayne hands over Lois to the cops, there is nothing made of the moment one way or the other.

Wayne certainly joins the Dirty Harry league of tough cops, sharing their indignation at legal niceties that leave criminals on the loose. His real anger is vented against the local drug king, Santiago (Al Lettieri). Wayne never believes the alternative theory advanced by Kosterman and encouraged by the scheming widow that his pal (and other policemen who have been killed) were victims of madmen or radicals. He even suspects Kosterman because the Captain is so keen on this theory. But Wayne does react to radicals: a long-haired youth seeks to anger him with gibes and follows him down a corridor at the police station. Wayne treats him like a pesky fly that needs to be brushed off, deftly kicking him in the shins. "He bumped into a chair," Wayne explains, ignoring the absence of any such item of furniture in the corridor. Wayne's real wrath is directed against professional criminals. He's remembered for putting one unconvicted hood in hospital and he remarks with satisfaction that the man's injuries kept him off the streets for six months. So Wayne doesn't hesitate to corner Santiago in a lavatory when he decides that he must have been responsible for the wave of murders. Wayne rams his head into a mirror attempting to make him talk and leaves him sprawled out ("He slipped on the wet floor and fell.") When the cops turn out to be the real crooks, cunningly pinning their crimes on Santiago, the gangster declares to Wayne, "See what the world has become!" — and for a moment the two men have a common viewpoint, an unholy bond of feeling.

But the bitter pill that Wayne has to swallow is sweetened by the film's emphasis on action. In this area, it compares well with others of its kind. A scene in which Wayne, in his car, is sandwiched between two trucks that crush it has a chilling sense of entrapment. The final car chase (in which Santiago makes a somewhat surprising appearance after the police villains have been disposed of) obtains a fresh look from being conducted along a beach at medium tide, with Wayne himself being visibly jarred behind the steering wheel as he races along.

In his first British film, Brannigan, Wayne is taken by Scotland Yard commander Richard Attenborough for a meal at the exclusive Garrick Club and takes it on the chin from the same policeman in a London pub.

93. Brannigan (1975)

McQ PERFORMED quite brightly at the American box office (helped, no doubt, by its exciting coming-attractions trailer). Wayne made a trip to England to work on a Glen Campbell TV special on the Old West, and gave *McQ* some useful publicity. His visit appears to have led to a decision to shoot a picture in Britain. It is surprising that Wayne had never done that before, but then he may have seemed just too quintessentially American to fit in—and indeed the difficulties of reconciling the Wayne character with the traditions of British life are exploited to the full by the scriptwriters.

Brannigan is a variation on *Coogan's Bluff,* being another story of a tough cop dropped into a strange environment. Wayne flies into Heathrow from Chicago (sportingly taking a British airline) to extradite a drug trafficker (John Vernon) whom Scotland Yard is keeping under surveilance. But the man is kidnapped before Wayne can grab him. He and Scotland Yard Commander Swann (Richard Attenborough) have to try and crack a ransom plot to get him back. Wayne also has to contend with a hit man (Daniel Pilon) who makes periodic attempts to fulfill the contract given him by the drug trafficker.

The plot is complicated and totally uninvolving (it's hard to care about the fate of such an odious kidnap victim or to believe in a twist that involves the willing sacrifice of a finger by amateurish amputation). Big John lives up to his character's surname with a crudely motivated, lavish but routine brannigan in a public house, but is more enjoyable out in the open against famous London landmarks splendidly photographed by Gerry Fisher. The use of such settings as Piccadilly Circus and Tower Bridge for complicated scenes (the latter involving some audacious and breathtaking stunt

Wayne meets his girl Friday (Judy Geeson) at Heathrow on his arrival from Chicago.

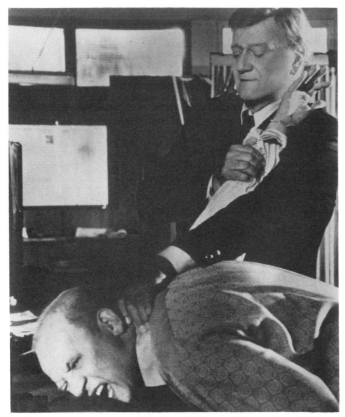

Wayne threatens the teeth of Brian Glover's villain, Jimmy the Bet.

There is an intriguing glimpse of Wayne turning to drink in a lonely Kensington flat but little real coloring to his role. John Vernon makes a powerful impression as the man he's after, but regrettably their hostility is an established fact before the film begins and is little developed by personal friction here.

Brannigan is insufficiently imaginative to open up Wayne's career at all; but it makes solid use of his still-powerful charisma. Like *McQ*, it passes the time pleasantly but not memorably.

Wayne takes aim at the assassin bearing down on him in a car at the end and (below) fires at the vehicle after he has nearly been run over.

work) shows a refreshing lack of inhibition (no recourse to back projection either) but also marks the film as an outsider's view of the city. It plays havoc with the geography of Central London in getting from one landmark to the next, and its dialogue and impression of the British character are both tailored to fit the preconceptions of American audiences rather than to surprise them with genuine local color. Thus, when Wayne strongarms a British thug into spurting out information by ramming his teeth against a hard surface and inquiring "Now would you like to apply for England's free dental treatment or will you answer my question?" the line is not so much directed at the character as at an American viewer whose ready knowledge of Britain is limited to such matters as its National Health system.

Here Wayne works for a British director, Douglas Hickox, who coaxed him into permitting some use of slow-motion to prolong moments of suspense and who shoots the picture in an aggressive style that generates some artificial excitement. Hickox does seem to have softened Wayne from his recent air of crabbiness, allowing him to appear more relaxed, especially with Judy Geeson in a thankless role as his exceptionally pretty and pleasant chauffeur who bestows on his cheek an affectionate peck because he's "Just so damn solid" in a variation on Jennifer O'Neill's "you're so comfortable" routine in snuggling up to him in *Rio Lobo*.

254

94. Rooster Cogburn (1975)

IT IS the rare sequel that recaptures the qualities of the original. Sequels are usually made for purely commercial reasons, nothing in the original being left open for future development; they are not expected to attract as large an audience but, with a wildly successful original, it only needs a sequel to do half as well to turn a nice profit. Still, there are rules; and one is that you try to make your follow-up while audiences still have the original fairly fresh in their minds. Production of *Rooster Cogburn* seems to have started exactly six years after *True Grit* went into production —hardly striking while the iron is still hot.

Still, *Rooster Cogburn* did start with a sizable coup: a first teaming of John Wayne and Katharine Hepburn. It was Miss Hepburn's first real western (1947's *Sea of Grass* is a borderline case) and came twenty years after she turned down the co-starring role in *Hondo*. In a striking change of location and co-star, Miss Hepburn hurried from partnering Laurence Olivier in the sophisticated comedy *Love Among the Ruins* to the Oregon location of the crude and boisterous *Rooster Cogburn*. Expectations ran high but the finished film proved to be, in the words of *Variety*, "a big disappointment," causing the journal to ponder "If Wayne and Hepburn can't attract today's cinemagoers, who can?"—the answer, of course, being stars nearer the age of the average filmgoer. Even so, *Rooster Cogburn* earned $4.5 million for its distributor in the North American market in 1975—not great, but not utterly disastrous.*

Why the film made little impact is all too clear. It leans on formulas worked to perfection in *True Grit* and *The African Queen*. Marshal Cogburn is again in trouble for his rough-and-ready ways of dispensing justice in the field—the last three of the sixty men he has killed in eight years are too much for Judge Parker to swallow—until a job calling for Rooster's special expertise comes along, i.e. apprehending a bunch of outlaws led by Hawk (Richard Jordan). Rooster is to bring them back alive: he doesn't, but is excused the lapse by Judge Parker in what might be seen as a right-wing nod to harsh justice, or perhaps a deserving fate for an indifferent bunch of badmen who provide very routine obstacles to delay their demise.

Where *True Grit* thrived on the age and attitudes gulf between Wayne and Kim Darby, the sequel concen-

trates on attitude and bolsters the antagonism by making Wayne's sparring partner more self-reliant and authoritative. It trades Kim Darby's way with a telling aphorism for Katharine Hepburn's command of biblical quotations. Since Wayne is still the coarse-mouthed imbiber of *True Grit,* Hepburn is contrasted as an especially respectable teetotaller. Since *True Grit* worked with Wayne yoked to a seemingly unsuitable female partner in hunting badmen, *Rooster Cogburn* uses the same trick. Again, the female's father is murdered and she insists on joining Wayne in apprehending the killer. As an expert marksman who saves Wayne's life, Hepburn also replaces Glen Campbell's La Boeuf from the earlier film.

Equally, though, an indebtedness to *The African Queen* can hardly be denied. Here is Hepburn again related to a priest killed off early in the film; and here is another perilous journey down a river with an explosive climax. Humphrey Bogart's Charlie Allnutt would have made a good drinking companion for Wayne's Rooster Cogburn.

Certainly, in its details, *Rooster Cogburn* strikes a course of its own. And, unlike many a sequel, it dovetails closely with the original in small ways, some so small that without a keen memory of the earlier film they would hardly be recognized. Wayne's rat-killing

*What was surprising was the film's total rejection by British audiences. Given a premiere before the Queen and Duke of Edinburgh at the prestigious Empire in London's West End and largely welcomed by the critics, it died a box-office death and subsequently had only a handful of bookings, mostly in support of the equally unpopular *Won Ton Ton, the Dog Who Saved Hollywood*.

Starring together for the first time: Katharine Hepburn and John Wayne.

episode and his liking for ''pulling a cork'' are recalled and utterances like ''Damn your murdering hide, meet your maker!'' are perfectly in character with the Rooster Cogburn of six years earlier. Wayne's family—the Chinaman Chen Lee (this time played by Tommy Lee, H. W. Gim having died in 1973) and the cat—are brought back. But the screenwriter Martin Julien (or more than one? An intriguing hint in a Canadian film magazine suggested that producer Hal Wallis's wife, Martha Hyer, leading lady in *The Sons of Katie Elder,* had a hand in writing the script), having established a close rapport with the original film and having created a strong characterization in Hepburn's Eula Goodnight, indulges in talk, talk, talk with a very episodic development of a boring plot. The badinage between Wayne and Hepburn is essentially light-hearted with no real conflict or threat to a continuing relationship—one knows that Rooster will soon regard Eula as ''quite a filly'' and that she will develop a caring regard for him. The roles lack shading and surprise; and director Stuart Millar (whose handling of *When the Legends Die* was memorably sensitive) does nothing to counter the drift towards indifference over the happenings on screen. Rooster Cogburn was not quite finished as a commercial property—Warren Oates later played the part in a TV film—but his return here gave Wayne disappointingly little to chew on. It also had one perhaps unfortunate repercussion. John Carpenter, the bright young writer-director of *Assault on Precinct 13* and *Halloween,* was then developing a western script for Wayne's company but the star finally decided against doing it because it was largely set on a river and Wayne felt it was too close to the film he had just made in this respect.

One-eyed, two-barrelled marksman:
Wayne as Rooster Cogburn.

Strother Martin, Katharine Hepburn, and John Wayne (carrying the wherewithal for an explosive climax).

95. The Shootist (1976)

THE SHOOTIST now seems the most grimly appropriate last film Wayne could have undertaken. Like the leading character, the dying gunfighter John Bernard Books who finds a way of ending his life with dignity, the film provided Wayne with a brave and honorable way of concluding his own big-screen career. Just as Books has outlived his time, so perhaps had Wayne as a film star outlived his—insurance and health problems were making it difficult for studios to use him, and both Paul Newman and George C. Scott had at one time accepted the role of the shootist ahead of Wayne. But Wayne is undoubtedly a better choice, not least for the way the film further narrows the gap between the part and the actor by using clips of Wayne in gunfights from *Red River, Hondo, Rio Bravo* and *El Dorado* to convey Books's past. But the main link between Books and Wayne was cancer: the disease that Wayne was thought to have licked for good and that is about to end Books' life painfully. Thus it was a part particularly

appropriate for Wayne, that he could identify with closely (as could, just as strikingly, his co-star Lauren Bacall as Humphrey Bogart's widow).

Wayne must have also liked the role for its broad similarity to the doomed title character in Henry King's *The Gunfighter* (1950). Wayne had wanted to play that role when he first saw William Bowers's script but lost it to Gregory Peck; however, twenty years on he was still known to talk about the way he could have handled particular moments. The role of Books is certainly less sympathetic than that of Peck's gunfighter. Books is proudly unrepentant about his past and his reputation as "the most celebrated shootist extant": "I don't believe I ever killed a man who didn't deserve it." He shoots down a holdup man encountered on his way into Carson City and leaves him wounded on the ground, just as the man would have left him—but in the process becoming as bad as the robber. When an ex-girl friend down on her luck,

Opening scene: Wayne is accosted by a robber and warns him, "You'd better find yourself another line of work—this sure don't fit your pistol!"

The last role: as John Bernard Books, the dying 'shootist.'

Wayne with James Stewart as the doc who tells him to expect the worst.

Wayne passes on a lifetime's experience as Ron Howard, playing young Gillom, takes aim.

Lauren Bacall as the landlady with Ron Howard as her son and Wayne as her boarder.

Serepta (Sheree North), proposes that he might marry her so that she can profit by being his widow and writing stories about him, his anger—"I won't be remembered for a pack of lies"—is understandable but also a little too self-righteous. Though the scavengers crowd around, Books's attitude is somewhat too holy and austere for a man of his unholy way of life and apparent past history. Actually, we get to know very little about him.

It is only our knowledge of his condition that makes us regard him with compassion. He is hardly ever offscreen (when he is, it seems like a regrettable lapse) and his impending demise is never forgotten. There is no playing for sympathy on either Wayne's part or that of director Don Siegel. Indeed, James Stewart, in a brief role as the doctor, drops his bumbling mannerisms and there seems to be a hint of relish in the way he confirms Wayne's worst fears about having a cancer and recommends suicide as a way of avoiding the pain. The film is handled with a classical austerity: tied to one setting (Carson City); emphasising the passage of time with titles that lead from "First Day January 22" to "Last Day January 29" and offer no escape from destiny; largely set indoors in gloomy rooms with yellow light from oil lamps. The use of unfamiliar, if authentic sounding, words like "shootist" for "gunfighter" or phrases like Wayne's "You have a fine color when you're on the scrap" to Lauren Bacall instead of "You look beautiful when you're mad," as well as the film's often odd names (like Thibido for the town's marshal), all serve to distance us somewhat from the characters and events. We feel as though we are watching from a long way away something that happened a long time ago—there is no immediacy. We are reminded of Queen Victoria, a real symbol of times past, for her death is news in Carson City as Wayne arrives, like him, she "outlived her time" but she is an inspiration in that she "never lost her dignity." It is 1901 and Wayne is in the wrong century. He rides into town and obstructs the bustling traffic, being greeted with "Hey, Methuselah!" like Joel McCrea's westerner in *Ride the High Country* being told "Get out of the way, old man!" in like circumstances.

260

"The most legendary shootist extant" deals with the newspaperman (Richard Lenz) who wants to write his life.

The last gunfight: Wayne takes up position by the mirror in which he can observe his adversaries dotted around the room.

The shootist dies with his boots on.

Wayne starts to make connections with the times as they are: there is the false hope of a family relationship in the attractive landlady (Lauren Bacall) and her son (Ronny Howard). But there is no time and, though Wayne can help the boy to become a good shot, the use of a gun is decisively rejected by the lad at the end of the film since he seems also to put behind him the shootist himself, once having used Wayne's gun to dispose of his killer.

The final shootout in the spacious but enclosed urban-style saloon with its fans rotating overhead allows Wayne to die with his boots on. Like Gregory Peck in *The Gunfighter,* he survives the obvious—the three chosen opponents—but succumbs to the unexpected, the shotgun of the bartender. There is little suspense in the confrontation; after all, Wayne wants to lose. There are no spectators, except the bartender who becomes a participant anyway. Here again, the film seems a little forced compared to, say, the more plausible arrangements made by the two washed-up gunfighters of Lamont Johnson's *A Gunfight* to conduct a duel for profit in public.

The film was widely acclaimed, but its rigorous approach seems to take away a lot without putting too much in its place. It is a film to admire but not one to like as one likes *Ride the High Country* or *She Wore a Yellow Ribbon.* Wayne was really more interesting *playing* old in the latter film than *being* old here in *The Shootist,* just as director Don Siegel is more interesting when his films allow for tension and suspense (like *Madigan*).

Perhaps Wayne had outlived his time. He and Siegel apparently feuded to the extent that Siegel ended up detesting Wayne, the trouble being that Wayne was no longer used to taking direction. Who, then, could he work with to make worthwhile films if even a well-established director like Siegel rubbed him the wrong way? There is one significant example of disagreement: as Books lies dying on the floor of the saloon, Wayne insisted that Siegel raise the camera so that it was no longer peering directly up his nostrils. It shows that Wayne was concerned with dignity—and it can certainly be said that *The Shootist* was a most dignified end to a career.

96. Feo, fuerte y formal

WITH *THE SHOOTIST*, John Wayne celebrated fifty years of working on motion pictures. Unknown to me when I wrote the first edition of this book is an assignment that Wayne has recalled in interviews of more recent date: while on the University of Southern California football team, he was paid $7.50 to double for Francis X. Bushman, Jr., running a hundred yards in a staged match and letting someone tackle him, as part of a film called *Brown of Harvard* (1926). (Wayne has also mentioned on a TV show that he worked as an extra on Michael Curtiz's *Noah's Ark* (1929) in the flood scene. And somewhere or other I have now picked up that Wayne took his name from the title character that intrigued him in a book called *Mad Anthony Wayne*.

The actor had no intention of retiring from the screen after *The Shootist*. He was keen to make a modern comedy, *Beau John*, but was still trying to get the script put right in 1978 and hoped to make it in 1979.

In March 1977, Wayne was a surprising guest at an Inaugural Concert for President Jimmy Carter. As he said to the audience, he was known as a member of the opposition, the loyal opposition. "Accent on the *loyal*," he said, "I would not have it any other way." It was a generous, touching little speech—one that Wayne had difficulty uttering, his voice husky but not with emotion. It was becoming difficult for him to say more than three words without pausing to take a breath. The mid sentence pause that had been an idiosyncrasy of delivery had now become a real encumbrance. An artery connecting his heart to his vocal chords was found to be at fault and in April 1978 he went into Massachusetts General Hospital for open heart surgery in which a defective valve was replaced

April, 1979: Sammy Davis Jr. greets the Duke after his appearance at the Academy Awards. Also seen: Yul Brynner, Johnny Carson, Shirley Jones.

by one from a pig. His recovery was complicated by hepatitis. Some 200,000 letters reached him from well-wishers.

Soon Wayne was working again, joining Bob Hope on a TV show, appearing on General Electric's 100th birthday home-screen special. But on January 10, 1979, Wayne was back in hospital for a gallstone operation that revealed cancer of the stomach and necessitated a nine-hour operation. Wayne seemed to be recovering and on April 9 he walked onstage to receive a standing ovation at the 51st Academy Awards. Though gaunt, he walked well, and he remarked of his welcome, "That's all the medicine a man really needs." He added, "I came to Hollywood at the same time as Oscar, in 1928, and we both plan to be around for a long time to come." He had the job of announcing the nominees for the year's best picture, a complicated business with the names of writers, producers, director and production companies appended to the titles. It seemed a strain. The winner was *The Deer Hunter:* fortunately, Wayne's difficulties with repeating that film's particularly lengthy credits were partly buried in the applause. What did Wayne, the producer-director-star of *The Green Berets,* feel at announcing the victory of *The Deer Hunter?* Whether willing or not, the same Wayne who had mellowed to salute a Democratic President appeared also to have accepted the new trends in filmmaking.

It was not long before Wayne was back in hospital—at UCLA Medical Center in Los Angeles—and it became clear that he was onto a losing battle with a return of "the Big C." Even that terrible disease had had to wait fifteen years for a man of Wayne's calibre after he first vanquished it in '64.

Suddenly Wayne was no longer a butt for the sophisticated sneerers, a victim of what Kingsley Amis thought might be "some secret fraternal oath, perhaps of Rosicrucian origin, that forbids any media-man to let that name pass unexecrated" (Amis was criticizing British television's Barry Norman). A move was afoot to have Wayne awarded a Congressional Medal of Honor as a "great American" and time was of the essence. Actress Maureen O'Hara made a movingly distraught appearance before a Congressional panel formed to consider the proposal; Elizabeth Taylor lent support, and President Carter approved in a written statement. Congress agreed, and late in May John Wayne became the thirty-second recipient in this century of the gold medal—inscribed, simply, "John Wayne, American".

Still in hospital, Wayne refused pain-killing drugs at times to be more alert when members of his family came to the bedside. In his general bearing, he gained the respect of his doctors who declared that his courage matched that of his image in the movies. Two weeks after the award of his Congressional Medal, two days after he became a convert to Catholicism, John Wayne died, aged 72, on June 11, 1979. He was buried shortly after daybreak on June 15 in a plot overlooking the ocean near his Newport Beach home at Pacific View Memorial Park in California. He left an estate worth $6.8 million. A new wing is to be built in his name at UCLA Medical Center, specializing in research to find a cure for cancer.

Quite often over the years Wayne was asked what he would like his epitaph to be. He always referred to a Mexican saying—*Feo, fuerte y formal*—which he translated as "He was ugly, he was tough, but he had dignity."

"If they say that about me when it's all over," he declared, "I'll be happy."

John Wayne Talking to Scott Eyman*

*Reprinted from *Focus on Film,* Spring, 1975.

JOHN WAYNE'S DRESSING-ROOM at CBS, where he is taping a segment of a TV special, is a spare, glaring room with sickly yellow paint and brash neon lighting.

Wayne, in his underwear, is sitting quietly facing a wall-sized mirror, solemnly looking at his own mountainous features while his make-up man, who looks like a shaggy, middle-aged William Powell, fusses over the proper look for Wayne's toupee.

Wayne, in the flesh, is enormous, both in size and presence; this is the man who fought the Indians in *Stagecoach,* his own adopted son in *Red River,* all comers in *The Quiet Man* and four desperate outlaws on horseback in *True Grit.* Yet, *The Man Who Shot Liberty Valance* retains the most astonishing humility imaginable.

Friendly, open, good-humored and polite, he has none of the typical Hollywood self-concealment or artifice. What there is is an almost intangible air of quietude, of loneliness, noticeable especially in moments of repose, when the eyes come to rest on nothing in particular and almost literally veil over in some private reverie of implicitly grave implications.

On stage, Wayne is the complete professional. Whether it be running over his lines written on enormous white cards placed out of camera range or taking direction from the stage manager, Wayne's patience is remarkable. Lights fail, an elevator that will lower Sid Caesar on to the stage fails to function and Caesar himself fails to show up. Through it all, Wayne is the soul of professional benevolence, passing the fast-moving hours by chatting about television, movies, sex, and politics, and even graciously intervening with an officious PR person who is about to throw me off the set because I don't represent Time-Life or The *New York Times,* evidently the only two printed media considered important enough to brook interference from.

The image this man carries is that of a dogmatic Puritan with the fiery righteousness of Moses. The man I met is a warmhearted, almost reticent legend who likes people too much to be iron-clad and dogmatic about them. Above everything else, John Wayne is a gentle man.

What were those early days of making serials and Westerns like?

Harry Cohn [head of Columbia] had taken a dislike to me and was trying to keep me out of pictures. For a year I couldn't get work and I was thinking of going into the fight racket, which I was too old for. Those serials paid me $500 for eighteen days work in which they got twenty-five cut reels of film. They'd change directors every day, but the leading man had to be there all the time. We never worked less than eighteen hours a day. Had to, just to get that much film cranked out. We'd do 101, 102 setups a day. Nowadays they get three or four or five. Back then, I think the most we ever got was 118 in one day. Some of those days lasted twenty-six hours.

Nat Levine produced the serials, didn't he?

Nat Levine was an interesting character. We had a party one day, lots of guests and everything. Levine had a diamond ring on, and, as a gag, they tried to take it off of him. Well, the sonofabitch put up one hell of a fight and ended the whole party. He wasn't gonna give up that diamond ring! And I know he was close with a buck; if the "thieves" had come to me first, I coulda told them not to bother.

What had Harry Cohn against you?

He thought I'd had something to do with his personal life, which was a goddam lie. But I'd been brought up to respect older people and he talked to me like I was a sewer rat. There was no communication at all. Today, when I look back on it, I realize I could have straightened the whole thing out if I would have spoken up, but the fact that he would accuse me of such a thing as he did,* I resented, resented to the point of counting to ten rather than throwing him out of the goddam window. But as you get older you get a sense of humor about these things.

It's just occurred to me that you never have made a picture for Columbia since then.

No, and there were plenty of opportunities. Harry would come and say, "Duke, you'd be just great in this—what do you want?" I'd say, "Gosh, Harry, I just haven't got time"—that's the only delight I ever had with that guy.

Can I ask you about The Long Voyage Home . . .

Beautiful picture.

Before you did that picture, had you read any O'Neill?

I've been to school; yes. But that wasn't what was tough about it. I was still under contract to Republic at the time. *Long Voyage Home* was right after *Stagecoach* but I was still doing six-day Westerns. I'd finished one Western at twelve o'clock at night and the next morning I had to start a picture where I was a Swedish sailor, presumably with an accent, with no chance for any coaching. I had to play a straight part as a Swede and my accent couldn't clash with John Qualen's who was playing a comic Swede. I wanna tell

---

*Cohn thought Wayne was carrying on with a starlet in whom he was keenly interested. According to Wayne: "I didn't even know her."

you, that was quite a switch from the night before, knocking people around and jumping on a horse.

Did Gregg Toland take longer to light a setup than the average cameraman?

No. He worked a lot with the art director so he'd know what values he'd have. And working with John Ford is a cameraman's dream. Gregg was probably the best cameraman in the world when it comes to set composition. Gregg was very helpful to Pappy Ford and Pappy was helpful to him. Between the two of them, they got about as beautiful a photographed picture as I've ever seen. Gregg was a wonderful guy; a dear, dear, man.

Why do you think Ford was a great director. Critics argue about it, but what's your view?

I think that as an administrator he could have been anything he wanted to be. Not necessarily in business, but in the military field, handling personalities and people. Nobody could handle actors and crew like Jack. He was the finest editor I've ever seen. When Dudley Nichols was doing *Stagecoach* he'd make Nichols write a scene five or six times till Nichols was just about drenched. And then he'd find three lines out of three scenes that Dudley had written and use them for that particular speech. He knew how to draw lines out that give character and progress your story at the same time.

The Quiet Man . . .

He had a beautiful short story called "The Quiet One." He gave that to the fellow who wrote "How Green Was My Valley," Richard Llewellyn, and had him write a novel out of it, just for him, Ford. Then he sat down with [Laurence] Stallings and [Frank S.] Nugent and from that he took his picture. Now that's preparation. He was the fastest reader I ever saw in my goddam life.

The Searchers . . .

I think that's the best picture Ford ever made.

Donovan's Reef . . .

He never should have used me in that picture. He should have picked some young guy. It didn't require much of him. All he had to be was a good-looking young guy and I wasn't young enough.

Didn't Ford generally have music on the set?

Yeah, Danny Borzage's accordion. We do it at Batjac all the time. It's easy to talk an actor into a scene that way. Ford, while they're lighting a set, talks to the actors very quietly, puts them through a scene. Now he calls the cameraman over. He watches them go through the scene. He talks to them. "Do you think you can go down over there instead of here?" "Yeah, sure." Now, when you start to do the scene you're at complete ease. You've walked through it, and as you're setting your lines you're in the right position. Some directors line the whole scene up the night

before and say, "You stand here and you stand there and when you say that line come over here." Well, when you say "Come over here on that line," instinctively it affects your performance. The other way, you're eased into it so beautifully, you're where he wants you for composition but you're also where you want to be for the lines. Ford wants the action to come out of the actor in a manner that is comfortable to him. After that's done, then he gives you the little touches that he wants. But he gets you at ease first. When you're working, though, there is no way you can do anything wrong.

What about William Wellman?

He's a wonderful old sonofabitch. Really wild. He had a metal plate in his head from some old accident and he'd go around belting all these big, tough guys and they'd be afraid to hit him back for fear they'd kill him. Wild Bill Wellman—a wonderful old guy!

Good director?

Fine director. He didn't delve into characters as much as some. I'll tell you the difference between directors: Hawks has tremendous patience with people. He'll keep working on a fellow, even if he's not cutting the mustard. Ford won't hire you unless he knows he can get it out of you. Wellman figures you're a pro and doesn't bother you much as an actor. If you don't deliver, he'll simply cut the part down. It's that easy.

And Hathaway?

Hathaway is a fine, instinctive creator. The problem with his career is that he worked at Fox for something like twenty years and he was the hatchet man—whenever things got too tough for everybody else, they'd give it to Hathaway. If they had an actor with one more picture to do on a contract and the director said, "Christ, I can't do this," they'd call Hathaway. He was a sort of story director. He never got the creative credit that I think is due him.

I've heard that he's been known to make grown actors cry.

Well, there's a legend built up around this man. I never saw him yell. He treats you very gently as an actor. He'll put down green boughs for you to walk on so you'll walk softly. Unless you are careless or not interested. Then he can be a sonofabitch. He treats a little mistake the same as a big one. He's a bludgeon on all mistakes. Ford, on the other hand, uses a rapier zinging in and out. Hawks never lets anything perturb him: he's the coldest character I've ever met in my life.

Do you have plans to do anything more with Hawks or Hathaway?

They just come up. I just keep working.

Would you like to do a picture with Bogdanovich?

We're talking. Sure, I'd love to. He likes what I like.

He loves Ford and Hawks and Hathaway and to my way of thinking they're the top.

You didn't get on with John Huston on The Barbarian and the Geisha.

I found it impossible to make any contact at all. When I look back at his career, Bogey and his dad helped him get started; outside the *Moulin Rouge* and *Asphalt Jungle,* I don't think he's made anything worthwhile when they weren't there to help him.

You didn't like Moby Dick?

Christ, of course not! I blamed Gregory Peck. There was no life in him. Then I started to work with Huston and found out that was how he was gonna have me play this drunken, riotous man, Townsend Harris, who had a great love of people. He had me started out dressed like Abe Lincoln and everybody knows I'm John Wayne. He had scenes where the Americans caused an epidemic of typhoid—wonderful chances to have me be something more than a textbook illustration, but no. There was a scene where the Japanese won't sell us food, so I wanted to go out and come back with a fish. The kids ask me where I got it, so I take them out and show them how to fish. There were all sorts of things he could have done to make us human beings but he was only concerned with his tapestry which he thought was more important than the human story. Huston? You can have him!

What prompted you to start your own production company? Bigger slice of the pie or what?

Yeah. A little more freedom to do what I wanted.

Why did you change the name of the company from Wayne-Fellows to Batjac?

Fellows was a friend of mine who came in and didn't quite do the job. Besides, I didn't like the idea of my name being on it. I got Batjac out of a picture I'd done, *Wake of the Red Witch,* in which there was a big Dutch company called Batjak. I told my partner and he thought it was a good idea, so we went ahead and changed the spelling.

You had James Arness under contract.

CBS came to me and asked me if I wanted to go into TV. I said that wouldn't be fair to the people who made my career. I told them that they would be smarter to take a young fellow like I had been, put top people around him, and they'd make a star. So they finally agreed to it. So I go back to Arness and I say, "Boy, I got it set for you." So he gets a long face and says, "You're ruining my career." "Your career, you sonofabitch, you can't get a job! Everybody says you're too goddam big to work with. I'm the only guy that'll work with you and I can't get enough parts to pay you this kind of money. This'll give you a chance to start like I did, with Saturday matinee-type of pictures." Well, he finally did it. Now he's been doing it for seventeen years and he's probably worth that

many million dollars. I guess he's happy about it.

Why, in your Batjac productions, do you tend to hire less domineering directors than when you're working outside of Batjac?

Oh, they're more reasonable. I like to work with young guys. The first guy I gave a break to was McLaglen's son, Andrew. I got him his first picture, I got him his director's card. What was the name of the first picture he did?

Man in the Vault. *I asked him about it once and he said that he'd tried to buy it up and burn it.*

It wasn't that bad.

Ten years after the fact, why do you think The Alamo *failed?*

Financially it didn't. Fifteen million the first time around. I didn't make a cent on it because I made a bad goddam deal. I know the rumor is out the picture was a bomb. Listen, I've only directed two pictures: both of them did fifteen million the first time around. Show me the other director who's done that.

Why did you pick The Green Berets *to direct?*

At the time we were in Vietnam, it was quite obvious that no one would tell the truth of why we were there. I'd been over there (this is before we'd sent 500,000 men over there and before the liberals had it as a point of obstruction for our country); I knew that the people of South Vietnam were being treated very badly, and that we had a goddam good right to be there. I tried to put that in the picture. Whether I succeeded or not, I don't know.

Why didn't you just hire Burt Kennedy or Andy McLaglen to direct it, like twenty other Batjac productions?

Because I wanted it to be a little better than that. I don't mean to say anything against the other gentlemen's ability, but it was something I was interested in and I wanted it told the way I saw it over there.

Do you have any other stories that you'd like to direct?

I have one good Western that some day I hope to do, but it'll have to be when pay television comes in, when they can afford to pay a little more. It won't be as expensive as most of these pictures that start out at three or four million and end up at ten million. (Look at *Darling Lili*—seventeen million dollars.) Well, I won't lie to anyone; I don't have to. When they want one of the best Westerns I've ever been stung by, they'll spend more money and we'll make this one. We at Batjac try to be within five per cent of our original estimated budget. That's a final budget, however. Then you go get the cast and everything else. Those prices change. At a studio they do another estimate. Then, after they're in the picture six weeks, they do another estimate and usually the picture comes in ten per cent over that. When we decide to make a picture, we've never been over ten per cent of what we said we'd originally make the picture for. I hope to continue in that way so that nobody'll ever be disappointed in anything that I'm connected with.

Do you mind being labelled a reactionary?

There is only one point that I'm a reactionary about. They've given me the credit for being one for years but this is the only thing I'm really a reactionary on. The motion picture business was intended to be a medium of illusion and all these young directors are trying to take the illusion out of it. I've knocked people on their ass, hit people over the head with chairs for years, and nobody ever said anything about it. But now they're specializing it. They tape a piece of liver to you and blow it out so it looks like your guts are coming out. They want a realism that I think is unnecessary. Their attitude is realism versus illusion, it's that goddam simple. As far as dying is concerned, I like the way they had me die in *Sands of Iwo Jima*. Dwan's a damn fine director. Guy hands you a cigarette, says stick around me, you'll live longer. Pow, and he's dead. That's all.

Aside from the realism kick, what do you think is wrong with pictures?

I don't say all that is wrong. I say it's different than my conception of it. Maybe they're right. All I know is that picture attendance has dropped off and they're no longer the most inexpensive attraction for the American people. It's no longer the American habit as it used to be. And it's obvious that it's due to the type of pictures that are being made; it doesn't take a soothsayer to figure that out.

When someone sends you a script, what do you look for?

I look for an interesting character. If I feel the character's interesting, I'll do it. I have a businessman's approach to motion pictures. My output is two pictures a year. One of them I might do because I think it'll be commercially successful, and the other one I might do because, Jesus, I really want to play that part.

How interested are you in politics?

I am not a political figure. I hate politics and most politicians. But when things get rough and people are saying things that aren't true, I sometimes open my mouth and eventually get in trouble.

You feel the press has quoted you out of context, blown up your remarks out of proportion?

They will not take a premise and take your point of view from that premise. I thought it was obvious what they did in the "Playboy" interview [May 1971]. Now I've done as much as any man to give human dignity to the Indian. My Indian in *Hondo* was a great guy, my Indian in *Fort Apache* was a great guy. I assume the Indians know that I have a great deal of respect for them. Well, this guy and I were talking about funny things and he says, "Well, what do you think about the Indians taking over Alcatraz?" Well, it's such a ridiculous thing. What did he want, a serious comment about the thing? So I said, "Let them have it. Nobody that ever lived there wants to go back and none of the guards want it. I think they ought to pay for it, just like we paid for Manhattan. And I hope they've been careful with their wampum." Now when it comes out in the magazine it comes right after something serious, so all of a sudden I get letters from the Indians. It looked like I was belittling them and I wasn't. I was talking about a bunch of jerks that had taken over the island, not the entire race. Good God, they're American citizens, they have every right we have and some we don't.

What springs to your mind when you think of the old days with Ford, Bond, Harry Carey, etc.?

Just a warm feeling when you mention those names. They were dear in my life and we had great times together.

Filmography

THIS FILMOGRAPHY lists all Wayne's work in the cinema that I have been able to establish with the exception of a few special appeals that Wayne filmed on behalf of charitable causes (these — or some of them — are listed in Karl Thiede's Wayne filmography referred to below). Wayne has also done some television work — guest appearances on shows like "The Rowan and Martin Laugh In," contributions to documentaries on John Ford, and two dramatic episodes in TV series under John Ford's direction (the latter listed in detail in Peter Bogdanovich's "John Ford" in the Movie Paperback series) — but this work is omitted here.

The following films are listed in order of appearance and the year date accompanying the titles is that of release. Where I have been able to locate production dates, these are given as well. The release dates usually recorded for both Britain and the United States are those of general distribution; where I have come across earlier *première* dates, I have noted these as well. Distributors are those that initially released each picture; other companies may have subsequently taken them over.

The credits of Wayne's films have been established from the films themselves, from contemporary publicity material and reviews, and cross-checked against reliable later research elsewhere, especially "The American Film Institute Catalog: Feature Films 1921-30" (New York, R.R. Bowker, 1971), "Who Wrote the Movie and What Else Did He Write?" (Los Angeles, Academy of Motion Picture Arts and Sciences, 1970), and the filmography in "John Ford" (London, Studio Vista, 1967). In addition, Karl Thiede's outline "John Wayne, a Comprehensive Filmography" in the magazine "Views and Reviews" (Fall 1969 issue, plus later additions) proved a valuable source for checking.

While I have restricted the extent of behind-camera credits to exclude such aspects as Set Decoration, these credits are otherwise in almost every case more complete than anything hitherto published. And, for making this possible, I am in no small way indebted to the unstinting help of two film enthusiasts who have devotedly extended my original research from their own files of information, especially in adding uncredited appearances to the official casts.

The experts concerned are John Brooker, who lavished attention on Wayne's B Westerns of the Thirties, and Pat Billings, who pored over all my work on Wayne's major films from *Stagecoach* onwards. This next section would have been much the poorer without their generous extension of my efforts.

THE DROP KICK (1927)
(American title)
GLITTER
(British title)

Director	Millard Webb
Production Company	
Distributor	First National

Released September 25 (U.S.); March 19, 1928 (G.B.)

Richard Barthelmess starred in this college drama which is reported to have featured Wayne as a member of the football team from the University of Southern California which was shown playing a game

---

HANGMAN'S HOUSE (1928)

Director	John Ford
Writers	Marion Orth
	Malcolm Stuart Boylan (titles)
	from an adaption by Philip Klein
	of the story by Donn Byrne
Cinematographer	George Schneiderman
Editor	Margaret V. Clancey
Production Company	
Distributor	Fox

80 minutes (approx.)

Citizen Hogan	Victor McLaglen
Connaught O'Brien	June Collyer
Lord Chief Justice James O'Brien	Hobart Bosworth
Dermot McDermot	Larry Kent
John D'Arcy	Earle Foxe
Anne McDermot	Belle Stoddard
Neddy Joe	Joseph Burke
Colonel of Legionnaires	Eric Mayne
Horse race spectator	John Wayne
	Jack Pennick

Released May 13 (U.S.); November 12 (G.B.)
Silent

WORDS AND MUSIC (1929)

Director	James Tinling
Associate	Frank Merlin
Writer	Andrew Bennison
	from a screen story by Frederick Hazlitt Brennan
	Jack McEdwards
Cinematographers	Charles G. Clarke
	Charles Van Enger
	Don Anderson
Musical director	Arthur Kay
Editor	Ralph Dixon
Executive producer	Chandler Sprague
Production Company	
Distributor	Fox

81 minutes (sound)

Mary Brown	Lois Moran
Phil Denning	David Percy
Dorothy Blake	Helen Twelvetrees
Pop Evans	William Orlamond
Dean Crockett	Elizabeth Patterson
Pete Donahue	Duke Morrison
Skeet Mulroy	Frank Albertson
Hannibal	Tom Patricola
Biltmore Quartet	Eddie Bush
	Paul Gibbons
	Bill Seckler
	Ches Kirkpatrick
Bubbles	Bubbles Crowell
Ward	Ward Bond

Richard Keene, Dorothy Ward, Collier Sisters, Muriel Gardner, Dorothy Jordan, Helen Parrish, Jack Wade, Vina Gale, Arthur Springer, Harriet Griffith, John Griffith, Helen Hunt, Charles Huff, etc.

Wayne was billed under his real name, Duke Morrison

Released August 18 (U.S.); December 6 (G.B.)

Also released in a silent version

SALUTE (1929)

Director	John Ford
Writers	James Kevin McGuinness
	Wilbur Morse Jr. (titles)
	from a screen story by Tristram Tupper
	John Stone

Cinematographer	Joseph August
Editor	Alex Troffey
Production Company	
Distributor	Fox
86 minutes	
Cadet John Randall	George O'Brien
Nancy Wayne	Helen Chandler
Midshipman Albert	
Edward Price	Frank Albertson
Midshipman	
Paul Randall	William Janney
Maj. Gen. Somers	Clifford Dempsey
Rear Admiral Randall	Lumsden Hare
Marion Wilson	Joyce Compton
Navy coach	David Butler
Smoke Screen	Stepin Fetchit
Cadet	Rex Bell
Midshipman	John Breeden
Football players	John Wayne
	Ward Bond

An early sound picture — titles credit probably applying to silent version
Released September 1 (U.S.);
January 27, 1930 (G.B.)

Words and Music: *Lois Moran, Wayne, Ward Bond (behind Wayne).*

MEN WITHOUT WOMEN (1930)

ROUGH ROMANCE (1930)

Director	John Ford
Stage Director	Andrew Bennison
Writer	Dudley Nichols
	from a screen story by
	John Ford
	James Kevin McGuinness
Cinematographer	Joseph August
Art Director	William Darling
Editor	Paul Weatherwax
Music	Peter Brunelli
	Glen Knight
Associate Producer	James Kevin McGuinness
Production Company	
Distributor	Fox
77 minutes	
Chief Torpedoman	
Burke	Kenneth MacKenna
Ensign Price	Frank Albertson
Handsome	Paul Page
Cobb	Walter McGrail
Kaufman	Warren Hymer
Costello	J. Farrell MacDonald
Jenkins	
(radio operator)	Stuart Erwin
Pollock	George LeGuere
Murphy	Ben Hendricks Jr.
Dutch Winkler	Harry Tenbrook
Lt. Com. Bridewell	Warner Richmond
Capt. Carson	Roy Stewart
Com. Weymouth	Charles Gerard
Lt. Digby	Pat Somerset
	John Wayne
	Robert Parrish

Premiere January 31, released February 9
(U.S.); July 14 (G.B.)

Director	A.F. Erickson
Writers	Elliott Lester
	Donald Davis (dialogue)
	from the story
	"The Girl Who Wasn't
	Wanted" by
	Kenneth B. Clarke
Cinematographer	Daniel B. Clark
Editor	Paul Weatherwax
Production Company	
Distributor	Fox
55 minutes	

Billy West	George O'Brien
Marna Reynolds	Helen Chandler
Loup La Tour	Antonio Moreno
Sheriff	
Milt Powers	Roy Stewart
Chick Carson	Harry Cording
"Dad" Reynolds	David Hartford
Laramie	Eddie Borden
Flossie	Noel Francis
Pop Nichols	Frank Lanning
	John Wayne

Released June 15 (U.S.); June 22 (G.B.)

Rough Romance: *George O'Brien, Wayne, Antonio Moreno.*

Cheer Up and Smile:
player, Arthur Lake, John Wayne.

The Big Trail:
Tully Marshall, John Wayne.

CHEER UP AND SMILE (1930)   THE BIG TRAIL (1930)

Director	Sidney Lanfield
Writer	Howard J. Green
	from the story
	"If I Was Alone
	with You"
	by Richard Connell
Cinematographer	Joseph Valentine
Editor	Ralph Dietrich
Associate Producer	Al Rockett
Production Company	
Distributor	Fox
76 minutes	
Margie	Dixie Lee
Eddie Fripp	Arthur Lake
Yvonne	Olga Baclanova
Himself	"Whispering"
	Jack Smith
Andy	Johnny Arthur
Pierre	Charles Judels
Tom	John Darrow
Paul	Sumner Getchell
Professor	Franklin Pangborn
Donald	Buddy Messinger
	John Wayne

Released June 22 (U.S.); November (G.B.)

Director	Raoul Walsh
Writers	Jack Peabody
	Marie Boyle
	Florence Postal
	from a screen story
	by Hal G. Evarts
Cinematographer	
(35mm)	Lucien Andriot
Cinematographer	
(70mm)	Arthur Edeson
Art Director	Harold Miles
	Fred Sersen
Editor	Jack Dennis
Music	Arthur Kay
Recording Engineers	George Leverett
	Don Flick
Production Company	
Distributor	Fox

158 minutes (70mm Grandeur)
125 minutes (35mm standard) (G.B.: 99 minutes)

Breck Coleman	John Wayne
Ruth Cameron	Marguerite Churchill
Gussie	El Brendel
Zeke, Breck's pal	Tully Marshall
Red Flack	Tyrone Power (Sr.)
Dave Cameron	David Rollins
Bill Thorpe	Ian Keith

Pa Bascom	Frederick Burton
Windy Bill	Russ Powell
Lopez	Charles Stevens
Honey Girl	Helen Parrish
Gussie's	
mother-in-law	Louise Carver
Wellmore	William V. Mong
Abigail	Dodo Newton
Bill Gillis	Jack Peabody
Sid Bascom	Ward Bond
Mrs. Riggs	Marcia Harris
Mary Riggs	Marjorie Leet
Sairey	Emslie Emerson
Ohio Man	Frank Rainboth
Ohio Man's son	Andy Shufford
Sisters from	Gertrude Van Lent
Missouri	Lucille Van Lent
Boat Captain	DeWitt Jennings
Marshall	Alphonz Ethier

Premiere October 24, released November 1 (U.S.); released April 30, 1931 (G.B.)

A German version, *Die Grosse Fahrt*, was also filmed with a German-speaking cast under Raoul Walsh's supervision; a French version was also made, *La Piste des Géants*, directed by P. Couderc

271

GIRLS DEMAND EXCITEMENT (1931)

Director	Seymour Felix
Writer	Harlan Thompson
Cinematographer	Charles Clarke
Editor	Jack Murray
Production Company	
Distributor	Fox
69 minutes	
Joan Madison	Virginia Cherrill
Peter Brooks	John Wayne
Miriam,	
Joan's friend	Marguerite Churchill
Freddie	William Janney
Harriet Mundy	Martha Sleeper
Gazella Perkins,	
college instructress	Helen Jerome Eddy
Tommy	Eddie Nugent
The Dean	Winter Hall
Sue Street	Addie McPhail

Ralph Welles, George Irving, Marion Bryon, Jerry Mandy, Ray Cooke, Emerson Treacy
Released February 8 (U.S.); July 20 (G.B.)

THREE GIRLS LOST (1931)

Director	Sidney Lanfield
Writer	Bradley King
	from a screen story by
	Robert D. Andrews
Cinematographer	L. William O'Connell
Editor	Ralph Dietrich
Production Company	
Distributor	Fox
80 minutes	
Noreen McMann	Loretta Young
Gordon Wales	John Wayne
William Marriott	Lew Cody
Edna Best	Joyce Compton
Marcia Tallant	Joan Marsh
Mrs. McGee	Katherine Clare Ward
Tony	Paul Fix
	Bert Roach

Released April 19 (U.S.); October 12 (G.B.)

MEN ARE LIKE THAT (1931)
(American title)
THE VIRTUOUS WIFE
(British title)

Director	George B. Seitz
Writers	Robert Riskin
	Dorothy Howell
	(continuity)
	from the play "Arizona"
	by Augustus Thomas
Cinematographer	Teddy Tetzlaff
Editor	Gene Milford
Production Company	
Distributor (U.S.)	Columbia

Three Girls Lost: *Wayne, Loretta Young, player.*

Men Are Like That: *June Clyde, John Wayne, Laura LaPlante.*

Distributor (G.B.)	United Artists
70 minutes	
Evelyn Palmer	Laura LaPlante
Lt. Bob Denton	John Wayne
Bonita Palmer	June Clyde
Col. Bonham	Forrest Stanley
Conchita	Nena Quartaro
Dot	Susan Fleming
Peggy	Loretta Sayers
Hank	Hugh Cummings

Released June 27 (U.S.); March 7, 1932 (G.B.)
First reviewed in America under the title *Arizona*

THE DECEIVER (1931)

Director	Louis King
Production Company Distributor	Columbia

Released December 1 (U.S.); July, 1932 (G.B)
Ian Keith played Thorpe and Wayne took over when the character became a corpse
The film starred Lloyd Hughes and Dorothy Sebastian

RANGE FEUD (1931)

Director	D. Ross Lederman
Writer	Milton Krims
Cinematographer	Ben Kline
Editor	Maurice Wright
Production Company Distributor (U.S.)	Columbia
Distributor (G.B.)	United Artists
64 minutes	
Sheriff Buck Gordon	Buck Jones
Clint Turner	John Wayne
Judy Walton	Susan Fleming
John Walton	Ed LeSaint
Dad Turner	William Walling
Hank	Wallace MacDonald
Vandall	Harry Woods
Biggers	Frank Austin

Released December 1 (U.S.); June 1932 (G.B.)

MAKER OF MEN (1931)

Director	Edward Sedgwick
Writer	Howard J. Green from a screen story by Howard J. Green Edward Sedgwick
Cinematographer	L. William O'Connell

Editor	Gene Milford
Production Company Distributor (U.S.)	Columbia
Distributor (G.B.)	United Artists
71 minutes	
Dudley	Jack Holt
Bob	Richard Cromwell
Dorothy	Joan Marsh
Chick	Robert Alden
Dusty	John Wayne
McNeill	Walter Catlett
Mrs. Rhodes	Natalie Moorhead
Mr. Rhodes	Richard Tucker
Aunt Martha	Ethel Wales

Titled *Yellow* during production
Released December 25 (U.S.); July 11, 1932 (G.B.)

THE VOICE OF HOLLYWOOD
Second series, No. 13 (1932)

Director	Mack D'Agostino
Production Company	Tiffany
12 minutes	

Wayne was the announcer who introduced various movie stars (George Bancroft, El Brendel, Jackie Cooper, Gary Cooper, Lupe Velez) within the series radio show background
Released January 17 (U.S.)

SHADOW OF THE EAGLE (1932)

Serial in 12 episodes:
1 The Carnival Mystery
2 Pinholes
3 The Eagle Strikes
4 The Man of a Million Voices
5 The Telephone Cipher
6 The Code of the Carnival
7 Eagle Vulture
8 On the Spot
9 When Thieves Fall Out
10 The Man Who Knew
11 The Eagle's Wings
12 The Shadow Unmasked

Director	Ford Beebe
Writers	Ford Beebe Colbert Clark Wyndham Gittens
Cinematographers	Ben Kline Victor Scheurich
Editor	Ray Snyder
Producer	Nat Levine
Production Company Distributor (U.S.)	Mascot
Craig McCoy	John Wayne
Jean Gregory	Dorothy Gulliver
Nathan Gregory	Edward Hearn
Evans	Richard Tucker
Green	Lloyd Whitlock
Danby	Walter Miller
Ward	Kenneth Harlan
Clark	Edmund Burns

Ames	Pat O'Malley
Midget	Little Billy
Strongman	Ivan Linow
Ventriloquist	James Bradbury Jr.
Kelly	Ernie S. Adams
Gardner	Bud Osborne
Boyle	Yakima Canutt
Clown	Billy West

Released February 1 (U.S.); no G.B. release traced

TEXAS CYCLONE (1932)

Director	D. Ross Lederman
Writer	Randall Faye from a story by William Colt MacDonald
Cinematographer	Ben Kline
Editor	Otto Meyer
Production Company Distributor (U.S.)	Columbia
Distributor (G.B.)	United Artists
63 minutes	
Pecos Grant	Tim McCoy
Helena Rawlins	Shirley Grey
Utah Becker	Wheeler Oakman
Steve Pickett	John Wayne
Nick Lawlor	Wallace MacDonald
Webb Oliver	James Farley
Jake Farwell	Harry Cording
Hefty	Vernon Dent
Lew Collins	Walter Brennan
Kate	Mary Gordon

Released February 24 (U.S.); December (G.B.)

TWO FISTED LAW (1932)

Director	D. Ross Lederman
Writer	Kurt Kempler from a story by William Colt MacDonald
Cinematographer	Benjamin Kline
Editor	Otto Meyer
Production Company Distributor (U.S.)	Columbia
Distributor (G.B.)	United Artists
64 minutes	
Tim Clark	Tim McCoy
Betty Owen	Alice Day
Bob Russell	Wheeler Oakman
Sheriff Malcolm	Tully Marshall
Artie	Wallace MacDonald
Duke	John Wayne
Deputy Sheriff Bendix	Walter Brennan
Zink Yokum	Richard Alexander

Released June 8 (U.S.); circa July (G.B.)

The Hurricane Express *(episode 8): players, Glenn Strange (leading gang), John Wayne.*

LADY AND GENT (1932)

Director	Stephen Roberts
Writers	Grover Jones
	William Slavens
	McNutt
Cinematographer	Harry Fischbeck
Production Company	
Distributor	Paramount
80 minutes	
Stag Bailey	George Bancroft
Puff Rogers	Wynne Gibson
Ted Streaver	Charles Starrett
Pin Streaver	James Gleason
Buzz Kinney	John Wayne
Cash Enright	Morgan Wallace
McSweeley	James Crane
Doc Hayes	William Halligan
Ted (aged 9)	Billy Butts
Betty	Joyce Compton
Principal	Frank McGlynn Sr.
Grocer	Charles Grapewin
Watchman	Frederick Wallace
Coroner	Lew Kelly

Joe	Sid Saylor
Second bartender	Russell Powell
Jim	Frank Darien
First bartender	Hal Price
Judge	A. S. Byron
Workman	John Beck
Small arena fighter	Tom Kennedy
Minister	Frank Dawson

Released July 15 (U.S.); July 11 (G.B.)
Known prior to release as *The Challenger*

THE HURRICANE EXPRESS (1932)

Serial in twelve
episodes:

1 The Wrecker
2 Flying Pirates
3 The Masked Menace
4 Buried Alive
5 Danger Lights
6 The Airport Mystery
7 Sealed Lips
8 Outside the Law
9 The Invincible Enemy
10 The Wrecker's Secret
11 Wings of Death
12 Unmasked

Directors	Armand Schaefer
	J. P. McGowan
Writers	George Morgan
	J. P. McGowan
	from a screen story
	by Colbert Clark
	Barney Sarecky
	Wyndham Gittens
Cinematographers	Ernest Miller
	Carl Wester
Editor	Ray Snyder
Producer	Nat Levine
Production Company	
Distributor (U.S.)	Mascot
Distributor (G.B.)	Ideal
Larry Baker	John Wayne
Gloria Martin	
(Stratton)	Shirley Grey
Mr. Edwards	Tully Marshall
Stevens	Conway Tearle

Jim Baker	J. Farrell MacDonald
Jordan	Matthew Betz
Hemingway	James Burtis
Walter Gray	Lloyd Whitlock
Matthews	Joseph Girard
Stratton	Edmund Breese
Carlson	Al Bridge
Barney	Ernie S. Adams
Mike	Charles King
Jim	Glenn Strange
Sandy	Al Ferguson

Released August 1 (U.S.)

THE HOLLYWOOD HANDICAP (1932)

Director	Charles Lamont
Production Companies	The Thalians Club Bryan Foy
Distributor	Universal

Wayne was a guest in this two reeler, part of a comedy series; other guests included Anita Stewart, Bert Wheeler, Dickie Moore and Tully Marshall

Released August 10 (U.S.)

RIDE HIM COWBOY (1932)
(American title)
THE HAWK
(British title)

Director	Fred Allen
Writer	Scott Mason from a story "Ride Him Cowboy" by Kenneth Perkins
Cinematographer	Ted McCord
Editor	William Clemens
Producer	Leon Schlesinger
Production Company Distributor	Warner Brothers
56 minutes	
John Drury	John Wayne
Ruth Gaunt	Ruth Hall
John Gaunt	Henry B. Walthall
Deputy Sheriff Clout	Harry Gribbon
Judge Jones	Otis Harlan
Judge Bartlett	Charles Sellon
Henry Suggs	Frank Hagney Duke the Devil Horse

Released August 27 (U.S.); January, 1933 (G.B.)
Re-make of *The Unknown Cavalier* (1926) in which Ken Maynard (as Tom Drury) played the Wayne role; Otis Harlan played the same part in both versions

Ride Him Cowboy: *Ruth Hall, Wayne, Harry Gribbon.*

Haunted Gold: *Harry Woods, Wayne, Erville Alderson, Otto Hoffman.*

275

Director	Tenny Wright
Writer	Kurt Kempler
	from a screen story
	by Marion Jackson
Cinematographer	Ted McCord
Editor	Frank Ware
Producer	Leon Schlesinger
Production Company	
Distributor	Warner Bros.
54 minutes	
John Steele	John Wayne
Sam Crew	Noah Berry
Ginger Malloy	Mae Madison
Sonora Joe	Luis Alberni
Gov. Lew Wallace	Berton Churchill
Arizona	Paul Hurst
Pat Malloy	Sherwood Bailey

Duke the Miracle Horse, Frank Ellis, Hank Bell, Lafe McKee

Released October 8 (U.S.); March, 1933 (G.B.)

Re-make of *Land beyond the Law* in which Ken Maynard (as Jerry Steele) played the Wayne role; re-made again under the original title with Dick Foran in the Maynard/Wayne role and released in 1936

Director	Mack V. Wright
Writer	Adele Buffington
Cinematographer	Nick Musuraca
Editor	William Clemens
Associate Producer	Sid Rogell
Producer	Leon Schlesinger
Production Company	
Distributor	Warner Bros.
58 minutes	
John Mason	John Wayne
Janet Carter	Shelia Terry
Benedict	Erville Alderson
Joe Ryan	Harry Woods
Simon	Otto Hoffman
Mrs. Herman	Martha Mattox
Clarence	Blue Washington
	Slim Whitaker

Released December 17 (U.S.); May, 1933 (G.B.)

Re-make of *The Phantom City* (1928) with Ken Maynard (as Tim Kelly) in the Wayne role; Blue Washington appeared in both versions

Director	Tenny Wright
Writer	Kurt Kempler
Cinematographer	Ted McCord
Editor	William Clemens
Producer	Leon Schlesinger
Production Company	
Distributor	Warner Bros.
55 minutes	
John Trent	John Wayne
Alice Ellis	Marceline Day
Sgt. Tippy	Frank McHugh
Zeke Keller	Otis Harlan
Gus Lynch	Albert J. Smith
"High Wolf"	Yakima Canutt
Lafe (oldtimer)	Lafe McKee
Cavalry commander	Clarence Geldert

Duke the Miracle Horse
Slim Whitaker, Frank Ellis

Released March 18 (U.S.); April 17 (G.B.)

Clip said to be featured in *Footlight Parade* (1933)

Action footage from *The Red Raiders* (1927)

The Telegraph Trail: *John Wayne, Frank McHugh.*

The Three Musketeers: *Wayne, Ruth Hall, Rodney Hildebrandt(?)*.

THE THREE MUSKETEERS (1933)

Serial in twelve episodes:

1 The Fiery Circle
2 One for All and All for One
3 The Master Spy
4 Pirates of the Desert
5 Rebels' Rifles
6 Death's Marathon
7 Naked Steel
8 The Master Strikes
9 The Fatal Cave
10 Trapped
11 The Measure of a Man
12 The Glory of Comrades

Directors	Armand Schaefer
	Colbert Clark
Writers	Norman S. Hall
	Colbert Clark
	Wyndham Gittens
	Ben Cohn
	Ella Arnold (dialogue)
	from the novel by
	Alexandre Dumas
Cinematographers	Ernest Miller
	Ed Lyons
Production Company	
Distributor (U.S.)	Mascot

Distributor (G.B.)	Wardour
Tom Wayne	John Wayne
Elaine Corday	Ruth Hall
Clancy	Jack Mulhall
Renard	Raymond Hatton
Schmidt	Francis X. Bushman Jr.
Stubbs	Noah Beery Jr.
Armand Corday	Creighton Chaney
	(Lon Chaney Jr.)
Ali	Al Ferguson
El Kador	Hooper Atchely
Ratkin	Edward Piel
El Maghreb	George Magrill
Col. Duval	Gordon DeMain
Capt. Boncour	William Desmond
Major Booth	Robert Frazer
Gen. Pelletier	Emile Chautard
Col. Brent	Robert Warwick
Demoyne	Rodney Hildebrandt

Released April 7 (U.S.)

Reissued in a 60 minute feature version under the title *Desert Command* by Favorite Films in 1946 (U.S.)

CENTRAL AIRPORT (1933)

Director	William A. Wellman
Writers	Rian James
	James Seymour
	from a story by
	Jack Moffitt
Cinematographer	Sid Hickox
Editor	James Morley
Production Company	
Distributor	Warner Bros.
71 minutes	
Jim	Richard Barthelmess
Jill	Sally Eilers
Neil	Tom Brown
Swarthy man	Harold Huber
Eddie	James Murray
Mr. Blaine	Grant Mitchell
Mrs. Blaine	Claire McDowell
Havana Manager	Willard Robertson
Amarillo Manager	Arthur Vinton
Man in wreck	Charles Sellon
	John Wayne

Released April 15 (U.S.);
September 25 (G.B.)

SOMEWHERE IN SONORA (1933)

Director	Mack V. Wright
Writer	Joe Roach from a magazine story and the novel "Somewhere South in Sonora" by Will Levington Comfort
Cinematographer	Ted McCord
Editor	William Clemens
Producer	Leon Schlesinger
Production Company Distributor	Warner Bros.
57 minutes	
John Bishop	John Wayne
Bob Leadly	Henry B. Walthall
Mary Burton	Shirley Palmer
Monte Black	J. P. McGowan
Patsy Ellis	Ann Fay
Riley	Frank Rice
Shorty	Billy Franey
Bart Leadly	Paul Fix
Burton	Ralph Lewis

Duke, the Miracle Horse
Released June 7 (U.S.); February, 1934 (G.B.)
Re-make of the 1927 release of the same title which starred Ken Maynard

Somewhere in Sonora: *Shirley Palmer, Ann Fay, John Wayne.*

HIS PRIVATE SECRETARY (1933)

Director	Philip H. Whitman
Writer	John Francis Natteford from a screen story by Lew Collins
Cinematographer	Abe Schultz
Editor	Bobby Ray
Supervisor	Al Alt
Production Company Distributor (U.S.)	Showmen's Pictures
Distributor (G.B.)	Gaumont Ideal
60 minutes	
Marion Hall	Evalyn Knapp
Dick Wallace	John Wayne
Doctor Hall	Alec B. Francis
Mr. Wallace	Reginald Barlow
Polly	Natalie Kingston
Little	Arthur Hoyt
Garage owner	Al St. John
Butler	Hugh Kidder
Boy	Mickey Rentschler Patrick Cunning

Released June 10 (U.S.); February 12, 1934 (G.B.)

THE LIFE OF JIMMY DOLAN (1933) (American title)
THE KID'S LAST FIGHT (British title)

Director	Archie Mayo

Writers	Erwin S. Gelsey David Boehm Bertram Millhauser Beulah Marie Dix from a story by Bertram Millhauser Beulah Marie Dix
Cinematographer	Arthur Edeson
Editor	Bert Levy
Production Company Distributor	Warner Bros.
89 minutes	
Jimmy Dolan	Douglas Fairbanks Jr.
Peggy	Loretta Young
Budgie	Fifi D'Orsay
Aunt	Aline MacMahon
Phlaxer	Guy Kibbee
Doc Wood	Lyle Talbot
Reggie Newman	Harold Huber
Sam	Farina
Mary Lou	Dawn O'Day (Anne Shirley)
George	David Durand
Goldie	Shirley Grey
Freckles	Mickey Rooney
Malvin	Arthur Hohl
Louie Primaro	Arthur Dekuh
Magee	George Meeker
Smith	John Wayne

Released June 14 (U.S.); September 25 (G.B.)
Remade as *They Made Me a Criminal* (1938)

BABY FACE (1933)

Director	Alfred E. Green
Writers	Gene Markey Kathryn Scola from a screen story by Mark Canfield (i.e. Darryl F. Zanuck)
Cinematographer	James Van Trees
Art Director	Anton Grot
Editor	Howard Bretherton
Production Company Distributor	Warner Bros.
76 minutes	
Lily (Baby Face)	Barbara Stanwyck
Trenholm	George Brent
Stevens	Donald Cook
Sipple	Arthur Hohl
Jimmy McCoy	John Wayne
Carter	Henry Kolker
Brakeman	James Murray
Nick Powers	Robert Barrat
Ann Carter	Margaret Lindsay
Brody	Douglas Dumbrille
Chico	Theresa Harris
The Girl	Renee Whitney
Stolvich	Nat Pendleton
Cragg	Alphonse Ethier
Doorman	Harry Gribbon
Lutza	Arthur De Kuh

Released July 1 (U.S.); December (G.B.)

THE MAN FROM MONTEREY (1933)

Director	Mack V. Wright
Writer	Lesley Mason
Cinematographer	Ted McCord
Editor	William Clemens
Producer	Leon Schlesinger
Production Company Distributor	Warner Bros.
57 minutes	
Capt. John Holmes	John Wayne
Dolores	Ruth Hall
Felipe	Luis Alberni
Don Pablo	Francis Ford
Anita Garcia	Nina Quartaro
Don Jose Castanares	Lafayette McKee
Don Luis Gonzales	Donald Reed
Juanita	Lillian Leighton
Jake Morgan	Charles Whitaker
Duke, the Devil Horse	

Released July 15 (U.S.); April 2, 1934 (G.B.)

RIDERS OF DESTINY (1933)

Director/Writer	R. N. Bradbury
Producer	Paul Malvern
Production Company	Lone Star
Distributor (U.S.A.)	Monogram
Distributor (G.B.)	Pathe
58 minutes	
Sandy Saunders ("Singin' Sandy")	John Wayne
Fay Denton	Cecelia Parker
Denton	George Hayes
Kincaid	Forrest Taylor
Bert	Al St. John
Pete (Stage Driver)	Heinie Conklin
Slip Morgan	Earl Dwire
Sheriff	Lafe McKee

Released October 10 (U.S.); July 16, 1934 (G.B.)

COLLEGE COACH (1933)
(American title)
FOOTBALL COACH
(British title)

Director	William A. Wellman
Writers	Niven Busch
	Manuel Seff
Cinematographer	Arthur Todd
Editor	Thomas Pratt
Production Company Distributor	Warner Bros.
75 minutes	
Phil Sargent	Pat O'Brien
Claire Gore	Ann Dvorak
Coach Gore	Dick Powell
Barnett	Hugh Herbert
Buck Weaver	Lyle Talbot
Dr. Philip Sargent	Arthur Byron

Matthews	Guinn Williams
Petrowski	Nat Pendleton
Editor	Phillip Faversham
Hauser	Charles C. Wilson
Spencer Trask	Donald Meek
Otis	Berton Churchill
Seymour Young	Arthur Hohl
Professor	Harry Beresford
Glantz	Herman Bing
Holcomb	Joe Sauers (Sawyer)
Westerman	Philip Reed
	John Wayne
	Ward Bond

Released November 4 (U.S.); April, 1934 (G.B.)

SAGEBRUSH TRAIL (1933)

Director	Armand Schaefer
Writer	Lindsley Parsons
Cinematographer	Archie Stout
Producer	Paul Malvern
Production Company	Lone Star
Distributor (U.S.A.)	Monogram
Distributor (G.B.)	Pathe
55 minutes	
John Brant	John Wayne
Sally Blake	Nancy Shubert
Bob Jones	Lane Chandler
Ed Walsh	Yakima Canutt
Deputy Sheriff	Wally Wales
Henchman	Art Mix
Sheriff Parker	Robert E. Burns
Dad Blake	Henry Hall
Blind Pete	Earl Dwire

Released December 15 (U.S.); March 4, 1935 (G.B.)

THE LUCKY TEXAN (1934)

Director/Writer	R. N. Bradbury
Cinematographer	Archie Stout
Editor	Carl Pierson
Producer	Paul Malvern
Production Company	Lone Star
Distributor (U.S.A.)	Monogram
Distributor (G.B.)	Pathe
56 minutes	
Jerry Mason	John Wayne
Betty	Barbara Sheldon
Jake Benson	George Hayes
Harris	Lloyd Whitlock
Cole	Yakima Canutt
Sheriff	Gordon DeMaine
Sheriff's son	Edward Parker
Banker	Earl Dwire

Released January 22 (U.S.); December 3 (G.B.)

WEST OF THE DIVIDE (1934)

Director/Writer	Robert N. Bradbury
Cinematographer	Archie Stout
Technical Director	E. R. Hickson
Recording Engineer	Dave Stower
Producer	Paul Malvern
Production Company	Lone Star
Distributor (U.S.A.)	Monogram
Distributor (G.B.)	Pathe
55 minutes	
Ted Hayden	John Wayne

Riders of Destiny: *Lafe McKee, Wayne, Earl Dwire, Forrest Taylor.*

Fay Winters	Virginia Browne Faire
Gentry	Lloyd Whitlock
Dusty Rhodes	George Hayes
Hank	Yakima Canutt
Spud	Billy O'Brien
Winters	Lafe McKee
Hutch	Blackie Whiteford
Red	Earl Dwire
Joe	Dick Dickinson

Released March 1 (U.S.); February 11, 1935 (G.B.)

BLUE STEEL (1934)

Director/Writer	Robert N. Bradbury
Cinematographer	Archie Stout
Editor	Carl Pierson
Technical Director	E. R. Hickson
Producer	Paul Malvern
Production Company	Lone Star
Distributor (U.S.A.)	Monogram
Distributor (G.B.)	Pathe
54 minutes	
John Carruthers	John Wayne
Betty Mason	Eleanor Hunt
Sheriff Jake	George Hayes
Melgrove	Ed Peil
Danti (The Polka Dot Bandit)	Yakima Canutt
Innkeeper (Hank)	George Cleveland
Bridegroom	George Nash
Dad Mason	Lafe McKee
Stagedriver	Hank Bell
Henchman	Earl Dwire

Released May 10 (U.S.); January 7, 1935 (G.B.)

THE MAN FROM UTAH (1934)

Director	Robert N. Bradbury
Writer	Lindsley Parsons
Cinematographer	Archie Stout
Editor	Carl Pierson
Producer	Paul Malvern
Production Company	Lone Star
Distributor (U.S.A.)	Monogram
Distributor (G.B.)	Pathe
55 minutes	
John Weston	John Wayne
Marjorie Carter	Polly Ann Young
George Higgins	George Hayes
Cheyenne Kent	Yakima Canutt
Barton	Ed Peil
Dolores	Anita Campillo
Judge Carter	Lafe McKee
Sheriff	George Cleveland

Released May 15 (U.S.); May, 1935 (G.B.)

The Man from Utah: *John Wayne, George Hayes.*

RANDY RIDES ALONE (1934)

Director	Harry Fraser
Writer	Lindsley Parsons
Cinematographer	Archie Stout
Technical Director	E. R. Hickson
Producer	Paul Malvern
Production Company	Lone Star
Distributor (U.S.A.)	Monogram
Distributor (G.B.)	Pathe
53 minutes	
Randy Bowers	John Wayne
Sally Rogers	Alberta Vaughn
Matt the Mute	George Hayes
Spike	Yakima Canutt
Sheriff	Earl Dwire
Deputy	Tex Phelps
Henchman	Arthur Ortega

Released June 5 (U.S.); April 8, 1935 (G.B.)

THE STAR PACKER (1934)

Director/Writer	Robert N. Bradbury
Cinematographer	Archie Stout
Editor	Carl Pierson
Technical Director	E. R. Hickson
Producer	Paul Malvern
Production Company	Lone Star
Distributor (U.S.A.)	Monogram

Distributor (G.B.)	Pathe
54 minutes	
John Travers	John Wayne
Anita	Verna Hillie
Matlock, alias The Shadow	George Hayes
Yak, the Indian	Yakima Canutt
Mason	Earl Dwire
Parker	Ed Parker
Pete	George Cleveland
Sheriff	Tom Lingham
Deputy	Arthur Ortega
Boy	Davie Aldrich
Stagecoach Driver	Tex Palmer

Released July 30 (U.S.); June 24, 1935 (G.B.)

THE TRAIL BEYOND (1934)

Director	Robert N. Bradbury
Writer	Lindsley Parsons from the novel "The Wolf Hunters" by James Oliver Curwood
Cinematographer	Archie Stout
Art Director	E. R. Hickson
Editor	Charles Hunt
Producer	Paul Malvern
Production Company	Lone Star
Distributor (U.S.A.)	Monogram
Distributor (C.B.)	Pathe
55 minutes	

Rod Drew	John Wayne
George Newsome	Noah Beery
Wabi	Noah Beery Jr.
Felice Newsome	Verna Hillie
Marie	Iris Lancaster
Jules LaRocque	Robert Frazer
Benoit	Earl Dwire
Ryan, the Mountie	Eddie Parker
	James Marcus
	Reed Howes

Released October 22 (U.S.);
May 27, 1935 (G.B.)
Previous version: *The Wolf Hunters*, 1926;
1949 release *The Wolf Hunters* was based
on the same source material with Lindsley
Parsons producing but not writing

THE LAWLESS FRONTIER
(1934)

Director/Writer	Robert N. Bradbury
Cinematographer	Archie Stout
Editor	Charles Hunt
Producer	Paul Malvern
Production Company	Lone Star
Distributor (U.S.A.)	Monogram
Distributor (G.B.)	Pathe
54 minutes	
John Tobin	John Wayne
Ruby	Sheila Terry
Dusty	George Hayes
Zanti	Earl Dwire
Joe	Yakima Canutt
Sheriff	Jack Rockwell
Miller	Gordon D. Woods

Released November 22 (U.S.); July 22,
1935 (G.B.)

'NEATH ARIZONA SKIES (1934)

Director	Harry Fraser
Writer	B. R. (Burl) Tuttle
Cinematographer	Archie Stout
Editor	Carl Pierson
Producer	Paul Malvern
Production Company	Lone Star
Distributor (U.S.A.)	Monogram
Distributor (G.B.)	Pathe
52 minutes	
Chris Morrell	John Wayne
Clara Moore	Sheila Terry
Jim Moore	Jay Wilsey (Buffalo Bill Jr.)
Nina	Shirley Ricketts
Matt Downing	George Hayes
Sam Black	Yakima Canutt
Vic Byrd	Jack Rockwell
Hodges	Phil Keefer
Express Agent	Frank Hall Crane

Released December 5 (U.S.); August 12,
1935 (G.B.)

The Trail Beyond: *Reed Howes, John Wayne, player.*

TEXAS TERROR (1935)

Director/Writer	Robert N. Bradbury
Cinematographer	Archie Stout
Editor	Carl Pierson
Producer	Paul Malvern
Production Company	Lone Star
Distributor (U.S.A.)	Monogram
Distributor (G.B.)	Pathe
58 minutes	
John Higgins	John Wayne
Beth Matthews	Lucille Brown
Joe Dickson	LeRoy Mason
Sheriff Williams	George Hayes
Blackie	Buffalo Bill Jr.
Red	Bert Dillard
Dan	Lloyd Ingraham

Released February 1 (U.S.); October 17
(G.B.)

RAINBOW VALLEY (1935)

Director	Robert N. Bradbury
Writer	Lindsley Parsons
Cinematographer	William Hyer
Editor	Carl Pierson
Technical Director	E. R. Hickson
Producer	Paul Malvern
Production Company	Lone Star
Distributor (U.S.A.)	Monogram

Distributor (G.B.)	Pathe
52 minutes	
John Martin	John Wayne
Eleanor	Lucille Brown
Rogers [Morgan?]	LeRoy Mason
George Hale	George Hayes
Galt	Buffalo Bill Jr.
Spike	Bert Dillard
Powell	Lloyd Ingraham
Storekeeper	Lafe McKee
Townsmen	Frank Ellis
	Art Dillard
	Frank Ball

Released March 15 (U.S.); September 9
(G.B.)

THE DESERT TRAIL (1935)

Director	Cullen Lewis
Writer	Lindsley Parsons
Cinematographer	Archie Stout
Editor	Carl Pierson
Producer	Paul Malvern
Production Company	Lone Star
Distributor (U.S.A.)	Republic
Distributor (G.B.)	Pathe
54 minutes	
John Scott	John Wayne
Anne	Mary Kornman
Jim	Paul Fix
Kansas Charlie	Edward Chandler
Juanita	Carmen LaRoux
Peter	Al Ferguson

Released April 22 (U.S.); November 18 (G.B.)

THE DAWN RIDER (1935)

Director/Writer	Robert N. Bradbury from a story by Lloyd Nosler
Cinematographer	Archie Stout
Editor	Carl Pierson
Producer	Paul Malvern
Production Company	Monogram
Distributor (U.S.A.)	Republic
Distributor (G.B.)	Pathe
56 minutes	
John Mason	John Wayne
Alice Gordon	Marion Burns
Barkeep	Yakima Canutt
Ben McClure	Reed Howes
Rudd Gordon	Denny Meadows (later Dennis Moore)
Buck	Bert Dillard
Black	Jack Jones
	James Sheridan

Released June 20 (U.S.); December 23 (G.B.)

PARADISE CANYON (1935)

Director	Carl Pierson
Writers	Lindsley Parsons Robert Emmett from a screen story by Lindsley Parsons
Cinematographer	Archie Stout
Editor	Gerald Roberts
Producer	Paul Malvern
Production Company	
Distributor (U.S.A.)	Monogram
Distributor (G.B.)	Exclusive
52 minutes	
John Wyatt	John Wayne
Linda Carter	Marion Burns
Doctor Carter	Earle Hodgins
Curly Joe Gale	Yakima Canutt
Trigger	Reed Howes
Ike	Perry Murdock
Mike	Gordon Clifford
Rurale Captain	Gino Corrado
	Tex Palmer

In production under title *Paradise Ranch*
Released July 20 (U.S.); late 1936 (G.B.)

WESTWARD HO (1935)

Director	Robert N. Bradbury
Writers	Lindsley Parsons Harry Friedman Robert Emmett from a screen story by Lindsley Parsons

Rainbow Valley: *LeRoy Mason, George Hayes, Wayne.*

Dawn Rider: *Wayne, Yakima Canutt, Denny Meadows.*

282

Cinematographer	Archie Stout
Editor	Carl Pierson
Producer	Paul Malvern
Production Company	
Distributor (U.S.A.)	Republic
Distributor (G.B.)	British Lion
60 minutes	
John Wyatt	John Wayne
Mary Gordon	Sheila Manners
Jim Wyatt	Frank McGlynn Jr.
Ballard	Jack Curtis
Red	Yakima Canutt
Young John	Bradley Metcalfe
Mark Wyatt	Hank Bell
Hannah Wyatt	Mary McLaren
Lafe Gordon	Jim Farley
Young Jim	Dickie Jones

Released August 19 (U.S.); May 1936 (G.B.)

THE NEW FRONTIER (1935)

Director	Carl Pierson
Writer	Robert Emmett
Cinematographer	Gus Peterson
Editor	Gerald Roberts
Producer	Paul Malvern
Production Company	
Distributor (U.S.A.)	Republic
Distributor (G.B.)	British Lion
59 minutes	
John Dawson	John Wayne
Hanna Lewis	Muriel Evans
Tom Lewis	Murdoch MacQuarrie
Padre	Alan Cavan
Ace Holmes	Warner Richmond
Kit	Al Bridge
Milt Dawson	Sam Flint
Norton	Glenn Strange
	Earl Dwire

Released October 5 (U.S.); circa April, 1936 (G.B.)

THE LAWLESS RANGE (1935)

Director	Robert N. Bradbury
Writer	Lindsley Parsons
Cinematographer	Archie Stout
Editor	Carl Pierson
Supervisor	Paul Malvern
Production	Trem Carr
Production Company	
Distributor (U.S.A.)	Republic
Distributor (G.B.)	British Lion
59 minutes	
John Middleton	John Wayne
Anne	Sheila Manners
Emmett	Earl Dwire
Carter	Frank McGlynn Jr.
Marshall	Jack Curtis
Burns	Yakima Canutt
Mason	Wally Howe

Released November 4 (U.S.); circa March, 1937 (G.B.)

The New Frontier: *Wayne, Murdoch MacQuarrie, Muriel Evans.*

The Oregon Trail: *player, Frank Rice, Wayne, Harry Harvey.*

283

THE OREGON TRAIL (1936)

Director	Scott Pembroke
Writers	Jack Natteford
	Robert Emmett
	Lindsley Parsons
	from a screen story by
	Robert Emmett
	Lindsley Parsons
Cinematographer	Gus Peterson
Editor	Carl Pierson
Producer	Paul Malvern
Production Company	
Distributor (U.S.A.)	Republic
Distributor (G.B.)	British Lion
59 minutes	
Capt. John Delmont	John Wayne
Anne Ridgley	Ann Rutherford
Col. Delmont	Joseph/Joe Girard
Tom Richards	Yakima Canutt
Red	Frank Rice
Jim Ridgley	E. H. Calvert
Major Harris	Ben Hendricks
Tim	Harry Harvey
Minnie	Fern Emmett
Benton	Jack Rutherford
Sis	Marian Farrell
Markey	Roland Ray
Forrenza	Gino Corrado
General Ferguson	Edward Le Saint
Don Miguel	Octavio Giraud

Released January 18 (U.S.); circa April (G.B.)

THE LAWLESS NINETIES (1936)

Director	Joseph Kane
Writer	Joseph Poland
	from a screen story by
	Joseph Poland
	Scott Pembroke
Cinematographer	William Nobles
Supervisor	Paul Malvern
Production Company	
Distributor (U.S.A.)	Republic
Distributor (G.B.)	British Lion
55 minutes	
John Tipton	John Wayne
Janet Carter	Ann Rutherford
Plummer	Harry Woods
Major Carter	George Hayes
Steele	Al Bridge
Bridger	Lane Chandler
Mose	Snowflake (Fred Toones)
Mandy Lou	Etta McDaniel
Marshall	Tom Brower
Davis	Cliff Lyons
Smith	Jack Rockwell
Red	Al Taylor
Hartley	Charles King
Green	George Cheseboro
Ward	Tom London
Pierce	Sam Flint
T. Roosevelt	Earl Seaman
Belden	Tracy Lane
Outlaw leader	Philo McCullough
Tex	Chuck Baldra
Telegraph operator	Jimmy Harrison

Released February 15 (U.S.); circa August (G.B.)

KING OF THE PECOS (1936)

Director	Joseph Kane
Writers	Bernard McConville
	Dorrell McGowan
	Stuart McGowan
	from a screen story by
	Bernard McConville
Cinematographer	Jack Marta
Supervising Editor	Joseph H. Lewis
Supervisor	Paul Malvern
Production Company	
Distributor (U.S.A.)	Republic
Distributor (G.B.)	British Lion
54 minutes	
John Clayborn	John Wayne
Belle	Muriel Evans
Stiles	Cy Kendall
Ash	Jack Clifford
Brewster	Frank Glendon
Josh	Herbert Heywood
Hank	Arthur Aylsworth
Clayborn Sr.	John Beak
Mrs. Clayborn	Mary McLaren
Little John	Bradley Metcalfe Jr.
Smith	Yakima Canutt

Released March 9 (U.S.); circa February, 1937 (G.B.)

The Lawless Nineties: *Snowflake, George Hayes, Ann Rutherford, Wayne, George Cheseboro.*

THE LONELY TRAIL (1936)

Director	Joseph Kane
Writers	Bernard McConville Jack Natteford from a screen story by Bernard McConville
Cinematographer	William Nobles
Editor	Lester Orlebeck
Producer	Nat Levine
Supervisor	Paul Malvern
Production Company *Distributor (U.S.A.)*	Republic
56 minutes	
John	John Wayne
Virginia	Ann Rutherford
Holden	Cy Kendall
Hays	Bob Kortman
Snowflake	Snowflake
Mammy	Etta McDaniel
Governor	Sam Flint
Terry	Denny Meadows (later Dennis Moore)
Jed	Jim Toney
Horrell	Yakima Canutt
Tucker	Lloyd Ingraham
Rancher	Bob Burns
Mayor	James Marcus
Captain of Cavalry	Rodney Hildebrand
Dancer	Eugene Jackson
Armstrong	Floyd Shackelford
Troopers	Jack Kirk Jack Ingram Bud Pope Tex Phelps Tracy Layne Clyde Kenney
Blaine	Leon Lord

Released May 25 (U.S.) ; circa April, 1937 (G.B.).

WINDS OF THE WASTELAND (1936)

Director	Mack V. Wright
Writer	Joseph Poland
Cinematographer	William Nobles
Supervisor	Paul Malvern
Producer	Nat Levine
Production Company *Distributor (U.S.A.)*	Republic
Distributor (G.B.)	British Lion
57 minutes	
John Blair	John Wayne
Barbara Forsythe	Phyllis Fraser
Cal Drake	Douglas Cosgrove
Smoky	Yakima Canutt
Larry	Lane Chandler
Dr. Forsythe	Sam Flint
Rocky	Lew Kelly
Cherokee Joe	Robert/Bob Kortman
Pike	Joe Yrigoyen

Jack Rockwell, W. M. McCormick, Ed Cassidy, Charles Loreker, Jack Ingram

Released July 6 (U.S.); circa June, 1937 (G.B.)

The Sea Spoilers: *William Bakewell, John Wayne.*

THE SEA SPOILERS (1936)

Director	Frank Strayer
Writer	George Waggner from a screen story by Dorrell McGowan Stuart E. McGowan
Cinematographer	Archie Stout
Editors	H. T. Fritch Ray Lockhart
Music Director	Herman S. Heller
Producer	Trem Carr
Production Company *Distributor (U.S.A.)*	Universal
Distributor (G.B.)	G.F.D.
63 minutes	
Bob Randall	John Wayne
Connie Dawson	Nan Grey
Lt. Mays	William Bakewell
Hogan	Fuzzy Knight
Phil Morgan	Russell Hicks
Commander Mays	George Irving
Marie	Lotus Long
Nick Austin	Harry Worth
Reggie	Ernest Hilliard
Hop Scotch	George Humbert
Louie	Ethan Laidlaw
Oil	Chester Gan
Detective	Cy Kendall
Fats	Harrison Green

Released October (U.S.); July 12, 1937 (G.B.)

CONFLICT (1936)

Director	David Howard
Writers	Charles Logue Walter Weems from the novel "The Abysmal Brute" by Jack London
Cinematographer	A. J. (Archie) Stout
Editor	Jack Ogilvie
Music Director	Herman Heller
Supervisor	Paul Malvern
Producer	Trem Carr
Production Company *Distributor (U.S.A.)*	Universal
Distributor (G.B.)	G.F.D.
60 minutes	
Pat	John Wayne
Maude	Jean Rogers
Tommy	Tommy Bupp
Spider	Eddie Borden
Sam	Frank Sheridan
Carrigan	Ward Bond
Ma Blake	Margaret Mann
Kelly	Harry Woods
City Editor	Bryant Washburn
Malone	Frank Hagney

Started shooting late September 1936

Released November 29 (U.S.); July 19, 1937 (G.B.)

Previously filmed under the novel's title for 1923 release, starring Reginald Denny

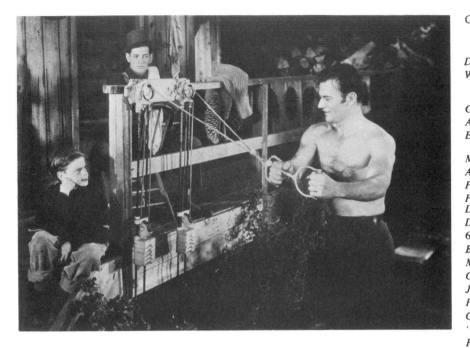

CALIFORNIA STRAIGHT AHEAD (1937)

Director	Arthur Lubin
Writer	Scott Darling from a screen story by Herman Boxer
Cinematographer	Harry Neumann
Art Director	E. R. Hickson
Editors	Charles Craft Erma Horseley
Musical Director	Charles Previn
Associate Producer	Paul Malvern
Producer	Trem Carr
Production Company *Distributor (U.S.A.)*	Universal
Distributor (G.B.)	G.F.D.
67 minutes	
Biff Smith	John Wayne
Mary Porter	Louise Latimer
Corrigan	Robert McWade
James Gifford	Theodore von Eltz
Harrison	Tully Marshall
Charlie Porter	Emerson Treacy
"Fish" McCorkle	Harry Allen
Padula	LeRoy Mason
Mrs. Porter	Grace Goodall
Huggins	Olaf Hytten
Clancy	Monty Vandergrift
Secretary	Lorin Raker

Released May 2 (U.S.); January 17, 1938 (G.B.)

Conflict: *Tommy Bupp, Eddie Borden, John Wayne.*

California Straight Ahead: *Wayne, Louise Latimer.*

I COVER THE WAR (1937)

Director	Arthur Lubin
Writer	George Waggner from a screen story suggestion by Bernard McConville
Cinematographer	Harry Neumann
Art Director	E.R. Hickson
Editor	Charles Craft
Associate Producer	Paul Malvern
Producer	Trem Carr
Production Company *Distributor (U.S.A.)*	Universal
Distributor (G.B.)	G.F.D.
68 minutes	
Bob Adams	John Wayne
Pamela	Gwen Gaze
Elmer Davis	Don Barclay
Archie	Pat Somerset
Col. Armitage	Major Sam Harris
El Kadar (Muffadi)	Charles Brokaw
Don Adams	James Bush
Logan	Arthur Aylsworth
Blake	Earl Hodgins
Graham	Jack Mack
Parker	Franklyn Parker
Mustapha	Frank Lackteen
Sir Herbert	Olaf Hytton
Sgt.-Major	Keith Kenneth
Abdul	Abdulla

Released July 4 (U.S.); April 4, 1938 (G.B.)

Adventure's End: *Jimmie Lucas (?), Wayne, Moroni Olsen, Maurice Black.*

IDOL OF THE CROWDS (1937)

Director	Arthur Lubin
Writers	George Waggner
	Harold Buckley
	from a screen story by
	George Waggner
Cinematographer	Harry Neumann
Art Director	Charles Clague
Editor	Charles Craft
Associate Producer	Paul Malvern
Producer	Trem Carr
Production Company	
Distributor (U.S.A.)	Universal
Distributor (G.B.)	G.F.D.
60 minutes	
Johnny Hanson	John Wayne
Helen Dale	Sheila Bromley
Jack Irwin	Charles Brokaw
Bobby	Billy Burrud
Peggy	Jane Johns
Harvey Castle	Huntley Gordon
Joe Garber	Frank Otto
Kelly	Russell Hopton
Mrs. Dale	Virginia Brissac
Andy Moore	Clem Bevans
Spike Regan	George Lloyd
Squat Bates	Hal Neiman
Swifty	Wayne Castle
Hank	Lloyd Ford
Elmer	Lee Ford

Released October 10 (U.S.); February 21, 1938 (G.B.)

ADVENTURE'S END (1937)

Director	Arthur Lubin
Writers	Ben Grauman Kohn
	Scott Darling
	Sid Sutherland
	from a screen story by
	Ben Ames Williams
Cinematographer	Gus Peterson
Editor	Charles Craft
Associate Producer	Paul Malvern
Producer	Trem Carr
Production Company	
Distributor (U.S.A.)	Universal
Distributor (G.B.)	G.F.D.
60 minutes	
Duke Slade	John Wayne
Janet Drew	Diana Gibson
Capt. Abner Drew	Montagu Love
Rand Husk, mate	Moroni Olsen
Blackie	Maurice Black
Kalo	Paul White
Slivers	Cameron Hall
Matt	Patrick J. Kelly
Tom	George Cleveland
Chips	Oscar W. Sundholm
Hooten	James T. Mack
Barzeck	Glenn Strange
Kierce	Wally Howe
Flench	Jimmie Lucas
Stantul	Ben Carter
Hardy	Britt Wood

Released December 5 (U.S.); May 2, 1938 (G.B.)

BORN TO THE WEST (1937)
HELL TOWN
(reissue title)

Director	Charles Barton
Writers	Stuart Anthony
	Robert Yost
	from the novel
	"Born to
	the West" by
	Zane Grey
Cinematographer	J. D. Jennings
Editor	John Link
Production Company	
Distributor	Paramount
59 minutes (G.B.: 50)	
Dare Rudd	John Wayne
Judith Worstall	Marsha Hunt
Tom Fillmore	Johnny Mack Brown
Bart Hammond	Monte Blue
Dinkey Hooley	Syd Saylor
Lynn Hardy	John Patterson
Jim Fallon	Nick Lukats
Cattle Buyer	Lucien Littlefield
Buck Brady	James Craig
Sheriff Stark	Jack Kennedy

Alan Ladd, Jennie Boyle, Lee Prather, Jack Daley, Vester Pegg

Released December 10 (U.S.); July 1938 (G.B.)

Previously filmed under title *Born to the West* as a 1926 release with Jack Holt in the Wayne role

Director	George Sherman	*Director*	George Sherman	*Director*	George Sherman
Writers	Stanley Roberts	*Writer*	Luci Ward	*Writers*	Luci Ward
	Betty Burbridge		from a screen story by		Betty Burbridge
	based on characters		Bernard McConville		from a screen story by
	created by William		Edmond Kelso		Luci Ward
	Colt MacDonald		based on characters		based on characters
Cinematographer	Reggie Lanning		created by William		created by
Editor	Tony Martinelli		Colt MacDonald		William Colt MacDonald
Music Director	Cy Feuer	*Cinematographer*	William Nobles	*Cinematographer*	Reggie Lanning
Associate Producer	William Berke	*Editor*	Tony Martinelli	*Editor*	Tony Martinelli
Production Company		*Associate Producer*	William Berke	*Music*	William Lava
Distributor (U.S.A.)	Republic	*Production Company*		*Associate Producer*	William Berke
Distributor (G.B.)	British Lion	*Distributor (U.S.A.)*	Republic	*Production Company*	
55 minutes		*Distributor (G.B.)*	British Lion	*Distributor (U.S.A.)*	Republic
Stony Brooke	John Wayne	55 minutes		*Distributor (G.B.)*	British Lion
Tucson Smith	Ray Corrigan	*Stony Brooke*	John Wayne	56 minutes	
Lullaby Joslin	Max Terhune	*Tucson Smith*	Ray Corrigan	*Stony Brooke*	John Wayne
Ann	Doreen McKay	*Lullaby Joslin*	Max Terhune	*Tucson Smith*	Ray Corrigan
Judge Hastings	Josef Forte	*Beth Hoyt*	Louise Brooks	*Lullaby Joslin*	Max Terhune
Paul Hartman	George Douglas	*Ned Hoyt*	Anthony Marsh	*Dave Carson*	William Farnum
Frank Paige	Frank Milan	*Bob Whitney*	Ralph Bowman	*Nancy Carson*	June Martel
Henry C. Gordon	Ted Adams		(later John Archer)	*Gil Byron*	LeRoy Mason
Hotel clerk	Harry Depp	*Mullins*	Gordon Hart	*Billy Carson*	Martin Spellman
Russian musician	Dave Weber	*Harmon*	Roy James	*Julie Jane Carson*	Genee Hall
Italian musician	Don Orlando	*Jake*	Olin Francis	*Harris*	Walter Wills
English musician	Charles Knight	*Ma Hawkins*	Fern Emmett	*Judge*	Ferris Taylor
Sheriff	Jack Kirk	*Sheriff*	Henry Otho	*Marshall*	Tom London
		Clanton	George Sherwood	*Sheriff*	Dick Rush
		Waddell	Archie Hall	*Newton*	James F. Cassidy
		Milton	Frank LaRue		

Released August 28 (U.S.); this and the following seven 3 Mesquiteers adventures had a "floating" release in Britain with no recorded date of first appearance.

Released September 20 (U.S.)

Shooting October, 1938

Released December 8 (U.S.)

Pals of the Saddle:
player, Wayne, Ted Adams.

RED RIVER RANGE (1938)

Director	George Sherman
Writers	Stanley Roberts
	Betty Burbridge
	Luci Ward
	from a screen story by Luci Ward
	based on characters created by William Colt MacDonald
Cinematographer	Jack Marta
Editor	Tony Martinelli
Music	William Lava
Associate Producer	William Berke
Production Company	
Distributor (U.S.A.)	Republic
Distributor (G.B.)	British Lion
56 minutes	
Stony Brooke	John Wayne
Tucson Smith	Ray Corrigan
Lullaby Joslin	Max Terhune
Mrs. Maxwell	Polly Moran
Jane Mason	Lorna Gray (later Adrian Booth)
Tex Reilly	Kirby Grant
Tommy	Sammy McKim
Payne	William Royle
Hartley	Perry Ivins
Randall	Stanley Blystone
Evelyn Maxwell	Lenore Bushman
Pop Mason	Burr Caruth
Sheriff	Roger Williams
	Earl Askam
	Olin Francis

Shooting November, 1938
Released December 22 (U.S.)

STAGECOACH (1939)

Director	John Ford
Writer	Dudley Nichols from the short story "Stage to Lordsburg" by Ernest Haycox
Cinematographer	Bert Glennon
Art Director	Alexander Toluboff
Editorial Supervisor	Otho Lovering
Editors	Dorothy Spencer
	Walter Reynolds
Music	Richard Hageman
	W. Franke Harling
	John Leipold
	Leo Shuken
	Louis Gruenberg
Producer	Walter Wanger
Production Company	Walter Wanger Productions
Distributor	United Artists
97 minutes	
Dallas	Claire Trevor
The Ringo Kid	John Wayne
Hatfield	John Carradine
Dr. Josiah Boone	Thomas Mitchell
Buck Rickabaugh	Andy Devine

Mr. Samuel Peacock	Donald Meek
Lucy Mallory	Louise Platt
Sheriff Curly Wilcox	George Bancroft
Henry Gatewood	Berton Churchill
Lt. Blanchard	Tim Holt
Luke Plummer	Tom Tyler
Chris	Chris Pin Martin
Yakima, Chris's wife	Elvira Rios
Billy Pickett	Francis Ford
Mrs. Pickett	Marga Daighton
Capt. Whitney	Cornelius Keefe
Billy Pickett Jr.	Kent Odell
Capt. Sickels	Walter McGrail
Indian scout	Chief Big Tree
Mrs. Gatewood	Brenda Fowler
Sheriff	Louis Mason
Mrs. Nancy Whitney	Florence Lake
Ike Plummer	Joseph Rickson
Hank Plummer	Vester Pegg
Cavalry scout	Yakima Canutt
Telegraph operator	Harry Tenbrook
Express agent	Paul McVey
Jerry, the bartender	Jack Pennick
Sergeant	William Hoffer (Hopper)?
Capt. Simmons	Bryant Washburn
Dr. Boone's housekeeper	Nora Cecil
Dancing girls	Helen Gibson
	Dorothy Appelby
Cowboys	Buddy Roosevelt
	Bill Cody
Indian Chief (Geronimo)	Chief White Horse
Sheriff of Lordsburg	Duke Lee
Lucy's baby	Mary Kathleen Walker
Saloon keeper	Ed Brady
Editor in Lordsburg	Robert Homans
Deputy	Franklyn Farnum
Jim (expressman)	Jim Mason
Ogler	Merrill McCormick
Barfly (Lordsburg)	Artie Ortega

Steve Clemente, Theodore Larch [Lorch?], Fritzi Brunette, Leonard Trainor, Chris Phillips, Tex Driscoll, Pat Wayne, Teddy Billings, Al Lee, John Eckert, Jack Mohr, Patsy Doyle, Wiggie Blowne, Margaret Smith, Si Jenks.

Filmed November-December 1938
Location shooting at Kernville, Dry Lake, Fremont Pass, Victorville, Calabasas, Chatsworth — in California; at Kayenta, Mesa, and Monument Valley — in Arizona.
Released March (U.S.); October 2 (G.B.)

THE NIGHT RIDERS (1939)

Director	George Sherman
Writers	Betty Burbridge
	Stanley Roberts
	based on characters created by William Colt MacDonald
Cinematographer	Jack Marta
Editor	Lester Orlebeck
Music	William Lava
Associate Producer	William Berke
Production Company	
Distributor (U.S.A.)	Republic
Distributor (G.B.)	British Lion
58 minutes	
Stony Brooke	John Wayne
Tucson Smith	Ray Corrigan
Lullaby Joslin	Max Terhune
Soledad	Doreen McKay
Susan Randall	Ruth Rogers
Talbot (alias Don Luis De Serrano)	George Douglas
Jackson	Tom Tyler
Sheriff	Kermit Maynard
Tim	Sammy McKim
Hazelton	Walter Wills
Andrews	Ethan Laidlaw
Harper	Edward Peil Sr.
Wilson	Tom London
Wilkins	Jack Ingram
Allen	William Nestell

In production from mid-February 1939 under title *Lone Star Bullets*
Released April 12 (U.S.)

THREE TEXAS STEERS (1939)
(American title)
DANGER RIDES THE RANGE
(British title)

Director	George Sherman
Writers	Betty Burbridge
	Stanley Roberts
	based on characters created by William Colt MacDonald
Cinematographer	Ernest Miller
Editor	Tony Martinelli
Music	William Lava
Associate Producer	William Berke
Production Company	
Distributor (U.S.A.)	Republic
Distributor (G.B.)	British Lion
57 minutes	
Stony Brooke	John Wayne
Tucson Smith	Ray Corrigan
Lullaby Joslin	Max Terhune
Nancy Evans	Carole Landis
George Ward	Ralph Graves
Sheriff	Roscoe Ates
Lillian	Collette Lyons
Hercules	Billy Curtis
Steve	Ted Adams
Rankin	Stanley Blystone
Tony	David Sharpe
Morgan	Ethan Laidlaw
Postman	Lew Kelly
Willie the Gorilla	Naba
Mike Abbott	John Merton
	Ted Mapes

In production by April, 1939
Released June 19 (U.S.)

WYOMING OUTLAW (1939)

Director	George Sherman
Writers	Betty Burbridge
	Jack Natteford
	from a screen story by
	Jack Natteford
	based on characters
	created by William Colt
	MacDonald
Cinematographer	Reggie Lanning
Editor	Tony Martinelli
Music	William Lava
Associate Producer	William Berke
Production Company	
Distributor (U.S.A.)	Republic
Distributor (G.B.)	British Lion
57 minutes	
Stony Brooke	John Wayne
Tucson Smith	Ray Corrigan
Rusty Joslin	Raymond Hatton
Will Parker	Donald Barry
Irene Parker	Adele Pearce
Balsinger	LeRoy Mason
Luke Parker	Charles Middleton
Mrs. Parker	Katherine Kenworthy
U.S. Marshal	Elmo Lincoln
Sheriff	Jack Ingram
Newt	David Sharpe
Amos	Jack Kenney
Ed Sims	Yakima Canutt

Released June 27 (U.S.)

New Frontier: *Ray Corrigan, Wayne, Hal Price, Raymond Hatton.*

NEW FRONTIER(1939)
FRONTIER HORIZON
(TV Title)

Director	George Sherman
Writers	Betty Burbridge
	Luci Ward
	based on characters
	created by William
	Colt MacDonald
Cinematographer	Reggie Lanning
Editor	Tony Martinelli
Music	William Lava
Associate Producer	William Berke
Production Company	
Distributor (U.S.A.)	Republic
Distributor (G.B.)	British Lion
57 minutes	
Stony Brooke	John Wayne
Tucson Smith	Ray Corrigan
Rusty Joslin	Raymond Hatton
Celia	Phyllis Isley
	(later Jennifer Jones)
Major Broderick	Eddy Waller
Stevie	Sammy McKim
Gilbert	LeRoy Mason
Proctor	Harrison Greene
Judge Lawson	Reginald Barlow
Doc Hall	Burr Caruth
Jason	Dave O'Brien
Sheriff	Hal Price
Harmon	Jack Ingram

290

Dickson	Bud Osborne
Turner	Charles Whitaker

Released August 10 (U.S.)

ALLEGHENY UPRISING (1939)
(American title)
THE FIRST REBEL
(British title)

Director	William A. Seiter
Writer	P. J. Wolfson
	from the factual story
	"The First Rebel"
	by Neil H. Swanson
Cinematographer	Nicholas Musuraca
Art Directors	Van Nest Polglase
	Albert D'Agostino
Editor	George Crone
Music	Anthony Collins
Producer	P. J. Wolfson
Production Company	
Distributor	RKO Radio
81 minutes (G.B.: 74)	
Janie McDougle	Claire Trevor
Jim Smith	John Wayne
Captain Swanson	George Sanders
Trader Callendar	Brian Donlevy
McDougle	Wilfrid Lawson
Magistrate Duncan	Robert Barrat
The Professor	John F. Hamilton
Tom Calhoon	Moroni Olsen
Will Anderson	Eddie Quillan
M'Cammon	Chill Wills
Poole	Ian Wolfe

Sgt. McGlashan	Wallis Clark
Morris	Monte Montague
Jailer	Eddy Waller
Governor John Penn	Clay Clement
General Gage	Olaf Hytten
Doctor Stokes	Charles Middleton
Prisoner in irons	Douglas Spencer

Released November 10 (U.S.); July 29,
1940 (G.B.)

THE DARK COMMAND (1940)

Director	Raoul Walsh
Writers	Grover Jones
	Lionel Houser
	F. Hugh Herbert
	from a novel by
	W. R. Burnett
	adaptation by Jan
	Fortune
Second Unit	Yakima Canutt
Directors	Cliff Lyons
Cinematographer	Jack Marta
Art Director	John Victor Mackay
Supervising Editor	Murray Seldeen
Editor	William Morgan
Music	Victor Young
Associate Producer	Sol. C. Siegel
Production Company	
Distributor (U.S.)	Republic
Distributor (G.B.)	British Lion
94 minutes	
Mary McCloud	Claire Trevor
Bob Seton	John Wayne

William Cantrell	Walter Pidgeon		
Fletch McCloud	Roy Rogers		
Doc Grunch	George Hayes		
Angus McCloud	Porter Hall		
Elizabeth Adams (Mrs. Cantrell)	Marjorie Main		
Judge Buckner	Raymond Walburn		
Bushropp	Joseph Sawyer		
Mrs. Hale	Helen MacKellar		
Dave	J. Farrell MacDonald		
Mr. Hale	Trevor Bardette		
Dental patient	Harry Woods		
Slave trader	Al Bridge		
Yankee	Glenn Strange		
Assassin	Jack Rockwell		
Townsman	Ernie S. Adams		
First juryman	Edward Hearn		
Third juryman	Edmund Cobb		
Vigilante	Hal Taliaferro		
Townsman	Yakima Canutt		
Sentry	Dick Alexander		
Messenger	Tom London		
Cantrell man	John Merton		
	Dick Rich		
	Harry Cording		

Shooting in February 1940
Released April 15 (U.S.); July 8 (G.B.)

THE LONG VOYAGE HOME (1940)

Director	John Ford
Writer	Dudley Nichols from the one-act plays "The Moon of the Caribbees," "In the Zone," "Bound East for Cardiff," and "The Long Voyage Home" by Eugene O'Neill
Cinematographer	Gregg Toland
Art Director	James Basevi
Editor	Sherman Todd
Music	Richard Hageman
Producer	Walter Wanger
Production Company	Walter Wanger
Distributor	United Artists
105 minutes	
Ole Olsen	John Wayne
Aloysius Driscoll	Thomas Mitchell
Smitty	Ian Hunter
Cocky	Barry Fitzgerald
Captain	Wilfrid Lawson
Freda	Mildred Natwick
Axel Swanson	John Qualen
Yank	Ward Bond
Davis	Joseph Sawyer
Donkeyman	Arthur Shields
Limehouse Crimp	J. M. Kerrigan
Tropical woman	Rafaela Ottiano
Scotty	David Hughes
Joe (Limehouse barman)	Billy Bevan
Mate	Cyril McLaglen
Paddy	Robert E. Perry
Johnny Bergman	Jack Pennick
Narvey	Constantin Frenke
Big Frank	Constantin Romanoff
Tim	Dan Borzage
Max	Harry Tenbrook
Second Lieut.	Douglas Walton
Girls in canoe	Carmen Morales Carmen d'Antonio
Captain of "Amindra"	Harry Woods

Edgar "Blue" Washington, Lionel Pape, Jane Crowley, Maureen Roden-Ryan
Shooting started late April, 1940
Released October 8 (U.S.); March 17, 1941 (G.B.)

THREE FACES WEST (1940)

Director	Bernard Vorhaus
Writers	F. Hugh Herbert Joseph Moncure March Samuel Ornitz Doris Anderson (uncredited)
Cinematographer	John Alton
Art Director	John Victor Mackay
Supervising Editor	Murray Seldeen
Editor	William Morgan
Music	Victor Young
Associate Producer	Sol C. Siegel
Production Company Distributor (U.S.)	Republic
Distributor (G.B.)	British Lion
79 minutes	
John Phillips	John Wayne
Dr. Braun	Charles Coburn
Leni Braun	Sigrid Gurie
Dr. "Nunk" Atterbury	Spencer Charters
Dr. Eric Von Scherer	Roland Varno
Clem Higgins	Trevor Bardette
Mrs. Welles	Helen MacKellar
Billy Welles	Sonny Bupp
Harris	Wade Boteler
Minister	Russell Simpson
Dr. Thorpe	Charles Waldron
Radio announcer	Wendell Niles
Bartender	Dewey Robinson

Filmed and originally trade shown as *The Refugee.*
Released July 12 (U.S.); November 11 (G.B.)

Seven Sinners.

SEVEN SINNERS (1940)

Director	Tay Garnett
Writers	John Meehan
	Harry Tugend
	from a story by
	Ladislas Fodor and
	Laslo Vadnai
Cinematographer	Rudolph Maté
Art Directors	Jack Otterson
	Martin Obzina
Editor	Ted J. Kent
Music	Frank Skinner
	Hans Salter
Songs	Frank Loesser
	Frederick Hollander
Producer	Joe Pasternak
Production Company	
Distributor (U.S.A.)	Universal
Distributor (Britain)	G.F.D.
87 minutes	
Bijou	Marlene Dietrich
Lt. Dan Brent	John Wayne
Dr. Martin	Albert Dekker
Little Ned (Edward	
Patrick Finnegan)	Broderick Crawford
Dorothy Henderson	Anna Lee
Sasha	Mischa Auer
Tony	Billy Gilbert
District Officer	Richard Carle
Governor	Samuel S. Hinds
Antro	Oscar Homolka
Capt. Church	Reginald Denny
Bartender	Vince Barnett
First mate	Herbert Rawlinson
Ensign	James Craig
Ensign	William Bakewell
Rubio	Antonio Moreno
First Governor	Russell Hicks
Police Chief	William B. Davidson

Shooting in August, 1940
Released October 25 (U.S.); April 28, 1941 (G.B.)
Reissued 1947 in Britain under title *Café of the Seven Sinners.*
A new screenplay from the same story was filmed as *South Sea Sinner* (1949), released in Britain as *East of Java.*

MELODY RANCH (1940)

Director	Joseph Santley
Production Company	
Distributor (U.S.A.)	Republic
Distributor (G.B.)	British Lion
84 minutes	

Wayne is reported to have performed the "car trolley crash stunt" in this Gene Autry musical Western with Jimmy Durante and Ann Miller.
Released November 4 (U.S.)

A Man Betrayed: *Wayne, Frances Dee.*

A MAN BETRAYED (1941)
(American title)
CITADEL OF CRIME
(British title)
WHEEL OF FORTUNE
(U.S. TV title)

Director	John H. Auer
Writer	Isabel Dawn
	from a story by Jack Moffitt
	adaptation by Tom Kilpatrick
Cinematographer	Jack Marta
Art Director	John Victor Mackay
Supervising Editor	Murray Seldeen
Editor	Charles Craft
Music Director	Cy Feuer.
Associate Producer	Armand Schaefer
Production Company	
Distributor (U.S.)	'Republic
Distributor (G.B.)	British Lion
80 minutes	
Lynn Hollister	John Wayne
Sabra Cameron	Frances Dee
Tom Cameron	Edward Ellis
Casey	Wallace Ford
Floyd	Ward Bond
Morris Slade	Harold Huber
T. Amato	Alexander Granach
George (butler)	Barnett Parker
Prosecutor	Ed Stanley
Mr. Wilson	Tim Ryan
Langworthy	Harry Hayden
Pringle	Russell Hicks
Governor	Pierre Watkin
Mayor	Ferris Taylor

Shooting (as *Citadel of Crime*) from early January to mid-February, 1941
Released March 7 (U.S.); October 27 (G.B.)

LADY FROM LOUISIANA (1941)

Director	Bernard Vorhaus
Writers	Vera Caspary
	Michael Hogan
	Guy Endore
	from a screen story by
	Edward James
	Francis Faragoh
Cinematographer	Jack Marta
Art Director	John Victor Mackay
Supervising Editor	Murray Seldeen
Editor	Edward Mann
Music Director	Cy Feuer
Associate Producer	Bernard Vorhaus
Production Company	
Distributor (U.S.)	Republic
Distributor (G.B.)	British Lion
82 minutes	
John Reynolds	John Wayne
Julie Mirbeau	Ona Munson
Blackie Williams	Ray Middleton
General Mirbeau	Henry Stephenson
Mrs. Brunot	Helen Westley
Cuffy	Jack Pennick
Felice	Dorothy Dandridge
Gaston	Shimen Ruskin
Pearl	Jacqueline Dalya
Judge Wilson	Paul Scardon
Senator Cassidy	Maj. James H. MacNamara
Littlefield	James C. Morton
Edwards	Maurice Costello

Shooting (as *Lady from New Orleans*) from early March to early April, 1941.
Released April 22 (U.S.); January 9, 1942 (G.B.)

THE SHEPHERD OF THE HILLS (1941)

Director	Henry Hathaway
Writers	Grover Jones
	Stuart Anthony
	from a story by
	Harold Bell Wright
	based on his novel
	"Shepherd of the Hills"
Cinematographers	Charles Lang
	W. Howard Greene
Art Directors	Hans Dreier
	Roland Anderson
Editor	Ellsworth Hoagland
Music	Gerard Carbonara
Producer	Jack Moss
Production Company	
Distributor	Paramount
98 minutes Technicolor	
Young Matt Matthews	John Wayne
Sammy Lane	Betty Field
Daniel Howitt	Harry Carey
Aunt Mollie	Beulah Bondi
Old Matt	James Barton
Granny Becky	Marjorie Main
Andy Beeler	Samuel S. Hinds
Coot Royal	John Qualen
Pete	Marc Lawrence

Jim Lane	Tom Fadden
Wash Gibbs	Ward Bond
Elvy Royal	Dorothy Adams
Corky (storekeeper)	Olin Howland
Mr. Palestrom	Fuzzy Knight
Charles (Deputy)	John Harmon
Revenuer	Carl Knowles
Mrs. Palestrom	Fern Emmett
Baby Royal	Vivita Campbell
Bald Knobbers	William Haade
	Robert Kortman
	Henry Brandon
	Jim Corey
Doctor	Selmer Jackson

Shooting from October 5 to late November, 1940.
Released July 18 (U.S.); December 8 (G.B.) London *première* opening: mid-September
Previously filmed under the same title as a 1927 release with John Boles in the Wayne role

---

LADY FOR A NIGHT (1942)

Director	Leigh Jason
Writers	Isabel Dawn
	Boyce De Gaw
	from a screen story by
	Garrett Fort
Cinematographer	Norbert Brodine
Art Director	John Victor Mackay
Supervising Editor	Murray Seldeen
Editor	Ernest Nims
Music	David Buttolph
Associate Producer	Albert J. Cohen
Production Company	
Distributor (U.S.)	Republic
Distributor (G.B.)	British Lion
87 minutes	
Jenny Blake	Joan Blondell
Jack Morgan	John Wayne
Alan Alderson	Ray Middleton
Stephen Alderson	Philip Merivale
Julia Alderson	Blanche Yurka

Lady for a Night: *Wayne, Joan Blondell.*

Katherine Alderson	Edith Barrett			Capt. Phillip Philpott	Lynne Overman
Boris	Leonid Kinskey			Commodore	
Chloe	Hattie Noel			Devereaux	Walter Hampden
Judge	Montagu Love			Maum Maria	Louise Beavers
Mayor's wife	Carmel Myers			Mrs. Claiborne	Elisabeth Risdon
Flo	Dorothy Burgess			Mrs. Mottram	Janet Beecher
Governor	Guy Usher			Aunt Henrietta	
Mayor	Ivan Miller			Beresford	Hedda Hopper
Mabel	Patricia Knox			Ivy Deveraux	Martha O'Driscoll
Napoleon	Lew Payton			Nathias Widgeon	Victor Kilian
Mary Lou	Marilyn Hare			Captain of the	
	The Hall Johnson Choir			"Tyfib"	Charles Bickford
	Dewey Robinson			Salt Meat	Oscar Polk

Jesse Lasky Jr.
Jeanie Macpherson
(Uncredited)
from a magazine story
by Thelma Strabel

Shooting from early October to late November 1941
Released January 5 (U.S.); April 13 (G.B.)

2nd Unit Director	Arthur Rosson
Cinematographers	Victor Milner
	William V. Skall
	Dewey Wrigley (under-water)
Art Directors	Hans Dreier
	Roland Anderson
Editor	Anne Bauchens
Music	Victor Young
Associate Producer	William H. Pine
Producer	Cecil B. DeMille
Production Company Distributor	Paramount

124 minutes   Technicolor

REAP THE WILD WIND (1942)

Director	Cecil B. DeMille
Writers	Alan LeMay
	Charles Bennett

Stephen Tolliver	Ray Milland
Capt. Jack Stuart	John Wayne
Loxi Claiborne	Paulette Goddard
King Cutler	Raymond Massey
Dan Cutler	Robert Preston
Drusilla Alston	Susan Hayward

Chinkapin	Ben Carter
The Lamb	Wee Willie (William) Davis
Sam, Philpott's mate	Lane Chandler
Captain of the "Pelican"	Lou Merrill
Dr. Jepson	Frank M. Thomas
Capt. Carruthers	Keith Richards
Lubbock (Cutler henchman)	Victor Varconi
Captain at conference	J. Farrell MacDonald

Reap the Wild Wind: *Paulette Goddard, John Wayne.*

Mace *(Cutler henchman)*	Harry Woods
Master Shipwright	Raymond Hatton
Lt. Farragut	Milburn Stone
"Claiborne" lookout	Dave Wengren
Cadge	Tony Patton
Charleston Ladies	Barbara Britton
	Julia Faye
	Ameda Lambert
Charleston	D'Arcy Miller
Gentlemen	Bruce Warren
Bixby (the emissary)	Byron Foulger
Cutler's co-counsel	Frank Ferguson
Seaman (first wreck)	William Haade
Jailer	Stanley Andrews
Judge Marvin	Davidson Clarke
Cutler henchman	Frank Lackteen
Servant at Mottram house	George Reed

Nestor Paiva, Emory Parnell, Monte Blue, George Melford, Forrest Taylor, John Sainpolis, Stanhope Wheatcroft, Ed Brady, Frank C. Shannon, Buddy Pepper, Tom Chatterton, Frank Richards, Hayden Stevenson, William Cabanne, Mildred Harris, Hope Landin, Claire McDowell, Dorothy Sebastian, Jack Lyden, Ottola Nesmith, Max Davidson, Gertrude Astor, Maurice Costello

(Not all the unplaced players may have survived into the film as finally edited)

In production from June to late August 1941
Released March 19 (U.S.); June 15 (G.B.)

THE SPOILERS (1942)

Director	Ray Enright
Writers	Lawrence Hazard
	Tom Reed
	from the novel by
	Rex Beach
Cinematographer	Milton Krasner
Art Director	Jack Otterson
	John B. Goodman
Editor	Clarence Kolster
Music	Hans J. Salter
Associate Producer	Lee Marcus
Producer	Frank Lloyd
Production Company	Charles K. Feldman Group
Distributor (U.S.A.)	Universal
Distributor (G.B.)	G.F.D.
87 minutes	
Cherry Malotte	Marlene Dietrich
Alexander McNamara	Randolph Scott
Roy Glennister	John Wayne
Helen Chester	Margaret Lindsay
Dextry	Harry Carey
Broncho Kid Farrell	Richard Barthelmess
Wheaton	William Farnum
Idabelle	Marietta Canty
Flapjack Simms	Russell Simpson
Banty	George Clevland
Judge Stillman	Samuel S. Hinds
Himself	Robert W. Service
Hotel proprietor	Irving Bacon

The Spoilers: *Randolph Scott, Marlene Dietrich, Wayne.*

Restaurateur	Robert McKenzie
Montrose	Chester Clute
Mr. Skinner (drunk)	Jack Norton
Complaining miner	Harry Woods
Jonathan Struve	Charles Halton
Ship's Captain	Robert Homans
Marshal	Bud Osborne
Marshal Thompson	William Gould
Deputy	William Haade
Chinaman in jail	Willie Fung
Kelly	Lloyd Ingraham
Deputy	Charles McMurphy
Mark	Ray Bennett

Shooting from mid-January to end of February 1942

Released May 8 (U.S.); July 13 (G.B.)

Previously filmed under the same title in 1914 (William Farnum in the Wayne role); 1923 (Milton Sills in the Wayne role); 1930 (Gary Cooper in the Wayne role); and subsequently filmed in 1955 (Jeff Chandler in the Wayne role)

IN OLD CALIFORNIA (1942)

Director	William McGann
Writers	Gertrude Purcell
	Frances Hyland
	from a screen story by
	J. Robert Bren
	Gladys Atwater
Cinematographer	Jack Marta
Art Director	Russell Kimball
Supervising Editor	Murray Seldeen
Editor	Howard O'Neill
Music	David Buttolph
Associate Producer	Robert North
Production Company	
Distributor (U.S.)	Republic
Distributor (G.B.)	British Lion
88 minutes	
Tom Craig	John Wayne
Lacey Miller	Binnie Barnes
Britt Dawson	Albert Dekker
Ellen Sanford	Helen Parrish
Helga	Patsy Kelly

Kegs McKeever	Edgar Kennedy
Joe Dawson	Dick Purcell
Mr. Carlin	Harry Shannon
Mr. Hayes	Charles Halton
Whitey	Emmett Lynn
Mr. Bates	Bob McKenzie
Mr. Tompkins	Milt Kibbee
Chick	Paul Sutton
Mrs. Tompkins	Anne O'Neal
	Frank McGlynn

Shooting from mid-March to mid-April, 1942

Released May 31 (U.S.); January 11, 1943 (G.B.)

FLYING TIGERS (1942)

Director	David Miller
Writers	Kenneth Gamet
	Barry Trivers
	from a screen story by
	Kenneth Gamet
Cinematographer	Jack Marta
Art Director	Russell Kimball
Editor	Ernest Nims
Music	Victor Young
Associate Producer	Edmund Grainger
Production Company	
Distributor (U.S.)	Republic
Distributor (G.B.)	British Lion
102 minutes	
Jim Gordon	John Wayne
Woody Jason	John Carroll
Brooke Elliott	Anna Lee
Hap Davis	Paul Kelly
Alabama Smith	Gordon Jones
Verna Bales	Mae Clarke
Col. Lindsay	Addison Richards
Blackie Bales	Edmund MacDonald
Dale	Bill Shirley
Reardon	Tom Neal
McIntosh	James Dodd
Tex Norton	Gregg Barton
Selby	John James
Mike	Chester Gan
Lt. Barton	David Bruce
McCurdy	Malcolm McTaggert
Airport official	Charles Lane
Barratt (new flyer)	Tom Seidel
Doctor	Richard Loo
Airfield radio man	Richard Crane
Jim, the waiter	Willie Fung

Shooting from early May to early July, 1942

Released October 8 (U.S.); March 29, 1943 (G.B.)

REUNION IN FRANCE (1942)
(American title)
MADEMOISELLE FRANCE
(British title)

Director	Jules Dassin
Writers	Jan Lustig
	Marvin Borowsky

Flying Tigers.

	Marc Connelly
	Charles Hoffman
	(uncredited)
	from a screen story by
	Ladislas Bus-Fekete
Cinematographer	Robert Planck
Art Director	Cedric Gibbons
Editor	Elmo Vernon
Music	Franz Waxman
Producer	Joseph L. Mankiewicz
Production Company	
Distributor	M-G-M
104 minutes	
Michèle de la Becque	Joan Crawford
Pat Talbot	John Wayne
Robert Cortot	Philip Dorn
Schultz (Pinkham)	Reginald Owen
General Hugo Schroeder	Albert Bassermann
Ulrich Windler	John Carradine
Juliette	Ann Ayars
Durand	J. Edward Bromberg
Paul Grebeau	Moroni Olsen
Emile Fleuron	Henry Daniell
Anton Stregel	Howard Da Silva
Honore	Charles Arnt
Martin	Morris Ankrum
Genevieve	Edith Evanson
Captain	Ernest Dorian
Clothilde	Margaret Laurence
Mme. Montanot	Odette Myrtil
Soldier	Petter Whitney

Shooting from early July to mid-September, 1942

Filmed and trade shown under title *Reunion*

Released December (U.S.); 24 May, 1943 (G.B.)

PITTSBURGH (1942)

Director	Lewis Seiler
Writers	Kenneth Gamet
	Tom Reed
	with additional dialogue
	by John Twist
	from a screen story
	by George Owen
	Tom Reed
Cinematographer	Robert De Grasse
Art Director	John Goodman
Editor	Paul Landres
Music	Frank Skinner
	Hans J. Salter
Associate Producer	Robert Fellows
Production Company	Charles K. Feldman
	Group
Distributor (U.S.A.)	Universal
Distributor (G.B.)	G.F.D.
91 minutes	
Josie "Hunky" Winters	Marlene Dietrich
Cash Evans	Randolph Scott
Charles "Pittsburgh" Markham	John Wayne
"Doc" Powers	Frank Craven
Shannon Prentiss	Louise Allbritton
Shorty the Tailor	Shemp Howard
Joe Malneck	Thomas Gomez
Dr. Grazlich	Ludwig Stossel
Morgan Prentiss	Samuel S. Hinds
Killer Kane	Sammy Stein
Burnside (mine operator)	Paul Fix
Wilson	John Dilson
Johnny (miner)	William Haade
Butler (Mike)	Charles Coleman

Barney (restaurateur)	Nestor Paiva
Miner	Harry Cording
Frawley (Josie's escort)	Douglas Fowley
Wise-guy reporter	Ray Walker
Building site labourer	Charles Arnt
Burns (Production manager)	William Gould

Shooting from early September to late October, 1942

Released December 11 (U.S.); March 8, 1943 (G.B.)

A LADY TAKES A CHANCE (1943)

Director	William A. Seiter
Writer	Robert Ardrey
	Garson Kanin (uncredited)
	from a screen story by Jo Swerling
Cinematographer	Frank Redman
Art Directors	Albert S. D'Agostino
	Alfred Herman
Editor	Theron Warth
Music	Roy Webb
Associate Producer	Richard Ross
Producer	Frank Ross
Production Company Distributor	RKO Radio
86 minutes	
Molly Truesdale	Jean Arthur
Duke Hudkins	John Wayne
Waco	Charles Winninger
Smiley Lambert	Phil Silvers
Florrie Bendix	Mary Field
Drunk	Don Costello
Storekeeper	John Philliber
Malcolm	Grady Sutton
Bob	Grant Withers
Gregg	Hans Conreid
Jitterbug	Peggy Carroll
Flossie	Ariel Heath
Linda Belle	Sugar Geise
Lilly	Joan Blair
Mullen	Tom Fadden
Bus station attendant	Ed Waller
Carmencita	Nina Quartaro
Bartender	Alex Melesh
Gambling House Boss	Cy Kendall
Second bartender	Paul Scott
Dr. Humbolt	Charles D. Brown
Sammy (horse)	Mysty Shot
	Butch and Buddy
	The Three Peppers

Shooting from mid-March to mid-April, 1943

Initially scheduled for release as *The Cowboy and the Girl*

Released August 19 (U.S.); December 13 (G.B.)

IN OLD OKLAHOMA (1943)
WAR OF THE WILDCATS
(reissue title)

Director	Albert S. Rogell
Writers	Ethel Hill
	Eleanore Griffin
	from adaptation by Thomas Burtis
	of his story "War of the Wildcats"

A Lady Takes A Chance: *John Wayne, Charles Winninger (right).*

Cinematographer	Jack Marta
Art Director	Russell Kimball
Editor	Ernest Nims
Music	Walter Scharf
Associate Producer	Robert North
Production Company	
Distributor (U.S.)	Republic
Distributor (G.B.)	British Lion
102 minutes	
Dan Somers	John Wayne
Catherine Allen	Martha Scott
Jim "Hunk" Gardner	Albert Dekker
Desprit Dean	George "Gabby" Hayes
Bessie Baxter	Marjorie Rambeau
"Cuddles" Walker	Dale Evans
Richardson	Grant Withers
Teddy Roosevelt	Sidney Blackmer
The Cherokee Kid	Paul Fix
Mrs. Ames	Cecil Cunningham
Ben (telegraph operator)	Irving Bacon
Wilkins	Byron Fougler
Mrs. Peabody	Anne O'Neal
Walter	Richard Graham
Big Tree	Robert Warwick
Mason (Indian agent)	Stanley Andrews
Doctor	Will Wright
Charlie Witherspoon	Harry Shannon
President Roosevelt's aide	Emmet Vogan
Joe (train conductor)	Charles Arnt
Kelsey (Waiter)	Edward Gargan
Al Dalton	Harry Woods
Tom	Tom London
Other men on train	Dick Rich
	Charles Whittaker
	LeRoy Mason
	Lane Chandler
	Arthur Loft

Rhonda Fleming is reputed to have made her first screen appearance in this film but she is not readily identifiable

Shooting from late August to mid-September, 1943

Released December 6 (U.S.); April 3, 1944 (G.B.)

THE FIGHTING SEABEES (1944)

Director	Edward Ludwig
Writers	Borden Chase
	Aeneas MacKenzie
	from a screen story by Borden Chase
2nd Unit Director	Howard Lydecker
Cinematographer	William Bradford
Art Director	Duncan Cramer
Editor	Richard Van Enger
Music	Walter Scharf
Associate Producer	Albert J. Cohen
Production Company	
Distributor (U.S.)	Republic
Distributor (G.B.)	British Lion
100 minutes	
Wedge Donovan	John Wayne
Lt. Commander Robert Yarrow	Dennis O'Keefe

Constance Chesley	Susan Hayward
Eddie Powers	William Frawley
Johnny Novasky	Leonid Kinskey
Sawyer Collins	J. M. Kerrigan
Whanger Spreckles	Grant Withers
Ding Jacobs	Paul Fix
Yump Lunkin	Ben Welden
Lieutenant Kerrick	William Forrest
Captain Joyce	Addison Richards
Joe Brick	Jay Norris
Juan	Duncan Renaldo
Johnson	Tom London
Seabee	Hal Taliaferro
Officer in charge of refueling	Crane Whitley

William Hall, Charles D. Brown, Roy Barcroft, Chief Thundercloud

Started production late September 1943, shooting completed by mid-December

Released March 10 (U.S.); July 10 (G.B.)

Reissued in Ireland as *Donovan's Army*

In Old Oklahoma: *John Wayne, Martha Scott.*

TALL IN THE SADDLE (1944)

Director	Edwin L. Marin
Writers	Michael Hogan
	Paul P. Fix
	from a magazine story, later novel, by Gordon Ray Young
Cinematographer	Robert De Grasse
Art Directors	Albert S. D'Agostino
	Ralph Berger
Editor	Philip Martin Jr.
Music	Roy Webb
Associate Producer	Theron Warth
Producer	Robert Fellows
Production Company	
Distributor	RKO Radio
87 minutes	
Rocklin	John Wayne
Arly Harolday	Ella Raines
"Judge" Garvey	Ward Bond
Clara Cardell	Audrey Long
Dave	George "Gabby" Hayes

Director	Joseph Kane
Writer	Borden Chase from a story by Prescott Chaplin
Cinematographer	Robert DeGrasse
Art Director	Gano Chittenden
Editor	Richard L. Van Enger
Music Direction	Morton Scott
Associate Producer	Joseph Kane
Production Company	
Distributor (U.S.)	Republic
Distributor (G.B.)	British Lion
91 minutes	
Duke Fergus	John Wayne
Flaxen Tarry	Ann Dvorak
Tito Morell	Joseph Schildkraut
Wolf Wylie	William Frawley
Rita Dane	Virginia Grey
Cyrus Danver	Russell Hicks
Byline Conners	Jack Norton
Calico Jim	Paul Fix
Doctor Gorman	Manart Kippen
Martha	Eve Lynne
Joe Disko	Marc Lawrence
Beulah	Butterfly McQueen
Collingswood (Headwaiter)	Rex Lease
Hank	Hank Bell
Horseshoe Brown	Al Murphy
Marie	Adele Mara
Rita's agent	Emmett Vogan

Shooting from mid-July to late August, 1944
Released May 28 (U.S.); July 23 (G.B.)

Above, Tall in the Saddle *production party: Paul Fix, Ella Raines, Wayne.*

Below, Flame of the Barbary Coast: *Wayne, William Frawley.*

Miss Martin	Elisabeth Risdon
Clint Harolday	Russell Wade
Mr. Harolday	Don Douglas
Tala	Frank Puglia
Jackson (sheriff)	Emory Parnell
Zeke	Raymond Hatton
Bob Clews	Paul P. Fix
George Clews	Harry Woods
Cap (bartender)	Cy Kendall
Doc Riding	Bob McKenzie
Ab Jenkins	Wheaton Chambers
Stan (at stage station	Walter Baldwin
Pat	Russell Simpson
Ferdy Davis	Frank Orth

George Chandler, Eddy Waller, Frank Darien, Clem Bevans, Erville Alderson, Russell Hopton

Shooting from late April to late June, 1944

Released September 29 (U.S.); May 7, 1945 (G.B.)

BACK TO BATAAN (1945)

Director	Edward Dmytryk
Writers	Ben Barzman
	Richard H. Landau
	from a screen story by
	Aeneas MacKenzie
	William Gordon
Cinematographer	Nicholas Musuraca
Art Directors	Albert S. D'Agostino
	Ralph Berger
Editor	Marston Fay
Music	Roy Webb
Associate Producer	Theron Warth
Executive Producer	Robert Fellows
Production Company	
Distributor	RKO Radio
95 minutes	
Colonel	
Joseph Madden	John Wayne
Captain	
Andres Bonifacio	Anthony Quinn
Bertha Barnes	Beulah Bondi
Dalisay Delgado	Fely Franquelli
Major Hasko	Richard Loo
Colonel Kuroki	Philip Ahn
Lt. Commander Waite	Lawrence Tierney
General Homma	Leonard Strong
Jackson	Paul Fix
Japanese Captain	
(at schoolhouse)	Abner Biberman
Maximo Cuenca	"Ducky" Louie
Senor Buenaventura J.	
Bello (Schoolteacher)	Vladimir Sokoloff
Sgt. Biernesa	J. Alex Havier
"Skinny"	
(General at H.Q.)	John Miljan
Prince Ito	Harold Fong
Officer making	
broadcast	Benson Fong
Elder Japanese	
at conference	Abner Biberman

Shooting (under title *The Invisible Army*) from mid-November, 1944, to mid-March 1945
Released May 31 (U.S.); April 24, 1950 (G.B.)

THEY WERE EXPENDABLE (1945)

Director	John Ford
Writer	Commander Frank
	Wead from the
	book by William
	L. White
2nd Unit Director	James C. Havens
Cinematographer	Joseph H. August
Art Directors	Cedric Gibbons
	Malcolm Brown
Editors	Frank E. Hull
	Douglass Biggs
Music	Herbert Stothart
Associate Producer	Cliff Reid
Producer	John Ford
Production Company	
Distributor	M-G-M
136 minutes	
Lt. John Brickley	Robert Montgomery
Lt. Rusty Ryan	John Wayne
Lt. Sandy Davyss	Donna Reed

General Martin	Jack Holt
"Boats" Mulcahey	
("Irish")	Ward Bond
Ens. "Snake"	
Gardner	Marshall Thompson
Ens. "Andy"	
Andrews	Paul Langton
Maj. James Morton	Leon Ames
Seaman Jones	Arthur Walsh
Lt. "Shorty" Long	Donald Curtis
Ens. George Cross	Cameron Mitchell
Ens. Tony Aiken	Jeff York
"Slug" Mahan	Murray Alper
"Squarehead"	
Larsen ("Cookie")	Harry Tenbrook
"Doc"	Jack Pennick
"Benny" Lecoco	Alex Havier
Admiral Blackwell	Charles Trowbridge
The General	
(MacArthur)	Robert Barrat
Elder Tompkins	Bruce Kellogg
Ens. Brant	Tim Murdock
"Ohio" (flyer	
in hospital)	Louis Jean Heydt
"Dad" Knowland	Russell Simpson
Army doctor	Vernon Steele
Bartender	Robert Emmett
	O'Connor
Bar proprietor	William B. Davidson
Officer on plane	Tom Tyler
Oriental bartender	Lee Tung Foo

Shooting from early March to late June 1945
Location filming in Florida
Released December 20 (U.S.); February 18, 1946 (G.B.)

DAKOTA (1945)

Director	Joseph Kane
Writer	Lawrence Hazard
	from a screen story by
	Carl Foreman,
	adaptation by Howard
	Estabrook
2nd Unit Director	Yakima Canutt
Cinematographer	Jack Marta
Art Directors	Russell Kimball
	Gano Chittenden
Editor	Fred Allen
Music	Walter Scharf
Associate Producer	Joseph Kane
Production Company	
Distributor	Republic
82 minutes	
John Devlin	John Wayne
Sandy Poli	Vera Hruba Ralston
Capt. Bounce	Walter Brennan
Jim Bender	Ward Bond
Bigtree Collins	Mike Mazurki
"Jersey" Thomas	Ona Munson
Marko Poli	Hugo Haas
Mrs. Stowe	Olive Blakeney
Nicodemus	Nicodemus Stewart
Carp	Paul Fix
Slagin	Grant Withers
Lieutenant	Robert Livingston
Devlin's driver	Olin Howlin
Wexton Geary	Pierre Watkin
Anson Stowe	Robert H. Barrat
Col. Wordin	Jonathan Hale
Little boy	Bobby Blake
Capt. Spotts	Paul Hurst
Stagecoach driver	Eddy Waller

Dakota: *Walter Brennan, Wayne, Vera Hruba Ralston.*

Mrs. Plummer	Sarah Padden
Suade	Jack LaRue
Mr. Plummer	George Cleveland
Dr. Judson	Selmer Jackson
Wahtonka	Claire DuBrey
Poli's driver	Roy Barcroft
	Cliff Lyons
	Fred Graham

Shooting from late July to early
September, 1945
Released December 25 (U.S.);
April 8, 1946 (G.B.)

WITHOUT RESERVATIONS (1946)

Director	Mervyn LeRoy
Writer	Andrew Solt from the novel "Thanks, God! I'll Take It from Here" by Jane Allen Mae Livingston
Cinematographer	Milton Krasner
Art Directors	Albert S. D'Agostino Ralph Berger
Editor	Jack Ruggiero
Music	Roy Webb
Producer	Jesse L. Lasky
Production Company Distributor	RKO Radio
107 minutes	
Christopher (Kit) Madden	Claudette Colbert
Rusty Thomas	John Wayne
Dink Watson	Don DeFore
Connie (Consuela Callaghan)	Anne Triola
Soldier	Phil Brown
Ortega	Frank Puglia
Henry Baldwin	Thurston Hall
Dolores	Dona Drake
Mexican boy	Fernando Alvarado
Salesman	Charles Arnt
Herself	Louella Parsons
Himself	Cary Grant
Himself (autograph hunter)	Jack Benny
Herself	Dolores Moran
Louis Burt	Charles Williams
Philip Jerome (the publisher)	Charles Evans
Jack	Frank Wilcox
Telegram boy	William Benedict
Randall (hotel clerk–Albuquerque)	Harry Hayden
Gibbs (reporter)	Ian Wolfe
Radio announcers	Robert "Bob" Anderson Marvin Miller
Women (Book Club members)	Esther Howard Minerva Urecal
Paul Gill	Raymond Burr
Ticket collectors	Griff Barnett Will Wright
Train porter	Sam McDaniel
Jailer	Houseley Stevenson

Lawyer	Cy Kendall
Flyer advising train porter	William Challee

Started shooting as *Thanks God, I'll Take It from Here* in late October, 1945;
completed by late January 1946
Released May 13 (U.S.); November 18 (G.B.)

Without Reservations: *Wayne, Claudette Colbert.*

ANGEL AND THE BADMAN (1947)

Director	James Edward Grant
Writer	James Edward Grant
2nd Unit Director	Yakima Canutt
Cinematographer	Archie J. Stout
Production Designer	Ernst Fegté
Editor	Harry Keller

Angel and the Badman: *Lee Dixon, Gail Russell, Wayne.*

Music	Richard Hageman
Producer	John Wayne
Production Company	
Distributor (U.S.A.)	Republic
Distributor (G.B.)	British Lion
100 minutes	
Quirt Evans	John Wayne
Penelope Worth	Gail Russell
Marshal Wistful	
McClintock	Harry Carey
Laredo Stevens	Bruce Cabot
Mrs. Worth	Irene Rich
Randy McCall	Lee Dixon
Johnny Worth	Stephen Grant
Dr. Mangrum	Tom Powers
Frederick Carson	Paul Hurst
Bradley	Olin Howlin
Thomas Worth	John Halloran
Lila Neal	Joan Barton
Ward Withers	Craig Woods
Nelson	Marshall Reed
Townsman	Hank Worden
Baker brother	Pat Flaherty

Shooting (under title *The Angel and the Outlaw*) from late April/early May to early July, 1946
Released February 15 (U.S.); circa March (G.B.)

TYCOON (1947)

Director	Richard Wallace
Writers	Borden Chase
	John Twist
	from the novel by
	C. E. Scoggins
Cinematographers	Harry J. Wild
	W. Howard Greene

Art Directors	Albert S. D'Agostino
	Carroll Clark
Editor	Frank Doyle
Music	Leigh Harline
Producer	Stephen Ames
Production Company	
Distributor	RKO Radio
128 minutes Technicolor	
Johnny Munroe	John Wayne
Maura Alexander	Laraine Day
Frederick Alexander	Sir Cedric Hardwicke
Miss Braithwhaite	Judith Anderson
Pop Mathews	James Gleason
Ricky Vegas	Anthony Quinn
Fog Harris	Grant Withers
Joe	Paul Fix
Chico (boy)	Fernando Alvarado
Holden	Harry Woods
Curly Massinger	Michael Harvey
Senor Tobar	Charles Trowbridge
Chavez	Martin Garralaga
	Nacho Galindo
	Eduardo Noriega

Shooting from early February to early May, 1947
Released December 27 (U.S.); May 2, 1949 (G.B.)

FORT APACHE (1948)

Director	John Ford
Writer	Frank S. Nugent
	from the short story
	"Massacre" by
	James Warner Bellah
2nd Unit Director	Cliff Lyons
Cinematographer	Archie Stout

Art Director	James Basevi
Editor	Jack Murray
Music	Richard Hageman
Producers	John Ford
	Merian C. Cooper
Production Company Argosy	
Distributor	RKO Radio
127 minutes	
Capt. Kirby York	John Wayne
Lt. Col. Owen	
Thursday	Henry Fonda
Philadelphia	
Thursday	Shirley Temple
Sgt. Beaufort	Pedro Armendariz
Lt. Michael O'Rourke	John Agar
Sgt. Maj. O'Rourke	Ward Bond
Mrs. Mary O'Rourke	Irene Rich
Capt. Sam	
Collingwood	George O'Brien
Mrs. Collingwood	Anna Lee
Sgt. Mulcahy	Victor McLaglen
Sgt. Quincannon	Dick Foran
Sgt. Shattuck	Jack Pennick
Dr. Wilkens	Guy Kibbee
Silas Meacham	Grant Withers
Cochise	Miguel Inclan
Mrs. Gates	Mae Marsh
Guadalupe	Movita Castenada
Shotgun guard	Francis Ford
Newspaperman	Frank Ferguson
Officer at dance	Mickey Simpson
Recruit	Ray Hyke
Ma (trading post	
owner)	Mary Gordon
Hick recruit	Hank Worden
Reporters	Archie Twitchell
	William Forrest
Stagecoach driver	Cliff Clark
Cavalryman	Fred Graham
	Philip Keiffer

Ben Johnson was Wayne's stunt double
Shooting (under title *War Party*) from mid-August to the end of September, 1947
Released March 9 (U.S.); July 26 (G.B.)

RED RIVER (1948)

Director	Howard Hawks
Writers	Borden Chase
	Charles Schnee
	from the magazine story/
	novel "The Chisholm
	Trail," also titled "Red
	River," by Borden Chase
2nd Unit Director	Arthur Rosson
Cinematographer	Russell Harlan
Art Director	John Datu Arensma
Editor	Christian Nyby
Music	Dimitri Tiomkin
Producer	Howard Hawks
Production Company Monterey	
Presentation	Charles K. Feldman
Distributor	United Artists
125 minutes (cut for 1963	
G.B. reissue to 112)	
Tom Dunson	John Wayne
Matthew Garth	Montgomery Clift
Tess Millay	Joanne Dru

Nadine Groot	Walter Brennan
Fen	Coleen Gray
Cherry Valance	John Ireland
Buster McGee	Noah Beery Jr.
Quo	Chief Yowlachie
Melville	Harry Carey Sr.
Dan Latimer	Harry Carey Jr.
Matthew as a boy	Mickey Kuhn
Teeler Yacey	Paul Fix
Sims	Hank Worden
Bunk Kenneally	Ivan Parry
Old Leather	Hal Taliaferro
Fernandez	Paul Fiero
Wounded wrangler	Billy Self
Walt Jergens	Ray Hyke
Maylor	Glenn Strange
A quitting wrangler	Tom Tyler
Laredo	Dan White
Colonel	Lane Chandler
Gamblers	Lee Phelps
	George Lloyd
Dancehall girl	Shelley Winters

Arthur Rosson is actually credited as "co-director" although he functioned as 2nd Unit director. Shelley Winters is briefly glimpsed as one of the girls in the wagon train under Indian attack. The credits give Colleen Gray, Chief Yowlatchie and Hal Talliaferro instead of the more usual spellings rendered above.
In production September-November 1946
Location filming at Elgin, Arizona
Released September 17 (U.S.); January 17, 1949 (G.B.)

THREE GODFATHERS (1949)

Director	John Ford
Writers	Laurence Stallings
	Frank S. Nugent
	from the story "The Three Godfathers" by Peter B. Kyne
Cinematographer	Winton C. Hoch
2nd Unit Cinematographer	Charles P. Boyle
Art Director	James Basevi
Editor	Jack Murray
Music	Richard Hageman
Producers	John Ford
	Merian C. Cooper
Production Company	Argosy
Distributor	M-G-M
106 minutes Technicolor	
Robert Marmaduke Hightower	John Wayne
"Pete" (Pedro Roca Fuerte)	Pedro Armendariz
William Kearney ("The Abilene Kid")	Harry Carey Jr.
Perley "Buck" Sweet	Ward Bond
The mother	Mildred Natwick
Mr. Latham	Charles Halton
Miss Florie	Jane Darwell
Mrs. Perley Sweet	Mae Marsh

Judge	Guy Kibbee
Ruby Latham	Dorothy Ford
Members of posse	Ben Johnson
	Michael Dugan
	Don Summers
Deputy Sheriff	Fred Libby
"Curly" (Deputy Sheriff)	Hank Worden
Luke (Train conductor)	Jack Pennick
Drunken old-timer at bar	Francis Ford
Saloon Pianist	Richard Hageman
Guard at Mojave Tanks	Cliff Lyons

Previously filmed as Marked Men (1919, with Harry Carey in the Wayne role); Hell's Heroes (1930, with Charles Bickford in the Wayne role) and Three Godfathers (1936, with Chester Morris in the Wayne role)
Shooting from mid-May to mid-June, 1948
Released January 14 (U.S.); May 2 (G.B.)

WAKE OF THE RED WITCH (1949)

Director	Edward Ludwig
Writers	Harry Brown
	Kenneth Gamet
	from the novel by Garland Roark
Cinematographer	Reggie Lanning
Art Director	James Sullivan
Editor	Richard L. Van Enger
Music	Nathan Scott
Associate Producer	Edmund Grainger
Production Company Distributor (U.S.A.)	Republic
Distributor (G.B.)	British Lion
106 minutes	
Captain Ralls	John Wayne
Angelique Desaix	Gail Russell
Sam Rosen	Gig Young
Teleia Van Schreeven	Adele Mara
Mayrant Ruysdaal Sidneye	Luther Adler
Harmenszoon Van Schreeven	Eduard Franz
Capt. Wilde Youngeur	Grant Withers
Jacques Desaix	Henry Daniell
Antonio "Ripper" Arrezo	Paul Fix
Captain Munsey	Dennis Hoey
Mr. Loring	Jeff Corey
Doktor Van Arken	Erskine Sanford
Va Nuke	Duke Kahanamoku
Prosecutor	John Wengraf
Kurinua (a native)	Henry Brandon
Seaman on "Red Witch"	Myron Healey
Second diver	John Pickard
Seaman handling diving line	Harlan Warde
Maru	Fernando Alvarado
Taluna	Jose Alvarado
Hekkim (cabin boy)	Carl Thompson
Second officer	Mickey Simpson

Dirk	Grant Means
First diver	Jim Nolan
Jarma	Harry Vegar
Mullins	David Clarke
Ship's surgeon	Fred Fox
Native servant	Al Kikume
Native priest	Leo C. Richmond
Kharma	Harold Lishman
Sailor (Lookout)	Fred Libbey
Young sailor	Robert Wood
Sailor (fight)	Fred Graham
Officer	Rory Mallinson
Lawyer	Norman Rainey
Sailor	Wallace Scott
Natives	Kuka Tuitama
	George Pliz

Shooting from mid-July to late October/early November, 1948
Released March 1 (U.S.); June 5 (G.B.)

THE FIGHTING KENTUCKIAN (1949)

Director	George Waggner
Writer	George Waggner
Cinematographer	Lee Garmes
Art Director	James Sullivan
Editor	Richard L. Van Enger
Music	George Antheil
Producer	John Wayne
Production Company Distributor (U.S.)	Republic
Distributor (G.B.)	British Lion
100 minutes	
John Breen	John Wayne
Fleurette DeMarchand	Vera Ralston
Colonel George Geraud	Philip Dorn
Willie Paine	Oliver Hardy
Ann Logan	Marie Windsor
Blake Randolph	John Howard
General Paul DeMarchand	Hugo Haas
Mme. DeMarchand	Odette Myrtil
George Hayden	Grant Withers
Beau Meritt	Paul Fix
Sister Hattie	Mae Marsh
Captain Dan Carroll	Jack Pennick
Jacques (the wrestler)	Mickey Simpson
Carter Ward	Fred Graham
Marie	Mabelle Koenig
Friends	Shy Waggner
	Crystal White
Announcer of wrestling contest	Hank Worden
Band Leader (Knox Brown)	Charles Cane
Driver	Cliff Lyons
	Chuck Roberson

Shooting (initially as A Strange Caravan) from mid-March to late April/early May, 1949
Released September 15 (U.S.); circa February 1950 (G.B.)

The Fighting Kentuckian.

She Wore a Yellow Ribbon.

SHE WORE A YELLOW RIBBON (1949)

Director	John Ford
Writers	Frank S. Nugent
	Laurence Stallings
	from two magazine
	stories "The Big
	Hunt" and "War
	Party" by James
	Warner Bellah
2nd Unit Director	Cliff Lyons
Cinematographer	Winton C. Hoch
2nd Unit	
Cinematographer	Charles P. Boyle
Art Director	James Basevi
Editor	Jack Murray
Music	Richard Hageman
Associate Producer	Lowell Farrell
Producers	John Ford
	Merian C. Cooper
Production Company	Argosy
Distributor	RKO Radio
103 minutes Technicolor	
Capt. Nathan	
Brittles	John Wayne
Olivia Dandridge	Joanne Dru
Lt. Flint Cohill	John Agar
Sgt. Tyree	Ben Johnson
Lt. Ross Pennell	Harry Carey Jr.
Sgt. Quincannon	Victor McLaglen
Mrs. Abby Allshard	Mildred Natwick
Major Allshard	George O'Brien
Dr. O'Laughlin	Arthur Shields
Barman	Francis Ford
Karl Rynders	Harry Woods
Poney-That-Walks	Chief Big Tree
Red Shirt	Noble Johnson
Trooper Cliff	Cliff Lyons
Quayne	Tom Tyler
Hochbauer	Michael Dugan
Wagner	Mickey Simpson
Bugler	Frank McGrath
Jenkin	Don Summers
Cpl. Krumrein	Fred Libbey
Sgt. Major	Jack Pennick
Courier	Billy Jones
N. C. O.	Bill Goettinger
Hench	Fred Graham
Badger	Fred Kennedy
Pvt. John Smith	Rudy Bowman
N. C. O.	Post Park
McCarthy	Ray Hyke
Interpreter	Lee Bradley
Chief Sky Eagle	Chief Sky Eagle
Bartender	Francis Ford
Rynder's partner	Paul Fix

In production early November to early
December 1948
Location filming at Monument Valley
Released October (U.S.); May 8, 1950 (G.B.)

SANDS OF IWO JIMA (1949)

Director	Allan Dwan
Writers	Harry Brown
	James Edward Grant
	from a screen story by
	Harry Brown
Cinematographer	Reggie Lanning
Art Director	James Sullivan
Editor	Richard L. Van Enger
Music	Victor Young
Associate Producer	Edmund Grainger
Production Company	
Distributor (U.S.)	Republic
Distributor (G.B.)	British Lion
100 minutes	
Sgt. John M.	
Stryker	John Wayne
Pfc. Peter Conway	John Agar
Allison Bromley	Adele Mara
Corporal Al Thomas	Forrest Tucker
Pfc. Benny Ragazzi	Wally Cassell
Pfc. Charlie Bass	James Brown
Pfc. Dan Shipley	Richard Webb
Corporal Robert	
Dunne	Arthur Franz
Mary	Julie Bishop
Pfc. Soames	James Holden
Pfc. Georgie	
Hellenopolis	Peter Coe
Pfc. Frank Flynn	Richard Jaeckel
Pfc. Eddie Flynn	Bill Murphy
Pfc. Harris	George Tyne
Pvt. "Ski" Choynski	Hal Fieberling
Captain Joyce	John McGuire
Pvt. Mike McHugh	Martin Milner

Pvt. Sid Stein	Leonard Gumley
Pvt. L. D. Fowler Jr.	William Self
Colonel in staff car	Don Haggerty
Themselves	Col. D. M. Shoup
	Lt.-Col. H. P. Crowe
	Capt. Harold G. Shrier
	Rene A. Gagnon
	Ira H. Hayes
	John H. Bradley

Shooting from mid-July to end of August,
1949
World première (San Francisco) December
14, generally released March 1, 1950
(U.S.); November 20, 1950 (G.B.)

RIO GRANDE (1950)

Director	John Ford
Writer	James Kevin McGuinness
	from the magazine story
	"Mission with No Record"
	by James Warner Bellah
2nd Unit Director	Cliff Lyons
Cinematographer	Bert Glennon
2nd Unit	
Cinematographer	Archie Stout

Sands of Iwo Jima: *Forrest Tucker, John Wayne.*

Art Director	Frank Hotaling
Editor	Jack Murray
Music	Victor Young
Songs	Stan Jones
	Dale Evans
	Tex Owens
Producers	John Ford
	Merian C. Cooper
Production Company	Argosy
Distributor	Republic
105 minutes	
Lt. Col. Kirby Yorke	John Wayne
Mrs. Kathleen Yorke	Maureen O'Hara
Trooper Tyree	Ben Johnson
Trooper Jeff Yorke	Claude Jarman Jr.
Trooper Daniel Boone	Harry Carey Jr.
Dr. Wilkins	Chill Wills
Gen. Philip Sheridan	J. Carrol Naish
Sgt.-Major	
Quincannon	Victor McLaglen
Deputy Marshal	Grant Withers
Capt. St. Jacques	Peter Ortiz
Capt. Prescott	Steve Pendleton
Margaret Mary	Karolyn Grimes
Lieutenant	Alberto Morin
Sergeant	Stan Jones
Heinze	Fred Kennedy
Officer	Chuck Roberson
Regimental Singers	The Sons of the
	Pioneers (Ken Curtis,
	Hugh Farr, Karl Farr,
	Lloyd Perryman, Shug
	Fisher, Tommy Doss)

Jack Pennick, Cliff Lyons, Pat Wayne
Shooting (as *Rio Bravo*) from mid-June to late
July, 1950
Released November 15 (U.S.); January 2,
1951 (G.B.)

OPERATION PACIFIC (1951)

Director	George Waggner
Writer	George Waggner
Cinematographer	Bert Glennon
Art Director	Leo K. Kuter
Editor	Alan Crosland Jr.
Music	Max Steiner
Producer	Louis F. Edelman
Production Company	
Distributor	Warner Bros.
111 minutes	
"Duke" Gifford	John Wayne
Mary Stuart	Patricia Neal
"Pop" Perry	Ward Bond
Larry	Scott Forbes
Bob Perry	Philip Carey
Jonesy	Paul Picerni
The Talker	William Campbell
Commander Steele	Kathryn Givney
Caldwell	Martin Milner
Comsubpac	Cliff Clark
The Chief	Jack Pennick
Sister Anne	Virginia Brissac
A Soundman	Vincent Forte
Squad Commander	Lewis Martin
Radarman	Louis Marconi

Flying Leathernecks: *Wayne, James Bell, Robert Ryan.*

Junior	Sam Edwards
"Mick"–shore patrol	
commander	James Flavin
Admiral's aide	Harlan Warde
Instructor	Carleton Young
Freddie	Harry Lauter

Shooting from early September to early
November, 1950
Released January 27 (U.S.); August
27 (G.B.)

FLYING LEATHERNECKS (1951)

Director	Nicholas Ray
Writer	James Edward Grant
	from a screen story by
	Kenneth Gamet
Cinematographer	William E. Snyder
Art Directors	Albert S. D'Agostino
	James W. Sullivan
Editor	Sherman Todd
Music	Roy Webb
Producer	Edmund Grainger
Distributor	RKO Radio
102 minutes Technicolor	
Major Dan Kirby	John Wayne
Capt. Carl Griffin	Robert Ryan
Lt. "Cowboy" Blithe	Don Taylor
Joan Kirby	Janis Carter
Master Sgt. Clancy	Jay C. Flippen
Lt. Commander	
Curan	William Harrigan
Colonel	James Bell
General	Barry Kelley
Shorty Vegay	Maurice Jara
Lieut. Malotke	Adam Williams
Pudge McCabe	James Dobson

Capt. McAllister	Carleton Young
Lieut. Jorgenson	Steve Flagg
Lieut. Ernie Stark	Brett King
Tommy Kirby	Gordon Gebert
Mess Sergeant	Dick Wessell
Virginia Blithe	Gail Davis
Ground Control	
Officer	Milburn Stone

Keith Larsen, Mack Williams
Shooting from late November, 1950, to
mid-February, 1951
Released August 28 (U.S.); October 22 (G.B.)

THE QUIET MAN (1952)

Director	John Ford
Writer	Frank S. Nugent
	from the short story
	"Green Rushes"
	by Maurice Walsh
Cinematographer	Winton C. Hoch
2nd Unit	
Cinematographer	Archie Stout
Art Director	Frank Hotaling
Editor	Jack Murray
Music	Victor Young
Producers	John Ford
	Merian C. Cooper
Production Company	Argosy
Distributor	Republic
129 minutes Technicolor	
Sean Thornton	John Wayne
Mary Kate Danaher	Maureen O'Hara
Michaeleen Flynn	Barry Fitzgerald
Father Peter	
Lonergan	Ward Bond

Red Will Danaher	Victor McLaglen	Mr. Nash	Peter Brocco	Art Director	James Basevi
Mrs. Sarah Tillane	Mildred Natwick	McLain's superior	William Forrest	Editor	Ralph Dawson
Dan Tobin	Francis Ford	Olaf	Gordon Jones	Music	Emil Newman
Mrs. Elizabeth		Truck driver	Peter Whitney	Producer	Robert Fellows
Playfair	Eileen Crowe	Waiter	Harry Tyler	Production Company	Wayne-Fellows

Red Will Danaher   Victor McLaglen
Mrs. Sarah Tillane   Mildred Natwick
Dan Tobin   Francis Ford
*Mrs. Elizabeth
Playfair*   Eileen Crowe
*Woman at railway
station*   May Craig
Rev. Cyril Playfair   Arthur Shields
Forbes   Charles FitzSimmons
Father Paul   James Lilburn
Owen Glynn   Sean McClory
Feeney   Jack McGowran
*Dermot Fahy
(ballad singer)*   Ken Curtis
*Father Paul's
mother*   Mae Marsh
Guard Maloney   Joseph O'Dea
*Engine Driver
Costello*   Eric Gorman
Fireman   Kevin Lawless
Porter   Paddy O'Donnell
Station Master   Web Overlander
Policeman   Harry Tenbrook
General   Maj. Sam Harris
*Pat Cohan
(the publican)*   Harry Tyler
The Children   Patrick Wayne
  Michael Wayne
  Melinda Wayne
  Antonia Wayne
  Elizabeth Jones

Shooting from early June to end August,
1951
Released August (U.S.); July 21 (G.B.)

BIG JIM McLAIN (1952)

Director   Edward Ludwig
Writers   James Edward Grant
  Richard English
  Eric Taylor
  from a screen story by
  Richard English
Cinematographer   Archie Stout
Art Director   Alfred Ybarra
Editor   Jack Murray
Music   Emil Newman
  Arthur Lange
  Paul Dunlap
Producer   Robert Fellows
Production Company   Wayne-Fellows
Distributor   Warner Bros.
90 minutes
Big Jim McLain   John Wayne
Nancy Vallon   Nancy Olson
Mal Baxter   James Arness
Sturak   Alan Napier
Madge   Veda Ann Borg
Dr. Gelster   Gayne Whitman
Poke   Hal Baylor
Edwin White   Robert Keys
Robert Henried   Hans Conreid
*Lt. Commander
Clint Grey*   John Hubbard
Mrs. Namaka   Mme. Soo Yong
Chief of Police   Dan Liu
Phil Briggs   Vernon (Red) McQueen
Mr. Lexiter   Paul Hurst
Mrs. Lexiter   Sara Padden

Mr. Nash   Peter Brocco
McLain's superior   William Forrest
Olaf   Gordon Jones
Truck driver   Peter Whitney
Waiter   Harry Tyler
Shooting (as *Jim McLain*) from mid-May to
late June/early July, 1952
Location filming in Honolulu
Released August 30 (U.S.); December 15
(G.B.)

TROUBLE ALONG THE WAY (1953)

Director   Michael Curtiz
Writers   Melville Shavelson
  Jack Rose
  from a screen story by
  Douglas Morrow
  Robert Hardy Andrews
2nd Unit Director   David C. Gardner
Cinematographer   Archie Stout
Art Director   Leo K. Kuter
Editor   Owen Marks
Music   Max Steiner
Producer   Melville Shavelson
Production Company   Warner Bros.
Distributor   Warner Bros.
110 minutes
*Steve Aloysius
Williams*   John Wayne
Alice Singleton   Donna Reed
Father Burke   Charles Coburn
Father Malone   Tom Tully
Carole Williams   Sherry Jackson
Anne McCormick   Marie Windsor
Harold McCormick   Tom Helmore
Father Mahoney   Dabbs Greer
Father Provincial   Leif Erickson
Procurator   Douglas Spencer
Cardinal O'Shea   Lester Matthews
Stan Schwegler   Chuck Connors
Moose McCall   Bill Radovich
Judge   Richard Garrick
Bus Driver   Murray Alper
*Buck Holman
(coach)*   James Flavin
Pool player   Ned Glass
Bishop   Phil Chambers
*Mike Edwards
(store proprietor)*   Frank Ferguson
*Polo grounds
manager*   Howard Petrie
Italian mother   Renata Vanni
Bill (team manager)   Tim Graham
Joe (team manager)   Robert Keys
Shooting (initially as *Alma Mater*) from
mid-October to early December, 1952
Released April 4 (U.S.); July 27 (G.B.)

ISLAND IN THE SKY (1953)

Director   William A. Wellman
Writer   Ernest K. Gann
  from his novel
Cinematographer   Archie Stout
*Aerial
Cinematographer*   William Clothier

Art Director   James Basevi
Editor   Ralph Dawson
Music   Emil Newman
Producer   Robert Fellows
Production Company   Wayne-Fellows
Distributor   Warner Bros.
109 minutes (G.B.: 102)
Capt. Dooley   John Wayne
Stutz   Lloyd Nolan
Col. Fuller   Walter Abel
McMullen   James Arness
Moon   Andy Devine
J. H. Handy   Allyn Joslyn
Murray, navigator   James Lydon
Hunt   Harry Carey Jr.
*Stankowski,
engineer*   Hal Baylor
*Frank Lovatt,
co-pilot*   Sean McClory
*D'Annunzia,
radioman*   Wally Cassell
Walrus   Gordon Jones
Capt. Turner   Frank Fenton
Major Ditson   Robert Keys
Lt. Cord   Sumner Getchell
Sgt. Harper   Regis Toomey
Miller   Paul Fix
Gidley   Jim Dugan
Rene   George Chandler
Fitch   Louis Jean Heydt
Wilson   Bob Steele
Swanson   Darryl Hickman
Gainer   Touch (Michael)
  Connors
Hopper   Carl Switzer
Stannish   Cass Gidley
Breezy   Guy Anderson
Ogden   Tony DeMario
Moon's wife   Ann Doran
Murray's wife   Dawn Bender
Girl in flashback   Phyllis Winger
Released September 5 (U.S.);
November 9 (G.B.)
Filmed at Donner Lake, near Truckee, California.

HONDO (1953)

Director   John Farrow
Writer   James Edward Grant
  from the story "The
  Gift of Cochise" by
  Louis L'Amour
*Second Unit
Directors*   Cliff Lyons
  John Ford (uncredited)
Cinematographers   Robert Burks
  Archie Stout
Art Director   Al Ybarra
Editor   Ralph Dawson
Music   Emil Newman
  Hugo Friedhofer
Producer   Robert Fellows
Production Company   Wayne-Fellows
Distributor   Warner Bros.
83 minutes   3-D   WarnerColor
Hondo Lane   John Wayne
Angie Lowe   Geraldine Page
Buffalo   Ward Bond
Vittoro   Michael Pate
Lennie   James Arness

The Quiet Man: *Wayne and John Ford enjoy a chat.*

Hondo: *Michael, John and Patrick Wayne on location.*

Hondo: *Wayne takes a break to look over a rough model of the ferry boat to be used in* Blood Alley.

Silva	Rodolfo Acosta
Ed Lowe	Leo Gordon
Lt. McKay	Tom Irish
Johnny Lowe	Lee Aaker
Major Sherry	Paul Fix
Pete	Rayford Barnes

Re-made by Wayne's production company in 1966 as *Hondo and the Apaches* with Ralph Taeger in the Wayne role, and subsequently developed into a TV series
Shooting from June 8 to early August 1953
Location shooting at Carmargo, Mexico
Released November 27 (U.S.); April 5, 1954 (G.B.)

THE HIGH AND THE MIGHTY (1954)

Director	William A. Wellman
Writer	Ernest K. Gann from his novel
Cinematographer	Archie Stout
Aerial cinematographer	William H. Clothier
Art Director	Al Ybarra
Editor	Ralph Dawson
Music	Dimitri Tiomkin
Producer	Robert Fellows
Production Company	Wayne-Fellows
Distributor	Warner Bros.
147 minutes CinemaScope WarnerColor	
Dan Roman	John Wayne
May Holst	Claire Trevor
Lydia Rice	Laraine Day
Sullivan	Robert Stack
Sally McKee	Jan Sterling
Ed Joseph	Phil Harris
Gustave Pardee	Robert Newton
Ken Childs	David Brian
Flaherty	Paul Kelly
Humphrey Agnew	Sidney Blackmer
Lillian Pardee	Julie Bishop
Gonzalez	Gonzalez-Gonzalez
Howard Rice	John Howard
Lenny Wilby (navigator)	Wally Brown
Hobie Wheeler	William Campbell
Mrs. Joseph	Ann Doran
Jose Locota	John Qualen
Frank Briscoe	Paul Fix
Ben Sneed	George Chandler
Dorothy Chen	Joy Kim
Toby Field (boy)	Michael Wellman
Alsop	Douglas Fowley
Garfield	Regis Toomey
Ensign Keim	Carl Switzer
Lt. Mowbray	Robert Keys
Roy	William DeWolf Hopper
Dispatcher	William Schallert
Susie	Julie Mitchum
Miss Spalding (stewardess)	Doe Avedon
Nell Buck	Karen Sharpe
Milo Buck	John Smith
	Robert Easton
	Philip Van Zandt

Shooting from November 16, 1953, to mid-January, 1954
Released July 3 (U.S.); November 1 (G.B.)

THE SEA CHASE (1955)

Director	John Farrow
Writers	James Warner Bellah
	John Twist
	from the novel
	by Andrew Geer
Cinematographer	William Clothier
Art Director	Franz Bachelin
Editor	William Ziegler
Music	Roy Webb
Producer	John Farrow
Production Company	
Distributor	Warner Bros.

117 minutes   CinemaScope   Warnercolor

Capt. Karl Ehrlich	John Wayne
Elsa Keller	Lana Turner
Commander Napier	David Farrar
Kirchner	Lyle Bettger
Cadet Wesser	Tab Hunter
Schlieter	James Arness
Cadet Walter	
Stemme	Richard Davalos
Chief Schmitt	John Qualen
Max Heinz	Paul Fix
Capt. Evans	Lowell Gilmore
Matz	Luis Van Rooten
Wentz	Alan Hole
Hepke	Wilton Graff
Bachman	Peter Whitney
Winkler	Claude Akins
Bos'n	John Doucette
Brounck	Alan Lee
Kruger (wireless	
operator)	Adam Williams
British officers	James Lilburn
	Gavin Muir
British High Official	Anthony Eustrel
Trawler survivor	Tudor Owen
French Governor	Jean de Briac
Warship officer	Patrick O'Moore

Gail Robinson, Gilbert Perkins
Shooting from late September to mid-
December, 1964
Location filming at Hawaii
Released June 4 (U.S.); August 22 (G.B.)

Blood Alley: *publicity pose.*

Blood Alley: *Wayne enjoys a visit from co-star Lauren Bacall's husband, Humphrey Bogart.*

BLOOD ALLEY (1955)

Director	William A. Wellman
Writer	A. S. Fleischman
	from his novel
Cinematographer	William H. Clothier
Art Director	Alfred Ybarra
Editor	Fred MacDowell
Music	Roy Webb
Production Company	Batjac
Distributor	Warner Bros.
115 minutes	(G.B.: 103)
	CinemaScope WarnerColor
Wilder	John Wayne
Cathy Grainger	Lauren Bacall
Mr. Tso	Paul Fix
Susu (Cathy's maid)	Joy Kim

Old Feng	Berry Kroger*
Big Han	Mike Mazurki
Wei Ling	Anita Ekberg
Mr. Han	W. T. Chang
Mr. Sing	George Chan
Tack (engineer)	Henry Nakamura
Feng's No. 1 nephew	Walter Soohoo
Feng's No. 2 nephew	Eddie Luke
Cpl. Wang	Victor Sen Yung
	Lowell Gilmore

Shooting from mid-January to mid-March, 1955

Location filming at San Rafael, California

Released October 1 (U.S.); January 16, 1956 (G.B.)

*more frequently spelt: Kroeger

THE CONQUEROR (1956)

Director	Dick Powell
Writer	Oscar Millard
2nd Unit Director	Cliff Lyons
Cinematographers	Joseph LaShelle
	Leo Tover
	Harry J. Wild
	William Snyder
Art Directors	Albert S. D'Agostino
	Carroll Clark
Editorial Supervision	Stuart Gilmore
Editors	Robert Ford
	Kennie Marstella
Music	Victor Young
Associate Producer	Richard Sokolove
Producer	Dick Powell
Production Company	
Distributor	RKO Radio

111 minutes   Cinemascope   Technicolor

Temujin	John Wayne
Bortai	Susan Hayward
Jamuga	Pedro Armendariz
Hunlun	Agnes Moorehead
Wang Khan	Thomas Gomez
Shaman	John Hoyt
Kasar	William Conrad
Kumlek	Ted de Corsia
Targutai	Leslie Bradley
Chepei	Lee Van Cleef
Bogurchi	Peter Mamakos
Tartar Captain	Leo Gordon
Captain of Wang's guard	Richard Loo
A guard	Ray Spiker
Solo Dancer	Sylvia Lewis
Girls in bath	Jarma Lewis
	Pat McMahon
Sibilant Sam	George E. Stone
Honest John	Phil Arnold
Scribe	Torben Meyer
Wang Khan's wives	Pat Lawler
	Pat Tiernan
Drummer boy	John George
A Mongol	Weaver Levy
1st chieftain	Michael Granger
2nd chieftain	Fred Aldrich

The Searchers: *John Wayne, Jeffrey Hunter.*

3rd chieftain	Paul Hoffman
4th chieftain	Lane Bradford
Merkit Captain	Carl Vernell
Subuya	Fred Graham
Jalair	Gregg Barton
Sorgan	Ken Terrell
Hochin	Jeanne Gerson
Mongol guards	Michael Wayne
	Norman Powell
Mongolian warriors	Members of the Chivwit Indian tribe

Shooting from May 17 to mid-August, 1954

Location filming in the Escalante Desert near St. George, Utah

World *première* (London) on February 2

Released February 21 (U.S.); April 9 (G.B.)

THE SEARCHERS (1956)

Director	John Ford
Writer	Frank S. Nugent
	from the novel by
	Alan LeMay
Cinematographer	Winton C. Hoch
2nd Unit Cinematographer	Alfred Gilks

Art Directors	Frank Hotaling
	James Basevi
Editor	Jack Murray
Music	Max Steiner
Title Song	Stan Jones
Associate Producer	Patrick Ford
Producers	Merian C. Cooper
	C. V. Whitney
Production Company	C. V Whitney
Distributor	Warner Bros.

119 minutes   VistaVision   Technicolor.

Ethan Edwards	John Wayne
Martin Pawley	Jeffrey Hunter
Laurie Jorgensen	Vera Miles
Capt. Reverend Samuel Johnson Clayton	Ward Bond
Debbie Edwards	Natalie Wood
Lars Jorgensen	John Qualen
Mrs. Jorgensen	Olive Carey
Chief Scar	Henry Brandon
Charlie McCorry	Ken Curtis
Brad Jorgensen	Harry Carey Jr.
Emilio Figueroa	Antonio Moreno
Mose Harper	Hank Worden
Debbie as a child	Lana Wood
Aaron Edwards	Walter Coy
Martha Edwards	Dorothy Jordan
Lucy Edwards	Pippa Scott
Lt. Greenhill	Pat Wayne
Look (the fat squaw)	Beulah Archuletta

311

Sergeant	Jack Pennick
Jerem Futterman	Peter Mamakos
Lawrence (Ranger)	Chuck Roberson
Mexican bartender	Nacho Galindo
Ben	Robert Lyden
Indian Chief	Chief Thundercloud
Col. Greenhill	Cliff Lyons

Mae Marsh, Dan Borzage

Shooting from mid-June to mid-August 1955

Location filming in Utah; studio work at RKO-Pathe

Released March 13 (U.S.); September 23 (G.B.)

THE WINGS OF EAGLES (1957)

Director	John Ford
Writers	Frank Fenton William Wister Haines from the life and writings of Commander Frank W. Wead, U.S.N. and the biography "Wings of Men"
Cinematographer	Paul C. Vogel
Art Directors	William A. Horning Malcolm Brown
Editor	Gene Ruggiero
Music	Jeff Alexander
Associate Producer	James E. Newcom
Producer	Charles Schnee
Distributor	Metro-Goldwyn-Mayer

110 minutes (G.B.: 196)   Metrocolor

Frank W. "Spig" Wead	John Wayne
Min Wead	Maureen O'Hara
"Jughead" Carson	Dan Dailey
John Dodge	Ward Bond
John Dale Price	Ken Curtis
Admiral Moffett	Edmund Lowe
Capt. Herbert Allen Hazard	Kenneth Tobey
Jack Travis	James Todd
Capt. Jock Clark	Barry Kelley
Party Manager	Sig Ruman
Capt. Spear	Henry O'Neill
Barton	Willis Bouchey
Rose Brentmann	Dorothy Jordan
Lt. Charles Dexter	Peter Ortiz
Dr. John Keye	Louis Jean Heydt
"Arizona" Pincus	Tige Andrews
Pete	Dan Borzage
Air Force Officer	William Tracy
Executive Officer	Harlan Warde
Joe McGuffey	Jack Pennick
Naval aide	Bill Henry
Second manager	Alberto Morin
Lila Wead	Mimi Gibson
Doris Wead	Evelyn Rudie
Admiral Crown	Charles Trowbridge
Nurse Crumley	Mae Marsh
Nurse	Janet Lake
Officer in brawl	Fred Graham
Producer	Stuart Holmes

The Wings of Eagles: *Louis Jean Heydt, John Wayne.*

Bridy O'Faolain	Olive Carey
Patient	Maj. Sam Harris
Nurse	May McEvoy
Wead's baby ("Commodore")	William Paul Lowery
Officer	Chuck Roberson
M. P. at garden party	James Flavin

Cliff Lyons, Veda Ann Borg, Christopher James

Shooting from end July to late September/early October, 1956

Released February 22 (U.S.); May 27 (G.B.)

JET PILOT (1957)

Director	Josef von Sternberg
Writer	Jules Furthman
Cinematographer	Winton C. Hoch
Art Directors	Albert S. D'Agostino Field Gray
Editorial Supervisor	James Wilkinson
Editors	Michael R. McAdam Harry Marker William M. Moore
Music	Bronislau Kaper
Producer	Jules Furthman
Production Company	Howard Hughes/ RKO Radio
Distributor (U.S.A.)	Universal-International (for RKO Radio)
Distributor (Britain)	RKO Radio

112 minutes

Released in RKO-Scope   Technicolor

Col. Shannon	John Wayne
Anna	Janet Leigh
Maj. Gen. Black	Jay C. Flippen
Maj. Rexford	Paul Fix

George Rivers	Richard Rober
Col. Sokolov	Roland Winters
Col. Matoff	Hans Conreid
Gen. Langrad	Ivan Triesault
Maj. Sinclair	John Bishop
Georgia Rexford	Perdita Chandler
Mrs. Simpson	Joyce Compton
Mr. Simpson	Denver Pyle

Jack Overman, Gene Roth, Don Haggerty,
Carleton Young
Initial shooting from mid-December, 1949,
to early May, 1950
Released October (U.S.); November 4 (G.B.)

LEGEND OF THE LOST (1957)

Director	Henry Hathaway
Writers	Robert Presnell Jr.
	Ben Hecht
Cinematographer	Jack Cardiff
Art Director	Alfred Ybarra
Editor	Bert Bates

Music	A. F. Lavagnino
Producer	Henry Hathaway
Production	Batjac/Robert Haggiag
Companies	Dear Film
Distributor	United Artists
109 minutes Technirama Technicolor	
Joe January	John Wayne
Dita	Sophia Loren
Paul Bonnard	Rossano Brazzi
Prefect Dukas	Kurt Kasznar
Girl	Sonia Moser
Girl	Angela Portaluri
Galli Galli	Ibrahim El Hadish

Location filming in Libyan Desert
Released December 17 (U.S.); March 2, 1958
(G.B.)

I MARRIED A WOMAN (1958)

Director	Hal Kanter
Writer	Goodman Ace
Cinematographer	Lucien Ballard

Art Directors	Albert S. D'Agostino
	Walter E. Keller
Editor	Otto Ludwig
Music	Cyril Mockridge
Producer	William Bloom
Distributor (U.S.)	Universal-
	International
	(for RKO Radio)
Distributor (G.B.)	RKO Radio
85 minutes RKO Scope	
	Technicolor sequence
Marshal Briggs	George Gobel
Janice Blake	Diana Dors
Sutton	Adolphe Menjou
Mother-in-law	Jessie Royce Landis
Miss Anderson	Nita Talbot
Eddie	William Redfield
Bob	Steve Dunne
Girard	John McGiver
Photographer	Steve Pendleton
Mrs. Wilkins	Cheerio Meredith
Camera Girl	Kay Buckley
Wife (in film)	Angie Dickinson
Himself	John Wayne

Shooting from July 16 to late August, 1956
Released March (U.S.); May (G.B.)

Legend of the Lost: *Wayne and director Henry Hathaway.*

THE BARBARIAN AND THE GEISHA (1958)

Director	John Huston
Writers	Charles Grayson
	Alfred Hayes (uncredited)
	Nigel Balchin (uncredited)
	from a screen story by
	Ellis St. Joseph
Cinematographer	Charles G. Clarke
Art Directors	Lyle R. Wheeler
	Jack Martin Smith
Editor	Stuart Gilmore
Music	Hugo Friedhofer
Producer	Eugene Frenke
Production Company	
Distributor	20th Century-Fox
105 minutes CinemaScope Eastman Colour	
Townsend Harris	John Wayne
Okichi	Eiko Ando
Henry Heusken	Sam Jaffe
Baron Tamura	So Yamamura
Capt. Edmunds	Norman Thomson
Lt. Fisher	James Robbins
Prime Minister	Morita
Daimyo	Kodaya Ichikawa
The Shogun	Hiroshi Yamato
Harusha	Tokujiro Iketaniuchi
Lord Hotta	Fuji Kasai
Chamberlain	Takeshi Kumagai

Shooting from December 1957 (as *The Townsend
Harris Story*) to February 1958 in Japan
Released September 30 (U.S.); November 9
(G.B.)

RIO BRAVO (1959)

Director	Howard Hawks

Writers	Jules Furthman
	Leigh Brackett
	from a short story by
	B. H. McCampbell
Cinematographer	Russell Harlan
Art Director	Leo K. Kuter
Editor	Folmar Blangsted
Music	Dimitri Tiomkin
Songs	Dimitri Tiomkin
	Paul Francis Webster
Producer	Howard Hawks
Production Company	Armada
Distributor	Warner Bros.
141 minutes Technicolor	
John T. Chance	John Wayne
Dude	Dean Martin
Colorado Ryan	Ricky Nelson
Feathers	Angie Dickinson
Stumpy	Walter Brennan
Pat Wheeler	Ward Bond
Nathan Burdette	John Russell
Carlos	Pedro Gonzalez-
	Gonzalez
Consuela	Estelita Rodriguez
Joe Burdette	Claude Akins
Harold	Harry Carey Jr.
Jake	Malcolm Atterbury
Matt Harris	Bob Steele
Cowboy murdered	
in saloon	Bing Russell
Burdette henchman	
in saloon	Myron Healey
1st Burdette man	
in shootout	Eugene Iglesias
2nd Burdette man	
in shootout	Fred Graham
Henchman	Tom Monroe
Messenger	Riley Hill

Shooting from beginning of May to mid-July 1958

Location filming at Old Tucson, near Tucson, Arizona

Released April 4 (U.S.); July 20 (G.B.)

THE HORSE SOLDIERS (1959)

Director	John Ford
Writers	John Lee Mahin
	Martin Rackin
	from the novel by
	Harold Sinclair
Cinematographer	William H. Clothier
Art Director	Frank Hotaling
Editor	Jack Murray
Music	David Buttolph
Song	Stan Jones
Producers	John Lee Mahin
	Martin Rackin
Production	
Companies	Mahin-Rackin/Mirisch
Distributor	United Artists
119 minutes Colour by DeLuxe	
Col. John Marlowe	John Wayne
Maj. Hank Kendall	William Holden
Hannah Hunter	Constance Towers
"Lukey"	Althea Gibson
Brown	Hoot Gibson

The Horse Soldiers: *director John Ford and Wayne.*

Mrs. Buford	Anna Lee
Henry Goodbody	
(Sheriff)	Russell Simpson
Gen. U. S. Grant	Stan Jones
Col. Jonathan Miles	Carleton Young
The Reverend	
(Commandant of	
Jefferson Military	
Academy)	Basil Ruysdael
Col. Phil Secord	Willis Bouchey
Wilkie	Ken Curtis
Otis "Hoppy"	
Hopkins (assistant	
medico)	O. Z. Whitehead
Sgt.-Major Kirby	Judson Pratt
Jagger Jo	Denver Pyle
Virgil	Strother Martin
The Deacon	Hank Worden
Union officer	Walter Reed
"Mitch"–Sgt.-Major	
Mitchell	Jack Pennick
Union soldier	Fred Graham
Union Captain	Chuck Hayward
Newton Station	
bartender	Charles Seel
Passengers to	Stuart Holmes
Newton Station	Maj. Sam Harris
Gen. Sherman	Richard Cutting
Dunker	Bing Russell
Major Gray	
(Confederate artillery)	William Leslie
The Bugler	Ron Haggerty

General Hurlbut	William Forrest,
	Fred Kennedy, Bill Henry, Dan Borzage

Shooting from late October 1958 to early/mid-January 1959

Location filming in Louisiana

Released June 12 (U.S.); January 10, 1960 (G.B.)

THE ALAMO (1960)

Director	John Wayne
Writer	James Edward Grant
2nd Unit Directors	Cliff Lyons
	John Ford (uncredited)
Cinematographer	William H. Clothier
Art Director	Alfred Ybarra
Editor	Stuart Gilmore
Music	Dimitri Tiomkin
Associate Producer	James Edward Grant
Producer	John Wayne
Production Company	Batjac
Distributor	United Artists
192 minutes (then 167, then 140).	
	Todd-AO Technicolor
Col. David Crockett	John Wayne
Col. James Bowie	Richard Widmark

Col. William Barret Travis	Laurence Harvey
Gen. Sam Houston	Richard Boone
Smitty	Frankie Avalon
Capt. James Butler Bonham	Patrick Wayne
Flaca	Linda Cristal
Mrs. Dickinson	Joan O'Brien
Beekeeper	Chill Wills
Juan Seguin	Joseph Calleia
Capt. Almeron Dickinson	Ken Curtis
Mexican Lieutenant	Carlos Arruza
Jethro (Negro)	Jester Hairston
Blind Nell	Veda Ann Borg
Jocko Robertson	John Dierkes
Gambler	Denver Pyle
Angelina (Lisa) Dickinson	Aissa Wayne
Parson	Hank Worden
Dr. Sutherland	Bill Henry
Col. Neill	Bill Daniel
Emile Sande	Wesley Lau
A Tennesseean	Chuck Roberson
Lt. Finn	Guinn Williams
Mrs. Dennisson	Olive Carey
Gen. Santa Anna	Ruben Padilla
Texan teenager	Carol Baxter
Sgt. Lightfoot	Jack Pennick
A Tennesseean	Red Morgan
Silvero Sequin	Julian Trevino
Bull	Tom Hennessey
Pete	Cy Malis
Bearded volunteer	Fred Graham
Woman	Le Jeanne Guye

Shooting from September 9 to mid-December 1959

Location filming at Bracketville, Texas

Released October 24 (U.S.); British premiere on October 27

NORTH TO ALASKA (1960)

Director	Henry Hathaway
Writers	John Lee Mahin
	Martin Rackin
	Claude Binyon
	Wendell Mayes (uncredited)
	from the play "Birthday Gift" by Laszlo Fodor
	from an idea by John Kafka
2nd Unit Director	Richard Talmadge
Cinematographer	Leon Shamroy
Art Directors	Duncan Cramer
	Jack Martin Smith
Editor	Dorothy Spencer
Music	Lionel Newman
Producer	Henry Hathaway
Distributor	20th Century-Fox
122 minutes	CinemaScope DeLuxe colour
Sam McCord	John Wayne
George Pratt	Stewart Granger
Frankie Canon	Ernie Kovacs
Billy Pratt	Fabian

Michelle (Angel)	Capucine
Peter Boggs	Mickey Shaughnessy
Lars Nordquist	Karl Swenson
Commissioner	Joe Sawyer
Lena Nordquist	Kathleen Freeman
Logger	John Qualen
Breezy	Stanley Adams
Duggan	Stephen Courtleigh
Lieutenant	Douglas Dick
Sergeant	Jerry O'Sullivan
Mack	Ollie O'Toole
Boat Captain	Tudor Owen
Jenny Lamont	Lilyan Chauvin
Jenny's husband (butler)	Marcel Hillaire
Angus (desk clerk)	Richard Deacon
Salvationist	James Griffith
Bish the waiter (Everett Bishop)	Max Hellinger
Skinny Sourdough	Richard Collier
Woman at picnic	Esther Dale
Loggers	Fortune Gordien
	Roy Jensen
Gold buyers	Charles Seel
	Rayford Barnes
Ole	Fred Graham
Bartender	Alan Carney
Olaf	Peter Bourne
Barber	Tom Dillon
Queen Lil	Arlene Harris

Paul Maxey, Oscar Beregi, Joel Faye, Johnny Lee, Kermit Maynard, Pamela Raymond, Maurice Delamore, Patty Wharton, Frank Faylen (?)

Shooting from May 9 (as *Go North*) to early August, 1960

Released November 7 (U.S.); January 1, 1961 (G.B.)

THE COMANCHEROS (1961)

Directors	Michael Curtiz
	John Wayne (uncredited)
Writers	James Edward Grant
	Clair Huffaker
	from the novel by Paul I. Wellman
2nd Unit Director	Cliff Lyons
Cinematographer	William H. Clothier
Art Directors	Jack Martin Smith
	Alfred Ybarra
Editor	Louis Loeffler
Music	Elmer Bernstein
Producer	George Sherman
Distributor	20th Century-Fox
107 minutes	CinemaScope DeLuxe colour
Jake Cutter	John Wayne
Paul Regret	Stuart Whitman
Pilar Graile	Ina Balin
Graile	Nehemiah Persoff
Tully Crow	Lee Marvin
Amelung	Michael Ansara
Tobe	Pat Wayne
Major Henry	Bruce Cabot
Melinda Marshall	Joan O'Brien

Horseface	Jack Elam
Judge Thaddeus Jackson Breen	Edgar Buchanan
Ed McBain	Guinn "Big Boy" Williams
Gireaux	Henry Daniell
Estevan	Richard Devon
Comanchero	Steve Baylor
Bill	John Dierkes
Bub Schofield	Roger Mobley
Pa Schofield	Bob Steele
Spanish dancer	Luisa Triana
Josefina	Iphigenie Castiglioni
Bessie Marshall	Aissa Wayne
Iron Shirt	George Lewis
Duel opponent	Gregg Palmer
Card dealer	Don Brodie
Elderly man on riverboat	Jon Lormer
Nervous man	Phil Arnold
Bartender	Alan Carney
Steward on riverboat	Ralph Volkie
	Dennis Cole

Wayne's directorial work was to help the ailing Michael Curtiz

Shooting from June 18 to early August 1961

Released October 30 (U.S.); January 29, 1962 (G.B.)

THE MAN WHO SHOT LIBERTY VALANCE (1962)

Director	John Ford
Writers	Willis Goldbeck
	James Warner Bellah
	from the short story by Dorothy M. Johnson
Cinematographer	William H. Clothier
Art Director	Hal Pereira
	Eddie Imazu
Editor	Otho Lovering
Music	Cyril J. Mockridge
Producer	Willis Goldbeck
Production Company	John Ford Prods.
Distributor	Paramount
122 minutes	
Ransom Stoddard	James Stewart
Tom Doniphon	John Wayne
Hallie Stoddard	Vera Miles
Liberty Valance	Lee Marvin
Dutton Peabody	Edmond O'Brien
Link Appleyard	Andy Devine
Doc Willoughby	Ken Murray
Major Cassius Starbuckle	John Carradine
Nora Ericson	Jeanette Nolan
Peter Ericson	John Qualen
Jason Tully	Willis Bouchey
Maxwell Scott	Carleton Young
Pompey	Woody Strode
Amos Carruthers	Denver Pyle
Floyd	Strother Martin
Reese	Lee Van Cleef
Handy Strong	Robert F. Simon
Herbert Carruthers	O. Z. Whitehead
Mayor Winder	Paul Birch

Hasbrouck	Joseph Hoover
Bartender	Jack Pennick
Widow in stage hold-up	Anna Lee
President of Election Council	Charles Seel
Drunk	Shug Fisher
Clue Dumphries	Earle Hodgins

Stuart Holmes, Dorothy Phillips, Buddy Roosevelt, Gertrude Astor, Eva Novak, Slim Talbot, Monty Montana, Bill Henry, John B. Whiteford, Helen Gibson, Major Sam Harris, Ted Mapes, Jack Kenny

Shooting from September 5 to early November 1961

Released April 22 (U.S.); May 28 (G.B.)

HATARI! (1962)

Director	Howard Hawks
Writer	Leigh Brackett from a story by Harry Kurnitz
2nd Unit Director	Paul Helmick
Cinematographers	Russell Harlan Joseph Brun
Art Directors	Hal Pereira Carl Anderson
Editor	Stuart Gilmore
Music	Henry Mancini
Associate Producer	Paul Helmick
Producer	Howard Hawks
Production Company	Malabar
Distributor	Paramount

157 minutes   Technicolor

Sean Mercer	John Wayne
"Dallas" (Anna Maria D'Allesandro)	Elsa Martinelli
Kurt Mueller	Hardy Kruger
"Pockets"	Red Buttons
"Chips" Chalmoy	Gérard Blain
"Brandy" de la Corte	Michèle Girardon
The Indian (Little Wolf)	Bruce Cabot
Luis Francisco Garcia Lopez	Valentin De Vargas
Dr. Sanderson	Eduard Franz

Filmed entirely in Tanganyika

Released May 24 (U.S.); February 18, 1963 (G.B.)

British *première* December 13

THE LONGEST DAY (1963)

Directors	Ken Annakin (British exterior episodes) Andrew Marton (American exterior episodes) Bernhard Wicki (German episodes) Darryl F. Zanuck (American interior episodes) Gerd Oswald

Hatari!: *Wayne gives his daughter Aissa an elephant ride between takes.*

	(Parachute drops on Ste. Mère Eglise)
Writers	Cornelius Ryan from his book with additional episodes by Romain Gary Jack Jones, David Pursall and Jack Seddon
Cinematographers	Jean Burgoin Henri Persin Walter Wottitz Guy Tabary Pierre Levent
Art Directors	Ted Haworth Leon Barsacq Vincent Korda
Editor	Samuel E. Beetley
Music	Maurice Jarre
Co-ordinator of battle episodes/ Associate Producer	Elmo Williams

Producer	Darryl F. Zanuck
Distributor	20th Century-Fox

180 minutes   CinemaScope

Col. Tom Newton	Eddie Albert
U.S. Ranger	Paul Anka
Mme. Barrault	Arletty
Father Roulland	Jean-Louis Barrault
Pvt. Schulz	Richard Beymer
Mayor of Colleville	Bourvil
R.A.F. Pilot	Richard Burton
Pvt. John Steele	Red Buttons
Pvt. Flanagan	Sean Connery
Capt. Frank	Ray Danton
Janine Boitard	Irina Demich
U.S. Ranger	Fabian
Maj.-Gen. Robert Haines	Mel Ferrer
Brig.-Gen. Theodore Roosevelt	Henry Fonda

Capt. Harding	Steve Forrest
Sgt. Kaffeeklatsch	Gert Fröbe
Brig.-Gen. Parker	Leo Genn
Gen. Dwight D. Eisenhower	Henry Grace
British Padre	John Gregson
Field-Marshal Gerd Von Rundstedt	Paul Hartmann
Field-Marshal Erwin Rommel	Werner Hinz
Sgt. Fuller	Jeffrey Hunter
Maj.-Gen. Gunther Blumontritt	Curt Jurgens
Maj. Gen. Walter Bedell Smith	Alexander Knox
Lord Lovat	Peter Lawford
Comm. Philippe Kieffer	Christian Marquand
Pvt. Morris	Roddy McDowall
Pvt. Martini	Sal Mineo
Brig.-Gen. Norman Cota	Robert Mitchum
Capt. Colin Maud	Kenneth More
Gen. Raymond O. Barton	Edmond O'Brien
Joe Williams	Ron Randell
Mother Superior	Madeleine Renaud
Brig.-Gen. James M. Gavin	Robert Ryan
U.S. Ranger	Tommy Sands
Destroyer Commander	Rod Steiger
Maj. John Howard	Richard Todd
Lt. Wilson	Tom Tryon
Lt.-Col. Ocker	Peter Van Eyck
U.S. Ranger	Robert Wagner
Lt. Sheen	Stuart Whitman
Lt.-Col. Benjamin Vandervoort	John Wayne
Pvt. Watney	Michael Medwin
Pvt. Clough	Norman Rossington
Admiral Sir Bertram Ramsey	John Robinson
Group Capt. J. N. Stagg	Patrick Barr
R.A.F. Officer	Leslie Phillips
R.A.F. Pilot	Donald Houston
Pvt. Coke	Frank Finlay
Lt. Walsh	Lyndon Brook
Ronald Callen	Bryan Coleman
Gen. Sir Bernard L. Montgomery	Trevor Reid
Air Chief Marshal Sir Trafford Leigh-Mallory	Simon Lack
Air Chief Marshal Sir Arthur William Tedder	Louis Mounier
Wren	Sian Phillips
Doctor	Howard Marion Crawford
British soldier	Richard Wattis
Alexandre Renaud	George Wilson
Louis	Fernand Ledoux
Maj. Werner Pluskat	Hans Christian Blech
Maj-Gen. Max Pemsel	Wolfgang Preiss
Col. Josef "Pips" Priller	Heinze Reincke
Gen. Erich Marcks	Richard Munch
Gen. Hans von Salmuth	Ernst Schroeder
Capt. Ernst During	Kurt Meisel

Lt. Col. Hellmuth Meyer	Heinz Spitzner
Meyer's aide	Robert Freytag
Col. Gen. Alfred Jodl	Wolfgang Luckschy
Capt. Hellmuth Lang	Til Kiwe
Maj.-Gen. Dr. Hans Speidel	Wolfgang Buttner
Frau Rommel	Ruth Hausmeister
Manfred Rommel	Michael Hinz
Col. Schiller	Paul Roth
Sgt. Bergsdorf	Harmut Rock
Luftwaffe General	Karl John
Luftwaffe Major	Dietmar Schonherr
Lt. Fritz Theen	Reiner Penkert
German commander	Kurt Pecher
German officer	Serge Tolstoy
Nazi soldier	Eugene Deckers
Pvt. Harris	Mark Damon
Pvt. Wilder	Dewey Martin
Col. Caffey	John Crawford
Lt. Gen. Omar N. Bradley	Nicholas Stuart
Rear Admiral Alan G. Kirk	John Meillon
Briefing Officer	Jack Hedley
Rangers Major	Fred Dur
1st Commando up cliff	George Segal
Sgt. Guy de Montlaur	Georges Rivière
Rear-Admiral Janjard	Jean Servais
Jean	Maurice Poli
Housekeeper	Alice Tissot
Naval Captain	Jo D'Avra

Bill Nagy, Harold Goodwin, Michael Beint, Harry Fowler, Peter Helm, Pauline Carton, Neil McCallum, Christopher Lee (several bits)
Shooting from late August 1961 to March 1962
World *première* (Paris) September 1962
London *première* October 1962, G.B. general release October 1963

HOW THE WEST WAS WON (1962)

Directors	John Ford (Wayne's "Civil War" episode)
	Henry Hathaway ("The Rivers," "The Plains," "The Outlaws")
	George Marshall ("The Railroad")
	Richard Thorpe (uncredited) (transitional historical sequences)
Writers	James R. Webb
	John Gay (uncredited)
Cinematographers	Joseph LaShelle (Wayne's "Civil War" episode)
	Charles Lang Jr. ("The Rivers")
	William Daniels
	Milton Krasner
	Harold Wellman
Art Directors	George W. Davis
	William Ferrari
	Addison Hehr
Editor	Harold F. Kress
Music	Alfred Newman
	Ken Darby

Narrator	Spencer Tracy
Producer	Bernard Smith
Distributor	Metro-Goldwyn-Mayer

162 minutes (G.B.: 155)
(Three camera) Cinerama   Metrocolor
"Civil War" Episode:

Gen. William T. Sherman	John Wayne
Gen. Ulysses S. Grant	Henry ("Harry") Morgan
Zeb Rawlings	George Peppard
Eve Prescott	Carroll Baker
Cpl. Peterson	Andy Devine
Deserter	Russ Tamblyn
Surgeon	Willis Bouchey
Jeremiah Rawlings	Claude Johnson
Ben (Union corporal)	Ken Curtis

Walter Reed, Carleton Young

Rest of Cast:

Marshal Lou Ramsey	Lee J. Cobb
Jethro Stuart	Henry Fonda
Julie Rawlings	Carolyn Jones
Zebulon Prescott	Karl Malden
Cleve Van Valen	Gregory Peck
Roger Morgan	Robert Preston
Lilith Prescott	Debbie Reynolds
Linus Rawlings	James Stewart
Charley Gant	Eli Wallach
Mike King	Richard Widmark
Dora	Brigid Bazlen
Col. Hawkins	Walter Brennan
Lilith's lawyer	David Brian
Abraham Lincoln	Raymond Massey
Rebecca Prescott	Agnes Moorehead
Aggie Clegg	Thelma Ritter
Deputy Stover	Mickey Shaughnessy
Outlaw (Gant gang)	Rodolfo Acosta
Outlaw	Dean Stanton
Marty	Lee Van Cleef
Sam Prescott	Kim Charney
Zeke Prescott	Bryan Russell
Train conductor	Karl Swenson
Gant henchman	Jack Lambert
Poker player	Christopher Dark
Huggins	Jay C. Flippen
Poker player (riverboat)	Gene Roth
Ship's officer	Joe Sawyer
Hylan Seabury	Clinton Sundberg
Poker player	James Griffith
Poker player (wagon)	Walter Burke
Grimes	John Larch
Auctioneer	Edward J. McKinley
Angus	Barry Harvey
Bruce	Jamie Ross
Colin	Mark Allen
James Marshall	Craig Duncan
Barker	Charles Briggs
Auctioneer's assistant	Paul Bryar
Parson Harvey	Tudor Owen

Beulah Archuletta, Chuck Roberson, Boyd "Red" Morgan, Jack Pennick (?)
Shooting from May 28 to mid-November, 1961
World *première* (London) November, 1962
Released February-March 1963 (U.S.)

McLintock!: *Wayne relaxes, sharing a joke with good friend Bruce Cabot and playing chess (his favorite pastime) with son Patrick (Michael Wayne observes the game).*

DONOVAN'S REEF (1963)

Director	John Ford
Writers	Frank Nugent
	James Edward Grant
	from a screen story by
	Edmund Beloin*
Cinematographer	William Clothier
Art Directors	Hal Pereira
	Eddie Imazu
Editor	Otho Lovering
Music	Cyril Mockridge
Producer	John Ford
Production Company	John Ford Prods.
Distributor	Paramount
106 minutes	Technicolor
Michael Patrick Donovan	John Wayne
Thomas Aloysius "Boats" Gilhooley	Lee Marvin
Amelia Sarah Dedham	Elizabeth Allen
Dr. William Dedham	Jack Warden
Marquis Andre De Lage	Cesar Romero
Miss Lafleur	Dorothy Lamour
Lelani Dedham	Jacqueline Malouf
Sgt. Menkowicz	Mike Mazurki
Father Cluzeot	Marcel Dalio
Mister Eu	Jon Fong
Sally Dedham	Cherylene Lee
Luki Dedham	Tim Stafford
Sister Gabrielle	Carmen Estrabeau
Sister Matthew	Yvonne Peattie
Capt. Martin	Frank Baker
Boston notary	Edgar Buchanan
Navy lieutenant	Patrick Wayne
Grand Uncle Sedley Atterbury	Charles Seel
Festus	Chuck Roberson
Irish Officer	Dick Foran
Officer	Cliff Lyons
Boston lady	Mae Marsh
Native girl (pool scene)	Aissa Wayne

Harold Fong, Maj. Sam Harris

Shooting from July 23 to late September, 1962

Location filming on the island of Lauai, Hawaii

Released July (U.S.); July 28 (G.B.)

*James Michener is credited with the original source material for the film on handouts but not on the film itself

---

McLINTOCK! (1963)

Director	Andrew V. McLaglen
Writer	James Edward Grant
Cinematographer	William H. Clothier
Art Directors	Hal Pereira
	Eddie Imazu
Editor	Otho Lovering
Music	Frank De Vol
Songs	Frank De Vol
	"By" Dunham
Production Supervisor	Robert E. Morrison
Producer	Michael Wayne
Production Company	Batjac
Distributor	United Artists
127 minutes	Panavision Technicolor
George Washington McLintock	John Wayne
Katherine McLintock	Maureen O'Hara
Louise Warren	Yvonne De Carlo
Devlin Warren	Patrick Wayne
Becky McLintock	Stefanie Powers
Birnbaum	Jack Kruschen
Drago	Chill Wills
Matt Douglas Jr.	Jerry Van Dyke
Bunny Dull	Edgar Buchanan
Ben Sage	Bruce Cabot
Davey Elk	Perry Lopez
Puma	Michael Pate
Agard	Strother Martin
Matt Douglas	Gordon Jones
Governor Cuthbert H. Humphrey	Robert Lowery
Ching	H. W. Gim
Young Ben Sage	Ed Faulkner
Alice Warren	Aissa Wayne
Sheriff Lord	Chuck Roberson
Camille	Mari Blanchard
Running Buffalo	John Stanley
Carter	Hal Needham
Carlos	Pedro Gonzales Jr.
Curly Butler	Hank Worden
Jones	Leo Gordon
Millie	Kari Noven
Train Engineer	Bob Steele
Fauntleroy	"Big" John Hamilton
Old Timer in Saloon	Ralph Volkie

Cliff Lyons was a consultant for the fight sequences

Shooting from October 24, 1962 to early January 1963

Released November 13 (U.S.); February 23, 1964 (G.B.)

The Magnificent Showman/Circus World: *Wayne and Claudia Cardinale between takes.*

THE MAGNIFICENT SHOWMAN (1964)
(British title)
CIRCUS WORLD
(American title)

Director	Henry Hathaway
Writers	Ben Hecht
	Julian Halevy
	James Edward Grant
	from a screen story by
	Philip Yordan
	Nicholas Ray
2nd Unit Director	Richard Talmadge
Cinematographer	Jack Hildyard
2nd Unit Cinematographer	Claude Renoir
Production Designer	John DeCuir
Editor	Dorothy Spencer
Music	Dimitri Tiomkin
Executive Associate Producer	Michael Waszynski
Producer	Samuel Bronston
Production Companies	Bronston/Midway
Distributor (Britain)	Rank
Distributor (U.S.)	Paramount

137 minutes (U.S.A.: 135)
   70mm Super Technirama Technicolor

Matt Masters	John Wayne
Toni Alfredo	Claudia Cardinale
Lili Alfredo	Rita Hayworth
Cap Carson	Lloyd Nolan
Aldo Alfredo	Richard Conte
Steve McCabe	John Smith
Emile Schuman	Henri Dantes
Mrs. Schuman	Wanda Rotha
Giovana	Katharyna
Flo Hunt	Kay Walsh
Anna	Margaret MacGrath
Molly	Katherine Ellison
Billy Hennigan	Miles Malleson
Hilda	Katharine Kath
Bartender	Moustache
Bartender (Madrid)	George Tyne

Franz Althoff and His Circus,
Robert Cunningham

Shooting in Spain from end September 1963
to early February 1964
Released July (U.S.) December (G.B.)
British *première* July 16

THE GREATEST STORY EVER TOLD
(1965)

Director	George Stevens
Writers	James Lee Barrett
	George Stevens
	from the Bible, other
	ancient writings, the book
	"The Greatest Story
	Ever Told" by Fulton
	Oursler, and writings
	by Henry Denker
Creative Associate	Carl Sandburg
Additional Direction (uncredited)	David Lean
	Jean Negulesco
2nd Unit Direction	Richard Talmadge
	William Hale

The Greatest Story Ever Told.

Cinematographers	William C. Mellor
	Loyal Griggs
Art Directors	Richard Day
	William Creber
	David Hall
Costumes	Vittorio Nino
	Novarese
Editors	Harold F. Kress
	Argyle Nelson
	Frank O'Neill
Music	Alfred Newman
Choral Supervision	Ken Darby
Executive Producer	Frank I. Davis
Associate Producers	George Stevens Jr.
	Antonio Vellani
Producer	George Stevens
Production Company	George Stevens
Distributor	United Artists

260 minutes, subsequently cut to
238, then 190, then 147 (G.B.: 197)
Ultra Panavision 70, originally presented in
Cinerama Technicolor

Jesus	Max Von Sydow
James the Younger	Michael Anderson Jr.
Veronica	Carroll Baker
Martha of Bethany	Ina Balin
Young Man at the Tomb	Pat Boone
Sorak	Victor Buono
Barabbas	Richard Conte
Mary Magdalene	Joanna Dunham
Herod Antipas	Jose Ferrer
Bar Amand	Van Heflin
John the Baptist	Charlton Heston
Caiaphas	Martin Landau
Claudia	Angela Lansbury
Mary of Bethany	Janet Margolin
Judas Iscariot	David McCallum
Matthew	Roddy McDowall
Mary	Dorothy McGuire
Uriah	Sal Mineo
Shemiah	Nehemiah Persoff
The Dark Hermit	Donald Pleasence
Simon of Cyrene	Sidney Poitier
Herod the Great	Claude Rains
Peter	Gary Raymond

Pontius Pilate	Telly Savalas
Nicodemus	Joseph Schildkraut
Questor	Paul Stewart
The Centurion	John Wayne
Woman of No Name	Shelley Winters
Old Aram	Ed Wynn
Joseph	Robert Loggia
Simon the Zealot	Robert Blake
Andrew	Burt Brinckerhoff
John	John Considine
Thaddaeus	Jamie Farr
Philip	David Hedison
Nathanael	Peter Mann
Thomas	Tom Reese
James the Elder	David Sheiner
Lazarus	Michael Tolan
Pilate's Aide	Johnny Seven
General Varus	Harold J. Stone
Emissary	Robert Busch
Alexander	John Crawford
Scribe	Russell Johnson
Speaker of Capernaum	John Lupton
Joseph of Arimathaea	Abraham Sofaer
Theophilus	Chet Stratton
Annas	Ron Whelan
Aben	John Abbott
Captain of Lancers	Rodolfo Acosta
Herod's Commander	Michael Ansara
Chuza	Philip Coolidge
Philip	Dal Jenkins
Archelaus	Joe Perry
Herodias	Marian Seldes
The Tormentor	Frank De Kova
Dumah	Joseph Sirola
Melchior	Cyril Delevanti
Caspar	Frank Silvera
Peter's 2nd accuser	John Pickard
Woman behind railings	Celia Lovsky
Rabble rouser	Mickey Simpson
Good Thief on Cross	Richard Bakalyan
Bad Thief on Cross	Marc Cavell
Weeping Woman	Renata Vanni

Frank Richards, Harry Wilson, Dorothy Neumann, Inbal Dance Theatre of Israel
Shooting from October 1962 to late July 1963
Released February 15 (U.S.); British *première* in April

IN HARM'S WAY (1965)

Director	Otto Preminger
Writer	Wendell Mayes from the novel by James Bassett
Cinematographer	Loyal Griggs
2nd Unit Cinematographer	Philip Lathrop
Production Designer	Lyle Wheeler
Art Director	Al Roelofs
Editors	George Tomasini Hugh S. Fowler
Music	Jerry Goldsmith
Titles	Saul Bass
Producer	Otto Preminger
Production Company	Sigma
Distributor	Paramount
167 minutes	Panavision
Capt. Rockwell Torrey	John Wayne
Cdr. Paul Eddington	Kirk Douglas
Maggie Haynes	Patricia Neal
Lt. William McConnel	Tom Tryon
Bev McConnel	Paula Prentiss
Jeremiah Torrey	Brandon de Wilde
Annalee	Jill Haworth
Admiral Broderick	Dana Andrews
Clayton Canfil	Stanley Holloway
Cdr. Egan Powell	Burgess Meredith
Cincpac I Admiral	Franchot Tone
Cincpac II Admiral	Henry Fonda
Cdr. Neal Owynn	Patrick O'Neal
Lt. Cdr. Burke	Carroll O'Connor
C.P.O. Culpepper	Slim Pickens
Ensign Griggs	James Mitchum
Col. Gregory	George Kennedy
Quartermaster Quoddy	Bruce Cabot
Liz Eddington	Barbara Bouchet
Liz's Officer friend	Hugh O'Brian
Capt. Tuthill	Tod Andrews
Lt. Cline	Larry Hagman
Ensign Balch	Stewart Moss
Lt. Tom Agar	Richard Le Pore
Ship's Doctor	Chet Stratton
Tearful woman	Soo Young
Boston	Dort Clark
PT-Boat Skipper	Phil Mattingly Christopher George

Shooting from June 24 to early September 1964
Location filming in Hawaii
World *première* (Cannes) May
London *première* May
Released June (U.S.)

THE SONS OF KATIE ELDER (1965)

Director	Henry Hathaway
Writers	William H. Wright Allan Weiss Harry Essex from a story by Talbot Jennings
Cinematographer	Lucien Ballard
Art Directors	Hal Pereira Walter Tyler
Editor	Warren Low
Music	Elmer Bernstein
Associate Producer	Paul Nathan
Producer	Hal Wallis
Production Company	Hal Wallis
Distributor	Paramount
122 minutes	Panavision Technicolor
John Elder	John Wayne
Tom Elder	Dean Martin
Mary Gordon	Martha Hyer
Bud Elder	Michael Anderson Jr.
Matt Elder	Earl Holliman
Deputy Sheriff Ben Latta	Jeremy Slate
Morgan Hastings	James Gregory
Sheriff Billy Wilson	Paul Fix
Curley	George Kennedy
Dave Hastings	Dennis Hopper
Judge Harry Evers	Sheldon Allman
Minister	John Litel
Undertaker Hyselman	John Doucette
Banker Venner	James Westerfield
Charlie Bob Striker	Rhys Williams
Charlie Biller	John Qualen
Bondie Adams	Rodolfo Acosta
Jeb Ross	Strother Martin
Storekeeper Peevey	Percy Helton
Doc Isdell/Bartender	Karl Swenson

Shooting from January 4 to early March 1965
Filmed on the Northern Plateau of Mexico near Durango, at El Saltito, Chupaderos, Casa Blanca, etc.; and at the Churubusco Studios in Mexico City
Released July 1 (U.S.); November 14 (G.B.)

CAST A GIANT SHADOW (1966)

Director/Writer	Melville Shavelson from the biography of Col. David Marcus by Ted Berkman
2nd Unit Direction	Jack Reddish
Cinematographer	Aldo Tonti
Production Designer	Michael Stringer
Art Director	Arrigo Equini
Editors	Bert Bates Gene Ruggiero
Music	Elmer Bernstein
Producers	Melville Shavelson Michael Wayne
Production Companies	Mirisch/Llenroc/ Batjac
Distributor	United Artists
141 minutes (G.B.: 135)	
Panavision Technicolor	
Col. David "Mickey" Marcus	Kirk Douglas
Asher Gonen	Yul Brynner
Magda Simon	Senta Berger
Spence Talmadge	Frank Sinatra
General Mike Randolph	John Wayne
Emma Marcus	Angie Dickinson
Jacob Zion	Luther Adler
Ram Oren	Stathis Giallelis
Major Safir	James Donald
James MacAfee	Gordon Jackson
Abou Ibn Kadir	Haym Topol
Mrs. Chaison	Ruth White
André Simon	Michael Shilo
Yussuf	Shlomo Hermon
Rona	Rina Gaynor
British Ambassador	Michael Hordern

The Sons of Katie Elder: *Earl Holliman and Wayne listen as director Henry Hathaway and Dean Martin discuss a point.*

Cast a Giant Shadow: *Wayne, Angie Dickinson, Kirk Douglas.*

Pentagon Chief of Staff	Gary Merrill
Immigration Officer	Allan Cuthbertson
Senior British Officer	Jeremy Kemp
Junior British Officer	Sean Barrett
Bert Harrison	Roland Bartrop
Mrs. Martinson	Vera Dolen
General Walsh	Robert Gardett
1st Sentry	Michael Balston
2nd Sentry	Claude Aliotti
Belly Dancer	Samra Dedes
Truck Driver	Michael Shagrir
U.N. Officers	Frank Latimore Ken Buckle
Aide to Randolph	Rodd Dana
Aide to Chief of Staff	Robert Ross
Officer	Arthur Hansell
Parachute Sgt.	Don Sturkie
Yaakov	Hillel Rave

(Gary Merrill's part was eliminated in cut British version)

Wayne's scenes filmed in Rome July-August 1965

Released April (U.S.); September 23 (G.B.)

THE WAR WAGON (1967)

Director	Burt Kennedy
Writer	Clair Huffaker from his novel "Badman"
2nd Unit Director	Cliff Lyons
Cinematographer	William H. Clothier
Art Director	Alfred Sweeney
Editor	Harry Gerstad
Music	Dimitri Tiomkin
Song "Ballad of the War Wagon"	Dimitri Tiomkin Ned Washington
Producer	Marvin Schwartz
Production Companies	Marvin Schwartz/ Batjac
Distributor (U.S.)	Universal
Distributor (G.B.)	Rank
101 minutes Panavision Technicolor	
Taw Jackson	John Wayne
Lomax	Kirk Douglas
Levi Walking Bear	Howard Keel
Billy Hyatt	Robert Walker
Wes Catlin	Keenan Wynn
Frank Pierce	Bruce Cabot
Kate	Valora Noland
Hoag	Gene Evans
Hammond	Bruce Dern
Sheriff Strike	Terry Wilson
Lola	Joanna Barnes
Shack	Don Collier
Dan Snyder	Sheb Woolley
Felicia	Ann McCrea
Calito	Emilio Fernandez
Bartender	Frank McGrath
Brown	Chuck Roberson
Early	Red Morgan
Hite	Hal Needham
Wild Horse	Marco Antonio
Rosita	Perla Walter
Oriental girls	Miko Mayama Midori Margarite Luna
Townsman at bar	Jose Trinidad Villa

Shooting from September 19 to early December, 1966
Location filming at Durango, Mexico
Released June (U.S.); December 31 (G.B.)

EL DORADO (1967)

Director	Howard Hawks
Writer	Leigh Brackett from the novel "The Stars in Their Courses" by Harry Brown
Cinematographer	Harold Rosson
Art Directors	Hal Pereira Carl Anderson
Editor	John Woodcock
Music	Nelson Riddle
Associate Producer	Paul Helmick
Producer	Howard Hawks
Production Company	Laurel

El Dorado: *sons and mothers (Wayne's and Robert Mitchum's).*

Distributor	Paramount
127 minutes Technicolor	
Cole Thornton	John Wayne
J. P. Harrah	Robert Mitchum
Alan Bourdillon Traherne called Mississippi	James Caan
Maudie	Charlene Holt
Joey MacDonald	Michele Carey
Bull Harris	Arthur Hunnicutt
Kevin MacDonald	R.G. Armstrong
Bart Jason	Edward Asner
Doc Miller	Paul Fix
Nelse McLeod	Christopher George
Milt	Robert Donner
Pedro	John Gabriel
Jim Purvis (Jason's Foreman)	Jim Davis
Maria	Marina Ghane
Saul MacDonald's wife	Anne Newman
Luke MacDonald	Johnny Crawford
Saul MacDonald	Robert Rothwell
Matt MacDonald	Adam Roarke
Jared MacDonald	Charles Courtney
Matt's wife	Diane Strom
Jared's wife	Victoria George
Dr. Donavan	Anthony Rogers
Swede Larsen (gunsmith)	Olaf Wieghorst
Sheriff Tod Draper	William (Bill) Henry
Mexican saloon keeper	Nacho Galindo
Bartender (Jason's saloon)	John Mitchum

Shooting from October 8 1965 to late January-early February, 1966
Location filming in Arizona
Released June (U.S.); August 6 (G.B.)

The Green Berets: *director at work.*

THE GREEN BERETS (1968)

Directors	John Wayne
	Ray Kellogg
Writer	James Lee Barrett
	from the novel by
	Robin Moore
2nd Unit Director	Cliff Lyons
Adviser	Mervyn LeRoy
	(uncredited)
Cinematographer	Winton C. Hoch
Production Designer	Walter M. Simonds
Editor	Otho Lovering
Music	Miklos Rozsa
Producer	Michael Wayne
Production Company	Batjac
Distributor (U.S.)	Warner Bros.—Seven Arts
Distributor (G.B.)	Warner-Pathe
141 minutes (G.B.: 138)	
Panavision Technicolor	
Col. Mike Kirby	John Wayne
George Beckworth	David Janssen
Sgt. Petersen	Jim Hutton
Sgt. Muldoon	Aldo Ray
Doc McGee	Raymond St. Jacques
Col. Cai	Jack Soo

Col. Morgan	Bruce Cabot
Capt. Nim	George Takei
Lt. Jamison	Patrick Wayne
Sgt. Provo	Luke Askew
Lin	Irene Tsu
Capt. MacDaniel	Edward Faulkner
Capt. Coleman	Jason Evers
Sgt. Kowalski	Mike Henry
Hamchunk	Craig Jue
Sgt. Griffin	Chuck Roberson
Sgt. Watson	Eddy Donno
Sgt. Parks	Rudy Robins
Collier	Richard "Cactus"
	Pryor
Phan Son Ti	William Olds
Bach Yen, Frank Koomen	

Shooting from August 9 to early December, 1967

Location filming at Fort Benning, Georgia

Released July (U.S.); August 15 (G.B. *première*)

HELLFIGHTERS (1969)

Director	Andrew V. McLaglen
Writer	Clair Huffaker
Cinematographer	William H. Clothier
Art Directors	Alexander Golitzen
	Frank Arrigo
Editor	Folmar Blangsted
Music	Leonard Rosenman
Producer	Robert Arthur
Production Company	
Distributor (U.S.)	Universal
Distributor (G.B.)	Rank
121 minutes (G.B.: 110)	
	Panavision Technicolor
Chance Buckman	John Wayne
Tish Buckman	Katharine Ross
Greg Parker	Jim Hutton
Madelyn Buckman	Vera Miles
Jack Lomax	Jay C. Flippen
Joe Horn	Bruce Cabot
George Harris	Edward Faulkner
Irene Foster	Barbara Stuart
Col. Valdez	Edmund Hashim
Amal Bokru	Valentin De Vargas

324

Wayne as Rooster Cogburn in True Grit.

Madame Loo	Frances Fong
Gen. Lopez	Alberto Morin
Harry York	Alan Caillou
Helen Meadows	Laraine Stephens
Jim Hatch	John Alderson
Dr. Songla	Lal Chand Mehra
Zamora	Rudy Diaz
Gumdrop	Bebe Louie
Hernando (house boy)	Pedro Gonzales Gonzales
Senor Caldez	Edward Colmans
Firefighter in airplane	Chuck Roberson

Shooting from March 14 to mid-June, 1968
Location filming at Houston, Texas, and Wyoming
Released December (U.S.); March, 1969 (G.B.)

TRUE GRIT (1969)

Director	Henry Hathaway
Writer	Marguerite Roberts from the novel by Charles Portis
Cinematographer	Lucien Ballard
Art Director	Walter Tyler
Editor	Warren Low
Music	Elmer Bernstein
Associate Producer	Paul Nathan
Producer	Hal Wallis
Production Company	Hal Wallis
Distributor	Paramount

128 minutes   Technicolor

Reuben J. "Rooster" Cogburn	John Wayne
La Boeuf	Glen Campbell
Mattie Ross	Kim Darby
Emmett Quincy	Jeremy Slate
Ned Pepper	Robert Duvall
Moon	Dennis Hopper
Goudy	Alfred Ryder
Col. G. Stonehill	Strother Martin
Tom Chaney	Jeff Corey
Capt. Boots Finch	Ron Soble
Lawyer J. Noble Daggett	John Fiedler
Judge Parker	James Westerfield
Sheriff	John Doucette
Barlow	Donald Woods
Mrs. Floyd	Edith Atwater
Dirty Bob	Carlos Rivas
Mrs. Bagby	Isabel Boniface
Chen Lee	H. W. Gim
Frank Ross	John Pickard
Mrs. Ross	Elizabeth Harrower
Yarnell	Ken Renard
Harold Parmalee	Jay Ripley
Farrell Parmalee	Kenneth Becker
A deputy	Myron Healey
Undertaker	Hank Worden
The hangman	Guy Wilkerson
Red, the ferryman	Red Morgan
	Robin Morse

Shooting from September 5 to early December 1968
Location filming around Montrose, Colorado, and Mammoth Lakes, California
Released July (U.S.); December 28 (G.B.)

THE UNDEFEATED (1969)

Director	Andrew V. McLaglen
Writer	James Lee Barrett from a screen story by Stanley L. Hough
Cinematographer	William Clothier
Art Director	Carl Anderson
Editor	Robert Simpson
Music	Hugo Montenegro
Producer	Robert L. Jacks
Production Company Distributor	20th Century-Fox

118 minutes   Panavision   Deluxe colour

Col. John Henry Thomas	John Wayne
Col. James Langdon	Rock Hudson
Gen. Rojas	Tony Aguilar
Blue Boy	Roman Gabriel
Ann Langdon	Marian McCargo
Margaret Langdon	Lee Meriwether
Big George	Merlin Olsen
Charlotte Langdon	Melissa Newman
Jeff Newby	Bruce Cabot
Bubba Wilkes	Michael Vincent
Short Grub	Ben Johnson
Anderson	Edward Faulkner
Webster	Harry Carey Jr.
Gen. Joe Masters	Paul Fix
Major Sanders	Royal Dano
Dan Morse	Richard Mulligan
Diaz	Carlos Rivas
Christian	John Agar
Giles	Guy Raymond
Goodyear	Don Collier
Mudlow	Big John Hamilton
McCartney, the cook	Dub Taylor
Thad Benedict	Henry Beckman
Major Tapia	Victor Junco
Judd Mailer	Robert Donner
Escalante	Pedro Armendariz Jr.
Jamison	James Dobson
Sanchez	Rudy Diaz
Petain	Richard Angarola
Jimmy Collins	James McEachin
Parker	Gregg Palmer
Col. Gomez	Juan Garcia
Union runner	Kiel Martin
Joe Hicks	Bob Gravage
Yankee officer at river crossing	Chuck Roberson

Shooting from February 4 to early May, 1969
Location filming at Durango, Mexico, and near Baton Rouge, Louisiana
Released November (U.S.); October 12 (G.B.)

CHISUM (1970)

Director	Andrew V. McLaglen
Writer	Andrew J. Fenady
Cinematographer	William H. Clothier
Art Director	Carl Anderson
Editor	Robert Simpson
Music	Dominic Frontiere
Songs	Dominic Frontiere Andrew J. Fenady Norman Gimbel
Producer	Andrew J. Fenady
Executive Producer	Michael A. Wayne
Production Company	Batjac
Distributor	Warner Bros.

110 minutes   Panavision   Technicolor

John Chisum	John Wayne
Lawrence Murphy	Forrest Tucker
Dan Nodeen	Christopher George
Sally Chisum	Pamela McMyler
William Bonney known as "Billy the Kid"	Geoffrey Deuel
James Pepper	Ben Johnson
Pat Garrett	Glenn Corbett
Sheriff Brady	Bruce Cabot
Alex McSween	Andrew Prine
John Tunstall	Patric Knowles
Jess Evans	Richard Jaeckel
Sue McSween	Lynda Day
Patton	John Agar
Neemo	Lloyd Battista
Morton	Robert Donner
Justice Wilson	Ray Teal
Dolan	Edward Faulkner
Bowdre	Ron Soble
Baker	John Mitchum
Dudley	Glenn Langan
Governor Axtell	Alan Baxter
Delgado	Alberto Morin
Jeff	William Bryant
Ben	Pedro Armendariz Jr.
O'Folliard	Christopher Mitchum
White Buffalo	Abraham Sofaer
Riker	Gregg Palmer
A trail herder	Chuck Roberson
Stage depot clerk	Hank Worden
Blacksmith	Ralph Volkie
Mexican rancher	Pedro Gonzales Gonzales
Aggressive Sergeant	John Pickard

Shooting from October 6 to early December 1969
Location filming at Durango, Mexico
Released July (U.S.); July 23 (G.B. première)

RIO LOBO (1970)

Director	Howard Hawks
Writers	Burton Wohl Leigh Brackett from a screen story by Burton Wohl
2nd Unit Direction	Yakima Canutt

Chisum: *Wayne and son Michael (the executive producer).*

Cinematographer	William Clothier
Production Designer	Robert Smith
Editor	John Woodcock
Music	Jerry Goldsmith
Associate Producer	Paul Helmick
Producer	Howard Hawks
Production Company	Malabar
Distributor (U.S.)	Cinema Center
Distributor (G.B.)	20th Century-Fox

114 minutes   Technicolor

Cord McNally	John Wayne
Pierre Cordona	Jorge Rivero
Shasta Delaney	Jennifer O'Neill
Phillips	Jack Elam
Ketcham	Victor French
Tuscarora	Chris Mitchum
Maria Carmen	Susana Dosamantes
Sheriff Hendricks	Mike Henry
Dr. Jones (dentist)	David Huddleston
Sheriff Cronin	Bill Williams
Lt. Harris	Edward Faulkner
Amelita	Sherry Lansing
Bitey	Dean Smith
Whitey Carter	Robert Donner
Riley	Jim Davis
Lt. Forsythe	Peter Jason
Whitey's henchmen	Robert Rothwell
	Chuck Courtney
	George Plimpton
Deputy	Bob Steele
Train engineer	Boy "Red" Morgan
Hank (hotel clerk)	Hank Worden
Soldier in baggage car/Guard at ranch	Chuck Roberson
John Ethan Wayne	

Shooting from mid-March (initially under title *San Timoteo*) to early June 1970
Location filming at Old Tucson, Arizona and Cuernavaca, Mexico
Released December (U.S.); December 17 (G.B. *première*)

BIG JAKE (1971)

Director	George Sherman
Writers	Harry Julian Fink
	R. M. Fink
2nd Unit Director	Cliff Lyons
Cinematographer	William Clothier
Art Director	Carl Anderson
Editor	Harry Gerstad
Music	Elmer Bernstein
Producer	Michael A. Wayne
Production Company	Batjac
Distributor (U.S.)	National General for Cinema Center
Distributor (G.B.)	20th Century-Fox

110 minutes   Technicolor   Panavision

Jacob McCandles	John Wayne
John Fain	Richard Boone
Martha McCandles	Maureen O'Hara
James McCandles	Patrick Wayne
Michael McCandles	Chris Mitchum
Jeff McCandles	Bobby Vinton
Sam Sharpnose	Bruce Cabot
O'Brien	Glenn Corbett
Pop Dawson	Harry Carey Jr.
Buck Dugan	John Doucette
Head of lynching party	Jim Davis
Bert Ryan	John Agar
John Goodfellow	Gregg Palmer
Will Fain	Robert Warner
Trooper	Jim Burke
James William (Kid) Duffy	Dean Smith
Little Jack McCandles	John Ethan Wayne
Delilah	Virginia Capers
Moses Brown	William Walker
Stubby	Jerry Gatlin
Saloon Brawler	Tom Hennesy
Saloon bully	Don Epperson
Walt Devries	Everett Creach
Billy Devries	Jeff Wingfield
Hank	Hank Worden
Hotel desk clerk	Jerry Summers
One of Dugan's men	Chuck Roberson
Scots sheepfarmer	Bernard Fox
Gunman in bath house	Roy Jenson

Shooting (as *The Million Dollar Kidnapping*), from early October to early December, 1970
Location filming at Durango, Mexico
Released June (U.S.); August 1 (G.B.— *première* July 8)

THE COWBOYS (1972)

Director	Mark Rydell
Writers	Irving Ravetch
	Harriet Frank Jr.
	William Dale Jennings
	from the novel by
	William Dale Jennings

Big Jake: *John Wayne and Maureen O'Hara.*

2nd Unit Director	Robert "Buzz" Henry	*Charlie Schwartz*	Stephen Hudis
Cinematographer	Robert Surtees	*Stuttering Bob*	Sean Kelly
Production Designer	Philip Jefferies	*Hardy Fimps*	Clay O'Brien
Editors	Robert Swink	*Jimmy Phillips*	Sam O'Brien
	Neil Travis	*Homer Weems*	Mike Pyeatt
Music	John Williams	*Kate*	Colleen Dewhurst
Associate Producer	Tim Zinnemann	*Anse*	Slim Pickens
Producer	Mark Rydell	*Preacher*	Lonny Chapman
Production Company	Sanford	*Annie Andersen*	Sarah Cunningham
Distributor (U.S.)	Warner Bros.	*Mr. Jenkins*	Charles Tyner
Distributor (G.B.)	Columbia-Warner	*Ellen Price*	Allyn Ann McLerie
128 minutes Technicolor Panavision 70		*Red Tucker*	Wallace Brooks
Will Andersen	John Wayne	*Pete*	Jim Burk
Jebediah Nightlinger	Roscoe Lee Browne	*Jake*	Larry Finley
Long Hair	Bruce Dern	*Phoebe*	Maggie Costain
Cimarron	A. Martinez	*Smiley*	Matt Clark
Singing Fats	Alfred Barker Jr,	*Howdy*	Jerry Gatlin
Four Eyes	Nicolas Beauvy	*Okay*	Walter Scott
Steve	Steve Benedict	*Henry Williams*	Dick Farnsworth
Slim Honeycutt	Robert Carradine	*Elizabeth*	Charise Cullin
Weedy	Norman Howell Jr.	*Rosemary*	Collette Poeppel

Jim's father	Norman Howell
Bob's mother	Margaret Kelly
Ben	Larry Randles

Fred Brookfield, Tap Canutt, Chuck Courtney, Gary Epper, Kent Hays, J.P. Randall, Henry Wills, Joe Yrigoyen

In production from April 5 to late July 1971

Filmed around San Cristobal ranch near Santa Fe, New Mexico

Released January (U.S.); March 21 (G.B. & European *première*)

CANCEL MY RESERVATION (1972)

Director	Paul Bogart
Writers	Arthur Marx
	Robert Fisher
	from the novel
	"The Broken Gun"
	by Louis L'Amour
Executive Producer	Bob Hope
Producer	Gordon Oliver
Production Company	Naho
Distributor (U.S.)	Warner Bros.
Distributor (G.B.)	MGM-EMI
99 minutes (G.B.: 86) Technicolor	

Bob Hope, Eva Marie Saint, Ralph Bellamy, Forrest Tucker, Anne Archer, Keenan Wynn

Released September (U.S.)

In this comedy Wayne made a cameo appearance along with Bing Crosby and Flip Wilson as a smiling figure in a brief nightmare sequence built around a lynching

THE TRAIN ROBBERS (1973)

Director	Burt Kennedy
Writer	Burt Kennedy
Cinematographer	William Clothier
Art Director	Al Sweeney
Editor	Frank Santillo
Music	Dominic Frontiere
Producer	Michael Wayne
Production Company	Batjac
Distributor (U.S.)	Warner Bros.
Distributor (G.B.)	Columbia-Warner
92 minutes Technicolor Panavision	
Lane	John Wayne
Mrs. Lowe	Ann-Margret
Grady	Rod Taylor
Jesse	Ben Johnson
Calhoun	Chris George
Ben	Bobby Vinton
Sam	Jerry Gatlin
Pinkerton Man	Ricardo Montalban

Cliff Lyons was stunt co-ordinator

Shooting from March 23 to early June 1972

Location filming at Durango, Mexico

Released February (U.S.); April (G.B.)

CAHILL, UNITED STATES MARSHAL
(1973) (American title)
CAHILL (British title)

Director	Andrew V. McLaglen
Writers	Harry Julian Fink
	Rita M. Fink
	from a story by
	Barney Slater
Cinematographer	Joseph Biroc
Production Designer	Walter Simonds
Editor	Robert L. Simpson
Music	Elmer Bernstein
Producer	Michael A. Wayne
Production Company	Batjac
Distibutor (U.S.)	Warner Bros.
Distributor (G.B.)	Columbia-Warner

103 minutes   Technicolor   Panavision

J. D. Cahill	John Wayne
Abe Fraser	George Kennedy
Danny Cahill	Gary Grimes
Lightfoot	Neville Brand
Billy Joe Cahill	Clay O'Brien
Mrs. Green (Hetty)	Marie Windsor
Struther	Morgan Paull
Brownie	Dan Vadis
MacDonald	Royal Dano
Ben Tildy	Scott Walker
Denver	Denver Pyle
Charlie Smith	Jackie Coogan
Pee Wee Simser	Rayford Barnes
Joe Meehan	Dan Kemp
Hunk	Harry Carey Jr.
Sheriff Grady	Walter Barnes
Old Man	Paul Fix
Hard Case	Pepper Martin
Negro	Vance Davis
Leader of Bunch	Chuck Roberson
Boy	Ken Wolger
Albert	Hank Worden
Doctor	James Nusser
Deputy Gordine	Murray MacLeod
Deputy Jim Kane	Hunter Von Leer

Shooting from November 13 to end of 1972
under title *Wednesday Morning*
Location filming at Durango, Mexico
Released circa July (U.S.), September (G.B.)

McQ (1974)

Director	John Sturges
Writer	Lawrence Roman
2nd Unit Director	Ron R. Rondell
Cinematographer	Harry Stradling Jr.
Production Designer	Walter Simonds
Editor	Bill Ziegler
Music	Elmer Bernstein
Producers	Jules Levy
	Arthur Gardner
	Lawrence Roman

Executive Producer	Michael Wayne
Production	Batjac
Companies	Levy-Gardner
Distributor (U.S.)	Warner Bros.
Distributor (G.B.)	Columbia-Warner

111 minutes   Technicolor   Panavision

Det. Lt. Lon McQ	John Wayne
Capt. Ed Kosterman	Eddie Albert
Lois Boyle	Diana Muldaur
Myra	Colleen Dewhurst
Franklin Toms	Clu Gulager
Edward M. "Pinky"	
Farrow	David Huddleston
J. C. Davis	Jim Watkins
Manny Santiago	Al Lettieri
Elaine Forrester	Julie Adams
Rosey	Roger E. Mosley
Sgt. Stan Boyle	William Bryant
LaSalle	Joe Tornatore
Ginger	Kim Sanford
Radical	Richard Kelton
Walter Forrester	Richard Eastham
Bob Mahoney	Dick Friel
Bodyguard	Fred Waugh
Bodyguard	Chuck Roberson

Shooting from June 4 to mid-August, 1973
Location filming in Seattle
U.S. *première*: February 6;
released March 3 (G.B.)

BRANNIGAN (1975)

Director	Douglas Hickox
Writers	Christopher Trumbo
	Michael Butler
	William P. McGivern
	William Norton
	from a screen story by
	Christopher Trumbo
	Michael Butler
Cinematographer	Gerry Fisher
Art Director	Ted Marshall
Editor	Malcolm Cooke
Music	Dominic Frontiere
Executive Producer	Michael Wayne
Producers	Jules Levy
	Arthur Gardner
Production Company	Wellborn
Distributor	United Artists

111 minutes   Panavision   Deluxe colour

Brannigan	John Wayne
Commander Sir	Richard
Charles Swann	Attenborough
Mel Fields	Mel Ferrer
Det.-Sgt. Jennifer	
Thatcher	Judy Geeson
Ben Larkin	John Vernon
Gorman	Daniel Pilon
Charlie the Handle	James Booth
Det.-Inspector	
Traven	John Stride
Freddy	Anthony Booth
Drexel	Del Henney

Geef	Don Henderson
Capt. Moretti	Ralph Meeker

Shooting from June 17 (under title
Joe Battle) to end of August, 1974
Studio work at Shepperton; location
shooting in the London area
Released March (U.S.); June 12
(British *première*)

ROOSTER COGBURN (1975)

Director	Stuart Millar
Writer	Martin Julien
	suggested by the
	character of
	Rooster Cogburn
	in the novel
	"True Grit" by
	Charles H. Portis
2nd Unit Director	Mickey Moore
Cinematographer	Harry Stradling Jr.
2nd Unit	
Cinematographer	Rexford Merz
Art Director	Preston Ames
Editor	Robert Swink
Music	Laurence Rosenthal
Associate Producer	Paul Nathan
Producer	Hal B. Wallis
Production Company	Hal B. Wallis
Distributor (U.S.)	Universal
Distributor (G.B.)	CIC

108 minutes   Technicolor   Panavision

Rooster Cogburn	John Wayne
Eula Goodnight	Katharine Hepburn
Breed	Anthony Zerbe
Hawk	Richard Jordan
Judge Isaac	
C. Parker	John McIntire
McCoy	Strother Martin
Luke	Paul Koslo
Red	Jack Colvin
Reverend Goodnight	Jon Lormer
Wolf	Richard Romancito
Leroy	Lane Smith
Dagby	Warren Vanders
Nose	Jerry Gatlin
Hambone	Mickey Gilbert
Jerry	Chuck Hayward
Emmett	Gary McLarty
Chen Lee	Tommy Lee

Shooting from September 5 to early
November, 1974
Location filming in the Deschutes National
Forest and Rogue River area of Oregon
Released November (U.S.); December 1
(British *première*)

THE SHOOTIST (1976)

Director	Don Siegel
Writers	Miles Hood Swarthout
	Scott Hale
	from the novel by
	Glendon Swarthout
Cinematographer	Bruce Surtees
Production Designer	Robert Boyle
Editor	Douglas Stewart
Music	Elmer Bernstein
Producers	M. J. Frankovich
	William Self
Production Company	Dino De Laurentiis
Distributor (U.S.)	Paramount
Distributor (G.B.)	CIC

100 minutes   Technicolor

John Bernard Books	John Wayne
Bond Rogers	Lauren Bacall
Gillom Rogers	Ron Howard
Dr. Hostetler	James Stewart
Mike Sweeney	Richard Boone
Pulford	Hugh O'Brian
Cobb	Bill McKinney
Marshal Thibido	Harry Morgan
Beckum	John Carradine
Serepta	Sheree North
Sam Dobkins	Richard Lenz
Moses	Scatman Crothers
Burly Man	Gregg Palmer
Barber	Alfred Dennis
Streetcar Driver	Dick Winslow
Girl on Streetcar	Melody Thomas
Schoolteacher	Kathleen O'Malley

Shooting from January 13 to early
March, 1976
Location filming at Carson City, Nevada
Released August (U.S.); October 7
(British *premiere*)

Appendix

Films produced by John Wayne or his Companies, Wayne-Fellows Productions and Batjac, in which he does not appear

BULLFIGHTER AND THE LADY
("A John Wayne Production")

Director	Budd Boetticher
Writer	James Edward Grant from a screen story by Budd Boetticher Ray Nazarro
Cinematographer	Jack Draper
Art Director	Alfred Ybarra
Editor	Richard L. Van Enger
Editorial Advisor	John Ford (uncredited)
Music	Victor Young
Production Company	
Distributor (U.S.)	Republic
Distributor (G.B.)	British Lion
87 minutes	

Robert Stack	Joy Page
Gilbert Roland	Virginia Grey
John Hubbard	Katy Jurado
Antonio Gomez	Ismael Perez
Rodolfo Acosta	Ruben Padilla
Dario Ramirez	

Released May 15, 1951

PLUNDER OF THE SUN
(A Wayne-Fellows Production)

Director	John Farrow
Writer	Jonathan Latimer from the novel by David Dodge
Cinematographer	Jack Draper
Art Director	Al Ybarra
Editor	Harry Marker
Music	Antonio D. Conde
Producer	Robert Fellows
Distributor	Warner Bros.
81 minutes	

Glenn Ford	Patricia Medina
Diana Lynn	Francis L. Sullivan
Sean McClory	Eduardo Noriega
Julio Villareal	Charles Rooner
Douglas Dumbrille	

Released August 29, 1953

RING OF FEAR
(A Wayne-Fellows Production)

Directors	James Edward Grant William A. Wellman (uncredited)
Writers	Paul Fix Philip MacDonald James Edward Grant
Cinematographer	Edwin B. DuPar
Editor	Fred MacDowell
Music	Emil Newman Arthur Lange
Associate Producer	D. Ross Lederman
Producer	Robert M. Fellows
93 minutes	CinemaScope WarnerColor

Clyde Beatty	Pat O'Brien
Mickey Spillane	Sean McClory
Marian Carr	John Bromfield
Gonzalez-Gonzalez	Emmett Lynn
Jack Stang	Kenneth Tobey
Kathy Cline	Clyde Beatty Circus

Released July 24, 1954
(U.S.); January 16, 1955 (G.B.)

TRACK OF THE CAT
(A Wayne-Fellows Production)

Director	William A. Wellman
Writer	A. I. Bezzerides from the novel by Walter Van Tilburg Clark
Cinematographer	William Clothier
Art Director	Al Ybarra
Editor	Fred MacDowell
Music	Roy Webb
Distributor	Warner Bros.
102 minutes	CinemaScope WarnerColor

Robert Mitchum	Teresa Wright
Diana Lynn	Tab Hunter
Beulah Bondi	Philip Tonge
William Hopper	Carl Switzer

Released November 27, 1954 (U.S.);
April 25, 1955 (G.B.)

GOODBYE, MY LADY
(A Batjac Production)

Director	William A. Wellman
Writer	Sid Fleischman from the novel by James Street
Cinematographer	William H. Clothier
Art Director	Donald A. Peters
Editor	Fred MacDowell
Music	Laurindo Almeida George Field

Distributor	Warner Bros.
95 minutes	

Walter Brennan	Phil Harris
Brandon De Wilde	Sidney Poitier
William Hopper	Louise Beavers

Released May 12, 1956

SEVEN MEN FROM NOW
(A Batjac Production)

Director	Budd Boetticher
Writer	Burt Kennedy
Cinematographer	William H. Clothier
Art Director	Leslie Thomas
Editor	Everett Sutherland
Music	Henry Vars
Producers	Andrew V. McLaglen Robert E. Morrison
Distributor	Warner Bros.
77 minutes	WarnerColor

Randolph Scott	Gail Russell
Lee Marvin	Walter Reed
John Larch	Donald Barry
Fred Graham	John Barradino
John Phillips	Chuck Roberson
Steve Mitchell	Pamela Duncan
Stuart Whitmore	

Released August 4, 1956

GUN THE MAN DOWN
(A Batjac Production)

Director	Andrew V. McLaglen
Writer	Burt Kennedy from a screen story by Sam C. Freedle
Cinematographer	William H. Clothier
Art Director	Al Ybarra
Editor	Eddie Sutherland
Music	Henry Vars
Producer	Robert E. Morrison
Distributor	United Artists
78 minutes	

James Arness	Angie Dickinson
Emile Meyer	Robert Wilke
Harry Carey Jr.	Michael Emmet
Don Megowan	Frank Fenton

Released November 1956

MAN IN THE VAULT
(A Batjac Production)

Director	Andrew V. McLaglen

Seven Men from Now: *Wayne visits star Randolph Scott and director Budd Boetticher.*

Writer	Burt Kennedy from the novel "The Lock and the Key" by Frank Gruber
Cinematographer	William H. Clothier
Editor	Everett Sutherland
Music	Henry Vars
Producer	Robert E. Morrison
Distributor (U.S.)	Universal for RKO Radio
Distributor (U.K.)	RKO Radio

73 minutes

William Campbell	Karen Sharpe
Anita Ekberg	Berry Kroeger
Paul Fix	James Seay
Mike Mazurki	Robert Keys
Gonzales Gonzales	Nancy Duke
Vivianne Lloyd	

Released December 1956

CHINA DOLL
(A Romina Production/Batjac
Enterprises)

Director	Frank Borzage
Writer	Kitty Buhler from a story by James Benson Nablo Thomas F. Kelly
Cinematographer	William H. Clothier
Editor	Jack Murray
Music	Henry Vars
Distributor	United Artists

85 minutes

Victor Mature	Li Li Hua
Ward Bond	Bob Mathias
Johnny Desmond	Elaine Curtis
Stuart Whitman	Ann McCrea
Danny Chang	Ken Perry
Tiger Andrews	Steve Mitchell
Don Barry	Anne Paif
Denver Pyle	Ti Ta

Released August 1958 (U.S.);
June 8, 1958 (G.B.)

ESCORT WEST
(A Romina Production/Batjac
Enterprises)

Director	Francis D. Lyon
Writers	Leo Gordon Fred Hartsook from a screen story by Steven Hayes
Cinematographer	William H. Clothier
Art Director	Alfred Ybarra
Editor	Otto Ludwig
Music	Henry Vars
Producers	Robert E. Morrison Nate H. Edwards
Distributor	United Artists

75 minutes   CinemaScope

Victor Mature	Elaine Stewart
Faith Domergue	Reba Waters
Noah Beery	Leo Gordon
Rex Ingram	John Hubbard
Harry Carey Jr.	Slim Pickens
Roy Barcroft	William Ching
Ken Curtis	Claire Dubrey
Syd Saylor	X. Brands
Chuck Hayward	Charles Soldani

Released January 1959 (U.S.);
November 2, 1958 (G.B.)

HONDO AND THE APACHES
(A Batjac/Fenady Associates
Production)

Director	Lee H. Katzin
Writer	Andrew J. Fenady from the screenplay for *Hondo* by James Edward Grant based on the story "The Gift of Cochise" by Louis L'Amour
Cinematographer	Lester Shorr
Music	Richard Markowitz
Associate Producer	Robert E. Morrison
Producer	Andrew J. Fenady
Distributor	MGM

85 minutes   MetroColor

Ralph Taeger	Kathie Browne
Michael Rennie	Gary Merrill
John Smith	Noah Beery
Gary Clark	Randy Boone
Buddy Foster	Michael Pate
Victor Lundin	Jim Davis
Steve Marlo	John Pickard
William Bryant	Robert Taylor

Re-make of Wayne's 1953 film, pilot for a
TV series

Released circa September 1967 (G.B.)

Acknowledgments

LASTLY, but not least, a note of warm appreciation — rather than mere acknowledgement — to all those who have helped me to amass this career study. I have already mentioned my great debt to John Brooker and Pat Billings in completing the Filmography, and along with these two experts I would like to single out David Meeker whose help enabled me to go much deeper into my subject than would otherwise have been possible, and Louise Brooks for generously entrusting her introductory essay to me.

Then, for providing snippets of information that eluded my grasp, for enabling me to see odd films that would have otherwise been inaccessible, for supplying stills from company files or private collections, or for words of advice I remain most grateful to: Robin Bean, DeWitt Bodeen, Peter Cowie, William K. Everson, Carole Fleming (and her successor, Barbara De Lord, at 20th Century-Fox), Carol Futrall (and Warner Bros.), Peter S. Haigh, Charles Hoyt, Alan Hutchinson (and Cinema International Corporation), Austin Lamont, Leonard Maltin, Philip Jenkinson, Gerald Pratley, Gene Ringgold, Jeanne Stein, Pat Suckling (and Paramount), Tom Vallance, Sandra Wake (and Lorrimer Publishing), Sheila Whitaker (and the Stills Library of the British Film Institute/National Film Archive), Christopher Wicking, William C. Wilson, Ken Wlaschin.

In addition, this book would not have been possible without the facilities of the Information Department of the British Film Institute.